TENTH EDITION

Archaeology

A Brief Introduction

Brian M. Fagan
University of California, Santa Barbara

Prentice Hall
Upper Saddle River London Singapore
Toronto Tokyo Sydney Hong Kong Mexico City

Editorial Director: Leah Jewell
AVP, Publisher: Nancy Roberts
Editor-in-Chief: Dickson Musslewhite
Editorial Assistant: Nart Varoqua
Director of Marketing: Brandy Dawson
Marketing Manager: Lindsey Prudhomme
AV Project Manager: Maria Piper
Supplements Editor: Mayda Bosco
Senior Media Editor: David Alick
Managing Editor: Maureen Richardson
Production Liaison: Shelly Kupperman
Senior Operations Supervisor: Mary Ann Gloriande
Manager, Rights and Permissions: Zina Arabia
Manager, Visual Research: Beth Brenzel
Manager, Cover Visual Research and Permissions: Karen Sanatar
Cover Coordinator: Rita Wenning
Image Permission Coordinator: Annette Linder
Image Researcher: Francelle Carapetyan
Cover Art Director: Jayne Conte
Cover Design: Bruce Kenselaar
Cover Image: Tibor Bognar/Corbis
Composition/Full-Service Project Management: Big Sky Composition/Kari Callaghan Mazzola and John P. Mazzola
Printer/Binder: Edwards Brothers, Inc.
Cover Printer: Lehigh-Phoenix Color

This book was set in 10/12 Sabon.

Grateful acknowledgment is made to the copyright holders on pages 328–329, which are hereby a continuation of this copyright page.

Library of Congress Cataloging-in-Publication Data

Fagan, Brian M.
Archaeology: a brief introduction/Brian M. Fagan—10th ed.
p. cm.
Includes bibliographical references and index.
ISBN 978-0-205-63338-8
1. Archaeology. I. Title.
CC165.F28 2009
930.1—dc22 2008047540

10 9 8 7 6 5 4 3 2 1

Prentice Hall
is an imprint of

PEARSON

www.pearsonhighered.com

ISBN 10: 0-205-63338-2
ISBN 13: 978-0-205-63338-8

To Lucia, Karen, and other friends at Whittier College,
who first gave me the idea for this book back in 1977.
And, as usual, to our cats, who were as subversive as ever.
They did everything to prevent me from revising the manuscript
by stepping on it with muddy paws and dancing intricate ballet
on the computer keyboard. As you can see, they failed!

---

*Imagine a dinner table set for a thousand guests,
in which each man is sitting between his own father and his own son.
At one end of the table might be a French Nobel laureate
in a white tie and tails, and with the Legion of Honor on his breast,
and at the other end a Cro-Magnon man dressed in animal skins
and with a necklace of cave-bear teeth.
Yet each one would be able to converse with his neighbors
on his left and right, who would either be his father or his son.
So the distance from then to now is not really great.*

—Björn Kurtén, *Singletusk: A Novel of the Ice Age*
(New York: Pantheon, 1986), p. 61

BRIEF CONTENTS

CONTENTS

Chapter 6
They Sought It Here, They Sought It There: Finding Archaeological Sites 109

Chapter 7
Excavation 131

PREFACE

Archaeology is a romantic subject, redolent of lost civilizations and grinning skeletons dripping with gold, the realm of pith-helmeted men and women who are adventurers and scholars at the same time, of movies like the Indiana Jones adventures. But is this reality? Most archaeologists have never worn a pith helmet, have never discovered gold, and will never unearth a long-forgotten civilization. Nor do most archaeological sites yield rich treasure or even human remains. The romance is not always there, but the world of modern archaeology is deeply fascinating all the same. This book is a journey through that world in all its intriguing diversity. It is designed to give you some idea of how archaeologists go about studying human behavior in the past.

This tenth edition of *Archaeology: A Brief Introduction* is a brief narrative introduction to the fundamental principles of method and theory in archaeology, beginning with the goals of archaeology, going on to consider the basic concepts of culture, time, and space, and discussing the finding and excavation of archaeological sites. The last six chapters summarize some of the ways in which archaeologists order and study their finds, as well as the management of the past for future generations. Throughout the book, I emphasize the ethics behind archaeology, ending with a discussion of careers in archaeology and how we should act as stewards of the finite records of the human past. This is a book with an ardently international perspective, for archaeology is the most global of all sciences, encompassing all humanity, not just, say, North America or Europe.

Most readers will encounter this simple book as a supplement to an introductory anthropology course, or as part of a broader archaeology offering. It is designed for complete beginners, so every attempt has been made to keep technical jargon to a minimum. Inevitably, a book of this length and scope glosses over many complex problems and smoldering controversies. I have proceeded on the assumption that, at this stage, a positive overstatement is better than a complex piece of inconclusive reasoning. Errors of overstatement can always be corrected in class or at a more advanced stage.

If there is a theme to this volume, it is that the patterning of archaeological artifacts we find in the ground can provide valuable insights into human behavior in the past. In pursuing this theme, I have attempted to focus on the basic concepts of archaeology and leave the instructor to impose his or her own theoretical viewpoints on the various chapters that follow. In the interests of simplicity, too, I have drawn again and again on a few relatively well-known sites from New World and Old World archaeology, such as Olduvai Gorge and Teotihuacán, rather than distracting readers with a multitude of site names. I have added brief descriptions of major sites in a special "Sites and Cultures" information section at the end of the book, where a Glossary of Technical Terms will also be found.

Highlights of the Tenth Edition

This is an exciting time to be writing about archaeology because major scientific advances in many fields are transforming our ability to reconstruct the remote past. Increasingly, archaeology is becoming a multidisciplinary field, and the tenth edition of this book reflects this fact. In general, however, the book remains much the same, because the basic principles of archaeology remain unchanged through the years, whatever new theoretical approaches or high-tech scientific methods are brought to bear on the past. These basic principles provide the foundation for all of the many research projects that archaeologists carry out, whether close to home or far afield, whether academic research or cultural resource management. And generations of instructors and students have told me that they like the current organization.

Updating and Rewriting

- *New perceptions of archaeology.* Chapter 4 includes a discussion of alternative perspectives on the past in archaeology, reflecting new thinking on this important topic and an update on contemporary archaeological theory.
- *Rearrangement of Chapter 4.* At the request of numerous users, "Explaining the Past" now appears earlier in the book, as a preliminary to the chapters discussing the acquisition of data through survey, excavation, and analysis, and reconstruction of the past. I have retained this arrangement in the tenth edition as it was well received in its first iteration.
- *Expanded coverage of ancient technologies.* In response to instructor and student requests, coverage of ancient technologies has been expanded within the space limits of the book.
- *Expanded coverage of environment and climate.* Chapter 10 summarizes ways in which scientists study long-term and short-term climatic change. The study of ancient climate and its impact on ancient societies has been revolutionized in recent years and reflects a major advance in archaeology.
- *Discussion of settlement and landscape.* Coverage of settlement and landscape has been updated extensively, especially to highlight an increasing interest in human conceptions of landscapes and ritual landscapes. We return to the archaeology of the intangible in Chapter 13, which deals with people of the past.
- *Discussion of bioarchaeology.* Bioarchaeology has expanded rapidly as a subspecialty in archaeology and is throwing important new light on both individuals and groups. I summarize its major contributions in Chapter 13, which is expanded throughout.
- *Management of the past.* Chapter 14 is a new stand-alone discussion of Cultural Resource Management and Public Archaeology at a basic level, reflecting an increasing interest in these subjects in beginning courses.
- *Career advice.* Chapter 15, as before, gives frank advice on archaeology as a career in an era when academic positions are shrinking and archaeology is becoming a profession. This turned out to be a very popular chapter in earlier editions.
- *Discovery boxes.* Feature boxes describing both well-known and recent discoveries have been added to each chapter. I have resisted the temptation to add more boxes on the grounds that they break up the narrative in a distracting way in a simple book like this one.
- *Previews.* I have added brief previews to the beginning of each chapter.
- *Revision and updating throughout.* The entire text and the Guide to Further Reading have been revised and updated on a page-by-page basis.

New and Revised Art Program

The tenth edition's art program has been expanded, with new photographs and fresh or revised line art. The new illustrations provide additional background on recent discoveries, amplify the narrative, or replace older art with new pictures. Some expanded captions serve to integrate the illustrations more closely into the text.

Ancillary Materials

The ancillary materials that accompany this textbook have been carefully created to enhance the topics being discussed.

MyAnthroKit (0-205-69040-8) This Web-based application contains book-specific resources to aid student learning and comprehension. MyAnthroKit includes a rich array of interactive tools enhanced with audio and video to engage students in their study of Anthropology and Archaeology. Features include practice tests to aid in comprehension of key textbook objectives, flashcards, Web links, maps, images, and additional multimedia resources.

Strategies in Teaching Anthropology (0-13-173371-0) Unique in focus and content, this book focuses on the "how" of teaching Anthropology across all of its sub-fields—Cultural Anthropology, Biological Anthropology, Archaeology, and Linguistics—to provide a wide array of associated learning outcomes and student activities. It is a valuable single-source compendium of strategies and "tricks of the trade" from a group of seasoned teaching anthropologists who are working in a variety of teaching settings and who share their pedagogical techniques, knowledge, and observations. Please contact your local Prentice Hall sales representative for more information.

The Dorling Kindersley/Prentice Hall Atlas of Anthropology (0-13-191879-6) Beautifully illustrated by Dorling Kindersley, with narrative by leading archaeology author Brian M. Fagan, this striking atlas features thirty full-color maps, timelines, and illustrations to offer a highly visual but explanatory geographical overview of topics from all four fields of anthropology. For packaging options, please contact your local Prentice Hall sales representative.

Archaeology and You (0-13-222623-5) Written by Brian M. Fagan, this brief book tells the story of the romance of archaeology and the detective work involved in studying the past. It discusses traveling in search of the past, museums, and ways in which archaeology contributes to the twenty-first-century world. For packaging options, please contact your local Prentice Hall sales representative.

Acknowledgments

The tenth edition has benefited from the expertise of many colleagues, too numerous to list here. I am deeply grateful for their encouragement and assistance.

My thanks go to my editor, Nancy Roberts, and her assistant, Nart Varoqua, for much encouragement and many kindnesses, and also to the production team, headed by Kari Callaghan Mazzola of Big Sky Composition. They have turned a complex manuscript into an attractive book and have done all they could to minimize unexpected difficulties.

As always, I would be most grateful for criticisms, comments, or details of new work, sent to me at brian@brianfagan.com.

Brian M. Fagan

AUTHOR'S NOTE

Glossaries

Key terms defined in the Glossary of Technical Terms at the end of the book are highlighted in **bold** type throughout the book. Archaeological sites, cultures, and civilizations whose names are *italicized* at first use in the book are described in the section on sites and cultures at the end of the book.

Dates

The following conventions are used in the text:

- Dates before 10,000 years ago are expressed in years Before Present (B.P.). This is common usage, although not commonly used in this particular book.
- Dates after 10,000 years ago are expressed in years Before Christ (B.C.) or Anno Domini (A.D.).

Another common convention is B.C.E./C.E. (Before Common Era/Common Era), which is not employed in this book. By scientific convention, "present" is A.D. 1950.

Please note that all radiocarbon dates and potassium-argon dates should be understood to have a plus and minus factor that is omitted from this book in the interests of clarity. They are statistical estimates. Where possible, radiocarbon dates have been calibrated with tree-ring chronologies, which adds a substantial element of accuracy (see Chapter 5). For tree-ring calibration of radiocarbon dates, see the journal *Radiocarbon,* 1998.

ABOUT THE AUTHOR

Brian Fagan is one of the world's leading archaeological writers and an internationally recognized authority on world prehistory. He studied archaeology and anthropology at Pembroke College, Cambridge University, and then spent seven years in sub-Saharan Africa working in museums and in monuments conservation and excavating early farming sites in Zambia and East Africa. He was one of the pioneers of multidisciplinary African history in the 1960s. From 1967 to 2003, he was Professor of Anthropology at the University of California, Santa Barbara, where he specialized in lecturing and writing about archaeology to wide audiences. He is now Emeritus Professor of Anthropology.

Brian Fagan has written several best-selling textbooks, all published by Prentice Hall—*Ancient Lives: An Introduction to Archaeology and Prehistory; In the Beginning: An Introduction to Archaeology; People of the Earth: An Introduction to World Prehistory; World Prehistory: A Brief Introduction; Ancient Civilizations* (with Chris Scarre); and this volume—which are used around the world. His general books include *The Rape of the Nile* (1965, 2004), a classic history of Egyptology; *The Adventure of Archaeology* (1985); *Time Detectives* (1995); *Ancient North America* (1990, 2005); *The Little Ice Age* (2001); *Egypt of the Pharaohs* (2001); and *The Great Warming* (2008). He also was General Editor of the *Oxford Companion to Archaeology* (1996). In addition, he has published several scholarly monographs on African archaeology and numerous specialized articles in national and international journals. An expert on multimedia teaching, he has received the Society for American Archaeology's first Public Education Award for his indefatigable efforts on behalf of archaeology and education.

Brian Fagan's other interests include bicycling, sailing, kayaking, and good food. He is married and lives in Santa Barbara with his wife and daughter, four cats (who supervise his writing), and last but not least, between six and twenty-four rabbits.

ONE

Fossils, Cities, and Civilizations

The Birth of a Science

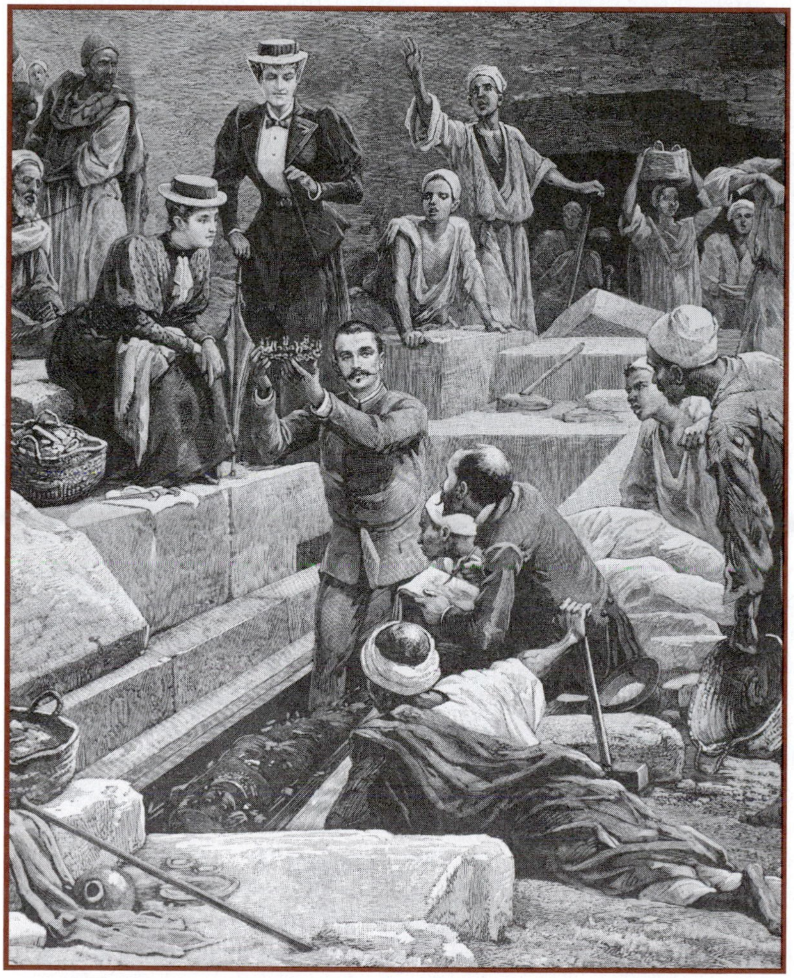

Discovery! Archaeologist Jacques de Morgan holds up the golden crown of Egyptian Queen Khnemet, wife of pharaoh Senusret II (nineteenth century B.C.). This romanticized picture appeared in the *Illustrated London News* in 1896.

CHAPTER OUTLINE

What Is Archaeology?

The Beginnings of Archaeology

The Three Ages and the Antiquity of Humankind

The Discovery of the Ancient Civilizations

The Ancient Egyptians

The Assyrians and Sumerians

Troy and Mycenae

Early American Archaeology

The "Moundbuilders"

Maya Civilization

Southwestern Archaeology and the Direct Historical Approach

Diversity, Diffusion, and Human Progress

"From Them to Us": Unilinear Evolution

Diffusionism: How Did Civilization Spread?

The Development of Modern Scientific Archaeology

Scientific Excavation

Archaeology and Ecology

Scientific Methods

"From Them to Us": Contemporary Archaeological Theory

Ecological/Evolutionary Approach

Historical Materialist Approach

PREVIEW

What is archaeology and how did it begin? Chapter 1 tells the story of the early archaeological discoveries that led to the development of scientific archaeology. We will enter the world of the early antiquarians and excavators and explore the controversies surrounding the antiquity of humankind. Then we will journey to Egypt, Mesopotamia, and the eastern Mediterranean to learn about the discovery of the world's earliest civilizations. Next, we will trace the beginnings of American archaeology with the controversies over the Moundbuilders and the spectacular discovery of Maya civilization in Central America by John Lloyd Stephens and Frederick Catherwood. Finally, we will examine some of the early theories that sought to explain the development of ancient human societies, culminating in the basic theoretical approaches of today.

These great towns and temples and buildings rising from the water, all made of stone, seemed like an enchanted vision. . . . I stood looking at it, and thought no land like it would ever be discovered in the whole world. . . . But today all that I then saw is overthrown and destroyed; nothing is left standing.

—Bernal Díaz del Castillo on the Aztec capital, Tenochtitlán, Mexico, 1519

The priests supervised the hasty digging of a vast pit in the royal cemetery at Ur in what is now southern Iraq over a few days in 2100 B.C. Dozens of workers carried basketloads of earth up a lengthening ramp and dumped their loads to one side. Next, in the bottom of the hole, a few masons built a stone burial chamber with a vaulted brick roof. A small procession of high officials carried the royal corpse into the empty sepulcher and laid the dead man out in all his finery. They arranged food offerings alongside the bier in gold and silver bowls. Then the dead man's closest personal attendants knelt silently by their master. They swallowed poison and accompanied the prince into eternity. The walled-up chamber stood at the back of the empty pit, where the priests presided over a lavish funeral feast.

A long line of soldiers, courtiers, and male and female servants filed into the mat-filled burial pit. The participants wore their finest robes, most brilliant uniforms, and badges of rank. Each courtier, soldier, or servant carried a small clay cup brimming with poison. The musicians bore their lyres. The royal charioteers drove the ox-drawn wagons down the ramp to their assigned place in the bottom of the great hole. Grooms calmed the restless animals as the drivers held the reins (see Figure 1.1 on page 3). Everyone lined up in his or her proper place in order of precedence.

Music played. A small detachment of soldiers guarded the top of the ramp with watchful eyes. At a quiet signal, everyone in the pit raised the clay cups to their lips and swallowed poison. Then they lay down to die, each in his or her correct place. As the bodies twitched, then lay still, a few men slipped into the pit and killed the oxen with quick blows. The royal court had embarked on its long journey to the afterlife.

The priests covered the grave pit with earth and a mudbrick structure before filling the hole and access ramp with layers of clay. A sacrificial victim marked each stratum until the royal sepulcher reached ground level.

Archaeology is the stuff dreams are made of—buried treasure, gold-laden pharaohs, and the romance of long-lost civilizations. Many people think of archaeologists as

Figure 1.1 A reconstruction of the burial ceremony at the Royal Cemetery at Ur. The ranked members of the court stand in their assigned places, the grooms tending their wheeled carts. (© Copyright The British Museum.)

romantic adventurers, like the film world's Indiana Jones. Cartoonists often depict us as eccentric scholars in pith helmets digging up inscribed tablets in the shadows of great pyramids. Popular legend would have us as absent-minded professors, so deeply absorbed in ancient times that we care little for the realities of modern life. Some discoveries, such as that of Tutankhamun's Tomb, do indeed foster visions of adventure and romance (see the Discovery box on page 4).

British archaeologist Sir Leonard Woolley reconstructed the Ur funeral from brilliant archaeological excavations made in 1926; he uncovered a layer of skeletons that seemed to be lying on a golden carpet. Woolley worked miracles of discovery under very harsh conditions. He excavated with only a handful of fellow experts and employed hundreds of workers. When the going got tough, he would hire a Euphrates River boatman to sing rhythmic boating songs with a lilting beat. Woolley cleared 2,000 commoners' graves and sixteen royal burials in four years, using paintbrushes and knives to clean each skeleton. He lifted a queen's head with its elaborate wig-like headdress in one piece after smothering the skull in liquid paraffin oil. Nearby, he noticed a hole in the soil, poured plaster of paris down it, and recovered the cast of the wooden sound box of a royal lyre. Woolley reconstructed a magnificent figure of a goat from tiny fragments. He called the cemetery excavation "a jigsaw in three dimensions" and wrote of the sacrificial victims: "A blaze of colour with the crimson coats, the silver, and the gold; clearly these people were not wretched slaves killed as oxen might be killed, but persons held in honour, wearing their robes of office" (Woolley, 1982: 123).

What Is Archaeology?

Although Indiana Jones is said to be a fictional composite of several early-twentieth-century excavators, I have never met a professional archaeologist who even vaguely resembled him, and only a handful who ever wore pith helmets. The heroic days when

Discovery

Tutankhamun's Tomb, Egypt, 1922

The small party of archaeologists and onlookers stood in front of the doorway that bore the seals of the long-dead pharaoh. They had waited six long years, from 1917 to 1922, for this moment. Silently, Howard Carter pried a hole through the ancient plaster. Hot air rushed out of the small cavity and massaged his face. Carter shone a flashlight through the hole and peered into the sepulcher. Gold objects swam in front of his eyes, and he was struck dumb with amazement (see Figure 1.2).

Lord Carnarvon fidgeted impatiently behind him, as Carter remained silent.

"What do you see?" Carnarvon asked, hoarse with excitement.

"Wonderful things," whispered Carter as he stepped back from the doorway (Carter et al., 1923–1933: 63).

They soon broke down the door. In a daze of amazement, Carter and Carnarvon wandered through the antechamber of the pharaoh Tutankhamun's tomb. They fingered golden funerary beads, admired beautifully inlaid wooden chests, and examined the pharaoh's chariots stacked against the wall. Gold was everywhere—on wooden statues, inlaid on thrones and boxes, in jewelry, even on children's stools (Reeves, 2007). Soon Tutankhamun was known as the golden pharaoh, and archaeology was known as the domain of buried treasure and royal sepulchers.

As for Carter and Carnarvon, they immediately installed an iron door to the tomb and placed a 24-hour guard at the entrance while they planned the clearance of the sepulcher. Late that night they returned on their own, chiseled a small hole in the sealed burial chamber, and slipped through to verify that the pharaoh lay undisturbed in his sarcophagus.

It took Howard Carter eight years to clear Tutankhamun's tomb, which was one of the greatest archaeological discoveries ever made. Unfortunately, Lord Carnarvon died of an infected mosquito bite shortly after the discovery of the sepulcher. Inevitably, there was journalistic talk of a "curse of the pharaohs" imposed by Ancient Egyptian priests on those who violated the tomb. This is complete hogwash. The fact that most people who worked on Tutankhamun lived into their eighties is conveniently forgotten.

one could discover an ancient civilization in a month and several royal palaces in a week are long gone. Today's archaeology is a sophisticated multidisciplinary science, with roots in anthropology and **history**.

Archaeology is the scientific study of the human past, of ancient human behavior, from the earliest times right up to the present. As such, most archaeology is part of a much wider discipline, **anthropology**, which studies all aspects of humanity, ancient and modern. But **archaeologists** are unique among scientists in that they study changes in human cultures over long periods of time.

Archaeology is the only academic discipline and profession that has an ancestry in treasure hunting. Nineteenth-century archaeology often consisted of a hasty search for lost cities or gold-laden royal burials. It was a time of high adventure, and, it must be admitted, a great deal of unbridled looting. The damage to the past was incalculable—royal tombs torn apart, temples ravaged, entire city mounds reduced to dust. Fortunately, treasure hunting gave way gradually to scientific excavation, and, eventually, to the highly sophisticated science we know today. The specialized science of today is a product not only of modern scientific innovation but also of the work of flamboyant pioneers who did indeed find lost civilizations in remote lands.

How, then, did archaeology begin? Here is an outline of some major developments and discoveries, out of hundreds of important finds.

Figure 1.2 Archaeologist Howard Carter peers through the doors of one of pharaoh Tutankhamun's golden shrines, undisturbed for more than 3,000 years. (Photography by Egyptian Expedition, The Metropolitan Museum of Art.)

The Beginnings of Archaeology

People have speculated about human origins and the remote past for centuries. As early as the eighth century B.C., the Greek writer Hesiod wrote that humanity had passed through five great ages of history. The earliest was an Age of Gold, when "people dwelt in ease," the last an Age of War, when everyone worked terribly hard and experienced great sorrow. In the sixth century B.C., the Babylonian monarch Nabonidus dug deep into ancient city mounds near the Tigris and Euphrates rivers. His workmen uncovered the foundations of the temple of the goddess Ishtar at Agade near Babylon. The find, says an ancient tablet, "made the king's heart glad and caused his countenance to brighten."

In later centuries, the Greeks and Romans were intensely curious about their primitive ancestors, about Scythian "barbarians" living on the northern plains who drank from cups made from human skulls, and about the Britons far to the northwest who painted themselves blue. Classical writers wrote of the long-term continuity of human life. "Thus the sum of things is ever being renewed," wrote the Roman poet Lucretius in the first century B.C. "Some races increase, others diminish, and in a short space the generations of living creatures are changed and like runners hand on the torch of life" (*De Rerum Natura* II: 75).

The history of archaeology really begins in the European Renaissance, which saw quickened intellectual curiosity, not only about the world beyond the narrow confines of Europe but also about the Classical civilizations. People of leisure and wealth began to follow the path of Renaissance scholars, traveling widely in Greece and Italy, studying antiquities, and collecting examples of Roman art. The same travelers were not above some illicit excavation to recover statuary from ancient temples and Roman villas. Soon the cabinets of wealthy collectors (**antiquarians**) bulged with fine art objects, and the study of Classical lands became a major scholarly preoccupation.

In 1738, Italy's King Charles III commissioned Spanish engineer Rocque Joaquin de Alcubierre to excavate the famed Roman city of Herculaneum, buried under deep layers of volcanic ash by an eruption of Vesuvius in A.D. 79. Alcubierre blasted and tunneled his way through rock-hard ash, tunneling sideways into underground galleries where he found jewelry, statues of well-known Herculaneans, and fragments of bronze horses. Visitors climbed down narrow shafts to walk through the buried theater, marble-columned houses, and frescoed rooms. Hundreds of men, including prisoners, labored below ground, recovering bronze busts, texts written on papyrus scrolls, and copies of now-lost Greek masterpieces. Toxic gases, slime, and collapsing tunnels brought an end to this glorified treasure hunt.

Many antiquarians were not wealthy enough to travel to Classical lands, so they stayed at home and searched for antiquities right in their own backyards. Stonehenge on the uplands of southern England was the most famous curiosity, a place where "stones of wonderful size have been erected after the manner of doorways" (Chippindale, 1994: 21). The antiquarians indulged their insatiable curiosity by digging into burial mounds and river gravels, recovering all manner of prehistoric finds—clay vessels, stone axes and adzes, bronze implements, even occasional gold ornaments. Their digging methods were brutally crude, usually little more than a hasty pit sunk into the center of a mound to recover a skeleton and its grave goods as quickly as possible (see Figure 1.3). Some fast-moving diggers would open two or three mounds a day. The accounts of their excavations frequently include complaints that a delicate find "crumbled to dust before their eyes"—hardly surprising, considering the crude digging methods they employed.

Until well into the nineteenth century, archaeology was little

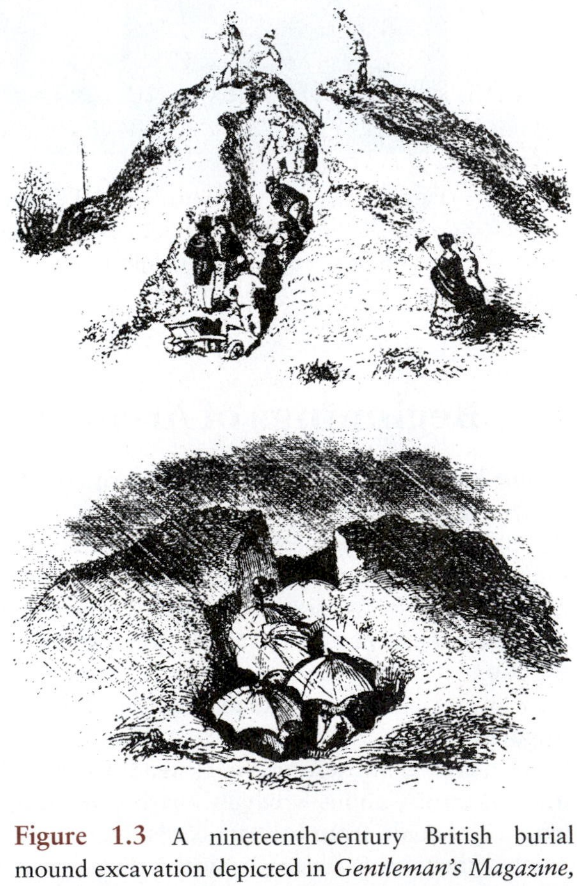

Figure 1.3 A nineteenth-century British burial mound excavation depicted in *Gentleman's Magazine*, 1840. The excursion was little more than a picnic. "Eight barrows were examined. . . . Most of them contained skeletons, more or less entire, with the remains of weapons in iron, bosses of shields, urns, beads, brooches . . . and occasionally more vessels."

more than a glorified treasure hunt, even a sport. Not only that, but also the archaeological record of prehistoric times was a complete jumble of stone and metal tools and clay vessels. "All that has come down to us . . . is wrapped in a thick fog," complained one Danish scholar in 1806.

The Three Ages and the Antiquity of Humankind

Although some eighteenth-century collectors were content to display their finds in cabinets, others puzzled over the people who had made these artifacts. Were they hunter-gatherers and farmers like the American Indians, or little more than animals? Had they developed more complex societies as time passed? What was needed was some way of classifying and dating the past.

The first breakthrough came in 1816, when Danish archaeologist Christian Jurgensen Thomsen opened the National Museum of Antiquities in Copenhagen to the public. For years, scholars had talked of three ages—a Stone Age when people had no metals, a Bronze Age, and an Iron Age. A man with a passion for order, Thomsen took the confusing jumble of artifacts in his museum and laid them out in different rooms. In one gallery he displayed implements of the Stone Age, "when little or nothing at all was known of metals." In another he showed those with stone and bronze but no iron, and in a third, grave finds belonging to the Iron Age.

His new scheme soon became known as the **Three-Age System**, a system still used to this day for classifying the prehistoric past. Thomsen knew his scheme was mere theory, but one of his assistants, Jens Jacob Worsaae, went out and excavated more burial mounds and other sites. Worsaae proved that Stone Age occupations did, in fact, underlie Bronze Age levels, and that Iron Age sites were the latest of all. The validity of the Three-Age System was now soundly established, and it was in widespread use by the 1860s.

But how long had human beings lived on earth? Between medieval times and the late eighteenth century, everyone in the Western world believed in the literal historical truth of the Scriptures. *Genesis* 1:1 stated that God had created the world and its inhabitants in six days. The story of Adam and Eve provided an entirely consistent explanation for the creation of humankind and the world's population. In the seventeenth century, Archbishop James Ussher used the genealogies in the Old Testament to calculate that the world had been created on the night preceding October 23, 4004 B.C. These bizarre calculations soon became theological dogma and were defended with great fanaticism by theologians in the early nineteenth century, when another group of experts showed that humans had lived on earth much longer than a mere 6,000 years.

The Industrial Revolution of the late eighteenth century with its massive canal-building and railroad-building schemes created a demand for a new breed of scientist—the field geologist. Men like Englishman William "Strata" Smith made their living surveying the earth's layers. Smith realized that the earth had been formed not by divine creation but by natural processes such as erosion, weathering, and sedimentation. These processes had been operating for a very long period of time—far longer than 6,000 years. This theory of the earth's formation became known as **uniformitarianism**. Many of Smith's geological strata contained the fossils of long-extinct animals, fossils that French scientist Georges Cuvier pieced together. Cuvier reconstructed pterodactyls and mammoths, and he used his fossils to place geological layers in order, each with its distinctive fossil animals. But how old were these strata? Cuvier believed that God had created each successive layer of the earth, after great floods had wiped out earlier life. Humans belonged to the time of the last flood. In other words, the world was only 6,000 years old.

Cuvier was wrong, for the proof that human beings had lived in far earlier times was right there in front of his nose. As early as 1600, elephant bones and a stone ax had been found in the heart of London; but no established scientist took these, or many subsequent finds of the same type, seriously. Uniformitarian theories were well established in geology by the 1830s, notably by the writings of British geologist Sir Charles Lyell, whose book *Principles of Geology* strongly influenced Charles Darwin.

In 1836, an eccentric French customs officer named Boucher de Perthes began digging for fossils in the gravels of the Somme River near *Abbeville* in northern France. He was surprised to find dozens of stone axes alongside the bones of animals such as an extinct form of hippopotamus. Boucher de Perthes claimed that these tools were the work of people who had lived long before the biblical flood, but scientists just laughed at him. It was not until stone artifacts and the bones of rhinoceroses, mammoths, and cave bears were found in the sealed layers of a cave near Brixham in southwestern England in 1858 that the scientific establishment finally sat up and took notice. There could be no doubt of the association, and a steady stream of British geologists and archaeologists crossed the Channel in 1859 to examine de Perthes's finds.

The same year—1859—saw the publication of Charles Darwin's book *Origin of Species,* the pivotal scientific essay of the nineteenth century. It described the theory and mechanisms of evolution and provided a theoretical framework for a human history that was not a mere 6,000 years long, but extended far back into the remote past. Darwin himself said little about human ancestry, but the assumption that human beings were descended from ape-like ancestors horrified many devout Victorians (see Figure 1.4). "My dear, let us hope it is not so," exclaimed one distraught mother. As the controversy over evolution raged, scientists began the long search for human ancestors, which continues to this day.

In 1857, quarrymen working in the *Neanderthal* cave near Düsseldorf in Germany unearthed an odd-looking skull with beetling brows quite unlike anything anatomists had seen before. Many experts dismissed the find as that of a modern hermit, or even as one of Napoleon's soldiers, but the great Victorian biologist Thomas Huxley thought otherwise. He examined the skull and compared it to those of modern humans and chimpanzees, pointing out that it had some ape-like characteristics. Here, then, was the first scientific evidence that humans had some evolutionary links to the apes. He called the evolutionary relationship between apes and humans "the question of questions," and it is a subject that still engages scientists.

In the decades that followed, the search for what was soon called the "missing link" between apes and humans took hold of the popular imagination. Even today, discoveries of early human fossils cause considerable excitement and often turn their finders into media celebrities. Raymond Dart caused an international furor when he announced the discovery of a primitive ape-human,

Figure 1.4 A Thomas Nast cartoon from the British humor magazine *Punch* lampooning Charles Darwin's linking of apes to humans.

Australopithecus ("southern ape human"), in South Africa in 1924. The celebrated Leakey family—Louis, Mary, son Richard and his wife Meave—have added more chapters to early human evolution than all other scientists put together, through a combination of expert fieldwork, intuition, and sheer patience. For example, Louis and Mary Leakey searched at *Olduvai Gorge* in Tanzania for human fossils for more than a quarter century before they unearthed a magnificent 1.75-million-year-old *Australopithecus* skull in 1959. Since then, attention has shifted northward to the Lake Turkana region of northern Kenya and the desolate Awash area of Ethiopia, which was covered by lush woodland 5 million years ago. Not that the numerous fossil finds of the past half century have dampened controversy. The ferocious debates over human evolution and early human behavior rage just as stormily today as they did in Darwin's time.

The Discovery of the Ancient Civilizations

The Ancient Egyptians

The Greeks and Romans considered the ancient Egyptians the fountain of wisdom and medical knowledge—the source of all the institutions of civilization. But ancient Egyptian civilization remained a mystery until French general Napoleon Bonaparte invaded Egypt in 1798 in an attempt to control the overland route to India. Napoleon professed an interest in science, so he took forty scientists along with him to record all that was known of Egypt, ancient and modern. The scholars, "Napoleon's donkeys," as the soldiers called them, were electrified by what they found. For six years they sketched and explored, collected antiquities, and compiled a magnificent record of an exotic civilization that had built temples and pyramids quite unlike anything in Greece or Italy. Among their finds was the famous Rosetta Stone, bearing a trilingual inscription that allowed the young French linguistic genius Jean François Champollion to decipher ancient Egyptian hieroglyphs in 1822. This was the scientific breakthrough that unlocked the secrets of civilization on the Nile, but by that time the scientists' remarkable discoveries had brought another breed of visitor to Egypt—the tomb robber.

Egyptian antiquities were so exotic and valuable that they commanded enormous prices in Europe, where the newly founded British Museum and the Louvre in Paris were competing for sensational exhibits. For the best part of a century, the Nile Valley attracted a remarkable procession of adventurers, treasure hunters, and scientists—a classic case of villains pitted against heroes.

Some of the tomb robbers were flamboyant characters such as circus strongman turned archaeologist Giovanni Belzoni. From 1817 to 1819, Belzoni blasted and tunneled his way from one end of Egypt to the other. He searched for papyrus inscriptions in mummy caves, where, he reported, "I contrived to sit, but when my weight bore on the body of an Egyptian, it crushed like a bandbox." He sank down "among the broken mummies, with a crash of bones, rags, and wooden cases," and had to wait for a quarter of an hour until the dust settled (Belzoni, 1820: 183). He found the (empty) royal tomb of Pharaoh Seti I in the *Valley of the Kings* near Thebes, and he was the first person in centuries to penetrate Pharaoh Ramses II's spectacular temple of *Abu Simbel.* A tall man of immense strength and considerable charm, Belzoni was an expert with levers, weights, and gunpowder—essential qualifications for an early-nineteenth-century tomb robber. He left Egypt precipitously in 1819 (after a fracas with his enemies in which shots were fired), exhibited some of his finds in London, and perished while searching for the source of the Niger River in West Africa.

Tomb robbing and looting continued unchecked in Egypt until the late nineteenth century; indeed, it persists to this day. But the mystery of hieroglyphs brought another kind of visitor to the Nile—the dedicated scientist. For example, Englishman John Gardiner Wilkinson spent ten years recording inscriptions in Egyptian tombs. He wrote a detailed account of the daily life of the ancient Egyptians, which revealed a colorful, cheerful civilization but one that was intensely conservative, deeply religious, and preoccupied with the afterlife.

All modern Egyptology has built on the work of Champollion and his contemporaries, and on the more scientific excavation methods introduced to the Nile in the late nineteenth century by the British archaeologist Flinders Petrie and others.

The Assyrians and Sumerians

"He will stretch out his hand and destroy Assyria," thundered the Old Testament prophet Zephaniah, "and will make Nineveh a desolation, and dry like a wilderness." To the occasional adventurous European visitor, the lands by the Tigris and Euphrates in what is now Iraq seemed like a confirmation of the prophet's fulminations. All that remained of *Nineveh* were some desolate earthen mounds covered with crumbling bricks. And all that survived of the Assyrians were some vague references in the Scriptures.

In 1840, the French government sent Paul-Emile Botta as consul to the small town of Mosul on the Tigris River opposite the ruins of Nineveh. His real assignment was to dig into Nineveh, to make spectacular archaeological finds as Napoleon's scientists had done in Egypt. Botta had no archaeological experience, and he did not excavate Nineveh deeply enough to find anything worthwhile. He listened with interest, though, when one of his men described the riches that lay under his home on another mound at *Khorsabad,* 14 miles (22.4 kilometers) away. The consul sent him away with a few helpers to see what he could find. A week later the man returned with tales of walls covered with carvings of strange animals. Visiting the site, Botta gasped at the bas-reliefs: winged, human-headed animals and processions of men with long beards. He put more than 300 men to work on what turned out to be the Assyrian King Sargon's palace, a vast multi-roomed structure adorned with grandiloquent reliefs that boasted of the monarch's triumphs.

Five years later, a restless young Englishman named Austen Henry Layard started digging at the city of *Nimrud* downstream from Nineveh. He found two Assyrian buildings the first day and was soon tunneling deep into magnificent palaces (see Figure 1.5 on page 11). This was the stuff of which archaeological legends were made. The visitor to Nimrud, and later Nineveh, where Layard worked with much greater success than Botta, wandered through deep earthen tunnels that followed the rooms of the palaces. Here one gazed at "the portly forms of kings . . . so life-like that they might almost be imagined to be stepping from the walls to question the rash intruder on their privacy" (Layard, 1849: 226).

Layard excavated with a small army of workmen and acted like a tribal chieftain. He arranged marriages, settled quarrels, supervised the dig all day, and recorded inscriptions until late at night. The young archaeologist was a brilliant writer; his books on Nineveh are still in print. His discoveries caused a sensation in Europe. Among other things, he uncovered a bas-relief of a royal lion hunt and a frieze that commemorated the siege of Lachish, a city of Judah mentioned in the Old Testament. His diggers even uncovered limestone slabs at the entrance to King Sennacherib's palace that bore the ruts made by his army's chariot wheels.

Layard's greatest discovery came at Nineveh, where he unearthed a complete royal library—piles of clay tablets lying a foot deep on the floor of a special chamber. He shoveled them into baskets and shipped them down the river, like all of his

Figure 1.5 Mesopotamian archaeology, nineteenth-century style: Austen Henry Layard's workmen recover a human-headed lion from an Assyrian palace at Nimrud, Iraq.

finds, on a wooden raft supported by inflated goatskins. A quarter century was to pass before even a small number of the tablets were deciphered, and when they were they yielded further sensations. In 1872, a young cuneiform expert named George Smith, who had never been to Mesopotamia, discovered a tablet that told of the prophet Hasisadra, who survived a great flood sent by the gods to punish humankind by building a large boat. Hasisadra's boat went aground on a mountain, and he sent out birds to find a resting place. The entire story bore a remarkable resemblance to the biblical story of the Great Flood. Seventeen lines of the story were missing, so Smith was sent to Iraq to find the missing lines. Incredible though it may seem, he discovered the tablet fragments in Layard's excavation dumps in a mere five days!

Those who believed in the historical truth of the Bible were, of course, electrified by the Flood tablets. But scholars were more interested in the evidence they gave for far earlier civilizations, for the Assyrians had merely copied the legend from earlier accounts. In 1877, another French diplomat, Ernest de Sarzec, excavated the ancient city of *Telloh* in southern Mesopotamia, where he discovered clay tablets and the remains of a great temple far older than those of the Assyrians. What Sarzec had found was the Sumerian civilization—the earliest literate society in the world and a civilization as old as, if not older than, that of the ancient Egyptians. A whole series of long-term excavations at other Sumerian cities like *Nippur* and Ur between the 1890s and 1930s chronicled many more details of this flamboyant, war-like civilization, a patchwork of small city-states that flourished 5,000 years ago between the Tigris and Euphrates rivers.

Troy and Mycenae

Many of the best-known nineteenth-century archaeologists were either professional travelers or adventurers. A few, like German businessman Heinrich Schliemann, were obsessed with the past. Schliemann became fascinated with the Greek poet Homer at an early age. He retired from business at the age of forty-six, determined to prove that Homer's *Iliad* and *Odyssey* were true stories. In 1871, he started excavations at *Hissarlik* in northwestern Turkey, which he soon proclaimed was the site of Homeric Troy. (Actually, British consul Frank Calvert had made the discovery before him.)

Figure 1.6 Heinrich and Sophia Schliemann. She wears the treasure allegedly found in a single hoard at Troy.

Schliemann thought and acted on a large scale. Employing engineers who had worked on the building of the Suez Canal in Egypt to supervise the work, he discovered seven ancient cities superimposed one on top of the other. His excavations culminated in the discovery of what Schliemann claimed to be a treasure of more than 8,000 gold ornaments and artifacts. He insisted that this was the Treasure of Priam, the Homeric king of Troy. Schliemann was no scientific saint—almost certainly his treasure was assembled from isolated gold pieces found over many months. Interestingly, the Treasure disappeared in the final days of World War II and was considered lost until it surfaced in Russia after the breakup of the Soviet Union. (See Figure 1.6.)

Schliemann's Troy discoveries caused a popular sensation, which reached a height when he moved his operations to *Mycenae* in Greece in 1876. This was, he thought, the legendary burial place of King Agamemnon, leader of the Greek armies at Troy. More than 125 men tore into Mycenae and uncovered a circle of stone slabs. Schliemann found more than fifteen burials at Mycenae, many of them with golden death masks and adorned with jewels and fine inlaid weapons. "I have gazed on the face of Agamemnon," cried Schliemann. He believed he had found the Homeric king; but archaeologists now date these finds to at least three or four centuries before the Trojan War, which raged in about 1190 B.C.

Heinrich Schliemann was the last of the great adventurer archaeologists to work in Mediterranean lands, for his methods were too unscientific even for his day. By the 1870s, Austrian and German archaeologists were working on Classical sites like *Olympia* with a new precision that was a far cry from the methods of Belzoni, Layard, or Schliemann. At Olympia, a team of architects worked with the archaeologists. The Germans renounced all claims to the finds, and they built a special museum for them at Olympia itself. A new era in archaeological research was beginning that put scientific recording before spectacular discovery, precise excavation before rapid shoveling.

Early American Archaeology

From the moment Christopher Columbus landed in the Bahamas in 1492, people speculated about the origins of the American Indians. In 1589, a Jesuit missionary named José de Acosta first proposed the general theory of their origins that provides the basis for modern thinking on the subject. He believed it was entirely possible that "small groups of savage hunters driven from their homelands by starvation or some other hardship" had taken an overland route through Asia to their present homelands with only "short stretches of navigation." He wrote this a century and a half before Vitus Bering sailed through the Bering Strait in 1728. Controversies over the routes taken by the first Americans and the date of their arrival continue to this day.

While some scholars speculated about Indian origins, others marveled at the great diversity of Native American populations. Some, like the Eskimo of the far north, were hunter-gatherers; others lived in large villages or, like the Aztec of Mexico and the Inka of Peru, in sophisticated civilizations. How could one account for this diversity, and why were some societies more complex than others? These questions still preoccupy archaeologists.

The "Moundbuilders"

When land-hungry colonists moved west of the Allegheny Mountains in the late eighteenth century, they were surprised to find large earthworks and burial mounds dotting the landscape. Those who dug into them found no gold, only human skeletons, copper and mica ornaments, and stone pipe bowls. Who had built these earthworks? Many colonists and intellectuals refused to believe that the "savage" Indians could have done so. They argued that they were the work of long-vanished civilizations from foreign lands.

Only a few scholars disagreed, among them Thomas Jefferson. Fascinated by what were already known as the Moundbuilders, he dug into a burial mound on his Virginia estate in the 1780s and uncovered several layers of human skeletons. Unlike many of his treasure-hunting contemporaries, Jefferson made careful note of the strata in the mound, making this the first stratigraphic excavation in the Americas.

The Moundbuilder controversy continued to smolder through the nineteenth century, pitting those who believed in an exotic explanation for the earthworks against more sober scholars like Samuel Haven of the American Antiquarian Society, who argued that the artifacts in the mounds often bore a resemblance to those used by living Native American groups. Writers churned out dozens of literary fantasies about the Moundbuilders, writing about "white people of great intelligence and skill" who had waged wars of conquest over the Midwest thousands of years ago. These racist theories had no foundation in scientific fact, but it was not until the 1890s that Cyrus Thomas of the Bureau of American Ethnology proved beyond all reasonable doubt that the mounds were in fact of Native American manufacture.

Maya Civilization

Farther south, "We were amazed on account of the great towers and buildings rising from the water. And some of our soldiers even asked whether the things we saw were not a dream," wrote conquistador Bernal Diaz of the Aztec capital in the Valley of Mexico. However, the Aztec and earlier Native American civilizations sank into almost complete historical oblivion. Dense forest covered the great Maya centers in the lowlands of Mexico and Guatemala. Only a few Catholic priests recorded details of Maya civilization before it vanished, among them Spanish bishop Diego de Landa. He visited Maya temples and recorded some of their script in 1566 while torturing and imprisoning Indians for refusing to accept the Christian faith, burning their unique hieroglyphic documents as well.

Only a few reports of temples and pyramids deep in the forest kept interest in the ancient Maya alive. It was these that excited the imaginations of two men who are among the immortals of early archaeology—lawyer-turned-traveler John Lloyd Stephens and artist Frederick Catherwood. Both were experienced archaeological travelers who had visited Egypt and the Holy Land. Stephens and Catherwood sailed for Central America in 1839, a journey that took them on foot and by mule into the depths of the tropical lowlands. They struggled through dense rain forest to the Maya city of *Copán,* where they found pyramids "some in workmanship equal to those of the finest monuments of the Egyptians." The jungle-covered ruins covered kilometers. While Catherwood settled down to draw the intricate carvings, Stephens tried to buy the site from the local people for $50 so he could exhibit his finds in New York. When the deal foundered, he contented himself with writing a famous description of Copán. "The only sounds that disturbed the quiet of this buried city were the noise of monkeys moving among the tops of the trees, and the cracking of dry branches broken by their weight. They moved over our heads in long and swift processions, forty or fifty at a time" (Stephens, 1841: 112).

Stephens and Catherwood recorded as much as they could of Copán, then visited *Palenque,* where they searched for parallels to ancient Egypt among the human figures at the site (see Figure 1.7). Back in New York, Stephens provided one of the first assessments of Maya civilization. "The works of these peoples, as revealed by the ruins, are different from the works of any known people," he wrote. "We have a conclusion far more interesting and wonderful than that of connecting the builders with the Egyptians or any other people. It is the spectacle of a people . . . originating and growing up here, having a distinct, separate, indigenous existence; like the plants and fruits of the soil, indigenous" (Stephens, 1841: 332). All subsequent scientific work on Maya civilization has been based on these famous words. Stephens and Catherwood were to journey to

Figure 1.7 John Lloyd Stephens and Frederick Catherwood examining a Maya temple deep in the Yucatán rain forest.

the Maya lowlands a second time, to study *Uxmal, Chichén Itza,* and other famous locations. These studies convinced Stephens that "these cities . . . are not the works of people who have passed" (332).

Like Austen Henry Layard, John Lloyd Stephens was a superb popular writer, and his books about the Maya became instant best-sellers. Frederick Catherwood's accompanying pictures of the ruins are among the finest of all archaeological illustrations. In writing his books, Stephens corresponded with the Boston historian William Prescott, whose *History of the Conquest of Mexico* set the Spanish Conquest against a background of the Aztecs' rapid rise to power. The books by these two men, more than any others, helped readers realize that there was more to America's past than merely Moundbuilders and mythical, exotic civilizations.

Southwestern Archaeology and the Direct Historical Approach

By the late 1800s, archaeologists and anthropologists were convinced that members of living American Indian societies were the descendants of the first Americans. So they began to work back from the present into the past. In 1879, Frank Hamilton Cushing of the Smithsonian Institution, among others, traveled to Zuñi Pueblo in New Mexico, intending to stay only three months. He ended up staying for nearly five years, observing Zuñi life in remarkable detail, even being initiated into a secret society: the Priesthood of the Bow. His widely read book *My Adventures in Zuñi* (1882) described the life and customs of a Pueblo society whose roots stretched far back into the past. His contemporary, anthropologist Adolph Bandelier, spent years wandering around the Southwest on a mule, tracking down oral histories at Pecos Pueblo and other locations (see Figure 1.8).

These oral traditions were to become a foundation of the archaeological research conducted by Alfred Kidder of Harvard University at *Pecos,* New Mexico, from 1915 to 1929. Bandelier and Cushing were two of the pioneers who showed the close relationship between anthropology, the study of living peoples, and archaeology, the study

Figure 1.8 Pecos Pueblo with the ruins of a Spanish colonial church built close to ancient pueblo kivas (subterranean chambers).

of past societies (see Chapter 2). Thus it was logical for Kidder to excavate the intricate strata of Pecos using a **direct historical approach**, working backward from well-documented historic levels far into prehistory. All American archaeology is based on the general principles developed by these and other pioneers, who showed the close links between ancient and modern Native American societies, between archaeology and anthropology.

Diversity, Diffusion, and Human Progress

As archaeologists began to study the early prehistory of humankind and the great civilizations, anthropologists were looking at the many diverse societies that explorers and missionaries were revealing every year. These societies ranged from simple hunter-gatherers such as the Tierra del Fuego Indians and Australian Aborigines to the complex and well-organized Japanese and the Pueblo Indians of the American Southwest. Then there were the ancient Egyptians and the Sumerians of Mesopotamia, civilizations that could be linked to the early development of Western civilization. How could one explain all of this diversity, and the change in human societies from hunting and gathering to city dwelling?

"From Them to Us": Unilinear Evolution

The nineteenth century was a period of remarkable industrial and technological change, to the point that notions of human progress and achievement dominated popular thinking. Darwin's theories of biological evolution seemed a natural extension of the doctrines of social progress. Archaeologists and anthropologists alike soon wrote of millennia of gradual human cultural evolution throughout early prehistory into modern times.

British anthropologist Edward Tylor (1832–1917) surveyed human development in all of its forms, from the crude stone axes of very early humans, to Maya temples in Mexico, to Victorian civilization. He developed a three-level sequence of human development, from simple hunting savagery, as he called it, through a stage of simple farming and pastoral nomadism, which he called barbarism, to civilization, the most complex of all human conditions. American anthropologist Lewis Henry Morgan (1818–1881) went even further and outlined no fewer than seven periods of human progress, starting with savagery and culminating in a "state of civilization."

Such notions of **unilinear cultural evolution**—of linear human progress from the simple to the complex—were easy to defend in a world whose frontiers were still being explored. Archaeology was still in its infancy, the remote past known mainly from Europe and the spectacular discoveries of ancient civilizations in southwestern Asia. It was easy for late-nineteenth-century scholars, living as they did in societies where doctrines of racial superiority were unchallenged, to speculate that human societies had evolved in a linear way, from simple unsophisticated hunter-gatherer bands to complex literate civilizations. Such simplistic hypotheses are long discredited.

Diffusionism: How Did Civilization Spread?

As more and more data accumulated from archaeological excavations all over the world, it became clear that a universal scheme of unilinear evolution was far too simplistic an explanation for the past. Could cultures have changed as a result of external influences? Did, for example, the ancient Egyptians spread the institutions of civilization to southwestern Asia, and perhaps even further afield? Could one account for the differences between human societies as the result of the diffusion of ideas and the migrations of peoples? In its more extreme forms, **diffusionism** is an assumption that many major human inventions originated in one place, then diffused to other parts of the world as a result of trade, migration, cultural contact, even exploration.

Diffusionist theories of prehistory were popular in the early twentieth century, when scholars like the Egyptologist Elliot Grafton Smith argued that the "Children of the Sun," the ancient Egyptians, had voyaged all over the world, taking sun worship and their civilization with them. Like unilinear cultural evolution, extreme diffusionism such as Grafton Smith's did not stand up to detailed scientific scrutiny, especially when twentieth-century archaeologists realized that they were dealing with very complex problems of culture change over very long periods of prehistoric time. It is tempting to write of bold Egyptians in great ships voyaging to America, or of sword-wielding Bronze Age chieftains fighting their way from Hungary to Belgium 3,500 years ago; but, unfortunately, the human past is much more complicated than that. Not that this deters the lunatic fringe, who still write of epic voyages and lost civilizations buried under Antarctic ice, to say nothing of ancient astronauts landing on earth and creating ancient Maya civilization.

By the 1920s, both unilinear evolution and diffusionism were discredited explanations for the past as archaeology became a fully fledged scientific discipline.

The Development of Modern Scientific Archaeology

The development of scientific archaeology and the discovery of the prehistoric past rank among the outstanding achievements of nineteenth- and twentieth-century science. The process of development began with the establishment of the antiquity of humankind and the development of the three-age system for subdividing prehistory. The crude excavations of Layard and Schliemann are part of the story, as are the pioneer efforts of Cushing and Bandelier to work from the present back into the past. But the technologically sophisticated archaeology of today can be said to stem from four major developments: the invention of modern scientific excavation techniques, the use of multidisciplinary approaches to study relationships between people and their environments, the increasing impact of science on archaeology, and the refinement of archaeological theory since the 1960s.

Scientific Excavation

The science of excavation as a systematic way of recording ancient human behavior began with the work of the Germans at Olympia in Greece during the 1870s. These meticulous excavators placed recording before spectacular discoveries.

An eccentric retired British Army general, Augustus Lane Fox Pitt-Rivers, refined the excavators' methods even further during the 1880s. Pitt-Rivers was a firearms expert who developed a passion for artifacts and the evolution of weapons. In later life, he inherited a vast fortune and huge land holdings in southern England and began devoting much of his time to excavating the ancient burial mounds and earthworks on his estates. Pitt-Rivers was no ordinary excavator. He ran his digs like military operations, employing expert supervisors who were trained surveyors. Unlike his contemporaries, who dug to find spectacular artifacts, Pitt-Rivers believed that every find, however small, was important. He insisted on accurate recording, built model reconstructions of his sites, and observed even the most minute details of the various layers (see Figure 1.9 on page 18). The military discipline of his work was apparent everywhere, even in his photographs. "The figure standing at attention in the foreground gives the scale," reads one of his captions.

Figure 1.9 A Pitt-Rivers excavation of a prehistoric burial mound at Wor Barrow, Cranborne Chase, in southern England during the early 1880s. His sites were remarkable for their careful excavation, precision, and attention to minute details. The general stands at the summit of the mound, with one of his cousins. (Courtesy of Salisbury & South Wiltshire Museum, © Anthony Pitt-Rivers.)

Pitt-Rivers's remarkable excavations went largely unheralded until the 1920s, when a new generation of field-workers refined his methods even further. The most famous was another British archaeologist, Mortimer Wheeler, who, between the 1920s and 1950s, carried out a series of beautifully executed excavations on Roman and Iron Age sites in Britain (see Figure 7.4 on page 138) and on cities of the *Harappan civilization* in Pakistan's Indus Valley. Wheeler also had a distinguished record as a military man. Like Pitt-Rivers, he insisted on precise recording, employed photographers and other experts, and pioneered the use of trained amateur diggers on his sites. Wheeler was a strict teacher who realized that all excavation was destruction. He also realized that scientific archaeology could be dull, and he did everything he could to enliven his writings about the past. "Dry archaeology is the driest dust that blows," he once remarked. How true!

Late-twentieth-century excavation still draws on the basic principles laid down by Wheeler (see Chapter 7). These include specialized methods for excavating waterlogged sites, minute recording methods using electronic instruments, and sophisticated ways of excavating minute discolorations, some of which even record the positions of long-vanished burials in sandy soil. Most important of all, today's archaeologists have moved away from the study of single sites to investigating large numbers of sites within regions (see Chapter 6). They also realize that all excavation is destruction, so that any digging should be kept to a minimum to preserve the finite record of the past for future generations.

Archaeology and Ecology

Few archaeologists thought of archaeological sites in their wider environmental context until the 1950s, although many of the tools for environmental reconstruction were developed early in the twentieth century. In 1916, Swedish scientist Lennart von Post invented the science of **palynology**, the study of minute fossil pollen grains as a means of studying ancient environments (see Chapter 10). Archaeologists eventually realized that this new technique offered a chance to study ancient societies in the context of their environments, but the study of *cultural ecology*, as it is called, did not reach a full level of sophistication until the 1950s and 1960s.

Cultural ecology is the study of the ecological relationships between human cultures and their environments, a study pioneered by anthropologist Julian Steward. Archaeologically, a concern with environmental relationships began in the late 1940s with British archaeologist Grahame Clark's excavations at the *Star Carr* hunter-gatherer site in northeast England. Using pollen analysis, plant remains, and animal bones, he was able to show that this 11,000-year-old hunting site once lay in a bed of reeds backed by birch forests. He even demonstrated that the site was occupied in late winter by studying the red deer antler in the deposits. (Clark's Star Carr interpretations have now been revised by later work; see Chapter 10.) Clark relied heavily on botanists and zoologists in his research. Today, teams of scientists from many disciplines routinely work together in the field, reconstructing the environments of late Ice Age societies in France, examining the landscape exploited by hunters 100,000 years ago in southern Africa, monitoring the modifications made by farmers to midwestern landscapes 1,200 years ago.

Scientific Methods

Archaeology is an integral part of history and of anthropology, the study of living peoples, but the high-tech methods of the sciences have had an ever-increasing impact on the field. Pollen analysis was one early contributor, as was aerial photography, which gave archaeologists an overhead view of the past (see Chapter 6). Perhaps the great revolution came in the 1950s, when **radiocarbon dating** revolutionized prehistoric chronologies, providing the first secure time scale for the last 40,000 years (see Chapter 5).

Since then, the impact of science on archaeology has been universal, in everything from computers to sophisticated ways of searching for archaeological sites through rainforest canopies, to methods for studying prehistoric diets through the carbon isotope content of human bones. The marriage between archaeology and other sciences is now so close that both the methods and theoretical approaches of many disciplines have affected the ways archaeologists go about their work. Many of these innovations are described in the pages that follow.

"From Them to Us": Contemporary Archaeological Theory

The impact of science and more scientific approaches has revolutionized explanations of the past, too. The simplistic unilinear and diffusionist theories of yesteryear are long gone, for archaeological theory has become far more sophisticated in recent years (see Chapter 4).

In archaeology, **theory** is the overall framework within which a researcher operates. Theory is still little developed in archaeology, as in the other social sciences, partly because working with highly varied human behavior is difficult, and also because of still inadequate research methods. Scientific archaeology is a constant dialogue between theory and observation, a more-or-less self-critical procedure that is very much based on inferences about the past, in turn built on phenomena found in the contemporary world.

Modern-day archaeological theory was born in the 1960s, when the well-known scholar Lewis Binford and others argued for more explicitly scientific approaches to the study of culture change in the past. The theoretical ferment has continued ever since, resulting in a considerable diversity of approaches. Some are concerned with the general processes of cultural change, others with the effects of individual and group actions on the ways cultures transform themselves through time.

Archaeological theory can be confusing, even for the expert, but the two major approaches currently in vogue are the ecological/evolutionary approach and the historical materialist approach.

Ecological/Evolutionary Approaches

Ecological/evolutionary theorists draw on a wide range of theoretical approaches, including highly sophisticated ecological and evolutionary theory. Archaeologists using this approach focus on interactions between ancient societies and their environments, and treat the former as part of holistic ecosystems.

Under this approach, culture change results from communal responses to stresses in the relationship between human societies and their ecosystems. Such stresses could include climate change—for example, a severe drought played a major role in inducing hunter-gatherers at the *Abu Hureyra* site in Syria's Euphrates Valley to switch to agriculture in about 10,000 B.C. Other stresses could be changes in the availability of such food sources as big game or acorns, rapid population increase, constraints on a group's ability to move about, or competition with other human, or even nonhuman, populations.

The ecological/evolutionary approach assumes that cultural and social change results from the complex interplay of many environmental and social factors. For instance, botanist Gordon Hillman has documented how the hunter-gatherers of the Euphrates Valley flourished in 11,000 B.C. by relying on fall nut harvests. A long drought linked to a 1,000-year cold snap in northern latitudes caused local forests to shrink. The people turned from nuts to wild grasses, a less-favored food but one that could be stored. Within a short time, they supplemented wild grasses with deliberately planted plots. After only a few generations, the foragers had become full-time farmers. When the drought ended in about 10,000 B.C., farming communities were flourishing over a wide area.

Ecological/evolutionary theory is widely used in archaeology, in part because a variety of scientific methods provide information on ancient environments and lifeways.

Historical Materialist Approaches

A second set of competing theoretical frameworks can be loosely described as "Historical Materialist," and covers a wide variety of approaches, including most research on gender and women in the past. Whereas ecological/evolutionary theorists regard human societies as an integrated, holistic system, the historical materialists view them as eclectic amalgams of competing individuals, factions, and social groups. Human existence is a constant negotiation with others—with one's spouse, one's family, those one works with, one's kin, entire communities. Each of these groups pursues its own strategies for survival and success, but they do so within the realities of the individual or collective power they possess and that of existing social inequality. Obviously, a king or a prime minister has more power to pursue his or her goals than a humble farmer hoeing his fields.

This approach places a major emphasis on the role of individual social actors in history. Historical materialists use all the same scientific methods as their ecological colleagues and develop and test hypotheses with as much rigor. They also share with ecologists a concern with human environmental interactions and have an interest in technology, the production of artifacts and commodities, the dynamics of social groups, and the control of labor and political power. But they see culture change as unfolding and being conditioned by human acts and interactions—by materialism.

Take the example of food production in the Euphrates Valley. Under the historical materialist rubric, one would theorize that with plenty of wild grain and abundant labor, more competitive individuals might deliberately intensify their collection and storage of wild grains, then foster their cultivation, as a deliberate strategy for acquiring surpluses to be used as social capital for increasing their own wealth and social status—by throwing feasts, engaging in ceremonial exchanges, and other devices. In other words, individuals are all-important in the changeover from foraging to agriculture.

The historical materialist approach places people at the center of the study of the past. We should never forget that archaeology, for all its scientific methods, is about the people of the past and the ways in which they made decisions about their lives.

Today's archaeological theory seems remote from the romantic days of archaeology, when Layard, Schliemann, Stephens, and others discovered entire civilizations in a few weeks. Modern archaeology is a serious, meticulous discipline with highly technical jargon and research methods. But the thrill of archaeological discovery is still there, even after a long day in the hot sun or the fog and cold wind.

Perhaps the greatest moment of archaeological discovery came in 1922, when Egyptologist Howard Carter pried a small hole through the sealed doorway leading to the tomb of the pharaoh Tutankhamun. He shone a candle through the aperture and was struck dumb with amazement. "What do you see?" his companion Lord Carnarvon asked impatiently. "Wonderful things," whispered Carter as he stepped back from the hole.

Few of us will ever be fortunate enough to experience a thrill as unique as Carter's, but the excitement of archaeology is just as great with smaller, less important finds—many of them pried from seemingly insignificant objects, or from discoveries as small as an individual seed.

In the pages that follow, we describe the principles and basic methods of archaeological research that make such moments possible.

SUMMARY

1. Archaeology began in the European Renaissance as travelers collected Classical antiquities.
2. Collecting led to excavation at the Roman city of Herculaneum in 1738, followed by widespread digging throughout Europe, especially into burial mounds.
3. The chaotic finds from these investigations were first classified by Danish museum curator Christian Jurgensen Thomsen, who developed the three-age system for subdividing prehistory in 1816.
4. The antiquity of humankind was established in 1859 after stratigraphic excavation of stone tools associated with the bones of extinct animals.
5. Other excavators in Egypt and Mesopotamia, like Englishman Austen Henry Layard, unearthed the early civilizations of southwestern Asia.
6. In the Americas, John Lloyd Stephens and Frederick Catherwood investigated ancient Maya civilization in the 1840s.
7. In North America, early archaeologists worked back from the present into the past investigating ancient Pueblo and Moundbuilder cultures in North America.
8. Early archaeological theories invoked unilinear cultural evolution and diffusion as explanations for such developments as the origins of civilization.
9. Modern scientific archaeology developed out of meticulous excavation techniques, a concern with environmental change, and explicitly scientific methods that allowed the development of two broad theoretical approaches, the one ecological and evolutionary, the other historical materialism.

TWO

Introducing Archaeology and Prehistory

The might of Rome: Hadrian's Wall, near the border of England and Scotland, built by Roman emperor Hadrian to keep the Scots out of the northernmost Roman province in the first century A.D.

CHAPTER OUTLINE

PREVIEW

Chapter 2 distinguishes between scientific and pseudoarchaeology. We will examine the differences between archaeology, anthropology, and history, the study of the past using written records. There are many specialties within archaeology, some of which will be described in this chapter. This chapter also answers a fundamental question: Why does archaeology matter in today's world? It is important as a source of information on human diversity, and it provides important tools for economic development, especially subsistence agriculture, and supports national economies through archaeological tourism. We will end with a summary of the major developments of human prehistory, as background for the chapters that follow.

In the absence of history, the spade is no mean historian.

—William A. Miles, *The Deverill Barrow,* 1826

In 7000 B.C., a small group of foragers camped in a sandy clearing near *Meer* in northern Belgium. One day, someone walked away from camp, sat down on a convenient boulder, and made some stone tools, using some carefully prepared flakes and lumps of flint he or she had brought along. A short time later, a second artisan sat down on the same boulder with a prepared flint cobble, struck off some blanks, and made some borers. Later, the same two stone workers used their finished tools to bore and groove some bone. When they finished, they left the debris from their work lying around the boulder.

When Belgian archaeologist Daniel Cahen excavated the site 9,000 years later, all he found were some scatters of stone debris. He plotted the clusters and painstakingly refitted the stone flakes onto their original stone cobbles. After months of work, he reconstructed the stone workers' activities and showed that the second one was left-handed.

This story, conjured up from a tiny scatter of inconspicuous stone tools, appears to be a miracle of archaeological detective work. In fact, it emerged from months of careful excavation, and especially laboratory work, which pieced together hundreds of stone fragments into a coherent reconstruction of ancient life. Modern scientific archaeology has an awesome ability to reconstruct the behavior of our forebears. The following pages take you on a journey through the world of scientific archaeology—an adventure as engaging as it is many-sided.

The Tourist, the Collector, and the Archaeologist

Any thinking person who visits an archaeological site faces the reality of the past, a vista of human experience that stretches far back in time. How, visitors may wonder, do archaeologists know how old a site is, and what do their finds mean? What do archaeologists really do? How do they unravel the complexities of early human societies? It seems very complicated to dig for the past. And the unchanging, incredibly ancient structures that surround one add to the sense of romance and awe (see the Discovery box on pages 24–25).

Discovery

An Anglo-Saxon Ship Burial at Sutton Hoo, England, 1939

In 1939, when British archaeologist James Brown asked landowner Elizabeth Pretty which of the burial mounds on her property at Sutton Hoo in eastern England she wanted opened, she pointed to the largest and asked, "What about this?" Her casual choice epitomized the archaeology of sixty years ago but led to a remarkable feat of archaeological excavation.

The work began that very afternoon with the cutting of a wide trench across the mound. Brown soon found five iron ship nails and suspected at once that he had found a funerary boat. With trowels and brushes, he and his workers cleared the bow and eleven frames of an Anglo-Saxon vessel. When he reached a sealed bulkhead, Brown wisely stopped the excavation and called in Charles

Figure 2.1a The Anglo-Saxon ship burial at Sutton Hoo, England. The ship's hull was exposed by excavating gray discolorations and iron nail fragments in the soil (Copyright: The British Museum).

Our complex world is full of unexplained mysteries and hidden surprises—phenomena that sometimes defy obvious explanation. Many people believe that the archaeologist lives in mysterious regions of our world, with "missing links" and long-lost civilizations. Enterprising authors and movie producers take us on fantasy rides into the strange territories of their specially selected archaeologists. From the comfort of our armchairs, via television, we can search for lost continents, reconstruct Noah's Ark, and trace the landing patterns of extraterrestrials' spaceships. Such searches are not only fantasy fun but are big business as well. Millions of dollars have been made from this type of archaeology—which, unfortunately, bears little resemblance to reality.

The romance of archaeology has taken people all over the world in search of the past. Every year thousands of tourists visit the pyramids of *Giza* in Egypt (see Figure 2.2 on page 26). To promote tourism, the Mexican government spent millions of pesos restoring the ancient city of Teotihuacán in the Valley of Mexico. Most popular package

Phillips of Cambridge University, an expert on Anglo-Saxon sites and on ancient timber structures. Phillips was a meticulous excavator. He followed gray discolorations in mound soil and traced the lines of the boat and the planked burial chamber that lay amidships. The diggers even found evidence of repairs to the hull (see Figure 2.1a). With infinite care, they opened the burial chamber, recording and conserving each find, however small. The chamber contained the treasure buried with a long-vanished body of a nobleman, including metal cauldrons, bowls, spears, axes, bottles, and thirty-seven coins dating to about A.D. 650. The boat was one of two in the burial mound. It was 89 feet (27 meters) long; it had no mast or sails and was propelled by thirty-eight oars, and it had been dragged overland 0.3 miles (1 kilometer) to its final resting place.

Phillips excavated Sutton Hoo with great skill, but later generations of archaeologists have been able to use far more sophisticated technology—metal detectors to find small buttons, ground-penetrating radar to map subsurface features, and ultraviolet light to detect the fragile outlines of bodies in the soil (see Figure 2.1b).

Figure 2.1b A more recent excavation of the burial ground at Sutton Hoo.

tours abroad now include visits to an archaeological site or two (for a map, see Figure 2.3 on pages 27–29). Many sites—for example, Stonehenge in England and the Stone Age painted cave at Lascaux in France—are in danger of permanent damage from the sheer volume of visiting tourists. As a result, you can no longer wander among the uprights at Stonehenge. The French government has built a magnificent replica of the Lascaux cave paintings for tourists to enjoy, but the original cave is closed to all but scientists (see Figure 2.4 on page 30).

Most such archaeological sites now boast a museum. Eagerly, the tourist peers into the display cases and admires the glittering gold of a fine necklace or the crude stone tools made by a human hand more than a million years ago. Perhaps the visitor pauses at the door to buy a replica of the archaeological find in the case. It is a pleasing reminder of a fleeting visit to the past, a memento to be displayed at home. But, unfortunately, many people are greedier—they covet the past and want to own a piece of the real thing.

Figure 2.2 The pyramids of Giza in Egypt: These pyramids were the culmination of more than a century of aggressive royal pyramid building by ancient Egyptian kings of the Old Kingdom, c. 2600 to 2100 B.C. Each served as the burial place for a king and was connected by a causeway to a mortuary temple where offerings were made to the deceased. The pyramid shape is thought to represent a symbolic sun-ray descending to earth through the clouds, a symbolic ladder for the divine king to ascend and join the sun god in the heavens.

Collectors and treasure hunters, many of whom regard themselves as legitimate archaeologists, are the curse of archaeology. The spiritual beliefs and vanity of the ancients decreed that they be buried with riches to accompany them in the afterlife. The greed of their descendants decrees that people today covet these riches. The antiquities dealer and the private collector pay enormous prices for painted pots and other fine antiquities looted from otherwise undisturbed sites. Major museums compete to acquire the finest specimens of prehistoric art. In perhaps the most blatant case of all, the Metropolitan Museum of Art in New York paid a cool million dollars for one Greek vase, which had been looted from an Italian tomb. The Museum is now returning the vase to Italy.

There seems to be some fundamental human desire to collect things and display them in the privacy of one's home. Collecting is a passion once described as "so violent that it is inferior to love or ambition only in the pettiness of its aims." People collect everything from barbed wire to beer cans, and many think of archaeology as the acquisition of objects. But when people collect archaeological finds, they are collecting a part of an endangered, finite resource that is rapidly vanishing, a unique archive that can never be replaced. Every object they buy or dig from a site is the product of ancient human behavior. This behavior can be partly reconstructed from objects found in the earth, but much of our insight depends on the contexts (positions) in time and space in which the objects occur in the ground. Removing an artifact from its context is an irreversible act that cheats us all of knowledge. (Perhaps it should be mentioned that professional archaeologists also destroy sites as they excavate them, but they record the context of their finds as they go along, a critical ingredient in scientific archaeology.)

Figure 2.3 The archaeological sites mentioned in this book. Obvious geographic place names are omitted.

Modern archaeology is not treasure hunting or collecting, nor is it a fantasy search for lost worlds; it is the systematic study of humanity in the past. This general definition includes not only ancient technology and human behavior, but also social organization, religious beliefs, and every aspect of human culture.

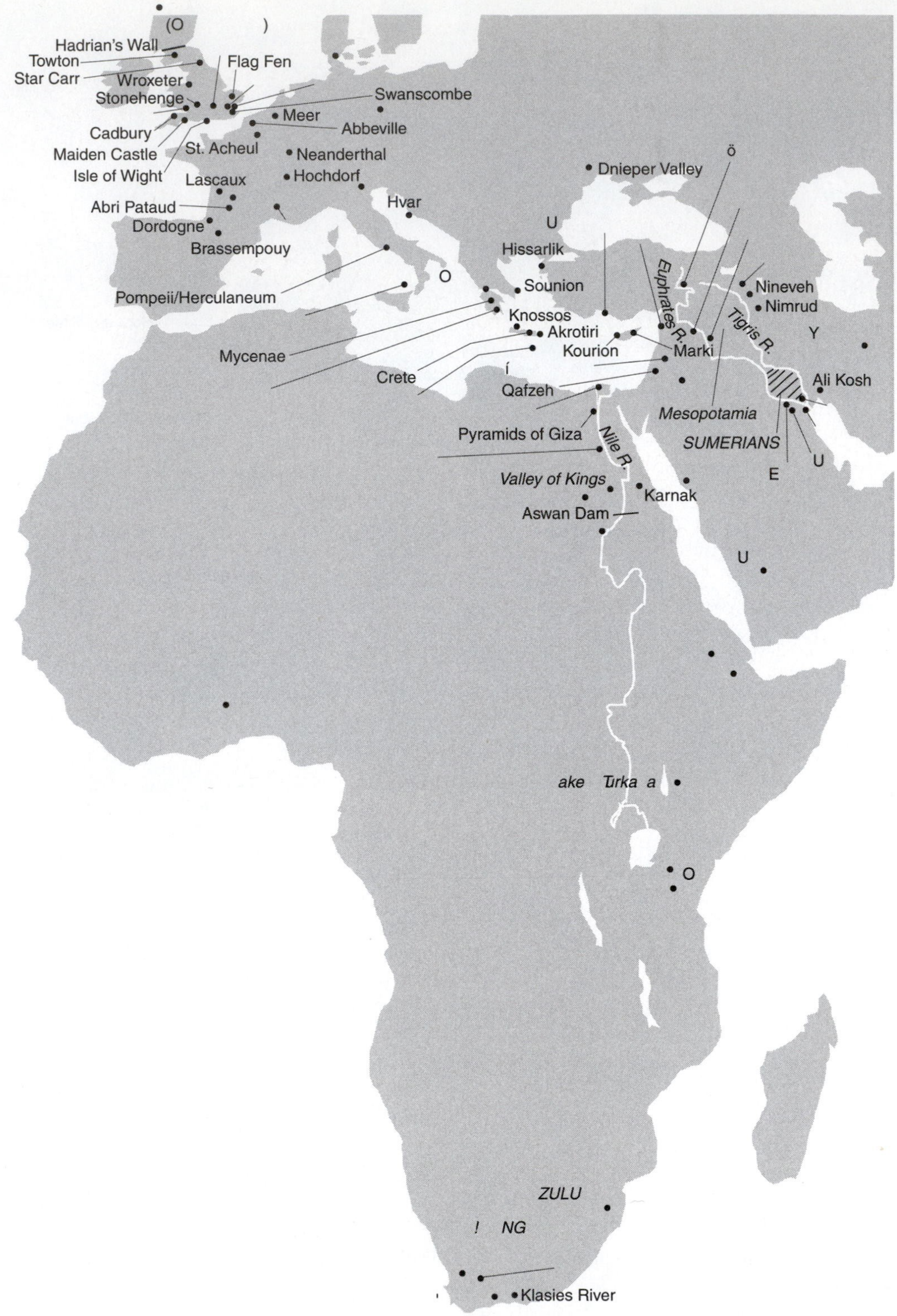

Figure 2.3 *(continued)*

Figure 2.3 *(continued)*

Figure 2.4 A great bull on the walls of Lascaux cave, painted about 17,000 years ago.

We must never forget that the archaeological sites that document the past are a finite, not renewable, resource. All of this raises a fundamental question: Who owns the past?

Who Needs and Owns the Past?

All societies have an interest in the past. It is always around them, haunting, mystifying, tantalizing, sometimes offering potential lessons for the present and future. The past is important because social life unfolds through time, embedded within a framework of cultural expectations and values. In the high Arctic, Inuit preserve their traditional attitudes, skills, and coping mechanisms in some of the harshest environments on earth. They do this by incorporating the lessons of the past into the present. In many societies, the ancestors are the guardians of the land, which symbolizes present, past, and future. Westerners have an intense scientific interest in the past, partly born of curiosity, but also out of a need for historical identity. There are many reasons to attempt to preserve an accurate record of the past. Nobody, least of all an archaeologist, should assume that he or she is uniquely privileged in his or her interest in the remains of that past.

We have no monopoly on history. Many non-Western societies do not perceive themselves as living in a changeless world. They make a fundamental distinction between the recent past, which lies within living memory, and the more remote past. For instance, the Australian Aborigine groups living in northeast Queensland distinguish between *kuma,* the span of events witnessed by living people, *anthantnama,* a long time ago, and *yilamu,* the period of the creation. Furthermore, many societies also accept that there was cultural change in the past. The Hadza hunter-gatherers of East Africa tell of their homeland's first inhabitants as being giants without fire or tools. These paradigms of the past take many forms, some involving mythic creators of culture—usually primordial ancestors, deities, or animals establishing contemporary social customs and the familiar landscape; others describing a more remote, discontinuous heroic era, such as that of the Greeks, which allowed such writers as the playwright Aeschylus to evaluate contemporary behavior.

Most human societies of the past were nonliterate, which meant that they transmitted knowledge and history orally, by word of mouth. The Aztec oral histories, partially set down after the Spanish Conquest in the sixteenth century A.D., are an excellent example of history transmitted by word of mouth. They were recited according to a well-defined narrative plot, which focused on great men, key events such as the dedication of the sun god Huitzilopochtli's temple in the Aztec capital in 1487, and the histories of favored groups. In these, as in other oral histories, there were formulas and themes, which formed the central ingredients of a story that varied considerably from one speaker to the next, even if the essential content was the same. Many oral histories are mixtures of factual data and parables that communicate moral and political values. But to those who hear them, they are publically sanctioned history, performed before a critical group, and subject to the critical evaluation of an audience that may have heard the same stories before.

Oral traditions are hard to use scientifically since their antiquity is very difficult to establish. In some cases—in Australia, for example—there are instances where oral histories and archaeology coincide in general terms. For example, the traditions speak of the arrival of the first people from overseas, of the flooding of coastal areas after the Ice Age, and of the hunting of giant marsupials (pouched animals like the kangaroo). So Australia's past can be said to come from two sources: archaeological data and oral traditions. In some instances, the archaeologists and the indigenous people have shared interests and come together to identify sacred and historic places, often to ensure they are preserved—even if the two groups disagree fundamentally on the "significance" of a particular location (for instance, a location where the archaeologist finds no buildings or artifacts, yet the local people consider it a "sacred place").

But, all too often, archaeologists and local communities have different interests in the past. To archaeologists, the past is scientific data to be studied with all the rigor of modern science. To local people, the past is often highly personalized and the property of the ancestors. Such accounts are valid alternative versions of history, which deserve respect and understanding, for they play a vital role in the creation and reaffirmation of cultural identity. And they raise a fundamental question, which lies behind many Native American objections to archaeological research. What do archaeologists have to offer to a cultural group that already has a valid version of its own history? Why should they be permitted to dig up the burial sites of the ancestors or other settlements and sacred places under the guise of studying what is, to the people, a known history? It is a question that archaeologists have barely begun to address. We should never forget that alternative, and often compelling, accounts of ancient times exist, and they play an important role in helping minority groups and others to maintain their traditional heritage as it existed before the arrival of the Westerner. There are many stakeholders in the past, not just archaeologists.

What Do Archaeologists Do?

What, then, do archaeologists do? Quite simply, we are a special kind of anthropologist and a special type of historian.

Anthropology, Archaeology, and History

Anthropology is the scientific study of humanity in the widest possible sense. Anthropologists study human beings as biological organisms and as people with a distinctive and unique characteristic—culture. They carry out research on contemporary human societies and on human development from the very earliest times. Thus, there is a close relationship between archaeology and anthropology, as there is between archaeology, history, and other disciplines.

This enormous field is divided into four major subdisciplines. **Physical** (or biological) **anthropology** involves the study of human biological evolution and the variations among different living populations. Physical anthropologists also study the behavior of living nonhuman primates, such as the chimpanzee and the gorilla, research that can suggest explanations for behavior among very early humans. **Cultural anthropology** deals with the analysis of human social life, both past and present. It is primarily the study of human culture and how culture adapts to the environment. Among cultural anthropologists, **ethnographers** describe the culture, technology, and economics of living and extinct societies, and **ethnologists** engage in comparative studies of societies, a process that involves attempts to reconstruct general principles of human behavior. **Social anthropologists** analyze social organization, ways in which people organize themselves. Finally, **linguistic anthropologists** study human languages, a field of research that is sometimes important to the study of the past.

Archaeology and cultural anthropology are part of the same discipline. However, archaeologists study past societies, ancient and relatively modern, which means that they cannot speak to their informants. Their excavations and site surveys yield the material remains of human behavior in the past—stone tools, pot fragments, broken animal bones, and so on—all manufactured or modified by deliberate actions possibly centuries, even millennia, ago. The archaeologist links these material remains to actual human behavior by developing theoretical models to explain such behavior and cultural change over long periods of time. As we have said, archaeology is a unique way of studying human culture change from the time of the earliest human beings 2.5 million years ago up to the present.

By studying ancient societies, archaeologists are also studying human history on a broad and long canvas, but with a difference. They use the material remains of the past to reconstruct the past, whereas historians use documents of all kinds. History reconstructed by archaeologists tends to be more anonymous, for archaeological chronologies rarely rival those of historians and can only occasionally pinpoint someone's lifetime. But we are a special kind of historian—an emphasis that is stronger in Europe, where there is continuity in history over thousands of years, than in the Americas, where continuous written records date back just a few centuries to Christopher Columbus in A.D. 1492.

Archaeologists on the Job

Modern-day archaeologists are far removed from the pith-helmeted professors beloved by cartoonists. As recently as the 1940s, you would have been correct to assume that most archaeologists spent their time in the field engaged in excavation and surveys. A half century ago, there were only a few hundred archaeologists throughout the world, most of them in Europe and North America. Today, there are archaeologists working in every corner of the globe—in Australia and on the Pacific Islands, in China and Siberia, in tropical Africa, Latin America, and the high Arctic. No one knows how many archaeologists there are worldwide, but the number must be near 10,000. Today, archaeology is a global science, a profession as much as an academic pursuit. There are even archaeologists engaged in the study of modern urban garbage.

The change began after World War II, as archaeologists became concerned about the wholesale destruction of archaeological sites with no effort being made to investigate them first. "Salvage archaeology" was born, notably with the international effort sponsored by UNESCO (United Nations Educational, Scientific, and Cultural Organization) to find archaeological sites in the vast area of the Nile Valley scheduled to be flooded by the Aswan Dam in the 1960s, and with the Glen Canyon Dam project in Utah. The realization that archaeological sites were vanishing rapidly in the face of looters and industrial development, and also due to deep plowing and mining, led to a stream of federal and state legislation from the 1960s through the 1980s designed to protect the past. Archaeology itself changed character in Europe and North America, as pure academic research gave way to field and laboratory research aimed at assessing and preserving the past, and also mitigating the effects of construction and other activities. Such **Cultural Resource Management (CRM)** is a type of archaeology concerned with the management and assessment of the significance of cultural resources such as archaeological sites. It is now the dominant activity in North American archaeology.

The shift toward CRM is mirrored in employment figures. In the 1960s, nearly all archaeologists were university or college professors or worked in museums. In a 1998 study of American archaeologists, Melinda Zeder of the Smithsonian Institution chronicled a dramatic shift in archaeological employment. Now only 35 percent of American archaeologists are academics; 8 percent labor in museums, and 23 percent work for federal, state, or local government, many in purely administrative functions. The fastest-growing segment of archaeological employment is in the private sector. In 1997, 18 percent of all American archaeologists worked for private consulting firms engaged in environmental monitoring and cultural resource management. The figure is still climbing.

The Zeder study shows that archaeology is changing rapidly from a purely academic discipline into a profession with strong roots in both government and private business. This is because the past is under siege from industrial civilization in the forms of deep plowing and mining, industrial development, road construction, and the inexorable expansion of huge cities—not to mention looters and pothunters, who think nothing of ravaging sites for valuable finds they can sell. Increasingly, archaeologists are managers rather than professors, supervising a precious and rapidly vanishing resource: the human past. The pith-helmeted professor of yesteryear is the cultural resource manager of today. An image further removed from the adventurer of a century-and-a-half ago is hard to envision.

Many Sites, Many Archaeologists

Archaeology is now a discipline and profession of specialists, often in dauntingly obscure topics. During the course of my career, I have worked with prehistorians, Egyptologists, and underwater archaeologists, to mention only a few relatively broad specialties. But I have also collaborated with experts on ancient Egyptian wine, cultural resource management, Ice Age earthworms, southern African mice, reindeer teeth growth rings, and eighteenth-century Colonial American gardens. All this without mentioning the many federal and state government archaeologists and private sector specialists who have crossed my path.

Here are some of the major specialties among academic archaeologists: **Prehistoric archaeologists (prehistorians)** study prehistoric times, from the time of the earliest human beings to the frontiers of written history. The numerous specialties within prehistoric archaeology include **paleoanthropology**, experts on the culture and artifacts of the earliest humans, on stone technology, art, and hunter-gatherers. There are specialists in the **prehistory** of the Old and New Worlds, Europe, the American Southwest, and many other regions.

Classical archaeologists study the remains of the great Classical civilizations of Greece and Rome (see Figure 2.5 on page 34). While many classical archaeologists study art and architecture, others study the same kinds of economic, settlement, and social issues that interest prehistorians.

Figure 2.5 The Parthenon in Athens.

Biblical archaeologists are experts on a variety of ethnic groups living in what is now Israel, Lebanon, and Syria. They attempt to link accounts in biblical and Canaanite literature with archaeological data.

Egyptologists, **Mayanists**, and **Assyriologists** are among the many specialist archaeologists who work on specific civilizations or time periods. Such specialties require unusual skills—for example, a knowledge of Egyptian hieroglyphs.

Historical archaeologists work on archaeological sites and study problems from periods in which written records exist. They excavate medieval cities such as Winchester and York in England, and study Colonial American settlements, Spanish missions, and nineteenth-century frontier forts in the American West.

Historical archaeology (sometimes called text-aided archaeology) is concerned mainly with the study of ancient human societies with the aid of written texts. (See Chapter 5.)

Underwater archaeologists study ancient sites and shipwrecks on the seabed and on lake beds, even under the rapids in Minnesota streams where fur traders once capsized and lost canoe loads of trade goods. Underwater archaeology uses diving technology, but its objectives are identical to those of archaeology on land—to reconstruct and interpret past cultures, as well as ancient seafaring (see the section on the Uluburun shipwreck in Chapter 13).

Industrial archaeologists study buildings and other structures of the Industrial Revolution such as Victorian factories.

Apart from area specialists, there are experts in all manner of archaeological methods, including **archaeobotanists**, who study ancient food remains; lithic technologists, who are experts on stone technology; and **zooarchaeologists**, specialists in ancient animal bones. There are even some archaeologists who specialize in forensics—ancient (and modern) crime.

Why Does Archaeology Matter?

Archaeology exercises a curious fascination. Cave people, golden pharaohs, lost cities hiding in swirling mist: The fantasies abound. So do spectacular discoveries, such as the *Moche* Lords of *Sipán,* Peru, found intact in an adobe platform where they were buried in A.D. 400 with all their gold and silver regalia (see Figure 2.6 and Figure 3.5 on page 55). Finds like Sipán or that of Ötzi the Ice Man, a Bronze Age traveler found deep-frozen high in the Italian Alps (see Figure 13.4 on page 263), are indeed fascinating, even romantic discoveries. Such scientific treasure troves appeal to the explorer and adventurer in all of us and bring the past to life in dramatic ways.

Few modern-day discoveries generate the excitement experienced by three French cave explorers when they entered a 30-inch-wide (76-centimeter-wide) cavity in the wall of a gorge in the Ardèche Mountains of southeastern France on December 18, 1994. Eliette Deschamps, Jean-Marie Chauvet, and Christian Hillaire squeezed through the narrow opening. They felt a draft flowing from a blocked duct, pulled out the boulders that blocked it, and saw a vast chamber 12 feet (3.6 meters) below them. Using a rope ladder, they descended into a network of chambers adorned with natural calcite columns. Calcified cave-bear bones and teeth lay on the floor, on which shallow depressions marked where the long-extinct beasts had hibernated. Suddenly, Deschamps cried out in surprise. Her lamp shone on a small mammoth figure painted on the wall. The explorers moved deeper into the chamber and came across more paintings—positive and negative hand imprints and figures of mammoths, rhinoceroses (see Figure 2.7 on page 36), and cave lions. As they gazed at the paintings, the three explorers felt as if time were abolished, as if the artists had left the cave only a few moments earlier. As one of them put it, "The artists' souls surrounded us. We felt we could feel their presence" (Chauvet, Deschamps, and Hillaire, 1996: 42).

Figure 2.6 A mannequin wears the full regalia of a Moche Lord of Sipán, northern coastal Peru, c. A.D. 400.

The *Grotte de Chauvet,* named after one of the discoverers, lay undisturbed from the time of the late Ice Age. Hearths on the floor looked as if they had been used the day before. The explorers found an extraordinary frieze of black wild horses and oxen and two woolly rhinoceroses facing one another. One 30-foot-long (9-meter-long) frieze of black figures depicted lionesses, rhinoceroses, bison, and mammoths. Far to the right stood a human figure wearing a bison-head mask, perhaps the shaman supervising the immense frieze. Radiocarbon tests reveal that Grotte de Chauvet was visited repeatedly between about 31,000 and 24,000 years ago, making it one of the earliest painted caves in the world.

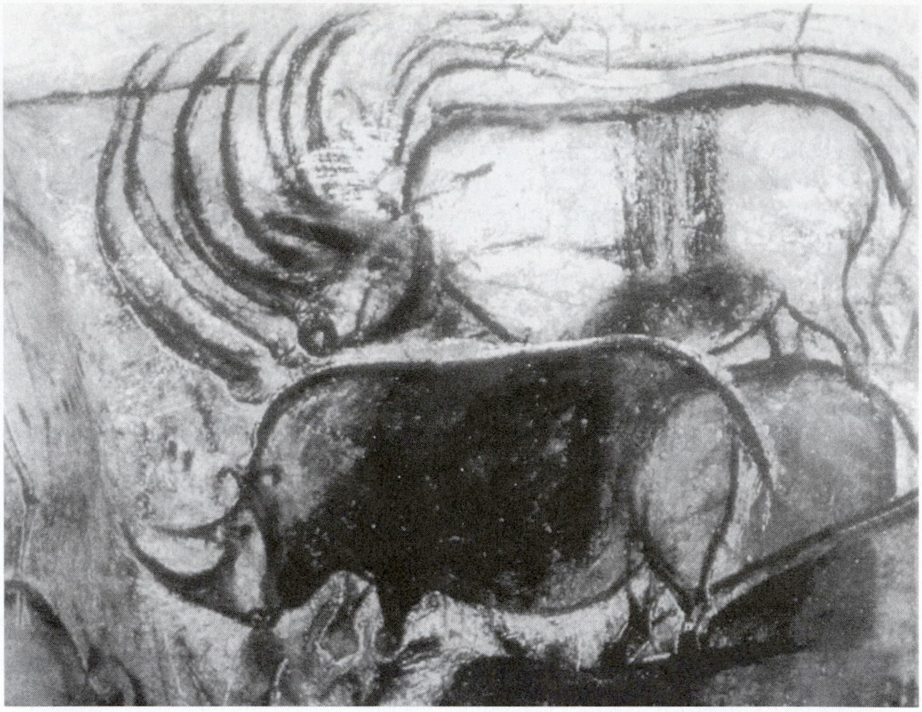

Figure 2.7 Grotte de Chauvet, France: Woolly rhinoceroses painted some 24,000 to 31,000 years ago by Cro-Magnon artists.

Mysteries of the Past

Chauvet's Ice Age animals caused an international sensation, like Tutankhamun's tomb and Ötzi the Ice Man. But the fascination with archaeology is much wider, for the past is redolent with unsolved mysteries and unexplained phenomena. You have only to watch fantasy movies—which cover such hoary old favorites as the search for Noah's Ark, the curse of the pharaohs (made especially realistic in a memorable performance by Boris Karloff as a hyperactive mummy in a movie of the 1930s), or the lost continent of Atlantis—for an example of this fascination with the past. But such fantasy stories are little more than pseudoarchaeology, no more historical fact than the Indiana Jones adventure movies. More legitimate archaeological puzzles, such as how the ancient Egyptians built the pyramids, or why the *Ancestral Pueblo (Anasazi)* people of *Chaco Canyon,* New Mexico, built roadways leading to nowhere (see Figure 5.10 on page 100), intrigue audiences that are much wider than merely archaeologists. Today, archaeology is as much a part of popular culture as football or the automobile. Thousands of people read archaeology books for entertainment, join archaeological societies, and flock to popular lectures on the past.

A Sideline: Pseudoarchaeology

Then there is pseudoarchaeology, which is not archaeology at all. Take a few intrepid adventurers in an ancient sailing vessel, some startlingly new religious cult, a handful of pyramids, lots of gold, and exotic civilizations swirling in ever-parting mists and you have the irresistible ingredients for an epic "archaeological" tale. Pseudoarchaeology is all the rage in a world where many people are fascinated by adventure, escapism, and space fiction. A distinctive literary genre tells compelling tales of a long-lost past. For instance, British journalist Graham Hancock has claimed that a great civilization flourished under

Antarctic ice 12,000 years ago. (Of course, its magnificent cities are buried under deep ice sheets, so we cannot excavate them!) Colonists supposedly spread to all parts of the world from this Antarctic home, colonizing such well-known sites as *Tiwanaku* in the Bolivian highlands and building the Sphinx by the banks of the Nile. Hancock weaves an ingenious story by piecing together all manner of controversial geological observations and isolated archaeological finds. He waves aside the obvious archaeologist's reaction, which asks where traces of these ancient colonies and civilizations are to be found. Hancock fervently believes in his far-fetched theory, and, being a good popular writer, he has managed to piece together a best-selling book, which reads like a "whodunit" written by an amateur sleuth.

Pseudoarchaeology appeals to people who are impatient with the deliberate pace of science and who like to believe that "there is always a faint possibility that . . . ." Some of these "cult archaeologies" show all the signs of becoming personality cults, even religious movements. The theories espoused by the leaders become articles of faith, the object of personal conversion. They are attempts to give meaning to being human and are often steeped in symbolism and religious activity. Almost invariably the cultists dismiss archaeologists as "elitists" or "scientific fuddy-duddies" because they reject wild theories that are unsupported by scientifically gathered evidence.

This book describes the science of archaeology, which, ironically, can be more interesting than the best fantasy tales.

Archaeology and Human Diversity

Archaeology's unique ability lies in its capacity to reach back over the millennia, to reconstruct and explain the cultures and lifeways of unimaginably ancient societies as they changed over many centuries and thousands of years. Why did some societies vanish without a trace, while others developed agriculture or highly complex urban civilizations? Who first tamed fire or invented the plow? How did bronze and iron smelting change the course of human history? Archaeology is fascinating because it enables us to study not only the remotest human origins, but also the ever-changing biological and cultural diversity of humankind.

We live in a complex world of almost bewildering human diversity. We can land people on the moon, send space probes to Mars, establish our position in the midst of tropical rain forests within inches, and build computers of mind-numbing speed and complexity. Yet our collective understanding of human diversity and our ability to collaborate with others from different cultural backgrounds and cultural heritages remains at an elementary level. We tend to fear diversity—people who are different from us, who speak alien languages or look at the world with cultural perspectives that differ from our own. We fear diversity because of apprehension, sometimes out of bigotry, but often just out of plain ignorance. Archaeology is one of the major educational weapons in the fight against such ignorance.

The most important lesson about diversity that archaeology teaches us is that we are all descended from what Harvard University biologist Stephen J. Gould once called "a common African twig." As long ago as 1871, the great Victorian biologist Charles Darwin of *Origin of Species* fame theorized that humanity originated in Africa, because this was where the greatest variety of apes dwelt. Today, we know that he was right. More controversially, thanks to DNA studies and archaeological finds, we also suspect that our own direct ancestors, *Homo sapiens,* originated on the same continent, then spread out of Africa, replacing much older human populations. Most important of all, both archaeology and DNA studies have shown that the relationships among all modern humans are closer than they are different. Above all, we are all humans with the identical abilities to conceptualize and shape our world, to make inventions, to love and hate, and to adapt to any environment on earth. We just happen to do it in different ways.

Archaeology studies diversity at its very beginnings, millennia before our intermingled industrial world was changed forever by the massive population movements of the nineteenth and twentieth centuries. We seek answers to fundamental questions. Why are we biologically and culturally diverse? In what ways are we similar or different? When did the great diversity of humankind first come into being, and why? Both geneticists and archaeologists suspect that we modern humans originated in tropical Africa, then spread throughout the world during the late Ice Age, after 100,000 years ago. This complex set of population movements and cultural changes was perhaps the seminal development of early human history. From it stemmed not only the brilliant biological and cultural diversity of modern humankind, but also art and religious life, agriculture and animal domestication, village life and urban civilization—the very roots of our own diverse and complex world.

Archaeology provides a constant reminder of our common, and recent, biological and cultural heritage in a world where racism is commonplace. Human artifacts are excellent barometers, not only of ancient behavior but also of cultural diversity. Early historic American society was much more diverse than we realize (see Chapter 13). Archaeologist Kathleen Deagan has excavated the site of Florida's *Fort Mose,* the first free African-American community in North America. This tiny hamlet of some thirty-seven families, 2 miles (3.2 kilometers) from Spanish St. Augustine on the Atlantic coast, was founded in 1738 and occupied until the Spanish abandoned Florida in 1763. In its heyday, the settlement of twenty-two thatched houses, a church, guardhouses, and a well lay behind earthen fortifications. Many of the inhabitants were of West African origin and used not only African artifacts, but also objects of English, Native American, and Spanish origin. Eventually, Deagan and her researchers hope to use the artifacts to decipher what cultural elements were important in the lives of the inhabitants.

Archaeology as a Political Tool

Rulers and governments have used the past to justify the present since civilization began. The Sumerians, who created the world's first urban civilization between the Euphrates and Tigris rivers in southern Iraq, created a heroic past personified by the Epic of Gilgamesh, a legendary king who ruled before a mythic flood that frightened even the gods. When the waters subsided, they restored kingship to earth at the city of *Kish,* where recorded history began.

The past has always served the present, for every society manufactures history. The Aztecs of highland Mexico were an obscure farming society in A.D. 1200. Only three centuries later, they ruled over all of *Mesoamerica,* that area of Central America where indigenous civilizations arose—an area straddling much of highland and lowland Mexico, Guatemala, Belize, and Honduras—from a dazzling capital, *Tenochtitlán,* in the Valley of Mexico (see Figure 6.4 on page 117). In 1426, a powerful official named Tlacaelel became the right-hand man to a series of fifteenth-century Aztec rulers in highland Mexico. He prevailed on his masters to burn all earlier historical records of other cities in the valley. In their place, he concocted a convincing rags-to-riches story that recounted the Aztecs' mercurial rise from obscurity to become masters of Mexico, as the chosen people of Huitzilopochtli, the Sun God himself. The new history was blatant political propaganda that justified a century of militant imperialism that made the Aztecs the rulers of a vast empire.

No one can look at the past objectively. We all bring our individual cultural biases to the study of history and archaeology, for we tend to look at past developments and events through the blinkered eyes of our own value system and society. Thus, any archaeological interpretation of the past is a form of narrative, which, by the nature of its evidence, is both a scientific and political/literary enterprise. As part of this enterprise, archaeological theory aims to explain the past as well as describe it.

Archaeology is peculiarly vulnerable to political misuse, because it deals with ancient societies and events that are little known, even from archaeological sources. Most people who use the past for nationalistic or political ends are searching for a glorious past, a simple story that justifies their own political agenda. The Nazis unashamedly used archaeology before World War II to propagate notions of a true "Nordic" race in ancient Europe. In the former Yugoslavia, the past has been a prize in endless political squabbles that go back centuries. Construction and ownership of a real or imagined past and its monuments serves as a vital political resource when seeking to sway public opinion. Such archaeologies are rarely based on scholarly standards of logic and evidence. Most, at best, stretch historical facts to their breaking points and promote bigotry, nationalism, and chicanery.

On the other side of the coin, archaeology, with its extended time perspectives, has added entire new chapters to human history in areas of the world where written records go back little more than a century. In parts of central Africa, for example, the first documentary history begins with the establishment of colonial rule in about 1890, with only a few Victorian explorers' accounts dating from earlier decades. The primary goal of archaeology in much of Africa is to write unwritten history as a way of fostering national identity, not from archives and documents, but from long-abandoned villages and rubbish heaps, the material remains of the past.

Archaeology and Economic Development

Bone-chilling cold descended on the high plains around Lake Titicaca, Bolivia, that night. White frost covered the dry hillsides where local farmers planted their potatoes in thin soil. Many families watched all night as their growing potatoes withered and turned brown before their eyes. As dawn spread, they wandered through their ruined fields, glancing down at a thin white blanket of warm air covering some experimental plots on the plain below. They had watched suspiciously as the archaeologists dug across long-abandoned ancient fields in the lowlands, then given one of their neighbors seed potatoes to plant in a replica of such a field. He piled up layers of gravel, clay, and soil, then dug shallow irrigation canals alongside the raised fields. The green shoots of the new potatoes grew far higher than those on the arid slopes. As the temperature dropped below freezing, a white cloud of warm air formed above the raised fields, hiding them from view. Now the warming sun dispersed the white blanket, revealing lush, green potato plants, their leaves only slightly browned by frost.

After months of ground survey, excavation, and controlled farming experiments, archaeologists had rediscovered the forgotten genius of ancient Andean farmers for the benefit of their descendants. The ancestors had used water to protect their crops against frost with such success that they supported the glittering city of Tiwanaku and its powerful kingdom for more than five centuries. Today, more than 1,500 modern farmers have rediscovered the benefits of raised fields (see Figure 2.8 on page 40). Dozens of nearby communities now clamor for training in ancient agriculture.

Archaeology shows how the traditional system has many advantages—high crop yields, no need for fertilizer, and much-reduced risks of frost or flood damage. Furthermore, high yields can be obtained with local labor, local crops, and no expensive outside capital. At last count, nearly 2,125 acres (860 hectares) had been rehabilitated, and many more fields are planned.

The Lake Titicaca raised-field experiments have been so successful that archaeologists are now actively involved in several other such projects in the Americas. Governments are slowly discovering something that archaeologists have known for a long time. The ancients knew their environments intimately and exploited them efficiently without expensive twentieth-century technology. There is nothing wrong with their often-forgotten ways of cultivating the soil and raising several crops a year, or with

Figure 2.8 Raised fields in the Bolivian altiplano. (Courtesy of Clark Erickson.)

their successful animal husbandry. Industrial-scale agriculture is not the universal answer to the world's food crisis.

Archaeologist William Rathje has applied archaeological methods to the study of modern garbage dumps in Tucson and other American cities for a long time. He has found that bags of abandoned household garbage never lie, for empty beer cans and liquor bottles are more eloquent testimony to a family's drinking habits than a questionnaire response that denies heavy alcohol consumption. Rathje's long-term research has revealed fascinating differences between the wasteful discard habits of many lower-income families and the habits of the wealthy, who are often more careful to consume leftovers. It's very easy to trivialize such research as being of greater use to cat-food companies than to archaeologists, but "garbagology" has much to tell us about the discard habits of modern industrial society. There are also important theoretical lessons for archaeologists investigating the middens of ancient Rome, Nineveh, or Thebes.

The Irresistible Lure of the Past

Armchair archaeology is one thing; to experience the sites and objects of the past firsthand is another. The monuments of antiquity cast an irresistible spell. The jetliner and the package tour have made archaeological tourism big business. Fifty years ago only the wealthy and privileged could take a tour up the Nile, visit Classical Greek temples, or explore Maya civilization. Now package tours can take you to Egypt, to the Parthenon (see Figure 2.5 on page 34), and to *Teotihuacán*, Mexico (see Figure 4.4 on page 70). The immense pyramids of *Giza* in Egypt (see Figure 2.2 on page 26) and the prodigious labor that built them, the white columns

Figure 2.9 The amphitheater at Epidauros, Greece.

of the Temple of Poseidon at *Sounion,* Greece, touched with pink by the setting sun, the ruins at the Maya city of *Tikal* bathed in the full moon's light—as sights alone, these overwhelm the senses.

I once sat in the great Classical amphitheater at *Epidauros,* Greece (see Figure 2.9), on a spring evening as the setting sun turned the world a pale pink. As I sat high above the stage, a small group of German tourists gathered around their learned guide. He sent them to the stall seats, stood at the center, and recited evocative stanzas from Euripides' play *Ion.* The ancient verses rolled and resonated through the still air. For a moment, I shut my eyes and imagined the theater crowded with a festive audience, incense wafting on the spring air, the stanzas gripping everyone's attention with electric tension, then pathos. . . . The guide's voice ceased. A deep silence fell and the magic of Epidauros's acoustics faded.

Visiting the past can be a deeply moving experience—the north wind blowing across *Hadrian's Wall* in northern England on a winter's day with a promise of snow (see the chapter-opener photo on page 22), or a muggy afternoon at *Moundville,* Alabama, when the air stands still and the thatched huts and imposing mounds come alive in your mind with fresh color, with the smell of wood smoke and the cries of children and barking of dogs.

You can get the same emotional connection the first time you see Pharaoh Tutankhamun's golden mask or the countenance of another great Egyptian, King Rameses II, which lifts us to a realm where achievement endures and perceptions seem of a higher order. Even humble artifacts such as a stone chopper or a finely made clay pot can evoke emotions of wonder and insight. Years ago, I turned a 2-million-year-old, jagged-edged chopper end over end in my hands. Suddenly, I realized from the flake scars that the ancient maker had been left-handed, and I felt a sudden bond with the past.

There are moments when the remote past reaches out to us, comforting, encouraging, offering precedent for human existence. We marvel at the achievements of the ancients, at their awesome legacy to all humankind. This book describes some of the basic methods and theoretical approaches that archaeologists use to study the human past, to reconstruct the long prehistory of humankind.

The Prehistory of Humankind According to Archaeologists

This book is concerned with the science of archaeology. So, before exploring the basic principles of archaeology, we need to take a brief journey through the 2.5 million years of human prehistory, so that you have a framework of the basic developments at the back of your mind as we delve deeper into archaeology (see Table 2.1 on page 43).

Prehistory, the human past before written records, covers an enormous span of time, starting more than 2.5 million years ago with the emergence of the first toolmaking hominins (human-like beings) in East Africa and extending right into modern times. A common, and conventional, distinction between prehistory and history is the existence of historical documentation for historic times. In these periods, archaeological finds can be amplified with documentary evidence. For example, there are inscribed clay tablets that form the archives of the Sumerian peoples of Mesopotamia some 5,000 years ago, so we are technically in historic times.

Prehistoric archaeologists are trying to document and understand the ways in which humanity adapted itself to the many and diverse environments of the globe. By studying these adaptations, we can begin to understand the astonishing diversity of human cultures that make up our world.

For the sake of convenience, we can divide prehistory into a series of broad chapters, each spanning long periods of time and increasingly complex cultural developments. In fact, it is more appropriate to refer to these chapters as "developments," for archaeologists are concerned, in the final analysis, with the study of evolving human cultures over very long periods of time.

Early Prehistory

The immensely long span of prehistoric time, from the emergence of toolmaking, upright-walking hominins in tropical Africa 2.5 million years ago, up to the time between 200,000 and 100,000 years ago when modern human beings first appeared, is known as early prehistory. (See Figure 2.10 on page 44.) This was the archaic world of early prehistoric times, when the hominins evolved slowly into more advanced *Homo erectus* some 1.9 million years ago. Cultural and social change was even more glacially slow, with little fundamental change in human lifeways or technology for more than a million years.

About 1.8 million years ago, human beings spread north out of the tropics into more temperate latitudes, into Europe and Asia, adapting to far greater climatic extremes. That they were able to do so was in part the result of the control of fire—for heat, perhaps for cooking, and certainly for protection against predators living in deep caves that were natural shelters for human beings.

For at least 800,000 years, these widely scattered *Homo erectus* populations evolved in the general direction of anatomically modern humans, showing great genetic and anatomical variation subsumed under the general term early *Homo sapiens.* Among these populations were the squat, heavily built Neanderthals of Eurasia, who flourished from before 100,000 until about 33,000 years ago, during the intensely cold climate of the last Ice Age glaciation.

The Origins and Spread of Modern Humans

Sometime between 200,000 and 100,000 years ago, anatomically modern humans evolved in the savanna woodlands of eastern and southern Africa. A minority of scientists believe, however, that *Homo sapiens* emerged in many parts of the Old World at roughly the same time. These modern people, known to us more from genetic studies than from fossils, were still hunter-gatherers, but apparently they were more efficient in their adaptations than their predecessors. By 100,000 years ago, *Homo sapiens* had spread out of Africa into southwestern Asia, coming into contact with other, earlier and archaic *Homo sapiens* hunter-gatherer populations.

Modern Times	A.D. 1492, Columbus lands in the New World Aztec and Inka civilizations flourish in Mexico and Peru.
A.D. 1000 or later	First settlement of New Zealand. Mesa Verde, Chaco Canyon
A.D. 1	Teotihuacán, 200 B.C. to A.D. 750 Maya civilization flourishes in Mesoamerican lowlands (before 600 B.C. to A.D. 900 and beyond)
1200 B.C.	Olmec civilization in Mesoamerica
1600 B.C.	Cretan and Mycenaean civilizations in Mediterranean, Shang civilization in China
2700 B.C.	Harappan civilization, Indus Valley, Pakistan
3100 B.C.	Ancient Egyptian and Sumerian civilizations emerge in the Near East
4000 B.C.	Uruk in Mesopotamia, a sizable settlement, near-city
5000 B.C.	Agriculture in Mesoamerica
6000 B.C. or earlier	Agriculture in China
9500 B.C.	Food production and animal domestication well established in the Near East
12,000 B.C.	End of the last Ice Age glaciation
15,000 B.C.	First human settlement of the Americas(?)
35,000 years ago	First settlement of Australia (May be earlier)
45,000 years ago	*Homo sapiens sapiens* begins settlement of Europe
75,000 years ago	Neanderthals widespread in Europe and Eurasia, also the Near East
100,000 to 200,000 years ago	Anatomically modern humans emerge, probably in tropical Africa
250,000 years ago	Early *Homo sapiens* evolving in many areas
400,000 years ago	*Homo erectus* in Europe and northern China
1.8 million years ago	*Homo erectus* spreads from tropical Africa into Asia
1.9 million years ago	Emergence of *Homo erectus* in Africa
1.75 million years ago	*Homo habilis* at Olduvai Gorge
2.5 million years ago	First toolmaking hominins in East Africa
4.5 million years ago	Earliest nontoolmaking, but bipedal (standing on two feet) hominins in Africa

Table 2.1 Major Developments in Human Prehistory.

Figure 2.10 Two hominins of the species *Australopithecus afarensis* walk across a soft bed of volcanic ash at *Laetoli,* Tanzania, 3.5 million years ago. Their footprints were perfectly preserved in the ash and were excavated by the great paleoanthropologist Mary Leakey in the 1970s.

In perhaps the most dramatic chapter of the human past, *Homo sapiens* spread widely over the Old World and into the New World (the Americas) during the closing millennia of the Ice Age. Human beings had crossed into Australia by 40,000 years ago. Less than 20,000 years later, people had developed the intricate technology needed to survive months of subzero winter cold. They flourished in a deep-frozen Ice Age Europe and on the open plains that stretched far northeast into Siberia. By 15,000 years ago, perhaps earlier, some tiny human bands had probably crossed into Alaska and the Americas. Only the far offshore islands of the Pacific remained uninhabited by humans, awaiting the development of deep-water canoes and offshore navigational techniques.

The Origins of Food Production

The worldwide thawing at the end of the Ice Age some 15,000 years ago led to dramatic changes in global climate and geography. Human populations in the Old World and the Americas had to adapt to radically new circumstances, to highly diverse postglacial environments. It was in about 10,000 B.C. that some largely sedentary hunter-gatherer communities in southwestern Asia started cultivating wild cereal grasses such as wheat and barley, perhaps in response to a severe drought triggered by a sudden cold snap that signaled a partial return to glacial conditions in the north. The new adaptation was highly successful, even if it was first adapted as a means of perpetuating traditional lifeways. Within a few centuries, village farmers were flourishing in many parts of the region, and soon further afield. The herding of goats, and then of cattle and pigs, soon replaced hunting as a primary means of subsistence.

The new economies spread like wildfire, south through the Nile Valley and north deep into Europe. Independent centers of plant and animal domestication may have developed in India, Southeast Asia, and China within a few millennia. The cultivation of indigenous plants and cereals began in the Americas by at least 4000 B.C., probably earlier.

Some of the major controversies in archaeology surround the origins of food production. Why did humans turn from hunting and gathering to agriculture and animal herding, a development that led to immediate, long-term changes in global environments because of overgrazing, forest clearance, and plowing? The first scholars to speculate about early agriculture searched for the village occupied by the genius who had first planted wheat grains and watched them germinate into a new and predictable food supply. No one has ever found this mythical genius. We now realize that farming and the domestication of animals were complex changes in human culture that took place over thousands of years, not only in southwestern Asia but in other areas of the world as well. Was climate change responsible for food production, or was a multiplicity of environmental, cultural, or social factors involved? The debate continues.

Throughout prehistory, human societies experimented with new ideas and technologies. Only a few caught on, and only a handful—among them agriculture, metalworking, writing, and wheeled transport—have profoundly affected the development of human societies on a global scale.

The Origins of States (Civilizations)

Before 3000 B.C., new, highly centralized urban societies appeared in Egypt and Mesopotamia (now southern Iraq). These were state-organized societies, civilizations headed by supreme rulers and governed by a bureaucracy of officials and priests (for more discussion of a state, see Chapter 13). People lived in much larger communities than in the past, in cities of more than 5,000 people, in societies with ranked social classes, under a social order where conformity was assured by the threat of force, and under an official religion that sanctified the deeds of the tiny minority who ruled the state.

The Sumerians of Mesopotamia, the ancient Egyptians, the Harappans of the Indus Valley in Pakistan, the Shang of northern China, and other early peoples were followed by much larger empires and imperial civilizations—for example, those of the Persians, Greeks, and Romans. The process of early state formation—still only partially understood—also took hold in the Americas, where European explorers like Hernán Cortes came into contact with amazingly sophisticated native American civilizations, such as the Aztecs of Mexico and the Inka of Peru, in the fifteenth century A.D.

A continuous historical record takes us from the Sumerians of Mesopotamia through biblical times right up to the conflicts and economic and technical achievements of Western civilization.

European Expansion

The final chapter of prehistory coincides with the expansion of Western civilization outward from its European homeland during the Age of Discovery after A.D. 1430. The five centuries that followed found Westerners coming into contact with all manner of human societies, covering the entire spectrum from Tasmanian hunting bands to the civilizations of the Khmer of Cambodia and the Inka of the Andes. These were the centuries when the world's diverse societies were first drawn into what historians and anthropologists often refer to as a world system—the system of economic and political interconnectedness that became pervasive in the late-twentieth-century world.

Prehistory, then, is the compelling story of unfolding human existence, a story that began at a few locations in tropical Africa. The recorded archives of history take us back to only a tiny fraction of our long past, which means that the study of prehistory has much to tell us about why we are so similar and why we are so different.

SUMMARY

1. Archaeology is the systematic study of humanity in the past, not only of human behavior and technology but also of every aspect of human culture.
2. The discipline is an integral part of anthropology, the study of humanity in the broadest sense, with archaeologists studying past societies from all time periods.
3. There are many types of archaeologists. Classical archaeologists study ancient Greece and Rome. Historical archaeologists study sites and societies that are also recorded in written documents. Underwater archaeologists are specialists in shipwrecks and other underwater features, which are excavated like those on land to acquire information about ancient societies. Cultural Resource Management (CRM) is a major area of archaeology that involves managing the finite remains of the past.
4. Archaeology faces a major crisis, as archaeological sites vanish in the face of looting and industrial development. Tourism, too, is having a major impact on popular sites now visited by tens of thousands of people.
5. Archaeologists have no monopoly on the past, for each society has its own worldview and perceptions of history.
6. World prehistory as practiced by archaeologists is a global study concerned with the following developments: early prehistory and human origins, the emergence and spread of modern humans, the origins of food production, and early civilization.

THREE

Culture and Context

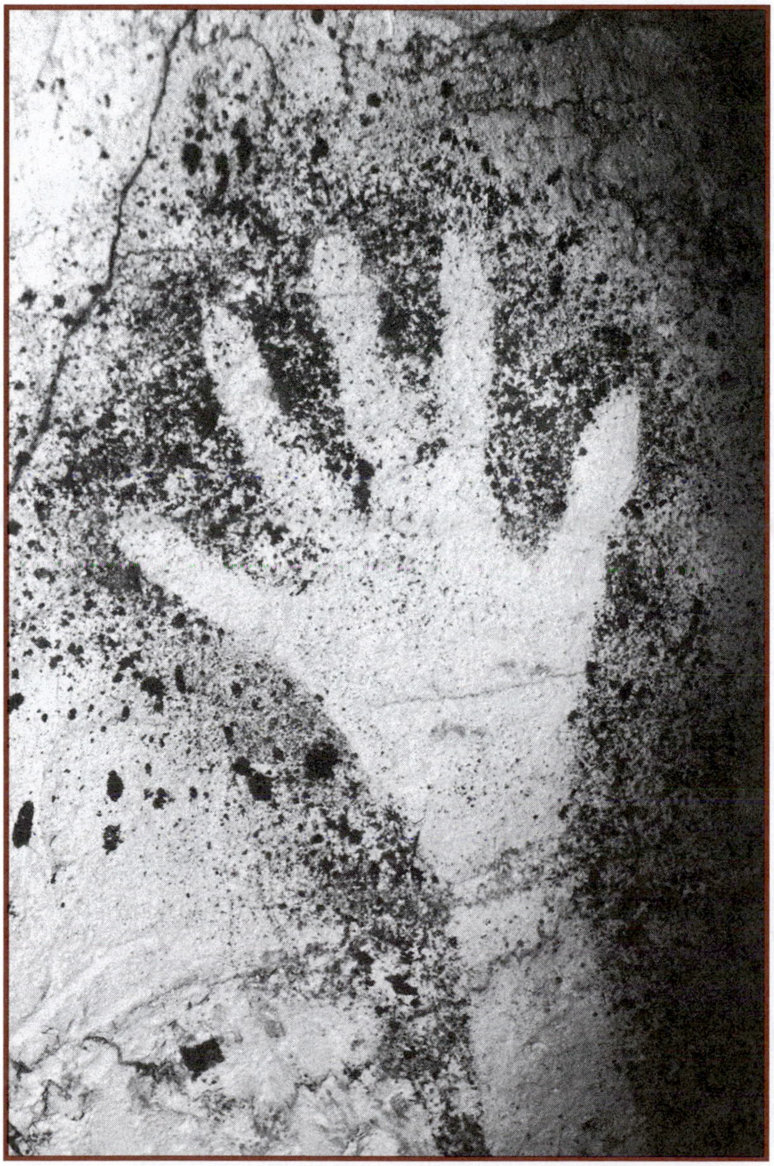

Handprint made by a Cro-Magnon on the wall of a French cave, c. 15,000 years ago.

CHAPTER OUTLINE

PREVIEW

This chapter is about the basic principles of archaeology, fundamental concepts upon which all archaeological research is based. Archaeologists study ancient human cultures, so we begin by discussing the concept of culture, then the notion of cultural systems, the assumption that human cultures are made up of many interacting components. We describe the importance of culture change, for archaeology is a unique way of studying changes in human society over long periods of time. The goals of archaeology embrace not only setting ancient human societies in time and space, but also reconstructing ancient human lifeways, explaining human behavior, and, above all, conserving the past for future generations. We end by defining the archaeological record and some of its components, all of which have a context in time and space.

> *An archaeologist of 6666 A.D. may find himself obliged to rely on the divergences between assemblages of kitchen utensils to help him recognize that by 1950, the United Kingdom and United States of America were not occupied by the same society.*
>
> —V. Gordon Childe, *Piecing Together the Past,* 1956

Many times, while excavating in Africa, I've awoken on a cool winter's morning deep in the bush and watched a modern-day farming village close to our site come alive as the sun rises. The air is still, a slight chill hugging the ground, where dew glistens in the soft light of dawn. You smell wood smoke and cattle dung, see figures wrapped in blankets moving out to cattle enclosures or huddling around fires. The thatched huts are still quiet as the timeless rhythm of another day begins. You sense the timelessness of it all, the annual cycles of planting and harvest, birth, life, and death. Again and again, I think of the continuity between ancient and modern, for, like it or not, we live with the past as well as the present. In places like Africa, where many people still live much as their predecessors did centuries ago, the links between past and present seem particularly strong. There, archaeology is anthropology as much as it is unwritten history. Experiences like this—the scent of wood smoke, cows moving restlessly in their pens, the soft murmurs of voices in the dawn—make you realize that archaeologists have only the shreds and patches of the past with which to study ancient cultures.

In this chapter, we discuss the fundamental concepts of **culture** and culture change and describe the goals of archaeology. We also describe the nature of archaeological evidence and the all-important issue of "context" and what it means to the study of the past (see the Discovery box on page 49).

Human Culture

Everyone lives within a cultural context, one that is qualified by a label like "middle-class American," "Roman," or "Sioux." These labels conjure up characteristic objects or behavior patterns typical of the particular culture. We associate hamburgers with middle-class American culture and kayaks with maritime Eskimos. Romans are thought to have spent their time conquering the world, Sioux wandering over the Great Plains. But such stereotypes are often crude, inaccurate generalizations. In fact, the label

Discovery

The Lords of Sicán, Peru, A.D. 900–1100

The Sicán culture flourished along the North Coast of Peru from about A.D. 800 to 1100. Sicán lords were buried with elaborate grave goods, including fine copper- and gold-alloy objects. For years, looters have targeted their burials, many of them associated with the 82-foot-high (25-meter-high) Huaca Loro pyramid at Sicán's capital. Izumi Shimada began long-term research at the capital in 1978. His work involved a study of tomb contents and construction and the excavation of a wide range of burials from all segments of Sicán society.

The Huaca Loro mound lies atop an elite cemetery. So far, Shimada has excavated two sepulchers. It took six months to excavate the East Tomb, a 33-foot (10-meter) vertical shaft, 10 feet (3 meters) square with seven sealed niches. Five skeletons lay in the tomb, as well as 12.2 tons of grave goods, two thirds of which consisted of copper, gold, and artifacts made of an alloy of gold, silver, and copper. The principal burial was that of a man 40 to 50 years old, whose body was mummified, painted with red cinnabar paint, and then dressed in his full ceremonial regalia (see Figure 3.1). His head was separated from his body, rotated right side up, and then placed in front of his inverted body. His regalia included pectorals made with amber, amethyst, and other semi-precious stones, also a gold ceremonial knife, ear spools, and a golden mask. A pair of golden gloves and a shin cover lay by the body. A nearby chest contained at least 24 layers of rattles, crowns, headbands, and other gold and alloy ritual objects.

Nearby lay a female adult with her legs flexed wide apart. Another woman sat in front of her with her hands placed close to the first woman's crotch. Shimada believes that the man and the women were carefully positioned to symbolize the rebirth of the former.

This Lord of Sicán owned a sumptuous array of gold objects, and also a huge assemblage of other artifacts that give an impression of his enormous wealth and power—15 bundles of unfinished cast bronze tools, 165 pounds (75 kg) of perforated, semiprecious beads, and about 1,100 pounds (500 kg) of hammered alloy sheet scraps. All of these products would have required thousands of hours to produce. The Lord lay with 179 *spondylus* shells and 141 *conus* shells, all imported from the coast of Ecuador and other areas far to the north. Clearly, Sicán's elite-controlled widespread trade routes, in which bronze and produce from irrigation agriculture were major players.

Shimada is now excavating the West Tomb, which lies 82 feet (25 meters) to the west. A man of 30 to 40 years lay in a central chamber, surrounded by hundreds of artifacts and flanked by two women. About 20 women, mostly between 18 and 22 years old, lay in an antechamber, placed in equal numbers on the north and south sides of the central chamber. Using DNA, ceramic styles, inherited dental characteristics, and general health profiles, Shimada established that the women on the south side were relatively healthy, included two kin groups, and were biologically close not only to one another, but to the principal individual buried in the tomb. They may even have married within their own community. In contrast, those to the north were more heterogeneous biologically and not as healthy. He theorizes that this group represented peoples conquered by the Sicán lords.

Figure 3.1 Reconstructed gold mask of a Lord of Sicán, Peru. The mask has emerald eyes and amber beads. The forehead ornament is a modified bat head. Height 39 in. (c. 100 cm).

"American Indian" or "Native American" is really a biological term that includes incredibly culturally diverse peoples, ranging from family-size hunter-gatherer bands to large, complex civilizations.

Each human society has its own recognizable cultural style, which shapes the behavior of its members, their political and judicial institutions, and their morals. Every traveler is familiar with the distinctive flavor of various cultures that one experiences when dining in a foreign restaurant or arriving in a new country. This distinctiveness results from a people's complex adaptation to greatly varied ecological, societal, and cultural factors.

Human culture is unique because much of its content is transmitted from generation to generation by sophisticated communication systems. Formal education, religious beliefs, and day-to-day social intercourse all transmit culture and allow societies to develop complex and continuing adaptations to aid their survival. Such communication systems also help rapid cultural change to take place, as when less technologically sophisticated societies come into contact with those with more effective technology. Culture is a potential guide for behavior created through generations of human experience. It provides a design for living that helps mold responses to different situations.

Human beings are the only animals to use culture as the primary means of adapting to the environment. Although biological evolution has protected the polar bear from arctic winters, only human beings make thick clothes and igloos in the Arctic and live in light thatched shelters in the tropics. Culture is an adaptive system; it is an interface between ourselves, the environment, and other human societies. Through the long millennia of prehistory, human culture became more elaborate. If this cultural buffer were now removed, we would be helpless and most probably doomed to extinction. As our primary means of adaptation, human culture is always adjusting to environmental, technological, and societal change.

Language, economics, technology, religion, and political and social organization are but a few of the interacting subdivisions of human culture. These elements shape one another and blend to form a whole. For instance, the distribution of water and food supplies as well as flexible social organization help determine the distribution of home bases among the San hunter-gatherers of the Kalahari Desert in southern Africa.

Culture is the dominant factor in determining social behavior; human society is the vehicle that carries our culture. Societies are groups of interacting organizers. Insects and other animals have societies, but only humans have culture as well.

What is culture? Anthropologists have tried to define this most elusive of theoretical formulations for generations—a half century ago, there were over 200 definitions, with many more in use today. All such definitions are concepts that are a means of explaining cultures and human behavior in terms of the learned, shared ideas held by a group of people. One of the best general definitions was that put forth by the great Victorian anthropologist Sir Edward Tylor more than a century ago. He wrote (1871: 4) that culture is "that complex whole which includes knowledge, belief, art, morals, law, custom, and any other capabilities and habits acquired by man as a member of society." To Tylor, culture was learned—which is fine as far as it goes, but his definition is too simple at anything but the most general level.

To make a sweeping generalization, archaeologists tend to look at culture in two distinct ways, with an adaptive view or with an ideational view.

Adaptive views assume that economics, technology, population densities, and ecology are key factors in shaping human behavior. Adaptive strategies adopted by humans ensure that their cultures operate in dynamic equilibrium with their **ecosystems**. Thus, many archaeologists prefer to define culture in general terms as the primary nonbiological means by which human societies adapt to and accommodate their environment. Culture regulates relationships with the environment through technology and social and belief systems.

Ideational approaches to culture focus on the complex sets of perceptions, conceptual designs, and shared beliefs and understandings that underlie the ways in which people live. In other words, culture is what people learn rather than what they make or do for a living. Under this approach, you cannot understand human behavior without decoding what went on in peoples' minds—what some scholars call a "cognitive code."

Both approaches have great value, especially when used together (see Chapter 4). Archaeology is the study of human behavior in the past, based on surviving remains of human behavior. Inevitably, these remains are mainly durable items such as stone tools and clay vessels. Many archaeologists throughout the world believe that ancient cultural behavior was driven by primarily impersonal processes, such as environmental change, population pressure, technological and economic innovation, and so on. Thus, they favor adaptive approaches to the study of culture and often look for general (and anonymous) laws of human behavior. This was the dominant approach to archaeology until the 1970s. Today, many archaeologists are more interested in ancient cultural behavior as something driven by beliefs, ideas, symbolic visions of the world, and other intangibles. What was the meaning of ancient artifacts? What roles did they play in the social environment of the day? Under this approach, people are all-important—their interactions with one another, the decisions they made that affected the outcome of historical events.

The debate over culture continues, with most archaeologists espousing an approach that probably lies between these two extremes. Certainly, few researchers would argue that one can look at human behavior only in people-oriented terms, for it is obvious that ecological factors, among them climate change, were of great importance in shaping human history.

The concept of culture provides anthropological archaeologists with a means for explaining the products of human activity. When archaeologists study **patterns of discard,** or the tangible remains of the past, they see a patterned reflection of the culture that produced them, of the shared behavior of a group of prehistoric people. This patterning of archaeological finds is critical, for it reflects patterned behavior in the past.

Cultural Systems

Archaeology can be very frustrating. I remember sitting in the middle of an ancient African farming village that I had excavated over many months. My laboratory was stacked high with boxes of animal bones, pot fragments, and other artifacts. Despite weeks of excavation under the hot sun, I felt a deep sense of frustration, for there was so much about the inhabitants that was hidden from me. As the afternoon shadows lengthened, I found myself conjuring up a living village on the now-silent mound. As images of huts and cattle enclosures passed through my mind, I felt an overwhelming desire for a few minutes of conversation with the ancient inhabitants. So much was lost, so much was intangible and beyond reconstruction with the archaeologist's spade.

Herein lies the great challenge of archaeology, whatever your theoretical approach to culture: not only reconstructing the material, but also trying to comprehend highly perishable aspects of human cultures—long-vanished religious beliefs and social interactions, the day-to-day transactions between individuals, within families, and with a wider world that make up our lives.

So far, no one has been able to dig up a religious philosophy or an unwritten language. Archaeologists have to work with the tangible remains of human activity that still survive in the ground. But these surviving remains of human activity are radically affected by intangible aspects of human culture. All cultures reflect their owners' worldview, their idea of the universe in which they live. In many ancient societies, the living and spiritual worlds were thought of as one, so that religious beliefs and symbolism affected architecture, art, and the design of ceremonial artifacts. Great Maya cities like Copán and Tikal were reproductions in stone and stucco of the supernatural world of trees (carved uprights), sacred mountains (pyramids), and openings to the Otherworld (caves and temple entrances). The same kinds of symbolism affected artifact design in many cultures. Eighteen hundred years ago, the *Hopewell* people of the American Midwest traded, over enormous distances, finely made ornaments fashioned of hammered copper sheet (see Figure 3.2). These ornaments turn up in Hopewell burial mounds. The copper technology that made them was simple, but the symbolism behind the artifacts was not. They were probably exchanged between important individuals as symbolic gifts, denoting kin ties, economic obligations, and other social meanings that are beyond the archaeologist's ability to recover. Thus the artifacts found in an excavation reflect not only ancient technology, but also the values and uses that a society placed on such objects. Ancient tools are not culture in themselves, but a patterned reflection of the culture that produced them. Such patternings provide a link between archaeological remains and the behavior of their makers.

When considering ancient relationships with the natural environment, I've always found it helpful to think of cultures as systems of different, interacting parts, which interact, in turn, with their ever-changing environments. In thinking this way, I, and many other archaeologists, have been strongly influenced by the work of anthropologist Leslie White. In the 1950s, he studied peoples' means of adapting to their environment. He argued that human culture is made up of many structurally different parts that articulate with one another within a total **cultural system** (see Figure 3.3 on page 53). This cultural system is the means whereby a human society adapts to its physical and social environment. White's formulation is a useful conceptual tool for studying the past, even if theoretical approaches to cultural systems vary widely from one archaeologist to another.

Under this perspective, all cultural systems articulate with other systems, which also are made up of interacting sets of variables. One such system is the natural environment. The links between cultural and environmental systems are such that a change in one system is linked to changes in the other. Thus a major objective of archaeology is to understand the linkage between the various parts of cultural and environmental systems as they are reflected in **archaeological data**. It follows that archaeologists studying cultural systems are more interested in the relationships between activities and tools within a cultural system than in the activities or tools themselves. They are profoundly interested in cultural systems within their environmental context, and in the intangible beliefs and values that helped create them.

To be workable, any human cultural system depends on its ability to adapt to the natural environment. A cultural system can be broken down into all manner of subsystems: religious and ritual subsystems, economic subsystems, and so on. Each of these is linked to the others. Changes in one subsystem, such as a shift from cattle herding to wheat growing, cause reactions in many others. Such relationships give the archaeologist a measure of the constant changes and variations in human culture that can accumulate over long periods as cultural systems respond to external and internal stimuli.

Figure 3.2 Hopewell bird claw in mica. The Hopewell people traded such prestigious objects over great distances in eastern North America during the first millennium B.C. (© The Field Museum, Neg. #A90925, Chicago.)

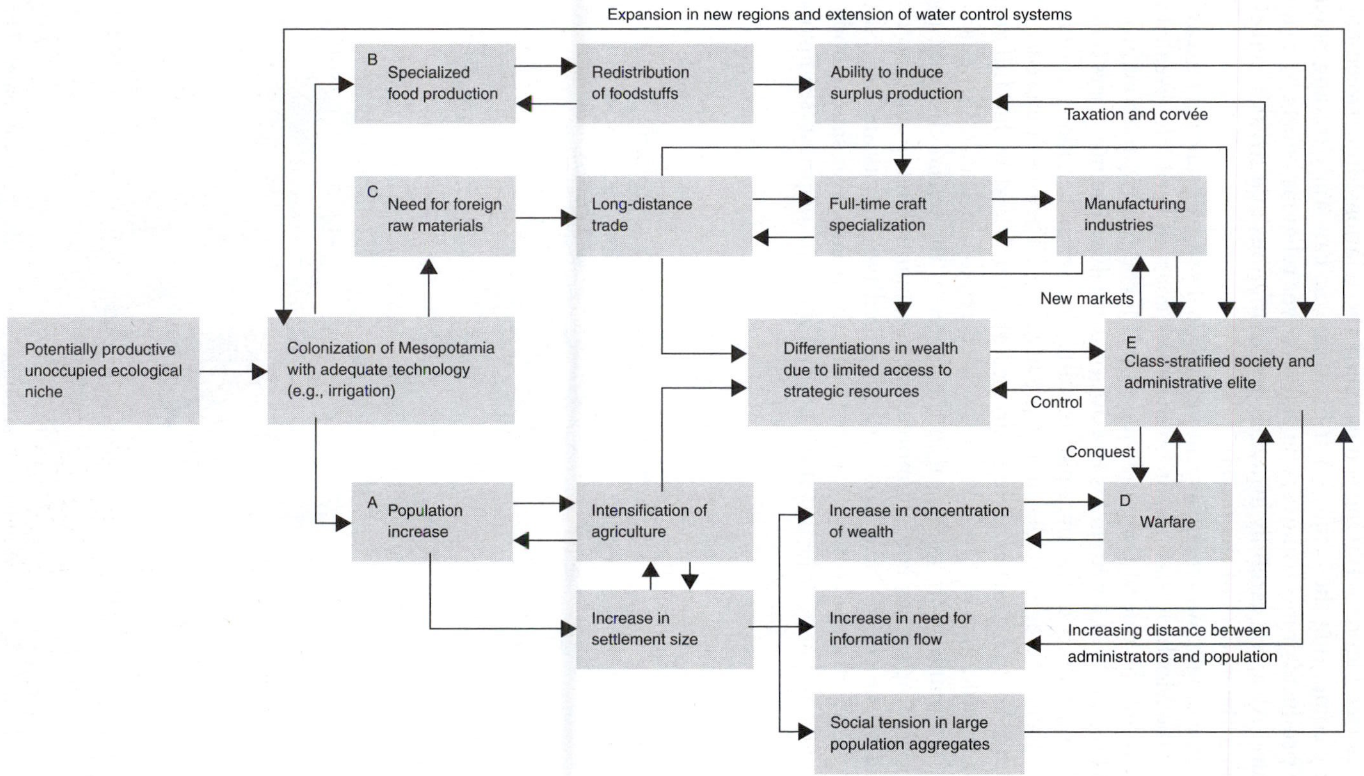

Figure 3.3 Cultural systems are, of course, theoretical formulations used by archaeologists to interpret the past. This systems model illustrates a systems approach to understanding human culture. It is an attempt to document the relationship between cultural and environmental variables that led to state-organized societies in Mesopotamia between 5000 and 2000 B.C. (Adapted from *The Rise of Civilization* by Charles L. Redman. © 1978 by W. H. Freeman and Company. Used with permission.)

The systems approach also has value when looking at the ideas and beliefs behind an ancient culture. By examining the systematic patternings of archaeological finds, we can discover more about the intangible aspects of human behavior. By dropping their possessions on the ground or burying their dead in certain ways, people have left vital information about many more elements in their cultural system than merely their tools or skeletal remains (see Figure 3.4). One can examine the relationship between individual households by comparing the artifacts left by each; one can study trading practices by analyzing the products of metalsmiths; one can discover religious beliefs by mapping temple architecture. Also, the carefully arranged grave offerings in a royal burial chamber tell much about the leaders of the society.

Peruvian archaeologist Walter Alva spent months in 1988 painstakingly excavating the royal tombs of the Moche lords of Sipán on the north coast of Peru. He revealed valuable information about the role of these individuals in Moche society in about A.D. 400.

Tomb I held the body of a man in his late 30s or early 40s. The mourners had built a brick burial chamber deep in the pyramid, building the sepulcher like a room, with solid mud-brick benches along the sides and at the head end. They set hundreds of clay pots in small niches in the benches. Priests dressed the dead lord in his full regalia, including a golden mask, and wrapped his corpse and regalia in textile shrouds. Then they placed him in a plank coffin and set it in the center of the burial chamber, the lid secured with copper straps. They laid out more ceramics, mainly fine spouted bottles, at the foot and head of the coffin. Next, someone sacrificed two llamas and placed them on either side of the foot of the coffin. At some point, the priests also sat the body of a nine- or ten-year-old child in poor health at the head of the warrior-priest (see Figure 3.5 on page 55).

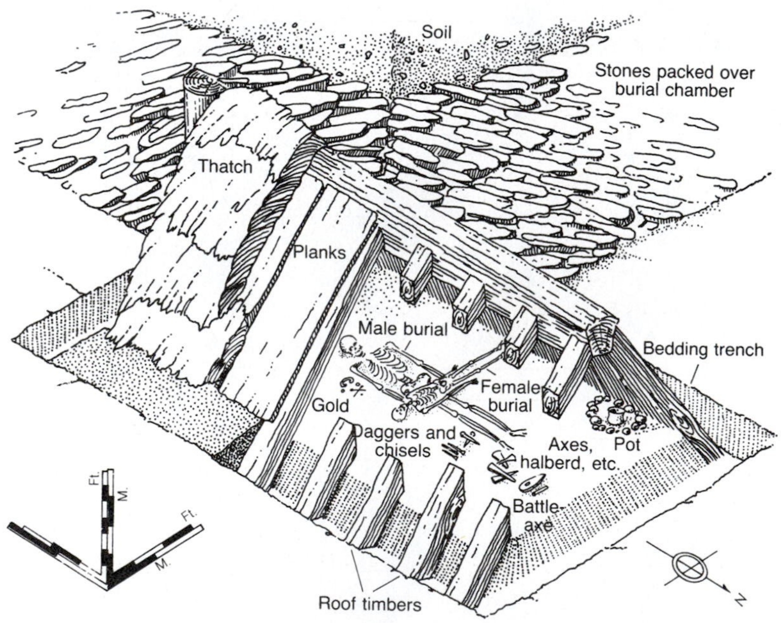

Figure 3.4 A wooden burial house from Leubingen, Germany. The two burials were deposited in a wooden house under a mound. The archaeologist not only recovers the burials and the objects with which the bodies were buried, but also reconstructs the burial layout and sequence of construction of the burial house. Further, the excavator tries to infer the funerary rituals from the artifact patterning and the structures under the mound.

Figure 3.5 Burial chamber of a lord of Sipán, Peru.

The mourners then lowered five cane coffins into the grave, each containing the body of an adult. The two male dead, perhaps bodyguards or members of the lord's entourage, were each laid on top of one of the llamas. One was a strongly built male, over 35 years old, adorned with copper ornaments and laid out with a war club. The other bore a beaded pectoral and was between 35 and 45 years old. Two of the three women's coffins lay at the head of the royal casket; in the third, at the foot of the coffin, the woman had been turned on her side. Interestingly, the women's disarticulated and jumbled bones suggest they were not sacrificial victims, for they had died long before the lord, and were partly decomposed at the time of their burial. Perhaps they had been wives, concubines, or servants. Once the coffins had been positioned, a low beam roof was set in place, too low for someone to stand inside the chamber. Then the tomb was covered, a footless male victim being laid out in the fill. Finally, a seated body with crossed legs watched over the burial chamber from a small niche in the south wall, about 3 feet (1 meter) above the roof.

The Sipán burial revealed not only minute details of lordly regalia, but priceless information on the intricate symbolism of the sun and moon that lay behind many of the ornaments (see Figure 4.7 on page 82). Archaeologist Christopher Donnan analyzed painted motifs on Moche pots to show that the buried lord was a warrior priest, buried in his full regalia, who had once presided over sacrifices of prisoners of war.

Culture Change

The notion of cultural systems is widely used in archaeology as a means of explaining cultural and social change. The argument is as follows. Every cultural system is in a constant state of change. Its various political, social, and technological subsystems adjust to changing circumstances. We ourselves live in a time of rapid cultural change, in which measurable differences set apart different ten-year periods. We would find it hard to identify the thousands of minor daily cultural changes that occur, but we can easily recognize the cumulative effects of these minor changes over a longer period.

Consider the many minor changes in automobile design over the past decades. In themselves the changes are not very striking, but if one looks at the cumulative effect of several years' steady change toward safer cars—energy-absorbing bumpers, padded steering wheels and dashboards, air bags, seat belts, more aerodynamic shapes—the change is striking. The automobile of today is different from that of the 1960s, and many of the changes are due to stricter governmental safety regulations, which in turn are due to greater public safety consciousness (see Figure 3.6). Here we see a major cumulative change in part of our enormous technological subsystem. By examining the relationship between technological and political subsystems, we can understand the processes by which culture changes.

The word **process** implies a patterned sequence of events, one event leading to another. A contractor builds a three-bedroom house in an ordered sequence of events, from foundation footings up to final painting. (Archaeological research itself has a process—designing a research project, collecting and interpreting data, publishing the results.) To analyze **cultural process**, we attempt to consider all of the factors that cause changes in human culture and how they affect one another.

How did human cultures change in the past? What cultural and social processes came into play when people began to cultivate the soil, or when complex and elaborate urban states developed 5,000 years ago?

As we saw in Chapter 1, new discoveries like agriculture or ironworking were once thought to have spread throughout the world by mass migrations or by long-distance trading over continents and oceans. But as more and more archaeological data have accumulated in all corners of the world, people have realized that such straightforward explanations of cultural process as universal evolution, or the spread of all ideas from one place of invention, are simplistic and do not reflect reality.

Most changes in human culture have been cumulative, occurring slowly over a long period of time. Ancient Egyptian civilization began with the unification of Upper and Lower Egypt into a single state by the pharaoh Horus-Aha in about 3100 B.C. Intensively conservative and seemingly unchanging, Egyptian civilization endured for 3,000 years, until the Nile Valley became part of the Roman Empire. This impression of unchanging civilization is misleading for, in fact, the institutions of Egyptian kingship developed long before the unification of the state and evolved constantly as circumstances changed along the Nile. The basic institutions remained much the same, but the pharaohs trimmed their rule to accommodate new technologies, new political and social circumstances. One of the reasons Egyptian civilization endured so long was that it was

Figure 3.6 Changing automobile styles reflect both design advances and safety considerations, as well as shifting fashions.

flexible enough to adjust to widely fluctuating Nile flood levels and changing outside political conditions. Studying these often subtle processes of cultural change requires highly sophisticated research work.

Processes of culture change in prehistory were the result of constantly changing adaptations to a myriad of external environments. Cultural systems were constantly adjusting and evolving in response to internal and external **feedback**. Clearly, no one element in a cultural system is a primary cause of culture change, because a complex range of factors—vegetation, technology, social restrictions, and population density, to mention only a few—interact with one another and react to a change in any element in the system. From the ecologist's point of view, therefore, human culture is merely one element of the ecosystem, a mechanism whereby people adapt to this environment. This viewpoint provides a useful framework for much modern archaeological research and for studying cultural process, although, of course, cultural systems encompass much more than merely environmental adaptation.

By no means does every researcher agree with the systems approach; some think that it promotes a mechanistic and anonymous way of studying culture change. They argue that other factors play an important role, especially the roles of individuals and groups in making history—archaeology being a part of history.

In truth, there is no one overarching perspective on culture and culture change that replaces either systems or more idea-based approaches. Today, there is tremendous theoretical diversity both in approaches to archaeology and in approaches to culture and culture change—which is probably healthy, given the enormous time range of the human past and the remarkable array of societies that have flourished on earth, all with their own perspectives on the world.

We look more closely at ways in which people have sought to interpret ancient cultural and social change in Chapter 4.

The Goals of Archaeology

The archaeologist has one primary and overriding priority: to preserve and conserve the material remains of the past for future generations.

Archaeological sites and their contents are a unique record of our forebears in every part of the world. Unlike trees, this archive of the past, the archaeological record, is finite. Once disturbed or excavated, the record is gone forever. Conserving this priceless asset is our greatest responsibility to the past, whether professional archaeologists or laypeople.

All archaeological research has four important goals, each of which builds on the others. The first three can be summarized as "form," "function," and "process" (see Figure 3.7 on page 58).

Constructing Culture History

Culture history is an approach to archaeology that assumes that artifacts can be used to build up generalized pictures of human culture in time and space, and that these can be interpreted. Culture history is the record of the human past described and classified in a context of time and space, which describes the past across the changing ancient landscape. In other words, it answers the fundamental question: What happened where and when?

Culture history relies on careful excavation, detailed classifications of finds of all kinds, and accurate sequences of human cultures defined through time and by spatial distribution.

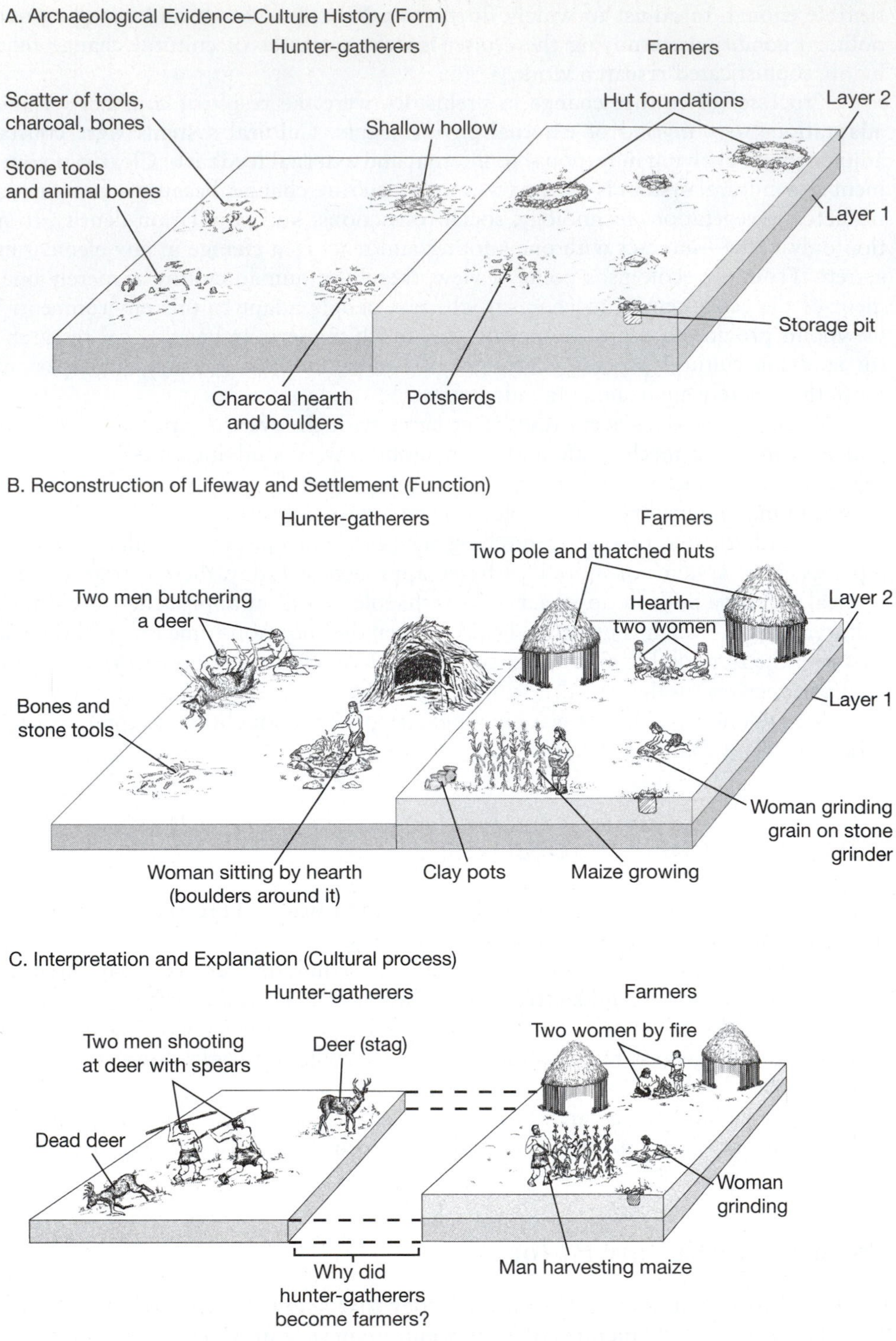

Figure 3.7 Three primary goals of archaeology.

Until the 1950s, culture history dominated archaeological research. For example, during the 1930s, teams of archaeologists surveyed major river valleys in the southeastern United States in advance of dam construction. They found hundreds of archaeological sites, which they dated using sequences of stone tool and pottery forms. These now-classic surveys tell us a great deal about what happened in these river valleys and when, but they tell us little about the ways in which the various river valley societies lived or why they became more complex and took up maize agriculture over the past 2,000 years.

Culture history is the vital first stage of all archaeological research. You cannot examine more detailed questions until you have a clear idea of what happened in a region and when. In many parts of the world—for example, Southeast Asia—archaeological research has hardly begun. Many archaeologists working in Cambodia or Thailand still have a primary concern for culture history. This focus will change once the basic framework of the past is in place. Some of the basic principles of culture history are described in Chapters 4 and 8.

Reconstructing Ancient Lifeways

Archaeology is also the study of ancient human behavior—of people, not their artifacts. Stone tools, **potsherds**, iron weapons, houses, and other material remains are indeed the raw materials for classifying the past, but we should never forget they were made by people—men and women, adults and children, members of different households, communities, and societies. Logically, then, our second major goal is the reconstruction of how people made their living, the study of ancient lifeways.

The word *lifeways* covers many human activities, everything from hunting and plant gathering to agriculture, interactions between individuals and groups, social organization, and religious beliefs. Some of archaeology's best detective work reconstructs these activities, which, for convenience, can be grouped into the following broad categories.

Subsistence How people make their living or acquire food—**subsistence**—is studied by using fragmentary animal bones, seeds, and other surviving evidence of ancient human diet and subsistence activities (see Chapter 11).

Environmental Modeling Subsistence activities depend heavily on a society's relationship with the natural environment. This means that studying ancient subsistence goes hand-in-hand with reconstruction of changing prehistoric environments (see Chapter 10).

Human Interactions People act out their lives at many levels: as individuals; as men, women, and children; as members of families, communities, and cultures. They may be divine rulers, merchants, artisans, common farmers, or slaves. Reconstructing lifeways means examining evidence of changing sex roles, assessing the importance of social ranking within societies, reconstructing the complex mechanisms by which people exchanged exotic raw materials or precious artifacts over enormous distances.

Much cutting-edge research revolves around "people" questions, especially such issues as changing gender roles and the distinctive activities of inconspicuous and often historically anonymous minorities in large cities. We identify people from their artifacts, which are the products of cultural traditions handed down over generations (see Chapter 13).

For instance, the great city of Teotihuacán in the Valley of Mexico attracted traders from every corner of the Mesoamerican world. The Teotihuacános ran a vast urban market that attracted people from all over the Mexican highlands and lowlands to trade everything from gold dust to tropical bird feathers. So lucrative and essential were some of these trading activities that the city authorities allowed foreigners from the distant Veracruz lowlands and the valley of Oaxaca to live in their own compounds in Teotihuacán. We know this because the distinctive clay vessels characteristic of these two areas have come to light in several of the city's neighborhoods.

Social Organization and Religious Beliefs Archaeologists are increasingly concerned with such intangibles as social organization and religious beliefs. Of course, we can never hope to capture the transitory events of the past such as the momentary ecstasy of a shaman's trance or a colorful dance performed in a plaza at Teotihuacán. However, artifacts, art styles, even entire temples and cities, are mirrors of the intangible, allowing us a fleeting glance into the social and spiritual worlds of ancient societies (see Chapter 4).

Explaining Cultural and Social Change

Archaeology is a search for both facts and explanations. The third major objective of archaeology is to study and explain cultural and social change (see Chapter 4). Such research attacks fundamental questions: After tens of thousands of years of hunting and plant gathering, why did people living over a huge area of southwestern Asia change over to agriculture before 10,000 B.C.? What caused Maya civilization in the southern Mesoamerican lowlands, with its huge cities and powerful lords, to collapse in A.D. 900? Why did no one settle the offshore islands of the Pacific until about 3,000 years ago?

Studying the processes of cultural and social change is among the most challenging parts of archaeological research. In Chapter 4, we describe some of the complex theoretical models that attempt to reconstruct such major developments as the origins of agriculture and the development of complex, urban civilizations. As we saw in Chapter 1, there are two broad schools of thought, one ecological and evolutionary, more concerned with ecosystems, and the second historical materialistic, placing major emphasis on the actions of people and groups in causing culture change.

The three main academic objectives of archaeology flow one into the other. A study of ancient lifeways depends on precise culture history, while an explanation of cultural processes requires large quantities of historical, environmental, and lifeway data of culture to be meaningful.

Preserving the Archaeological Record

The fourth and most fundamental objective of all is to conserve, manage, and preserve the archaeological record of the past for future generations. This overriding objective has assumed major importance in recent years. Archaeological sites are precious, finite resources, and they are vanishing at a breathtaking speed. Already, most archaeological fieldwork around the world is devoted to salvage work and general management of the surviving archives of the past, often called Cultural Resource Management (CRM). It is now the dominant paradigm in archaeology.

The Archaeological Record

Archaeologists construct ancient cultures from archaeological data, the material remains of the past. This material data, archaeological evidence if you will, comes in many forms—as an entire city, a humble farmer's dwelling, the golden mask of the Egyptian pharaoh Tutankhamun, or a scatter of broken bones or stone tools. Such data makes up the **archaeological record.**

Archaeology is based on the scientific recovery of data from the ground—on the systematic excavation and recording of the archaeological record as it survives in sites as artifacts, food remains, and other finds.

Archaeological Sites

The archaeological **site** is a place where traces of ancient human activity are to be found. It is the archaeologist's archive, in much the same way as government files can yield a day-by-day record of historical events. Sites are normally identified through the manufactured tools, or **artifacts**, found in them. They can range in size from a huge prehistoric city, such as Teotihuacán, in the Valley of Mexico, to a small meat cache used by hunter-gatherers at Olduvai Gorge, Tanzania. An archaeological site can consist of a human burial, a huge rockshelter occupied over millennia, or a simple scatter of stone tools found on the floor of Death Valley, California. Sites are limited in number and variety by preservation conditions and the activities of the people who occupied them. Some were used for a few short hours, others for a generation or two. Some, like Mesopotamian city mounds, were major settlements for hundreds, even thousands, of years and contain numerous separate occupation layers. The great mounds of the city of Ur in Mesopotamia contain many occupation levels, which tell the story of a long-established ancient city that was abandoned when the river Euphrates changed its course away from the settlement (see Figure 1.1 on page 3).

Archaeological sites are most commonly classified according to the activities that occurred there. Thus cemeteries and other sepulchers, like Tutankhamun's tomb, are referred to as *burial sites*. A 20,000-year-old Stone Age site in the Dnieper Valley of the Ukraine, with mammoth-bone houses, hearths, and other signs of domestic activity, is a *habitation site*. So are many other sites, such as caves and rockshelters, early Mesoamerican farming villages, and Mesopotamian cities—in all of these, people lived and carried out greatly diverse activities. *Kill sites* consist of bones of slaughtered game animals and the weapons that killed them. They are found in East Africa and on the North American Great Plains. *Quarry sites*—where people mined stone or metals to make specific tools—are another type of specialized site. Prized raw materials, such as **obsidian,** a volcanic glass used for fine knives, were widely traded in prehistoric times and are of profound interest to the archaeologist. Then there are spectacular *ceremonial and religious sites* such as the stone circles of Stonehenge in southern England; the Temple of Amun at *Karnak*, Egypt; and the great ceremonial precincts of lowland Maya centers in Central America at Tikal, Copán, and Palenque (see Figure 3.8 on page 62). *Art sites* are common in southwestern France (see Figure 2.7 on page 36), southern Africa, and parts of North America, where prehistoric people painted or engraved magnificent displays with deep, and still little understood, symbolic meaning. Some French art sites are more than 30,000 years old. Each of these site types reflects a form of human activity, which is represented in the archaeological record by specific artifact patterns and surface indications found and recorded by the archaeologist.

Artifacts, Features, and Ecofacts

Artifacts are objects found in archaeological sites that exhibit features resulting from human activity. The term covers every form of portable archaeological find, from stone axes to gold ornaments, as well as food residues such as broken bones. **Features** are structures such as houses, hearths, storage pits, and so on. They can also include buried fields, workshop areas, and drainage systems. Artifacts are distinguished from nonartifacts simply because artifacts display patterns of humanly caused features, or attributes. These objects can be classified according to their distinctive attributes. Artifacts are the product of human ideas, ideas that people had about the way objects should look or be used. Every culture has its own rules that limit and dictate the form of artifacts. Our own society has definite ideas of what a fork should look like, or an automobile, or a pair of shoes. We are so familiar with the artifacts of other cultures that seeing, say, a skin kayak, we at once identify it as "Eskimo" (in Canada, Inuit).

Most craft skills, such as stone toolmaking, pottery manufacture, basketry, and metallurgy, are learned by each new generation. Each generation passes the skills on to the next, usually resulting in relatively slow, sometimes very slow, changes in artifacts and artifact technology. This inborn conservatism, which we might call tradition, strongly influences perpetuation of artifact forms.

Figure 3.8 The Acropolis complex at Copán, Honduras, as drawn by Tatiana Proskouriakoff. The ceremonial precincts of Copán are surrounded by several square kilometers of residential quarters and outlying settlements, making it one of the largest pre-Columbian cities in the Americas. The pyramids and plazas of central Copán were laid out as a symbolic representation of the Maya sacred world, complete with sacred mountains (pyramids), with the temple entrance at the top of the pyramid serving as the symbolic entrance to the underworld.

The variation in a group of similar artifacts, such as stone projectile points, may reflect varied ideas behind them. Archaeologists study and classify artifacts, as we discuss in Chapter 8. These **classifications** are really research devices by which we study the products of human behavior and, indirectly, human behavior itself. For the archaeologist, every artifact has a number of attributes—identifiable properties that combine to give the object its distinctive form.

The vessel illustrated in Figure 3.9 on page 63 has several obvious attributes: painted motif, rounded base, and so on. Each of these **attributes** contributes to the form of the pot and each was part of the mental template that produced it. Each attribute has a different reason for being there. The band of decoration is purely ornamental, part of the decorative tradition among the people who made it. The shape of the pot is determined by its function—it was designed for carrying liquids and for cooking, for which a bag-shaped, round-bottomed body is essential. Attributes can be present because of traditional, functional, technological, or other reasons. Occasionally a new attribute appears—a new decorative motif, perhaps—which may vanish just as fast as it appeared. Why? Because it did not catch on with other potmakers. Occasionally, too, a new attribute may achieve wide popularity and be adopted by everyone. Then the innovation becomes part of the pottery tradition.

The dictates of fashion and style play an important role in the changes that occur in attributes over short and long periods of time. These fashions and the styles associated with them are a major factor in studying culture change. To take a relatively modern **analogy**, Victorian explorers who penetrated deep into the East African interior traveled in caravans laden with cheap imported goods such as glass beads, cotton cloth,

Figure 3.9 Mimbres painted vessel from the American Southwest. Attributes include rim shape, height, paint colors, design motif, clay composition, and so on.

and iron hoes. Sometimes they would find that the trade goods they brought with them to barter for food—goods once thought to be prime commodities—were no longer of interest to people in the interior. Fashions had changed, and different bead colors had assumed greater desirability. If one were to investigate sites where such trade was taking place over several centuries, one would find changes in proportions of different bead types, shapes, and colors. In this case, they are the result of changing fashions.

The archaeologist is deeply concerned with how artifacts vary and with the changing forms of the many manufactured objects found in archaeological sites. Variation in the form of artifacts is a complex subject, but one of critical importance to archaeologists. It's the cumulative result of thousands of minor changes in dozens of different artifacts that provides the tangible evidence for culture change in the prehistoric past. And that, as we have seen, is a major concern to anyone studying prehistory.

Ecofacts are archaeological finds of cultural significance that were not manufactured by humans. These include bones and plant remains.

The archaeological record, whether a site or an artifact, a seed or an entire city, has a context in time and space, which we must now define.

Context

The thin line of the 1,000-year-old cattle-dung-covered hut floor appeared in the bottom of the trench, a hard semicircular patch of fire-baked clay lined on its outer side with the charred bases of wall posts. We removed the overlying ashy soil with slow care, using trowels, then paintbrushes, to ease the matrix off the long-abandoned floor surface. Three large boulders appeared in the soil. We brushed them off, exposing a patch of charcoal between them, also a broken ox jaw and the broken fragments of a small clay pot. The exposed floor was about 10 feet (3 meters) across, with the hearth set near the center of the house. Before we lifted the hearth, artifacts, and hut floor, we measured the exact position of every find and feature three-dimensionally, tying our measurements into a site grid linked in turn to the map of the area. I remember thinking as we took up the boulders that in themselves they were just three large stones. Taken together, plotted in relationship to the charcoal and artifacts, they became something quite different. They told a story of long-forgotten household behavior. The finds had a **context**.

Artifacts are found in archaeological sites. Archaeological sites are far more than just a concentration of artifacts, however. They can hold the remains of dwellings, burials, storage pits, craft activities, and sometimes several occupation levels. Each artifact, each broken bone or tiny seed, every dwelling, has a relationship in space and time to all of the other finds made in the site. An artifact can be earlier than, contemporary with, or later than its neighbors in the soil. A thousand obsidian flakes and half-completed projectile heads scattered over an area several square feet in diameter are, in themselves, merely stone fragments. But the spatial patterning of all the fragments is significant, for it tells us something of the various manufacturing activities carried out by the person who flaked the thousand fragments from chunks of obsidian. In this instance, and many others, the context of the artifacts in time and space is vital (see the section on site-formation processes in Chapter 9).

To every archaeologist, an artifact is of limited value without this context. The museums and art galleries of the world are filled with magnificent artifacts that have been collected under circumstances that can only be described as highly unscientific. Generations of treasure hunters have ravaged ancient Egyptian cemeteries and dug up thousands of pre-Columbian pots for museums and private collectors. Few of these objects have any **archaeological context.** Any expert can look at a pre-Columbian pot and say at once, "Classic Maya." But, tragically, rarely will our expert be able to consult excavation records and say, "Classic Maya, Level VIB from Temple of the Inscriptions, Palenque, excavation c. 1976, associated with burial of an adult male, 35 years old, date about A.D. 680." An artifact removed from its context in space and time in an archaeological site is merely an object that yields only limited cultural information. An artifact carefully excavated from a recorded archaeological context is an integral part of history, and as such has far more significance.

Archaeologists distinguish **primary context**, the original position of an artifact in time and space. This can be a situation like, for example, an undisturbed burial in an earthen mound, where the original context in time and space still exists. **Secondary contexts** arise when a primary context is disturbed by later human or natural activity. For instance, a few generations later, another burial may be deposited in the same mound, partially disturbing the earlier grave.

In Chapter 5, we explore the context of time and space, all-important dimensions of the archaeological record.

SUMMARY

1. Archaeologists are concerned with the study of ancient cultures and societies.
2. Human culture is unique, its content transmitted from one generation to the next, allowing societies to develop and continue adapting to aid their survival. Humans are the only animals to use culture as the primary means of adapting to the environment.
3. Archaeologists differ considerably in their definitions of culture. Many think of it as an adaptive system, which reflects the constant adjustments to environmental, technological, and societal change. Others argue that culture is predominantly ideational, made up of human ideas, interactions, and beliefs.
4. The great diversity of approaches to culture is reflected in constant theoretical debates, which surround the issue of cultural and social change through time.
5. Archaeology has four basic goals: the construction of culture history, the reconstruction of ancient lifeways, the explanation of cultural and social change, and the conservation of the archaeological record.
6. The archaeological record comprises all kinds of archaeological finds, from vast cities to small scatters of stone artifacts.

FOUR

Explaining the Past

Bas-relief of the goddess Maat, goddess of rightness. Painted stone relief, Egypt, nineteenth dynasty. (Museo Archeologico, Florence, Italy. Copyright Scala/Art Resource, NY.)

CHAPTER OUTLINE

PREVIEW

Studying culture change, the subject of Chapter 4, is one of the major goals of archaeology. All archaeological research begins with culture history, which is concerned with ancient societies in time and space. We discuss the classic mechanisms of culture change—inevitable variation, invention, diffusion, and migration, also noncultural models for such change. Culture history is a descriptive process, which may invoke mechanisms of change, but it does not explain *why* such changes took place. Two major changes to the study of cultural process dominate archaeology. Ecological and environmental approaches, processual archaeology, are concerned with cultural and ecological systems, and multilinear cultural evolution. Postprocessual archaeology, a reaction against processual approaches, is profoundly concerned with people as much as cultural processes. We end with a discussion of current theoretical trends, which offer potential for future study of culture change.

> *Academics in universities are often theorists, intoxicated by theory or haunted by it. To the field-worker, their theories compete and multiply like insects in a hot house, the dominant species being variously social, processual, analytical, behavioural, cognitive, structural, symbolic, or contextual, each with its own plumage and coterie.*
>
> —M. O. H. Carver, 1989

In Chapter 3, we described some important basic principles of archaeology, among them human cultural systems and culture change. We also discussed the goals of archaeology, one of which was "explaining cultural and social change." Before exploring the ways in which archaeologists collect and analyze data and reconstruct ancient lifeways, we must look more closely at archaeology's most important task beyond preserving the past—explaining *why* things happened in ancient times, the study of cultural process.

Culture history is the record of the past in time and space, the basis for all study of culture change in the past.

Interpretation of Culture History

The ordering of archaeological data is a descriptive process. It highlights the patterning and regularities in archaeological data. The concepts and units of culture historical studies are devices used to organize data as a preliminary to studying culture change. These classificatory units, described in Chapter 8, put artifacts and other culture traits into a time and space context by using such tools as site distribution maps, observations of layered occupations in ancient settlements, and a variety of dating methods (see Chapter 5).

Culture history is a sound way of describing the past, but it is of minimal use for explaining why artifacts, sites, and human societies were similar or different—why they displayed variability. It's based on inductive research methods, the development of generalizations about a research problem that are based on numerous specific observations, and on a **normative view** of culture. This assumes that abstract rules govern what a culture considers normal behavior.

The normative view of culture is a descriptive one, one that can be used to describe culture during one particular time period or throughout time. Archaeologists base it on the assumption that surviving artifacts, such as potsherds, display stylistic and other changes that represent the changing norms of human behavior through time.

The archaeological record does not invariably reflect an orderly and smooth chronicle of culture change. A radical new artifact inventory may suddenly appear in occupation levels at several sites while earlier tool kits suddenly vanish. The economy of sites in a local sequence may change completely within a century as the plow revolutionizes agricultural methods. Such changes are readily observed in thousands of local sequences all over the world. But how did these changes come about? What processes of cultural change were at work to cause major and minor alterations in the archaeological record? A number of descriptive models have been formulated to characterize mechanisms of culture change—some cultural, others noncultural. Several involve internal change, others external influence. These descriptive models include inevitable variation and cultural selection, invention, diffusion, and migration.

Inevitable Variation

Inevitable variation is somewhat akin to the well-known phenomenon of genetic drift in biology. As people learn the behavior patterns of their society, inevitably some differences in learned behavior appear from generation to generation, which, although minor in themselves, accumulate over a long time, especially in isolated populations. The snowball effect of inevitable variation and slow-moving cultural evolution can be detected in dozens of prehistoric societies. The great variation in Acheulian hand ax technology throughout Europe and Africa between a million and 150,000 years ago may be in part the result of the effects of inevitable variation.

Inevitable variation often results from isolation—a very low density of humans per square kilometer. It should not be confused with broad trends in human prehistory that grew over long periods. For example, the more and more complex burial rituals in the Adena and Hopewell cultures of the American Midwest between 500 B.C. and A.D. 300 probably resulted from trends toward greater complexity in religious beliefs and rituals as well as from political and economic organization over a long time, and not from isolation.

Inevitable variation is also quite different from what happens when a society recognizes that certain culture changes or inventions may be advantageous. Perhaps many hunter-gatherer societies deliberately took up cultivating the soil once they saw the advantages it gave neighboring peoples, who had already adopted the new economies.

Invention

Invention is the creation or evolution of a new idea. Many inventions, such as new social institutions or religious beliefs, leave no trace in the archaeological record. But some innovations are reflected in new types of surviving artifacts, such as the plow or the iron ax. If an invention such as plowing is sufficiently useful to be attractive to more than a few people, the new idea, or a product of the idea, spreads widely and often rapidly.

By tracing from their place of origin the distribution of such distinctive artifacts as plowshares, archaeologists have studied ways in which inventions spread. The earliest occurrence of iron making was in northern Turkey in about 1500 B.C. Iron tools first appear in the archaeological record of Europe and Egypt much later (see Figure 4.1 on page 68). Because the earliest presently known and dated iron artifacts occurred in Turkey, we can say that iron making may have been invented there.

In the early days of archaeology, people assumed that metallurgy and other major inventions were invented in only one place—in many cases southwestern Asia. These

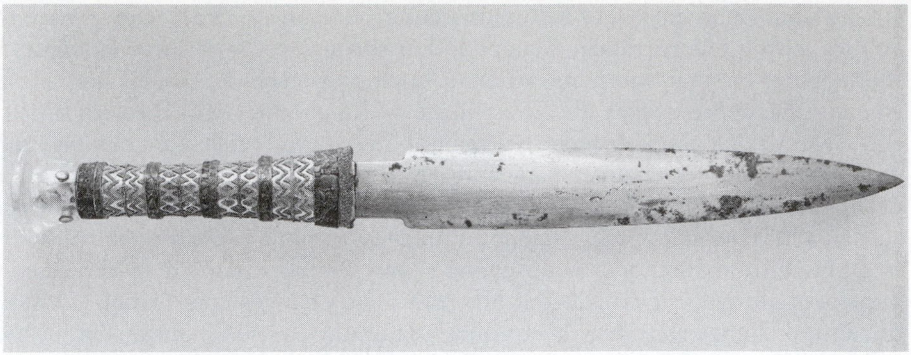

Figure 4.1 Iron technology, a revolutionary invention: Pharaoh Tutankhamun's iron-bladed dagger, from his tomb, c. 1323 B.C. Iron objects were of enormous value in Egypt at the time, as iron metallurgy was a closely guarded secret held by the Hittites of modern-day Turkey. This particular artifact was probably made of native hammered iron. (Photograph by the Egyptian Expedition, The Metropolitan Museum of Art.)

innovations were then assumed to have spread all over the world as other societies realized how important the new ideas were. But as the importance of environment and adaptation in the development of human culture has become better understood, this simple view of invention has been rejected. We now know that agriculture developed quite independently in southwest and southeast Asia, Mesoamerica, and the Andean area. Complex adaptive processes occurred in all of these areas. Scholars now try to identify the many interacting factors that caused people to modify their lifestyles to adopt food production. The genius of humanity was that it recognized opportunities when they came along and adapted to new circumstances. The issue is not to discover who first cultivated corn but rather to study the dozens of major and minor alterations in human culture that were the result of adaptive changes over time.

Diffusion

The spread of ideas, over short or long distances, is termed **diffusion**. Ideas can be transmitted in many ways other than by the movements of entire societies or communities. Regular trade between neighboring villages or more distant peoples results in the exchange not only of goods but of ideas as well, especially when much of this trade is conducted reciprocally. Reciprocity implies a two-sided relationship in which both parties exchange goods, services, and, of course, ideas. Ideas such as a new religious belief are transmitted from individual to individual and ultimately from group to group. But neither the exchange of ideas nor that of technological innovations necessarily involves actual movements of people. Even the spread of material objects and abstract ideas can have a quite different effect in a new area. For instance, the Hopi Indians of the Southwest received American trade goods but still retained their own culture, trading objects but rejecting the ideas of an alien culture.

Let us say that a new type of painted pot is invented in one village in A.D. 1400. The advantages of this new vessel are such that villagers 9 miles (14 kilometers) away learn about it at a celebration a year later. Within ten years, their potters are making similar receptacles. In a short time the pot form is found commonly in villages 10 miles (16 kilometers) farther away. Half a century later, communities in a 50-mile (80-kilometer) radius are making the now well-established vessel design. If we put this stirring tale on paper, we end up with the cone effect shown in Figure 4.2 on page 69. The cone effect is the type of distribution we study when identifying diffusion in the archaeological record.

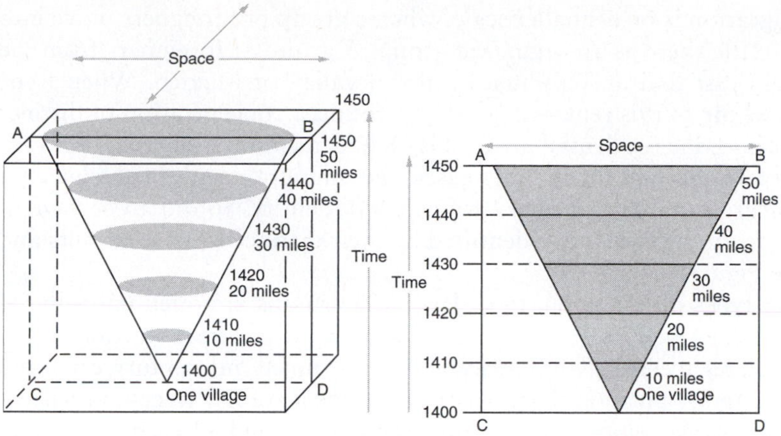

Figure 4.2 The spread of a culture trait in time and space: the cone effect.

Archaeologically, diffusion is difficult to identify unless one can use very distinctive artifacts, obviously of common origin, to demonstrate that the artifacts were invented in only one place, then trace the distribution of the artifact in space and time from its origin point to neighboring areas. To do so means establishing that the tool was made first in one place and later in other sites nearby (see Figure 4.2). Instances of diffusion in prehistory are common. A classic example is the Chavín art style of Peru, which diffused widely over the lowlands from a homeland in the highlands, where it appeared about 900 B.C. (see Figure 4.3).

Migration

Migration takes place when entire societies deliberately decide to expand their sphere of influence. English settlers moved to North America, taking their own culture with them. Spanish conquistadors occupied Mexico. Migration involves not only the movement of ideas but a mass shift of people that results in social and cultural changes on a large scale. A classic prehistoric migration was that of groups of Polynesians who deliberately voyaged from the Society Islands to Rapa Nui (Easter Island) and New Zealand, where they settled. In each case, new land masses were found by purposeful exploration, then colonized by small numbers of people who moved to an uninhabited island.

Figure 4.3 A Chavín shaman transforms himself into a jaguar. From Chavín de Huantar, Peru.

These types of mass migration were rare in prehistoric times. They would be reflected in the archaeological record by totally new components and phases or by skeletons of a totally new physical type. To be proved, the migration would have to show up as new complexes in the cultural sequence at many neighboring sites.

A second type of migration is on a smaller scale, when a group of foreigners move into another region and settle there as an organized group. A group of foreigners from the Valley of Oaxaca did just that at Teotihuacán in the Valley of Mexico. When René Millon mapped the whole of this remarkable city, he found a concentration of distinctive Oaxacan artifacts in one residential area. This Oaxacan colony flourished for centuries in an alien city. In this and many other cases, the immigrants adopted some features of the host culture but retained their own cultural identity. So did an enclave of Veracruz merchants from the lowlands, identified by their distinctive circular huts and painted pottery (see Figure 4.4).

There are other types of migration, too. Slaves and artisans are often unorganized migrants, sometimes taking new technological devices with them. Great warrior migrations, like those of Zulu regiments in South Africa in the early nineteenth century, can cause widespread disruption and population shifts. Such migrations leave few traces in archaeological sites. Within a few generations, the warriors settle down and adopt the sedentary life of the conquered. Only a few new weapon forms reveal the presence of strangers.

It's important to realize that migrations are not only physical movements over distance but incidents that involve major, sometimes fundamental social change.

Noncultural Models

Culture change triggered by alterations in the natural environment is an integral part of culture history. Earlier noncultural models tended to be simple, stating, for example, that agriculture began in southwestern Asia when population pressure caused game and

Figure 4.4 Reconstruction of the Veracruz enclave at Teotihuacán, Mexico.

plant food shortages, causing people to turn to farming instead. However, the most recent research in archaeology has focused heavily on specific details of the relationship between environment and prehistoric cultures. The complex models that are emerging from this research show that earlier explanations were far too general to explain these ever-changing environment-culture relationships.

One needs large quantities of data to identify invention, diffusion, or migration in the archaeological record. The identification of these classic cultural mechanisms is largely a mechanical, descriptive activity because the artifacts used, be they stone axes, pots, or swords, are considered in isolation and not as an element of the cultural system of which they are part. The explanation of culture change requires more sophisticated research models, based on the notion that not only are human cultural systems made up of many complex interacting elements—religious beliefs, technology, subsistence, and so on—but these cultural systems also interact with the natural environment and other complex systems.

Genetics and DNA

An increasingly powerful tool for studying human population movements comes from molecular biology. All humans carry in their genes the record of their history. Modern molecular biological techniques have made it possible to detect and analyze new polymorphic genes (genes present in slightly different forms in different people) that might have medical or anthropological interest. Most of our genetic information is in the form of 46 chromosomes inside the nuclei of each cell in our bodies. This nuclear DNA is easy to study in living populations, but degrades quickly and is no longer intact when a body decomposes. In recent years, studies of mitochondrial DNA (mtDNA) present outside the cell nuclei in small structures called mitochondria have attracted particular attention. Mitochondrial DNA is useful when studying the past because it has three distinctive properties. It is preserved in thousands of copies in each cell. MtDNA is inherited through the female line and is passed from mothers to offspring virtually unaltered except for rare changes caused by mutation. It also changes at a steady rate and in a distinctive way, being transferred from one generation to the next intact, changing through time only as a result of random mutations. MtDNA changes faster than nuclear DNA, so much so that it has been used as a clock for dating such major events as the appearance of modern humans. Large-scale studies of human mtDNA in present-day populations from all parts of the world have shown that there is relatively little mtDNA variation throughout the globe, suggesting that there was a relatively recent branching-out of human populations. The African mtDNAs were the most variable, having had more time to accumulate genetic changes, consistent with the theory that the African human lineages are the oldest ones.

The first ancient DNA sequences were reported by Swedish scientist Svaante Pääbo, who extracted and characterized DNA from the skin of a Predynastic Egyptian of about 4000 B.C. in 1985. Since then, DNA has been extracted from bones, teeth, and plant remains using a new technique called polymerase chain reaction (PCR). Pääbo used this technique on a human brain of 3000 B.C. from a hunter-gatherer site at Windover, Florida, and identified an mtDNA strain not previously observed in North America. In recent years, scientists have succeeded in extracting DNA from a Neanderthal bone over 50,000 years old and have shown that these archaic Europeans were genetically distinct from the modern humans who succeeded them. Mitochondrial DNA analysis of ancient human skeletons from Rape Nui (Easter Island) in the Pacific has also shown that the ultimate origins of the Easter Islanders lie in Polynesia, for this remote landmass had been colonized from the Society Islands (the Tahiti region) by A.D. 500.

As molecular biology assumes even great sophistication, it will play an important role in the study of such major issues as the origins of modern humans, the first Americans, and the first arrival of farming societies in Europe.

Ecological/Environmental (Processual) Archaeology

Many archaeologists espouse an ecological/evolutionary approach to explaining the past. This approach, sometimes called **processual archaeology**, is based on deductive research methodology that employs research design, formulation of explicit research hypotheses, and testing of these against basic data. Its methods are cumulative; that is, initial hypotheses are designed that propose a working model to explain culture change. These hypotheses are tested against basic data and some are discarded; others are refined again and again until the factors that affect cultural change are isolated in highly specific form.

The processual approach is firmly based on culture history and data obtained from deductive research. It must be, for the chronological and spatial frameworks for prehistory come from such investigations. The difference between the processual and systems-ecological approaches lies in the orientation of the research. Processual archaeologists rely on deductive strategies, formulate testable hypotheses, and then gather data to test them. Very often, however, the initial hypotheses are based on data derived from inductive culture history.

Systems and Cultural Ecology

Deductive research is extremely valuable for the study of the past, provided that realistic account is taken of the uniqueness of archaeological data. In many respects, the numerous theoretical problems archaeologists are grappling with are the same as those encountered by biologists working on change in living organisms. It is for this reason that evolutionary theory is playing an increasingly important part in archaeology.

The most common processual approach deals with the ways in which cultural systems function, both internally and in relation to external factors such as the natural environment. The systems-ecological approach involves three basic models of cultural change: systems models, which are based on **general systems theory**, cultural ecology, which provides complicated models of the interaction between human cultures and their environment, and multilinear evolution, which is a theory of the cumulative evolution of culture over long periods through complex adaptations to the environment. It is, as archaeologist Kent Flannery (1976: 16) once put it, "the search for the ways human populations (in their own way) do the things that other systems do."General systems theory came to archaeology from other sciences and has caused archaeologists to think of human cultures as open systems, regulated in part by external stimuli. This general concept is most applicable to human cultures that interact intimately with the natural environment. Systems theory is little more than a general concept in archaeology, with the advantage that it frees us from having to look at only one agent of culture change, such as migration or diffusion. It allows us to focus instead on relationships between different components of a cultural system and between a cultural system and its environment.

Cultural ecology is a means of studying human culture that gives a picture of the way in which human populations adapt to, and transform, their environments. Human cultural systems have to adapt to other cultures and to the natural environment. Indeed, so many factors influence cultural systems that the processes by which cultural similarities and differences are generated are not easy to understand. Cultural ecologists see human cultures as subsystems interacting with other major subsystems, among them the biotic community and the physical environment. Thus the key to understanding cultural process lies in the interactions among these various subsystems.

Effective subsistence strategies and technological artifices are the cornerstones of any society's successful adaptation to its environment. But social organization and religious beliefs are important in ensuring cooperative exploitation of the environment as well as technological cooperation. For instance, religious life provided an integrating force in many societies, not least among them the Maya of Mesoamerica and the Sumerians of Mesopotamia. There are obvious difficulties in studying the interactions between people and their environment, especially when preservation conditions limit the artifacts and other data available for study. Fortunately, however, artifacts and other elements of the technological subsystem often survive. Because technology is a primary way in which different cultures adapt to their environment, detailed models of technological subsystems allow archaeologists to obtain a relatively comprehensive picture of the cultural system as a whole.

Multilinear Cultural Evolution

Multilinear cultural evolution is a branching, cumulative process that results from cultural adaptations over long periods. Multilinear evolution recognizes that there are many evolutionary tracks, the differences resulting from individual adaptive solutions. Thus cultural adaptations are complex processes that are fine-tuned to local conditions, with long-term cumulative effects. These adaptations can be studied on a large and small scale by a systems-ecological approach. Multilinear cultural evolution, then, is the vital integrative force that brings systems theory and cultural ecology together into a closely knit, highly flexible way of studying and explaining cultural process.

The systems-ecological approach produces very complex interpretations of major developments in prehistory—for example, the origins of literate civilization in southwestern Asia. Early theories invoked single causes, such as population pressure, the invention of irrigation agriculture, even warfare or trade, as the ultimate single causes—prime movers, if you will—of civilization. Systems-ecological models argue that a whole series of important variables with complex interrelationships and variations caused the emergence of civilization. Under this rubric, the rise of civilization should be thought of as a series of interacting and cumulative processes that were triggered by favorable cultural and ecological conditions, which continued to develop cumulatively as a result of continuous positive feedback.

For example, farming communities were established in the low-lying Mesopotamian delta between the Tigris and Euphrates by at least 6000 B.C. These settlements triggered three processes that set up critical feedback relationships: slow but steady population growth within the delta, increased specialization in food production by different groups within society, and a demand for and acquisition of raw materials from outside the delta region. Each of these processes set off feedback reactions that became more and more complex as time went on. A need for more fields to feed more people, more centralized planning and administration, larger and more densely populated settlements that took up a minimum of agricultural land, irrigation farming, and finally an administrative elite that controlled people's access to resources—all were complex reactions to long-term processes of cultural change.

Historical Materialist Approaches

Archaeology is based on the optimistic belief that knowledge about human societies has accumulated gradually, through rational inquiry modeled on the hard sciences and mathematics. This notion of cumulative science and knowledge is vital to understanding the convoluted history of archaeological theory since the 1960s.

In the 1960s and 1970s, archaeologists were talking about a so-called "new" archaeology, a revolutionary approach to the past that promised to overcome the many limitations of the archaeological record. In fact, this "new" archaeology, processual archaeology, failed to deliver on many of its promises. Processual archaeology has emphasized subsistence and settlement patterns, animal bones, plant remains, and ancient population distributions, topics covered extensively in this book. Its many practitioners embraced methodological rigor and interpreted the past in terms of cultural systems, with a strong emphasis on material objects. Many of its once new tenets are part of today's mainstream archaeology.

Back in the 1960s, Lewis Binford and others believed that processual archaeology would allow researchers to investigate all aspects of human experience, including intangibles such as beliefs. But, eventually, many discouraged processual archaeologists dismissed religion, ideology, and human ideas as marginal to the central enterprise of studying subsistence and settlement.

Inevitably, there was a reaction against the processual approach, which seemed to dehumanize the past in a quest for processes of cultural change. During the late 1970s and 1980s, more researchers began thinking about the entire spectrum of human behavior—the development and expression of human consciousness, religion and belief, symbolism and iconography, as part of a more holistic archaeology. Thus was born what is sometimes called **postprocessual archaeology**, a sometimes violent antidote to its predecessor—in general terms a reaction against the relatively anonymous processual approach that emphasized cultural processes over people and individuals.

Postprocessual archaeology is a loosely defined term that covers several often aggressively expressed intellectual developments that often parallel schools of thought in literature and anthropology. The term is used more extensively in Europe than in North America, although the same theoretical concerns arise on both sides of the Atlantic. It is a convenient term that embraces an enormous range of different, and often transitory, theoretical approaches, as eclectic as those who propose them. These approaches coincide, in general, with what one can call historical materialist approaches to the past and cover much contemporary research into the past, including research on ethnic minorities, gender, and women. Whereas ecological/evolutionary theorists regard human societies as integrated, holistic systems, the historical materialists view them as eclectic amalgams of competing individuals, factions, and social groups. In other words, people lie at the core of cultural and social change in the past. Individuals, households, kin groups, and other entities are agencies for change. **Agency** in archaeology is the notion that the past was inhabited by people rather than anonymous "cultures."

The historical materialist (or postprocessual) approach covers a formidable morass of ever-changing theory. As British archaeologist John Bintcliff has pointed out, archaeological theory has unfolded not in a cumulative manner but by a process of almost total renewal every ten years or so. In each case, the leading proponents of the new approach write off the previous paradigm as useless and introduce new concepts, often derived from attractive theoretical approaches developed in other disciplines, and not in archaeology itself.

Postprocessualism introduced a long period of theoretical instability in the 1970s and 1980s, which saw some archaeologists, notably British scholar Ian Hodder, turning to spatial analysis, then structuralism and postmodernism. Almost without exception, the new approaches arrived within archaeology via what Bintcliff (1991: 277) called "a novel bibliography of intellectual traditions [from other academic disciplines] likely to be esoteric and unpalatable to their predecessors—who 'write themselves out' of the debate by failing to read the new sacred texts." Very often, their original authors in, say, sociology, had never thought about archaeology in their lives! With such constant renewal going on, there was often very little debate or even dialogue between people who adhered to or had developed new theoretical approaches. Very often, their predecessors were too busy testing their own laboriously developed approaches in the field.

It's easy to be cynical about the cross-currents of archaeological theory, but good theory is always like that—ever-changing, brimming with original (and not-so-original) ideas, and in a constant state of flux. Archaeology, like other sciences, would soon shrivel into insignificance without constant theoretical debates. The best theorists are bold, controversial, and not afraid to go out on a limb. We cannot have enough of them!

For all of their constantly shifting paradigms, historical materialist (postprocessual) approaches have made three positive and important contributions.

First, meaning is more important than materialism. No longer can we interpret the past in terms of purely ecological, technological, and other material considerations. Culture is interactive. In other words, people are actors who create, use, and manipulate their symbolic capabilities to make and remake the world they live in.

Second, archaeologists must critically examine their social responsibilities, looking beyond their specialties to the broader aims of the discipline, and to issues of moral and emotional involvement with the past in contemporary society. How does the public interact with the past?

Third, many perspectives on ancient society have been neglected, among them those of women, ethnic minorities, and what are often called "the people without history"—anonymous, often illiterate commoners.

Considerable debate surrounds the third of these issues, for some archaeologists believe that their interpretations of the past are Eurocentric and culturally biased, making them unacceptable to those whose history they claim to study. In other words, they are imposing their culture and view of the past on others such as Australian Aborigines and Native Americans, who may have entirely different perspectives. The controversy is still unresolved, but there is no question that in the future archaeologists will have to work more closely with those they study, or they are in real danger of becoming marginalized as a source of history. One helpful approach considers the archaeologist as a form of "active mediator" between the present and the past. The debate continues.

Cognitive-Processual Archaeology

Many archaeologists still firmly believe in the ecological/evolutionary approach, especially in North America. But even the most diehard processualists are now paying closer attention to the role of people in the past. People are like actors, interacting with their culture—this concept is the major difference in approach between archaeologists using an ecological/evolutionary approach to the past and those who are concerned with symbolic meaning, structure, and the rules that once governed society. After intensive debate, the beginning of a theoretical consensus is emerging, under the broad label of **cognitive-processual archaeology**. This label covers numerous approaches to cultural and social change, which are as eclectic as their users. The important point is that the latest approaches combine science and more intuitive ideas.

The *Oxford English Dictionary,* the ultimate arbiter of the English language, even for Americans, defines cognition as "the action or faculty of knowing taken in its widest sense, including sensation, perception, conception, etc." From an archaeological perspective, the term **cognitive archaeology** covers the whole spectrum of human behavior, especially religion and belief, and also the development and expression of human consciousness. Since the very early days of archaeology, researchers have been concerned with ancient religion, belief, and expression, the subject matter of cognitive archaeology—what has sometimes been called the "archaeology of mind." How can one define cognitive archaeology? Is it possible to study human cognition from the material remains of the archaeological record, even granting that we cannot afford to ignore it? Some of the best minds in archaeology are debating these questions and attempting to create a cognitive-processual approach, which creates a new framework for archaeology, drawing on both old and new models and methods. This is an important exercise because the archaeology of today is built on solid scientific foundations, not on **hermeneutics**, interpretive approaches that allow insight to play a key role. That is the approach used by those who believe there are ancient civilizations lying under Antarctic ice or that astronauts from outer space founded Maya civilization. Thus cognitive-processualists never claim they can establish what people thought, but they can give insights into *how* they thought.

Cognitive archaeology covers all of the human past, but it can be divided into two broad areas of concern. One involves the study of the cognitive facilities of early hominins and archaic humans, the relationships between toolmaking and cognitive abilities, the origins of language, and the social contexts of early human behavior. The other covers the past 40,000 years—the cognitive aspects of such major developments as the origins of food production and civilization. British archaeologist Colin Renfrew considers the challenge for cognitive archaeology to be establishing how the formation of symbolic systems in, say, the Near East or early Mesoamerica molded and conditioned later cultural developments—for example, in Maya civilization. He considers that humans use symbols in about six ways: for design and planning, for measurement and social relations (using symbols to structure and regulate interpersonal behavior), for representation, and for mediating between the human and supernatural worlds. He also believes the reason that cognitive archaeology has been neglected is that it lacks a coherent methodology. This methodology may emerge from the convergence of such diverse fields as cognitive psychology, artificial intelligence, computer simulation, and cognitive archaeology itself. But this convergence, and the potential intellectual leap forward that might result, will not occur until archaeologists interested in human cognition develop a rigorous and explicit methodology that will substitute for many of the simplistic generalizations that masquerade under the label of postprocessual archaeology.

Archaeologists Kent Flannery and Joyce Marcus have long been interested in cognition. Their earliest work was an attempt to understand ancient Zapotec subsistence behavior in Mexico's Valley of Oaxaca by taking into account what early Spanish accounts told of local Indian cosmology. They believe this kind of approach, which makes use of critically analyzed historical documents and other sources, to be productive, as opposed to the inspired speculation so common in the 1980s. Flannery and Marcus consider cognitive archaeology to be the study of all those aspects of ancient culture that are the product of the ancient mind. This includes cosmology, religion, ideology, iconography, and all forms of human intellectual and symbolic behavior. They also firmly state that effective cognitive archaeology depends on rigorous research methods. Thus it can only be used when the body of supporting data is rich. Otherwise, it becomes (1993: 264) "little more than speculation, a kind of bungee jump into the Land of Fantasy." In practical terms, and for obvious reasons, cognitive archaeology is usually most effective when historical records are available to amplify the archaeological record, as they are when working with archaeological evidence and Maya inscriptions.

Under this approach, cognitive archaeology has considerable limitations. All cultures have a theory of the universe in which they live. Their cosmology, like that of Western civilization based on modern astronomy, constitutes a theory of the origin of the universe, defines space and time, and can provide a structure for religion and ideology. Many cultures, among them the ancient Greek and Maya, envisage a cosmos inhabited by supernatural beings, another link to religious beliefs. Although cosmology can have a strong influence on both settlement and subsistence—as, for example, in cases where certain aspects of the environment such as pristine forest may be held sacred—it is difficult, if not impossible, to reconstruct cosmology from animal and plant remains alone.

Religious beliefs provide ethics and values, often within the framework of a quest for the values of an ideal life. A well-defined worldview links cosmology and religion, the latter providing the rituals and practices that help the worshiper attain the ideal. Clearly, these ethics and values can have a powerful effect on human behavior, even on such pragmatic areas of life as obtaining food and trading. Religion can provide a powerful catalyst for social and political change, as was the case, for example, when Buddhist merchants brought their religion to Southeast Asia and changed the course of history by providing the spiritual inspiration for a series of brilliant kingdoms, like those of the Khmer of Cambodia (see Figure 4.5).

Flannery and Marcus believe that one approach to reconstructing ancient religions is to construct models from ethnohistoric sources, then to isolate temples, artifacts, art styles, and other cultural elements that can be identified archaeologically. These are studied in their cultural context, and the observed archaeological remains compared with the model from ethnohistoric documents. Ideology is a product of society and politics, "a body of doctrine, myth, and symbolism associated with a social movement, an institution, class, or group of individuals, often with reference to some political or cultural plan, along with the strategies for putting the doctrine into operation" (Flannery and Marcus, 1993: 266). For example, any archaeologist concerned with the appearance of ranked, as opposed to egalitarian, societies is studying fundamental changes in ideology, simply because egalitarian societies tend to have leveling mechanisms that prevent one individual or group from attaining superior rank. Again, these changes can only be documented by a judicious use of historical analogies and artifacts.

For instance, in the Valley of Oaxaca, many village farming communities functioned without any apparent ranking between 1400 and 1150 B.C. Between 1150 and 850 B.C. the first artistic depictions of supernatural lineage of ancestors appear. Some may represent the earth, others the sky, in the form of lightning or a fire serpent. Some form of hereditary social ranking seems to accompany the new art. Then the Zapotec state came into being, with a powerful elite ruling from Monte Albán—a tiny minority associated with depictions of sky and lightning, while earth and earthquake symbols

Figure 4.5 *Angkor Wat*, Cambodia, a Khmer representation of the Hindu universe with its sacred mountain peaks, A.D. 1117.

faded into obscurity. It is as if those who rose to prominence were associated with lightning's descendants, in an ideological shift where hereditary social inequality is condoned for the first time.

Cognitive-processual researches are highly effective if they use established analytical techniques and draw on information from many sources. Cognitive archaeology reaches a high degree of refinement when document-aided, as is the case with the Aztec civilization of Mexico or the Inka of the Andes. But earlier societies, like, for instance, the first farming societies of the Near East with their mysterious female figures and plastered human skulls, offer much greater challenges. It is all too easy to call each female figure a "fertility figurine" and to talk of ancient Mother Goddesses, when there is, in fact, no scientific basis for such conclusions.

Cognitive archaeology is no shortcut, but an approach to ancient beliefs, cosmology, religion, and other intangibles based on rigorous analysis and data from many sources.

All of the historical materialist approaches to the past are reactions to the feeling that modern archaeology has become too dehumanized, too divorced from its proper role in modern society. In a sense, this is a process of archaeologists becoming more critical of their own place in the unfolding intellectual development of Western scholarship.

Archaeological Theory Today and Tomorrow: "Processual Plus"

Most of today's archaeologists would agree that theory does not comprise a rigid framework into which they must squeeze their work at all costs—as has sometimes happened in the past. As Michelle Hegmon has pointed out, "Theory is, or should be, a set of general guiding principles that help us—as researchers and as curious human beings—make sense of specific cases and of the world around us" (Hegmon, 2003: 213). Theory is a tool to identify, label, and explain the past. As Hegmon points out, most American archaeologists (and, indeed, researchers elsewhere in the world) tend to combine a broad array of theoretical approaches into what she calls "processual-plus." Evolutionary theory in various forms is much used; so are many new approaches for conceptualizing society, and the notion of individuals as agents of change. The past has been "engendered"—a perspective that developed in parallel with postprocessual archaeology with a strong base in feminist theory. Studying what men and women did in the past, and the implications of this activity for gender relations, is now a part of mainstream archaeology.

The theoretical approaches known as processual and postprocessual archaeology are now pushing against one another to produce research that invokes a number of avenues, everything from Marxist perspectives to attempts at historical narratives of households and communities. Today, most archaeologists are more interested in exploring the archaeological record and its implications than in theory alone. Nevertheless, there are many theoretical disagreements, which keep archaeology dynamic and exciting. Much of this dynamism comes from a focus on major issues like gender and agency that cut across all kinds of theoretical approaches.

Our interpretations of the past are likely to become more sophisticated in the future, as archaeological theory matures. New actors are coming on stage as well, among them the increasingly urgent need to focus on conservation and management of the archaeological record and the increased influence of cultural resource management as a primary source of archaeological research. At present, archaeology draws on theoretical approaches from many academic disciplines and there is little agreement as to a dominant approach. This makes it doubly hard to discern what lies ahead.

Discovery

THE ROYAL TOMBS OF QATNA, SYRIA, C. SIXTEENTH CENTURY B.C.

The ancient city of Qatna lies about 125 miles (200 km) north of Damascus in Syria, on a strategic route between the eastern Mediterranean coast and Mesopotamia and a route from Egypt to Anatolia. Qatna's palace stands on a high cliff, stretched about 490 feet (150 m) from east to west. A lavish structure, the main audience hall boasted a wooden roof supported by four massive wooden columns and led to a throne room and large ceremonial hall. In 2002, the excavators unearthed a long corridor at the foot of a stairway that descended beneath the palace from the ceremonial hall. A sealed door blocked off the passageway. They followed the stairway past the remains of a second and third doorway to the outer wall of the palace. The 130-foot-long (40-m-long) passage led to an entryway on the right that opened into a 16-foot (5-m) shaft. At the bottom was a doorway cut into solid bedrock, guarded by two identical basalt figures, perhaps idealized depictions of kingship. Perhaps it was here that Qatna's kings made food offerings to, and communicated with, their ancestors.

The tomb entrance was blocked with debris, but the contents were undisturbed. After testing for infectious mold, the researchers cleared the sepulcher with the utmost care, recording the position of over 2,000 objects, working lying on planks suspended above the floor. The sepulcher comprised a central chamber and three side rooms. An open sarcophagus held the remains of three individuals, who had originally been buried elsewhere. Four wooden biers that had rotted away once held other burials—the outlines could be traced on the floor. Chemical analysis of the residue showed that the corpses had once been covered in purple cloth. Hundreds of gold and stone beads, also spearheads, lay on the biers, as well as the remains of an amber cosmetic box in the shape of a lion head. A golden hand, once mounted on a wooden stick, may have served to present offerings. Stone benches with numerous bowls and jars on and under them lined two walls. One of them was an Egyptian calcite jar dating to the sixteenth century B.C. Under the benches were numerous animal bones, believed to be the remains of communal meals between the living and the dead, ritual feasts known from ancient literature as *skip*-offerings (see Figure 4.6).

One of the side chambers may have been the dead ruler's banqueting room, where vessels were deposited at the foot of a wooden bench. The westernmost side chamber held a stone bench that supported the only fully articulated skeleton in the tomb, probably the most recent burial and the only one in its original resting place. Remarkably, the body had been heated to around 392–482 F (200–259 C) for at least an hour before being placed in a wooden box, of which only the bronze clamps at the corners remained. The box was then covered with a multicolored cloth. Why the body was heated is a mystery—perhaps to preserve it or to reduce odors. The deceased wore a girdle of gold and semi-precious stones suspended on a golden thread. A second basalt sarcophagus on the other side of the chamber held the remains of two bodies, a golden bowl, and several clay and stone vessels. The final side chamber on the eastern side was an ossuary with layers of animal and human bones and offering bowls. Here the dead were deposited after they were moved from the other chambers, but, judging from the offering bowls, the older ancestors were still revered and given food offerings.

The Qatna burials provide vivid insights into royal burial practices in Syria at a time when it was a major cultural and commercial center of the eastern Mediterranean world, and when Egypt was at the height of its powers.

Figure 4.6 Main chamber of the royal tomb at Qatna, Syria, with stone benches for feasting and storage jars for food offerings.

I believe that major advances in archaeological theory will come from several already identifiable trends.

Multidisciplinary Perspectives

Archaeology is becoming ever more multidisciplinary in its perspective and in its research. More and more, a researcher working on, say, an early agricultural settlement draws on a diverse range of tools, not just the methods of archaeology alone. Genetics alone is changing the face of human prehistory. I think that future archaeological theory will be driven by this broad, multidisciplinary perspective. The result: an increasingly eclectic body of archaeological theory.

Alternative Histories

As part of this multidisciplinary endeavor, a new generation of archaeological theory will take increasing account of ethnohistorical researches and traditional oral histories to offer new perspectives on the past. In the American Southwest, for example, Native American Indian groups such as the Hopi, Navajo, and Zuñi have formed their own archaeological units and conduct important CRM research. But the dialogue between archaeologists and indigenous peoples everywhere has hardly begun.

DNA Studies

A great deal will be learned from DNA studies of ancient human bones, and from DNA preserved in other specimens such as **coprolites**. The study of mitochondrial DNA has thrown important light on the origins of modern humans in tropical Africa and on their spread from their original homeland.

Ecology and Evolutionary Theory

Both ecology and evolutionary theory will be important in the study of cultural change and the birth of complex societies. The most useful evolutionary perspective in archaeology, concerned as it is with change through time, is one that focuses on individuals as dynamic persons, constantly adjusting their behavior as their social and physical environments alter. These same individuals are people capable of creative thinking, a uniquely human characteristic.

Thought is a driving force in cultural change, in decision making and learning, and in the process of adaptation. There are, of course, limits on human knowledge—problems we cannot cope with, processes of comprehension that are beyond us, mistakes we can make through mental confusion. These limits place a premium on cooperation between individuals in the solving of problems, such as finding a way to kill large numbers of bison at one time.

This form of evolutionary archaeology will involve developing new methodologies that integrate evolutionary ecology and human psychology and ways of relating short-term individual behavior to the inevitably generalized data from the archaeological record. Many new and sometimes arcane approaches will characterize the next generation of evolutionary archaeology, including everything from computer simulations to cost-benefit analysis. In many ways, the biologist and the archaeologist are facing the same problem: How do forms, whether living or cultural, emerge and stabilize?

Understanding the Role of the Human Mind

The ecological/evolutionary approach may give us a better understanding of what archaeologists know, but this is useless without a better comprehension of what human behavior produced the archaeological record. Today, many archaeologists believe that human behavior is less orderly than many cultural evolutionists would like us to believe, yet not entirely random, as some historical materialist scholars assume. There are sufficient regularities in cultural developments in different regions—such as, for example, in the development of agriculture and village life in the Near East and Mesoamerica—to suggest that recurrent operations of cause and effect do result in the evolution of similar forms of behavior in widely separated areas. There is much we do not know about the nature of cultural and social systems. Does a change in one subsystem affect all others, as many archaeologists assume? It is by no means certain that this is the case.

Humans never adjust to the physical world as it really is but to this same world as they perceive it through their own cultural conditioning. Thus the human ability to reason and adjust cultural perceptions plays an essential role in the ways in which people interact with one another and with the environment. In other words, the human mind plays an important role in all aspects of human behavior. As the Canadian archaeologist Bruce Trigger wrote (1991: 567), we should view human behavior as "the product of interaction between the ability of individual human beings to foresee at least some of the consequences of what they do and the sorts of constraints on human behavior, both physical and imagined, that such calculations must take into account."

External and Internal Constraints

These constraints can be external. Processual archaeologists have made important studies of the ecological, technological, and economic constraints that act on human societies: Witness important research into changes in settlement patterns in the Basin of Mexico and on the rise of Mesopotamian civilization. But many noneconomic and noneecological factors also influence human behavior. So do actual physical limitations of the human body and the nature of our brains. So instead of saying that the environment is responsible for cultural change, one can argue that it constrains human behavior. Finally, general systems research has shown convincingly that there are only a limited number of alternative ways to process information and make decisions. This limits the number of social and political organizations that are viable for human societies. For instance, decision making by consensus, so typical of small-scale societies, only works well in groups of 300 people or fewer. Some form of coercion is essential when more than 1,500 people live in the same group.

In general terms, the larger the scale of the society, the more complex and bureaucratized the institutions that regulate it. There are only a limited number of viable social and political structures that human societies can adopt, which accounts for the striking similarities in general organization between, say, Sumerian and Maya civilization in different corners of the world.

Internal constraints also operate on our behavior. These include knowledge, beliefs, values, and other culturally conditioned habits, all of them different in each culture. Yet some of them are shared by cultures flourishing thousands of miles apart. For instance, two widely separated cultures may develop bronze metallurgy, which is based on a common body of technological know-how; but the cultural context of that knowledge is radically different, as it was, say, in the Shang civilization of China and Moche culture in coastal Peru (see Figure 4.7 on page 82). Some symbols, like the common practice of elevating chiefs or kings on a dais, or associations between rulers and the sun, have developed in many places. That does not mean they are connected, as early

Figure 4.7 Moche gold ear ornament in hammered gold from the tomb of a Lord of Sipán. The warrior wears a turquoise tunic and holds a detachable war club. He wears an earplug, minute bells on his belt, and carries a removable circular shield. Every part of this intricate ornament had intense symbolic meaning in Moche society. (Courtesy of UCLA Fowler Museum of Cultural History.)

diffusionists would have argued, but simply reflect more or less uniform operations of the human mind.

According to this perspective, human cultures are historical phenomena shaped by both external and internal constraints. Our ability to use our imaginations to make calculated decisions plays a significant part in streamlining any form of innovation. Our culture has a store of ideas and social values that channel and restrict innovation. In other words, information transmitted from one generation to the next provides most of the knowledge that an individual needs to deal with ecological and social realities. Each generation reworks this information and its accompanying cultural constraints to reflect the realities of its own circumstances, a process that transformed human societies and at times led to new social institutions.

Cultural traditions provide guidance for coping with the environment—a force that can operate against innovation—and a body of intellectual information that changes constantly from one generation to the next. They are as important as ecological factors in influencing human behavior. The individual is the one who has perception, who takes steps to make changes. So external and internal constraints on human behavior are equally important, and complement each other throughout human history. Ecological and other external factors can be culturally mediated, but they operate independently of human actions, which makes them susceptible to understanding in terms of evolutionary theory and other such generalizations. Cultural traditions, the internal constraints, are far more idiosyncratic, far more haphazard. This makes it difficult to impose evolutionary order on human history because, despite external constraints, much cultural change is contingent on ever-changing circumstances and cultural traditions. Human culture's open-ended capacity for further elaboration creates a need for order to make its diversity understandable. By studying individual cultural traditions, archaeologists can explain the distinctive features of cultures in ways that evolutionists and cultural ecologists can never hope to.

I believe that archaeologists will have to explain the past in terms of constraints. There are those of a natural order, such as environment, technology, and limitations placed on social organization by the cultural system. Such general factors can best be explained through applications of middle-range theory and ethnoarchaeological data (see Chapter 9). This research will be combined with inquiries into cultural meanings, using refinements of the direct historical method that employ documents, archaeology, linguistics, and oral traditions to provide cultural meaning for the generalizations of middle-range theory.

Archaeological understandings of all the constraints that have shaped ancient societies will vary considerably from one culture to another. Although the direct historical method can take us back many millennia, there are many societies—for example, those of the European Cro-Magnons of 20,000 years ago—that will always be known to us mainly from the perspective of external constraints. This does not mean, of course, that archaeologists despair of ever understanding the behavior of very early human societies. It is simply that they have a lively perception of the limitations of archaeological data. At the same time, they are striving to make archaeology more human-centered than the kind of impersonal science that characterized much of earlier processual archaeology.

A General Theoretical Framework?

Some theoreticians will continue their attempts to construct a general theoretical framework for archaeology, an elusive and frustrating task. Any general framework will have to pay careful attention to ecological and cultural approaches to the past, and also to advances in biological anthropology, pyschology, and neuroscience. Those who develop it will wrestle with complex problems. For example, under what circumstances is learned behavior more powerful than individual innovation in determining whether innovations become established in society? Under what circumstances does natural selection favor certain behavioral characteristics or types of society over others? What kinds of ancient human behavior result from thought patterns that are part of being human? How profoundly can cultural and social factors influence them? Much of this research will depend on very detailed studies of single ancient societies or cultural traditions, as a basis for generalizing about others. As a dispassionate observer of archaeological theory, the late Canadian archaeologist Bruce Trigger noted that the best way to develop a general theoretical framework will be on the basis of long-term, intensive research into ancient peoples, cultures, and regions, a major task for future generations.

This is an exciting time to become an archaeologist. A new generation of highly sophisticated methods and multidisciplinary research is rapidly changing the ways in which archaeologists explain the past. There will never be consensus about archaeological theory, but it offers remarkable opportunities for fresh insights into ancient times.

SUMMARY

1. Chapter 4 is concerned with the explanation of culture change. Culture history is descriptive archaeology, based on inductive research methods, the development of generalizations based on numerous specific observations, and on a normative view of culture.
2. Culture historians use four descriptive models to characterize culture change: inevitable variation, invention, diffusion, and migration.
3. The processual approach to culture change uses deductive research and is most commonly concerned with the ways in which cultural systems function. This systems-ecological approach uses systems models, cultural ecology, and multilinear evolution to produce complex interpretations of such developments as the origins of agriculture.
4. Many archaeologists have reacted against the materialist processual approach and have focused on the entire spectrum of human behavior. Such reactions form the complex field of historical materialist (postprocessual) archaeology, which emphasizes the importance of individuals and groups in cultural change, including women and minorities, and also the role of the modern-day archaeologist as an interpreter of the past.
5. In recent years, a synthesis between processual and what is sometimes called cognitive archaeology has begun to develop, which combines scientific approaches with studies of human consciousness, religion, and belief.
6. The debate over a new, more human-centered archaeology is in its infancy. Most archaeologists in North America and elsewhere use a combination of theoretical approaches to explore the archaeological record.
7. New generations of multidisciplinary research, evolutionary inquiry, and studies of the constraints of human behavior will revolutionize archaeological theory in the future. Developing a general theoretical framework for archaeology will involve drawing on many other disciplines, among them biological anthropology and psychology.

FIVE

Space and Time

Two boys exchanging fisticuffs on a frieze from the Minoan village at Akrotiri, Santorini Island, Greece., c. 1600 B.C.

CHAPTER OUTLINE

PREVIEW

Chapter 5 discusses time and space, the two ingredients of archaeological context. Space in archaeology is closely tied to patterns of human behavior, associations of artifacts, food remains, and other structures with one another in the ground. We discuss the all-important Law of Association, which governs artifact patternings, also the Law of Superposition, which governs relative chronology, the establishment of chronological relationships between different occupation, layers, etc. in archaeological sites. We also discuss absolute chronology, dating in calendar years and some of the chronological methods that are used to do this. These include tree-ring chronology, radiocarbon dating, and potassium argon methods.

What seest thou else in the dark backward and abysm of time?

—William Shakespeare, *The Tempest*

An Egyptian pharaoh lying in his tomb surrounded by all his riches; a house destroyed during an earthquake, the inhabitants buried inside; a mass bison kill on the North American Plains—all moments from the past frozen in time and space. Having traveled briefly through the world of archaeological theory, we must now focus on the basic principles of archaeology. Chapter 5 examines the critical elements of space and time, the basis of archaeological context.

Space

Space—not the limitless space of the heavens, but a precisely defined location for every find made during an archaeological survey and excavation—is a vital dimension of archaeological context.

Every archaeological find has an exact location in latitude, longitude, and depth measurement, which together identify any point in space absolutely and uniquely. (The universal transverse Mercator international grid system is often used as an alternative.) The telltale debris from stone toolmaking, heavy butchery tools and broken animal bones from a Plains bison kill site, carbonized loaves and clay ovens at an ancient Egyptian bakery: All tell stories of long-forgotten human behavior in villages, houses, and workshops. All depend on the dimension of space. Spatial location is indispensable to archaeologists because it enables them to establish the distances between objects or dwellings, or between entire settlements, or between settlements and key vegetational zones and landmarks. Such distances may be a few inches of level ground between a fine clay pot and the skeleton of its dead owner, or 10 miles (16 km) separating two seasonal camps. A team of fieldworkers may record the distance between dozens of villages that traded luxury goods such as seashells over hundreds of miles. For example, the research teams that studied the hinterland of the great Maya city of Copán in Honduras located more than 2,500 outlying towns, villages, and small hamlets. They used this spatial data to document the buildup and collapse of rural populations around the city between A.D. 400 and 1200.

When carrying out surface surveys or excavations, archaeologists use special methods to record the precise positions of artifacts, dwellings, and other finds. They tie in the position of each site to accurate survey maps so they can use the grid coordinates on the map to define the location precisely on the landscape. By using geographic positioning systems (GPS) (see Chapter 6), they can combine their spatial data with environmental, topographic, and vegetational information in digitized databases, then examine changing settlement distributions over time. The same precision operates at the site level. When investigating an individual site, excavators lay out recording grids made up of equal squares over the entire site, using the grids or, more commonly, electronic measuring devices, to record the position of each artifact, each feature (see Figure 7.8 on page 142 for a site grid).

Spatial analysis is the analysis of spatial relationships both within sites and over much larger areas.

Space involves archaeologists in three directions of inquiry:

- The process of describing one's finds, of determining the cultural origins of artifacts. This procedure of ordering is described more fully in Chapter 8, where we discuss some of the arbitrary analytical devices that archaeologists use.
- Studying specific activities—economic, religious, social, technological—within a human settlement. These patternings may reflect the activities of a person, a household, or an entire community.
- The study of **settlement patterns**, the changing distributions of human settlement over ancient landscapes (see Chapter 12).

The Law of Association

Context in space is based on **associations** between artifacts and other evidence of human behavior around them. Let us say you find a beer can opener in a plowed field. An expert on such artifacts—and they can be found—usually can date your opener to within a few years of its manufacture by going to manufacturers' files or U.S. Patent Office records. But your beer can opener was an isolated find. No other signs of human activity were discovered nearby. You would have difficulty, if you were not a twenty-first-century American, making the inference that the artifact was used for opening a can. But had you found the can opener in association with a dozen punctured beer cans of similar age, you could then infer the general activity that took place and you could draw some conclusions about the purposes for which the artifact was designed.

The law of (stratigraphic) association is based on the principle that an artifact is contemporary with the other objects found in the precise archaeological horizon (see Figure 5.1 on page 88). The mummy of Egyptian pharaoh Tutankhamun was associated with an astonishing treasury of household possessions and ritual objects. This association provided unique information on Egyptian life in 1323 B.C. The mummy alone would have been far less informative.

The law of association is of great importance when ordering artifacts in chronological sequences. Many prehistoric societies buried their dead with grave furniture—clay pots, bronze ornaments, seashells, or stone axes. In some cases, the objects buried with a corpse were obviously in use when their owner died. Occasionally, they may be prized heirlooms, passed down from generation to generation. Together they are an association of artifacts, a grave group that may be found duplicated in dozens of other contemporary graves. But later graves may be found to contain quite different furniture, vessels of a slightly altered form. Obviously some cultural changes have taken place. When dozens of burial groups are analyzed in this way, the associations and changing artifact styles may provide a basis for dividing the burials into different chronological groups (see Figure 5.2 on page 89).

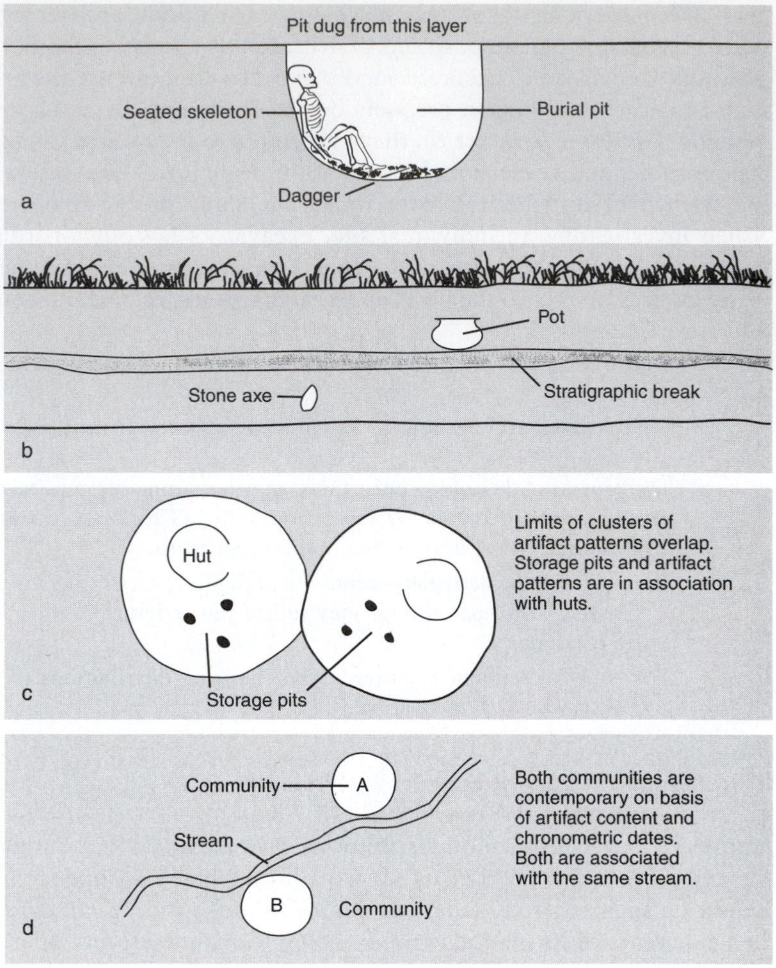

Figure 5.1 The law of association: (a) a skeleton associated with a dagger; (b) a pot and a stone ax, separated by a stratigraphic break, which are not in association; (c) two contemporary household clusters associated with each other; (d) an association of communities that are contemporary.

Assemblages and Subassemblages

Human behavior can be individual and totally unique, or shared with other members of one's family or clan, or common to all members of the community. All of these levels of cultural behavior should, theoretically, be reflected in artifact patterns and associations in the archaeological record. The iron projectile point found in the backbone of a British war casualty of A.D. 43 is the consequence of one person's behavior, but that behavior is clearly related to the common cultural behavior of the warrior's society (see Figure 5.3 on page 90).

Archaeologists use a hierarchy of units to group artifact associations, the lower levels of which are as follows (for higher units, see Chapter 8):

- *Subassemblages* A collection of artifacts associated with a single individual. For example, a hunter uses a bow and arrows, which are carried in a quiver. An auto mechanic employs a tool kit of wrenches, screwdrivers, and gauges.

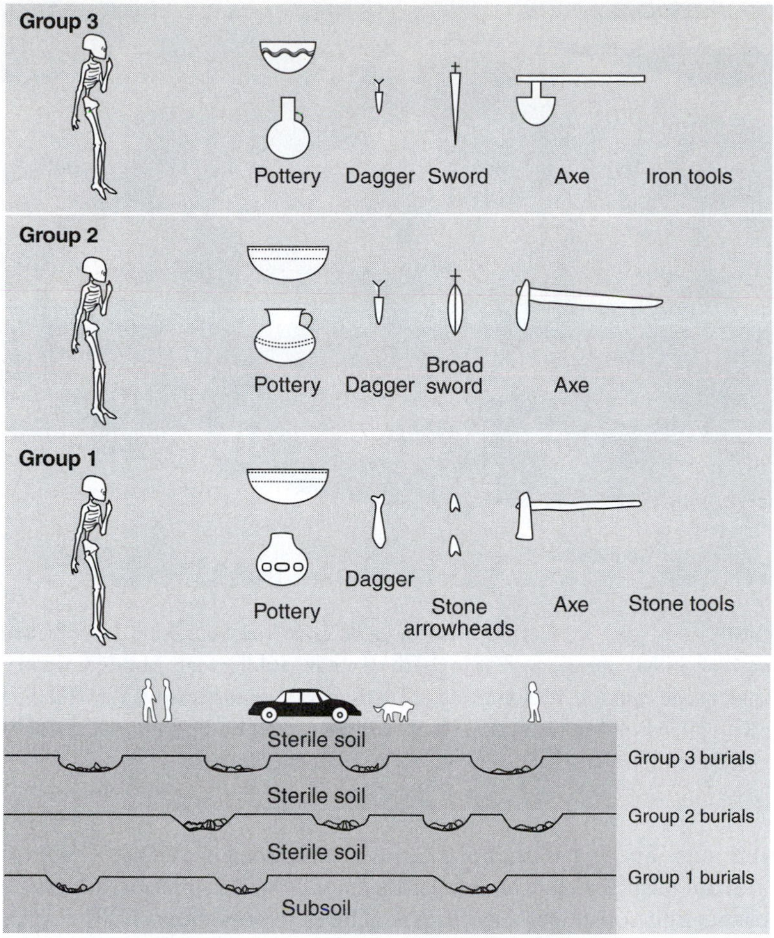

Figure 5.2 Burial groups divided into chronological groups by assessing associated artifacts. Group 1 burials contain no metal artifacts but simple decorated shallow bowls that were made by all burial groups and show cultural continuity through time. The stone arrowheads of Group 1 are replaced by metal swords; daggers continue in use, made successively of stone, bronze, and iron. Continuity of artifacts is sufficient to place groups in sequence using the law of association; this grouping was in fact confirmed by stratigraphic observation, shown at the bottom.

- *Assemblages* Dissimilar subassemblages of artifacts—let us say, hunting weapons and baskets and also digging sticks used in collecting plant foods—that occur in association. The artifacts together reflect in their patterning the shared activity of a group—an assemblage. This shared behavior is also reflected in the remains of houses—in the nonportable artifacts such as storage pits and hearths, inside and outside the house—and in community settlement patterns.
- *Industries* Similar subassemblages at a site, which were made at the same time by the same population.

The distinctions are straightforward. Some early Mexican villages consisted of groupings of square thatched houses. Each house contained subassemblages that reflected the behavior of individual males and females—subassemblages inferred from artifact

Figure 5.3 An iron arrowhead embedded in the backbone of a British warrior killed during a battle with Roman soldiers at Maiden Castle, England, in A.D. 43. This important Celtic Iron Age fortress was stormed by a Roman legion in that year, a battle reconstructed by British archaeologist Mortimer Wheeler from excavations at the fort entrance.

associations and patternings. For instance, the houses in the ancient Maya village at *Cerén,* preserved by volcanic ash, have revealed evidence of female domestic activities: food preparation, cooking, and so on (see Chapter 9). The patterned household groups in the village—that is, the associations of those subassemblages and the features associated with them—make up the larger assemblage of human behavior in space that constitutes the entire community.

Time

Time—our hectic lives depend on it. Only the other day, a harried student made an appointment with me after sifting through the crowded pages of her day-planner. I could see that every half hour of the day was crammed with lectures, meetings, and sports practice. We both commented on the tyranny of schedules, which never seem to get easier, only more hectic. The hours of the day are the framework of our daily lives, of our jobs and leisure time. Not for us the broad sweep of changing seasons or days measured by sunrise and sunset. We depend on the clock to guide us through the day, to regulate our lives. I write these words at precisely 10:18 A.M. and could, if I wished, obtain a reading for the exact second that I write the number 10. We Westerners are obsessed with the passage and measurement of time.

Our sense of linear history spans our own lives and those of our parents and grandparents. I have a dim memory of balloons on my second birthday, and continuous recollection from about age eight. My parents saw the elderly Queen Victoria driving in a carriage in a London park in 1898—more than a century ago. An Irish archaeological colleague's father talked regularly to an elderly woman in his village, who remembered French soldiers landing in Ireland in 1798. Two centuries is a long span of living memory, but the history books give us a linear past that extends back to the beginnings of writing in southwestern Asia more than 5,000 years ago. They tell us that Washington, D.C., was founded in A.D. 1790, that Rome was established in 753 B.C., and that the famous Egyptian pharaoh Rameses II reigned from 1304 to 1237 B.C.

Looking earlier than 3000 B.C., however, we enter a chronological vacuum, a blank that archaeologists have labored to fill with carefully assembled sequences of sites and artifacts. Except in a very few areas, such as the American Southwest and parts of Europe and the eastern Mediterranean, where tree rings can be used to date prehistoric sites very accurately, time must be measured in centuries and millennia, rather than individual years. We may know that Washington, D.C., was founded in A.D. 1790, but we will be lucky if we can ever date the beginnings of the city of Teotihuacán in Mexico to closer than 200 ± 100 years B.C. Some idea of the scale of the problem can be gained by piling up 100 quarters to represent the time that humankind has been on earth. The length of time covered by historical records is considerably less than the thickness of one quarter, because 99.9 percent of human experience lies in prehistoric times. Small wonder that time is important in archaeology.

The prehistoric past is like a vast, empty landscape, which archaeologists have peopled with thousands of archaeological sites large and small, each with its own characteristic artifacts and other traces of long-forgotten human behavior. Each of these sites with their contents has a precise context in time and space. Some sites, like Teotihuacán, were occupied for hundreds of years. Other localities, such as Olduvai Gorge, were inhabited for hundreds of thousands of years. Without dates, prehistory would be a jumble of confusing sites and cultures devoid of order. How, then, do archaeologists date the past?

Linear and Cyclical Time

Westerners think of the passage of the human past along a straight, if branching, highway of time. The great nineteenth-century German statesman Otto von Bismarck called this the "stream of time," on which all human societies ride for a time. The analogy is apt if you think of time in a linear fashion, as archaeologists do.

An unfolding, linear past is not the only way of conceptualizing ancient times. Many non-Western societies, ancient and modern, think of time as a cyclical phenomenon, or sometimes as a combination of the linear and the cyclical. The cyclical perspective stems from the passage of seasons and of heavenly bodies, from the close relationships between foragers and village farmers and their natural environments. It is also based on the eternal verities of human life: fertility and birth, life, growth, and death. The endlessly repeating seasons of planting and harvest, of game movements or salmon runs, and of ripening wild foods governed human existence in deeply significant ways. The ancient Maya developed an elaborate cyclical system of interlocking secular and religious calendars to measure the passage of the seasons and to regulate religious ceremonies.

But we should not assume that societies with a cyclical view of time did not have linear chronologies as well. The celebrated Maya "Long Count" was a linear chronology that formed an integral part of the close relationship between Maya rulers and the cosmos. The ancient Egyptians developed a linear chronology for administrative purposes. But, in general, societies develop linear chronologies only when they need them. For example, Western societies use linear time to regulate times of prayer, to control the working day, and for airline schedules. It is hard to generalize, but societies with centralized political systems tend to use the reigns of chiefs or kings as signposts along a linear time scale. For instance, the history of the rulers of the state of *Benin* in West Africa shows a significant shift in the interpretation of time. Before the fourteenth century A.D., Benin history is essentially mythological, with inaccurate chronology and a variable number of kings. But with the founding of the Yoruba dynasty, the deeds and reigns of every *oba* (king) are remembered in detail with chronological accuracy right down to modern times.

Archaeologists refer to three types of chronology:

- *Relative chronology,* which establishes chronological relationships between sites and cultures
- *Absolute chronology* (as it is sometimes called), which refers to dates in calendar years
- *Chronometric chronology,* which are dates in the form of date ranges established by statistical probability.

Relative Chronology

My aged gray cat Caractacus has just come into my study. Bulging with breakfast, he gives me a plaintive meow and looks for a patch of sunlight on the carpet. He spots one, just where I have laid down a pile of important papers. Thump! With a sigh, he settles down on top of the documents and dozes blissfully as I write. Time passes. I realize that I need one of the articles in the pile under my faithful beast. I debate whether to have a cup of coffee and procrastinate or to disturb Caractacus, knowing there will be angry claws. In the end, writing deadlines prevail and I gently elevate the cat and slip the papers out from under him. He protests half-heartedly and settles down again as I congratulate myself on escaping grievous injury.

The case of Caractacus and the papers is a classic example of relative chronology in action. Consider the sequence of four events. I am sitting at my computer, consult some documents, then lay them aside on the floor. This is the first event in the sequence. Some time later, the second event takes place. The cat settles on the publications and goes to sleep. More time passes. I need an article in the pile, lift the cat, and remove the papers. The final act of this stirring drama unfolds as the cat goes back to sleep. We have observed a sequence of events. However, beyond establishing that they took place "after breakfast," we have no idea exactly how much time passed between each event in the sequence. In other words, we have a relative chronology of human (and feline) behavior (see Figure 5.4 on page 93).

The Law of Superposition

Our relative chronology of the cat and the papers is based on a fundamental principle of archaeology and relative chronology: the law of superposition. **Superposition**, the notion that underlying levels are earlier than those that cover them, came to archaeology from geology. The geological layers of the earth are superimposed one upon another, almost like layers of a cake. Easily viewed examples are cliffs by the seashore or road cuts along the highway, which show a series of geological levels. Obviously, any object deposited in the lower horizons usually got there before the upper strata were accumulated. In other words, the lower levels are relatively earlier than the later strata. The deposition of a series of occupation levels or geological strata in order can be achieved by many processes: wind, water, earthquakes, and other factors. The fundamental principles of context in time and space are borrowed straight from geology, where observations of fossils and other phenomena in geological layers provide the framework of geological time.

Superposition is fundamental to the study of the **stratigraphy** of archaeological sites, for many settlements, such as desert caves in western North America or Mesopotamian mounds, were occupied more or less continuously for hundreds, even thousands, of years. Human occupation of any site results in the accumulation of all kinds of rubbish. Objects are lost and become embedded in the ground. Buildings fall

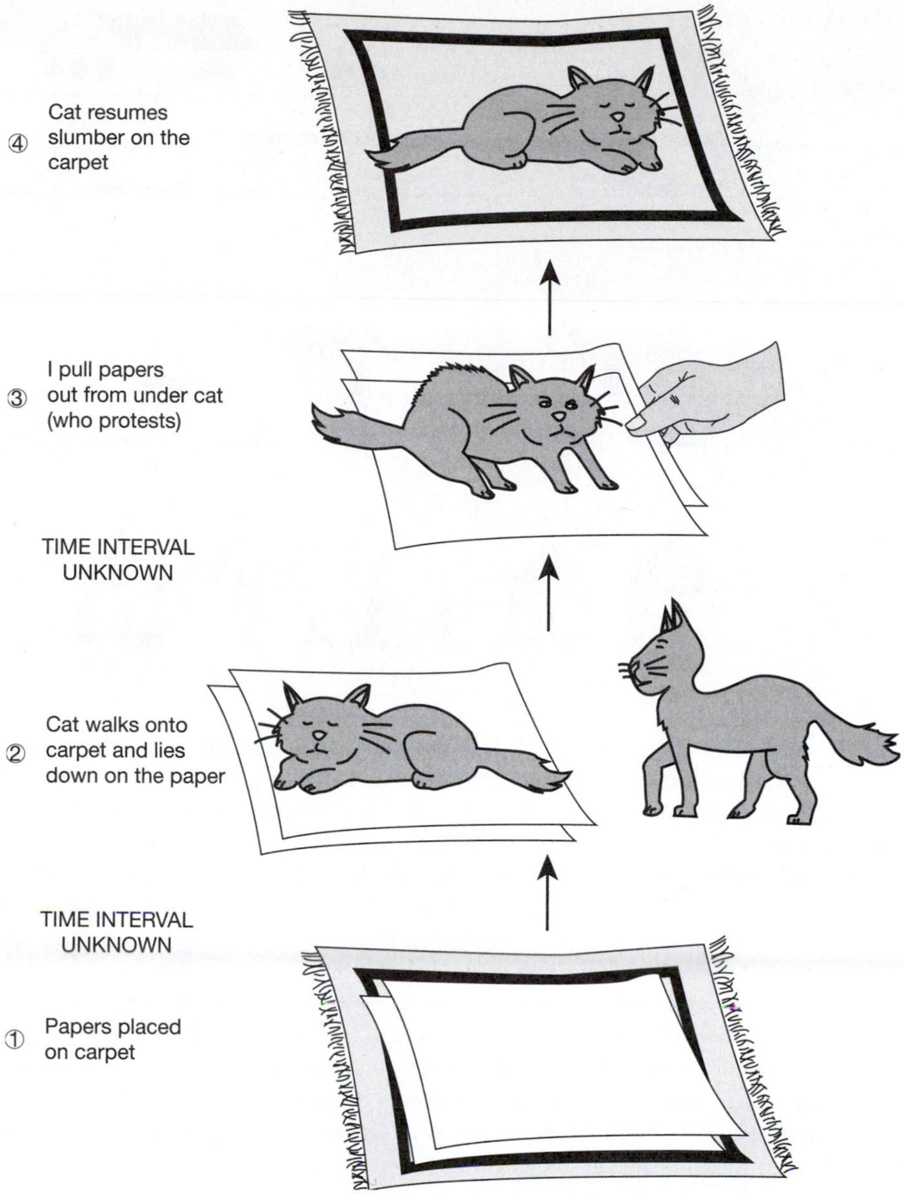

Figure 5.4 The relative chronology of the cat Caractacus. (Caractacus was an ancient British chieftain.)

into disrepair and are leveled to make way for new ones. A flood may wipe out a village and deposit a thick layer of silt. A new village may rise on the same spot years later. The sequence of these superimposed occupation levels is carefully recorded as the excavation of a site proceeds. Of course, not all settlements were occupied several times. Single occupation sites, even very temporary camps, are studied just as carefully.

The sequence of natural and humanly accumulated layers on an archaeological site is the basis for all stratigraphic observations in archaeology. But as Figure 5.5 on page 94 shows, it is not only the carefully observed layers but their detailed contents as well that provide us with relative cultural chronologies. Each level in a settlement has its associated artifacts, objects that the archaeologist uses as indicators of technological, economic, social, or even religious change.

Figure 5.5 The principle of superposition. (a) A flourishing farming village 5,000 years ago. After a time, the village is abandoned and the huts fall into disrepair. Accumulating earth and vegetation covers the ruins. (b) After an interval, a second village is built on the same site, with different architectural styles. This village in turn is abandoned; the houses collapse into piles of rubble and are covered by accumulating earth. (c) Twenty-first-century people park their cars on top of both village sites and drop litter and coins that, when uncovered, reveal to the archaeologist that the top layer is modern. An archaeologist digging this site would find that the modern layer is underlain by two prehistoric occupation levels, that square houses were in use in the upper of the two, which is the later (law of superposition), and that round huts are stratigraphically earlier than square ones here. Therefore, village 1 is earlier than village 2, but when either was occupied or how many years separate village 1 from 2 cannot be known without using absolute dating methods.

Artifacts and Relative Chronology

Manufactured artifacts are the fundamental data archaeologists use to study past human behavior. These artifacts have changed with passing time in radical ways. One has only to look at the humble stone chopper of the earliest humans and compare it with modern-day surgical instruments to get the point. Most artifact changes in prehistory are extremely small; minor changes in such characteristics as the shape, decoration, or lip angle of clay pots accumulate slowly as they lead ultimately to a vessel form that is hardly recognizable as originating from its ancestors.

The popularity of any artifact form is fleeting. Women's skirt lengths rise above the knee, then fall to mid-calf; clothing styles change from month to month. Recordings hit the Top 40 but soon pass into oblivion. Other artifacts have a far longer life. The crude stone flakes of the earliest humans were a major element in early toolkits for hundreds of thousands of years. People used candles for centuries before they turned to kerosene and gas lamps. But each has its period of maximum popularity, or frequency of occurrence, whether it lasts for millennia or for only a few months. Archaeologists use **seriation techniques** to place artifacts in chronological order, on the assumption that the popularity of any artifact, be it a specific model of automobile, pottery types, stone artifact forms, or other objects, peaks at a specific moment in time. If we plot the frequencies with which these objects occur as a set of bars, they look like the hull of a battleship glimpsed from an aircraft (see Figure 5.6). The center of the hull bulges outward amidships, where the armor is thickest, coinciding with the period of greatest popularity. This phenomenon is sometimes called the battleship curve. Thus, it is argued, when sites within a restricted geographic area contain similar pottery and other artifacts at an equivalent rate of popularity, they are of approximately the same age. If the samples are statistically reliable, a series of sites can be linked in a relative chronology, even though, without dates in years, one cannot tell when they were occupied.

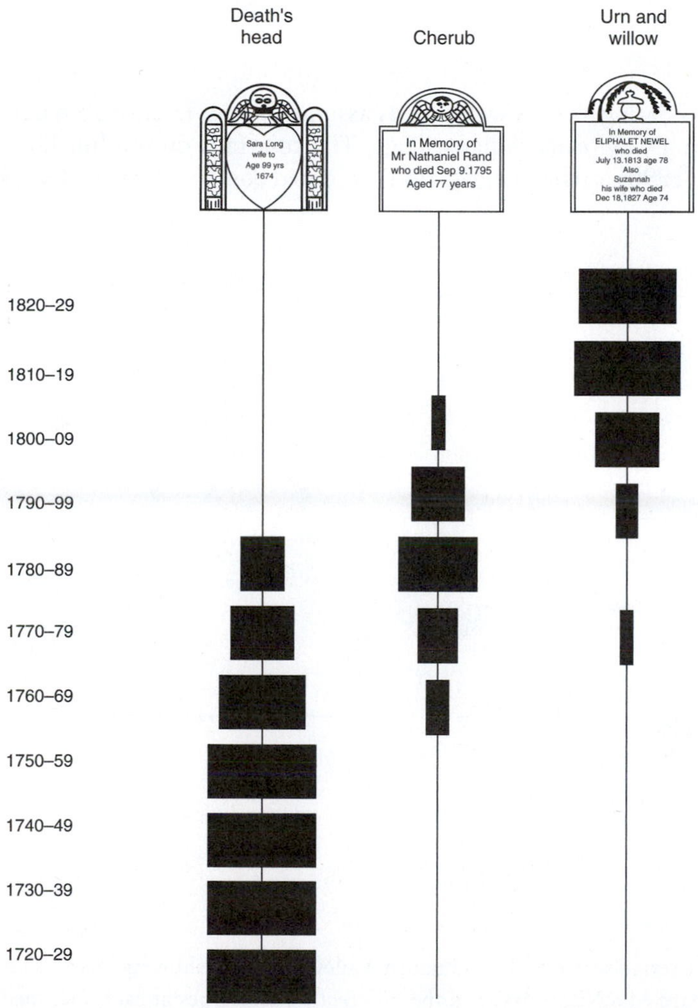

Figure 5.6 A classic example of seriation: The changing styles of New England gravestones, from Stoneham, Massachusetts, between 1720 and 1829, seriated in three styles. Notice how each style rises to a peak of maximum popularity and then declines as another comes into fashion. The cherub style shows the classic battleship curve. Each horizontal bar represents the percentage of a gravestone type at that date; for example, between 1720 and 1729 death's heads were at 100 percent. (From *Invitation to Archaeology* by James Deetz, copyright © 1967 by James Deetz. Used by permission of Doubleday, a division of Random House, Inc.)

A generation ago, archaeologists Edwin Dethlefsen and James Deetz tested this battleship-curve assumption against the changing decorative styles on dated gravestones in New England colonial cemeteries (see Figure 5.6 on page 95). They found that the changing styles of death's heads, cherubs, and urns succeeded one another in an almost perfect series of battleship curves. Because the dates of the gravestones were known from their inscriptions, the experiment could be conducted and tested within a precise chronological context.

A series of archaeological sites may contain many different artifacts that appear and vanish over relatively short periods. By applying seriation, it is possible to place the different forms of artifacts in a series of relative chronologies, such as that from the *Tehuacán Valley,* Mexico, illustrated in Figure 5.7. Each occupation level of each site contains different proportions of each artifact form manufactured during that period. And once you have a sequence of changing artifact frequencies, it is possible to fit isolated, newly discovered sites into a relative chronology.

Cross-Dating

Seriation is effective for cross-dating sites as well. Let us assume that an English coin dating to A.D. 1825 is traded in a California Indian village. The coin falls onto a hut floor and is lost in the dust. In the 1990s, archaeologists find this dated coin in a stratified level

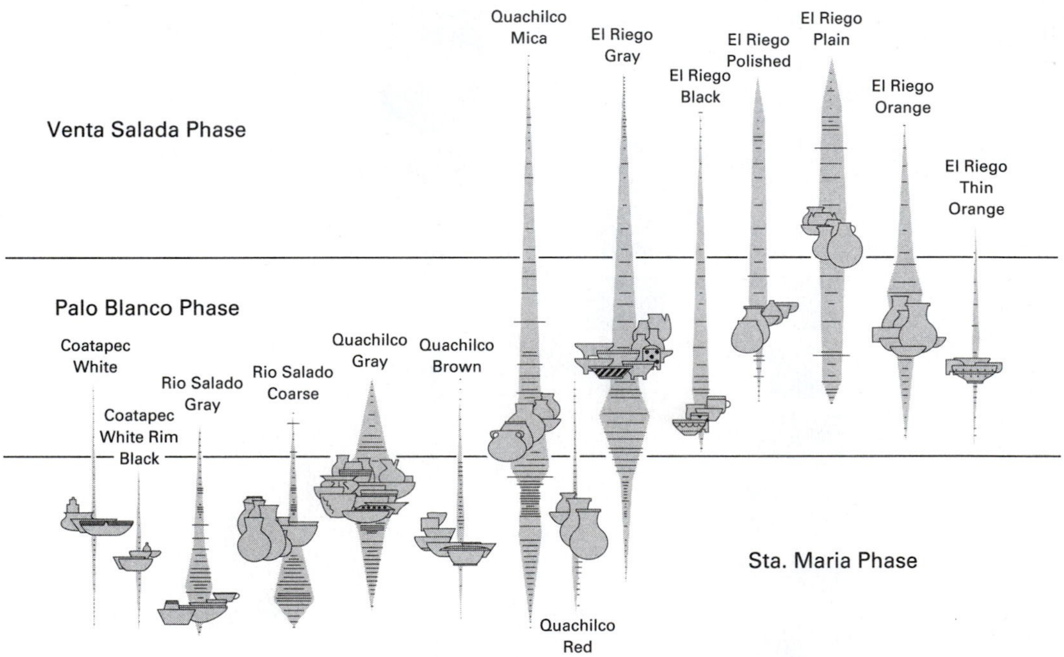

Figure 5.7 A classic pottery style seriation from the Tehuacán Valley, Mexico, showing many sites ordered into a single sequence. Richard MacNeish classified the different pottery types at each site, then placed them in chronological order on the basis of periods of maximum popularity for each type. Here the battleship curve principle is used to develop a sequence of changing pottery forms, each site being "fitted" into the sequence on the basis of the percentage of each type represented. (Adapted from R. S. MacNeish, F. A. Peterson, and K. V. Flannery, *The Prehistory of the Tehuacan Valley,* vol. 3. Austin: Published for the Robert S. Peabody Foundation, Phillips Academy, Andover, MA, by the University of Texas Press, 1970. © Robert S. Peabody Museum of Archaeology, Phillips Academy, Andover, MA. All Rights Reserved.)

of the ancient village. They know it was traded into the settlement no earlier than its date of minting, so the village was flourishing in, or after, 1825. They may find more sites with the same Indian artifacts in similar proportions—but no coins—a few miles away. When they seriate the finds, they will be able to cross-date the undated settlements because their artifact frequencies are the same. This **cross-dating** technique has been widely applied to central European prehistoric sites whose inhabitants traded with literate civilizations in the Mediterranean basin, exchanging copper and other raw materials for ornaments and other luxuries whose age is known.

Absolute Chronology

Figure 5.8 shows the chronological spans of the major absolute and chronometric methods used to date the past.

Historical Records and Objects of Known Age

Historical records cover only the very smallest fraction of the human experience. King lists and genealogies in early Egyptian and Mesopotamian archives give us dates in years that go back to at least 3100 B.C. Recorded history starts in about 750 B.C. in the central Mediterranean, about 55 B.C. in Britain. The first historical records for the Americas begin with the Spanish Conquest, although the recently deciphered Maya script gives us invaluable information about Classic Maya civilization 1,500 years ago. Parts of Africa entered "history" in A.D. 1890.

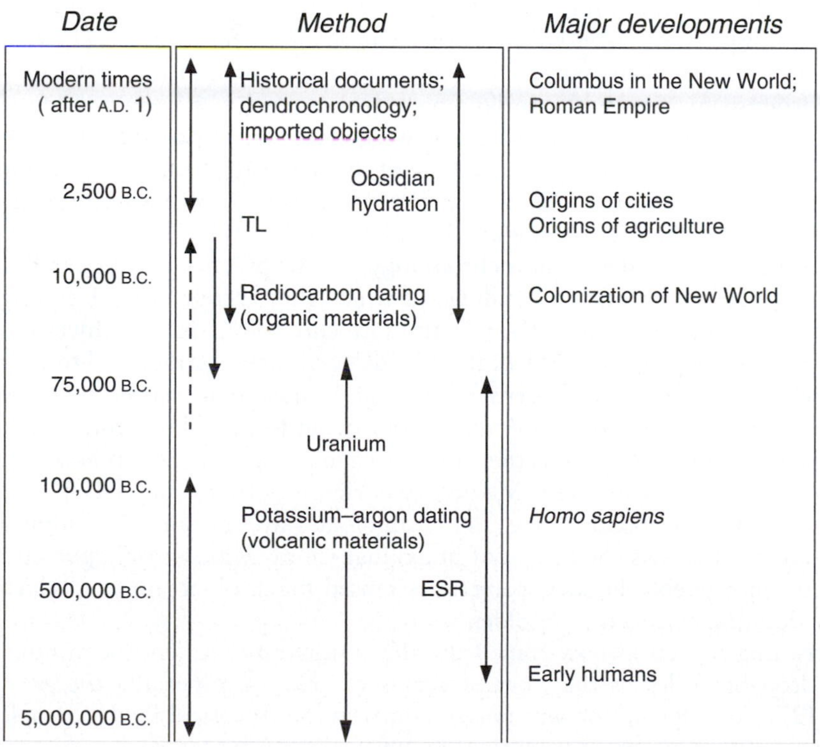

Figure 5.8 Major chronological methods in prehistory. Experimental methods eliminated for clarity.

Fortunately, the literate civilizations of three or four thousand years ago traded their products far and wide, so cross-dating is possible. The Egyptians traded fine ornaments to Crete; the Cretans sent wine and fine pottery to the Nile. When archaeologist Arthur Evans discovered Crete's *Minoan civilization* in 1900, he dated the Palace of *Knossos* by means of Minoan pottery fragments that had been excavated in faraway Egypt, in levels whose precise historical date was known. In recent years, German archaeologists have found brilliantly painted Minoan friezes on the walls of *Avaris* in Lower Egypt, confirming earlier evidence for trading connections.

Coins and other imports of known age can be used to date buildings or refuse pits in which they were dropped centuries earlier. A bewildering array of dated objects are used by archaeologists dealing with the recent periods of prehistory. These include glass bottles and beads, seals, imported Chinese porcelain, even military buttons. Each of these objects has the advantage of its age being exactly known. Objects of known age—even such artifacts as barbed wire, beer and Coca-Cola bottles, and leather shoes—provide excellent dating evidence on historic sites of the past four or five centuries.

Tree-Ring Dating (Dendrochronology)

Everyone is familiar with the concentric growth rings that can be seen in the cross section of the trunk of a felled tree. These rings, formed in most trees, are of special importance to archaeologists in areas such as the American Southwest, where the seasonal weather changes markedly and growth is concentrated during a few months of the year. Normally trees produce two growth rings each year, which are formed by the **cambium** between the wood and the bark. Each year's growth forms a distinct ring that varies in thickness according to the tree's age and annual climatic variations. Weather variations in the Southwest tend to run in cycles of wet and dry years, which are reflected in patterns of thicker and thinner rings on the trees.

The tree-ring samples are taken with a borer from living or felled trees. The ring sequences from the borer are then compared to each other and to a master chronology of rings built up from many trees with overlapping sequences tied to a known terminal date. The patterns of thick and thin rings for the new sequences are matched to the master sequence and dated on the basis of their accurate fit to the master sequence. By using the California bristlecone pine, tree-ring experts have developed a master chronology over 8,000 years back into the past (see Figure 5.9 on page 99).

Tree-ring dating, usually called **dendrochronology**, can be practiced on long-felled wood beams to date the Indian pueblo buildings of which they were a part. Tree-ring experts have been able to develop an extremely accurate chronology for Southwestern sites that extend back as long ago as 322 B.C. It was a difficult task, for they had to connect a prehistoric chronology from dozens of ancient beams to a master tree-ring chronology connected to modern times obtained from living trees of known age. The dates of such famed Southwestern sites as the Cliff Palace in *Mesa Verde,* Colorado, and *Pueblo Bonito* in Chaco Canyon, New Mexico (see Figure 5.10 on page 100), are known to within a few years because tree-ring chronologies are accurate to within a year. Such precision even allows the dating of individual rooms within single pueblos. This requires care, since pueblo builders sometimes reused much older timbers, which would give dates decades, even centuries older.

So many tree-ring sequences now come from the Southwest that dendrochronologists can study drought cycles as they spread across the region, especially the great drought of A.D. 1276 to 1299, which was one reason why the Ancestral Pueblo people of the Four Corners region dispersed from their homeland (see Chapter 10).

Dendrochronology has been used in other areas of the world as well—in Alaska and the American Southeast, and with great success in Greece, Ireland, and Germany. The bristlecone pine is to the Southwest as oaks are to Europe. European tree-ring

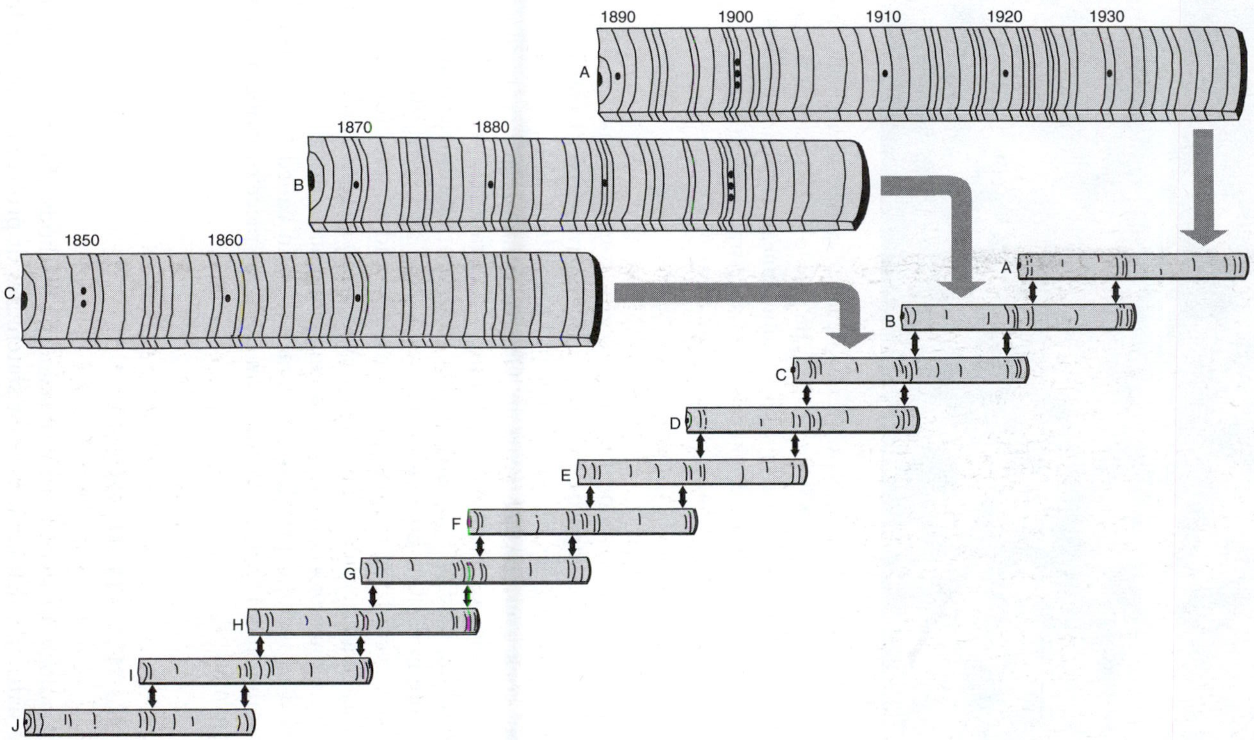

Figure 5.9 Building a tree-ring chronology: (A) a boring taken from a living tree after the 1939 growing season; (B–J) specimens taken from old houses and progressively older ruins. The ring patterns match and overlap back into prehistoric times.

Figure 5.10 Pueblo Bonito, New Mexico, a large southwestern pueblo built and occupied between about A.D. 850 and 1130. The pueblo had five stories of rooms in a semicircle. The round structures are kivas, subterranean ceremonial rooms. Pueblo Bonito was part of the Chaco Phenomenon, an ancestral pueblo (Anasazi) trade and ritual network centered on Chaco Canyon, New Mexico.

experts have collected large numbers of tree-ring records from oaks that lived 150 years or so. By visual and statistical comparison they have linked living trees to farmhouse and church beams and to ancient trees found in bogs and prehistoric sites, providing a tree-ring sequence that goes back 10,021 years in Germany and 7,289 years in Ireland. European master chronologies are now astoundingly accurate. For example, tree-ring samples dated the felling date of a massive timber from a mysterious ceremonial circle found on the seashore in eastern England to between April and June, 2050 B.C. Dutch tree-ring experts have even dated the oak panels used by old masters for backing their oil paintings as a way of authenticating paintings. And, in an elegant application of tree-ring dating, British archaeologists have used a ring sequence from the Italian Alps to date the spruce used to make a priceless Stradivarius violin called "The Messiah" to 1682. They also established that it was made from the same piece of wood as two other violins made by the master!

Chronometric Chronology

Chronometric chronology involves the use of scientific methods of dating the past that yield not absolute dates in calendar years, but statements of probability in the form of date ranges. Such dating methods are used for the earlier millennia of the past.

Radiocarbon Dating

Radiocarbon dating, developed by physicists J. R. Arnold and W. F. Libby in 1949, is the best known of all chronometric methods. Cosmic radiation produces neutrons that enter the earth's atmosphere and react with nitrogen to produce the carbon isotope carbon 14

(14C, or radiocarbon), which has eight rather than the usual six neutrons in its nucleus. With these additional neutrons, the nucleus is unstable and subject to radioactive decay. Arnold and Libby calculated that it took 5,568 years for half of the 14C in any sample to decay, the so-called **half-life** of 14C. (The half-life is now more accurately measured at 5,730 years.)

The 14C isotope is believed to behave just like ordinary carbon (12C) from a chemical standpoint. Together with 12C it enters into the carbon dioxide of the atmosphere. Because living vegetation builds up its own organic matter by photosynthesis and by using atmospheric carbon dioxide, the ratio of 14C to 12C in living vegetation and the animals that eat it is equal to that in the atmosphere (see Figure 5.11). As soon as an organism dies, no further radiocarbon is incorporated into it. The radiocarbon present in the dead organism continues to disintegrate, so that after 5,730 years half of the original amount is left; after about 11,400 years, a quarter; and so on. Thus, measuring the amount of 14C still present in plant and animal remains and emitting radiation enables us to determine the time that has elapsed since death. By calculating the difference between the amount of 14C originally present and that now present, and comparing the difference with the known rate of decay, we can compute the time elapsed in years.

The amount of 14C in a fresh sample emits particles at a rate of about 15 particles per minute per gram of carbon. A sample with an emission rate of half that amount

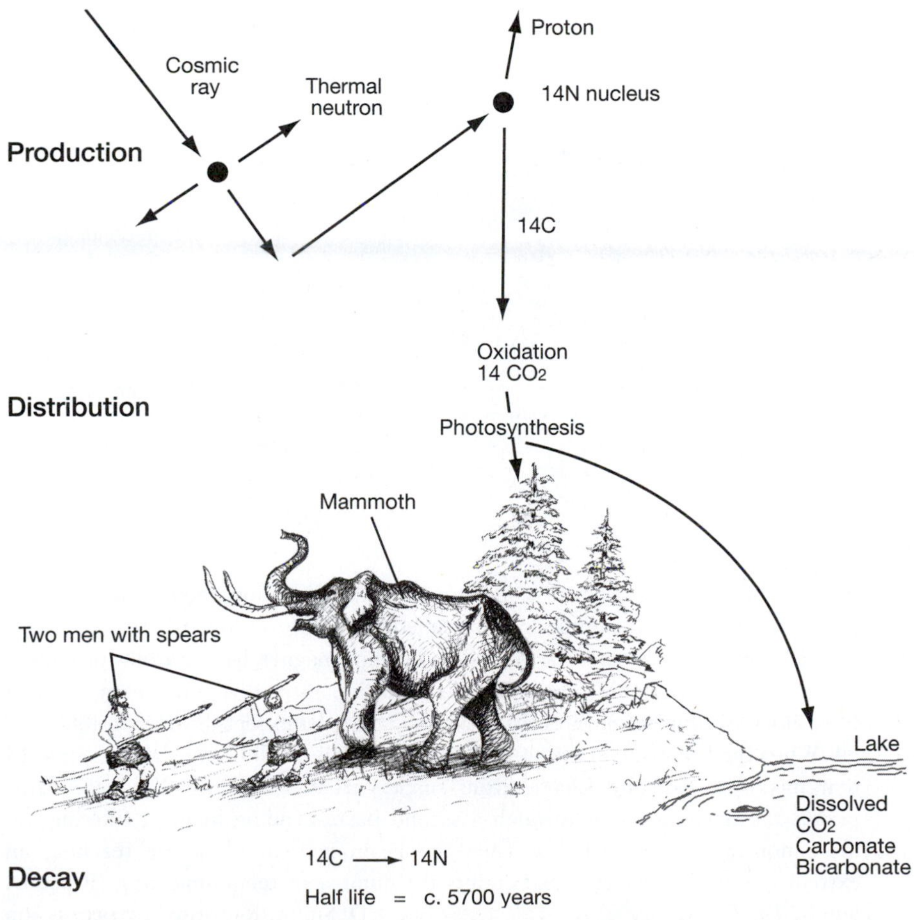

Figure 5.11 The principle of the radiocarbon dating method—production, distribution, and decay of 14C.

would be approximately 5,730 years old, the time needed for one half the original radioactive material to disintegrate (the half-life of 14C). When a 14C date comes from a laboratory, it bears a statistical plus or minus factor. For example, 3,600 ± 200 years (200 years represents one standard deviation) means that chances are 2 out of 3 that the correct date is between the span of 3,400 and 3,800. If we double the deviation, chances are 19 out of 20 that the span 3,200 to 4,000 is correct. Radiocarbon dates should be recognized for what they are—statistical approximations.

Radiocarbon samples can be taken from many organic materials: charcoal, burned bone, shell, hair, wood, or other organic substances. The samples themselves are collected with meticulous care from particular stratigraphic contexts so that an exact location, or a specific structure, is dated. For years, dating laboratories used a beta ray decay rate to date 14C samples. They now use **accelerator mass spectrometry (AMS)**, which allows radiocarbon dating to be carried out by direct counting of 14C atoms rather than by counting radioactive disintegrations (see Figure 5.12). The samples required are so small that it is possible, for example, to date an individual tree ring.

Accelerator dating is especially useful for dating the amino acids from bone collagen, but one can date almost any material, even tiny wood fragments preserved in the haft sockets of metal spearheads. This makes it possible, for example, to date an actual corncob in a Southwestern cave, a much better way of dating early agriculture than by merely using the principle of association to link a cob with a dated feature or isolated charcoal sample.

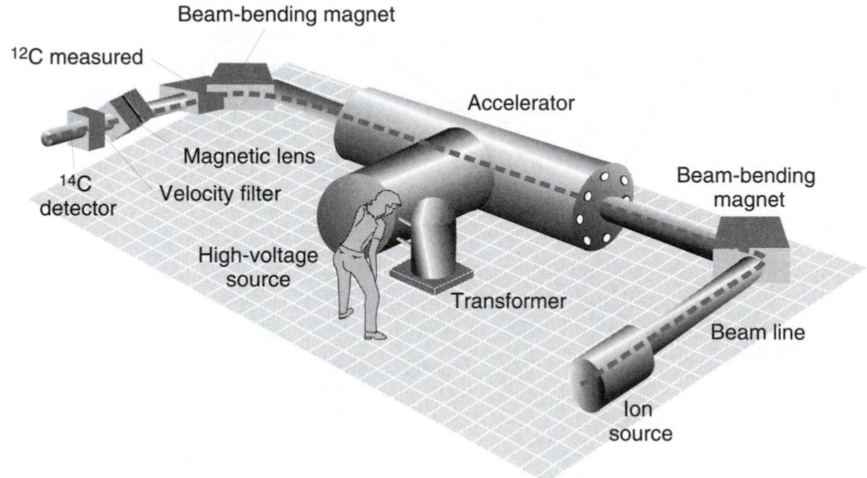

Figure 5.12 Accelerator mass spectrometry (AMS) radiocarbon dating. Ionized carbon atoms from the sample are first pulled in beam form toward the accelerator. As the beam passes through the first beam-bending magnet, lighter atoms turn more sharply than heavier ones. They move to the inside of the diverging beam, where a filter blocks the further progress of all charged particles except those of atomic mass 14. When the beam enters the accelerator, it is stripped of all molecules of mass 14 that might be indistinguishable from single carbon-14 atoms. The accelerator pushes the remaining ions through a second beam-bending magnet, filtering out more non-carbon-14 particles. Then the beam is focused before reaching an extremely sensitive detector that counts the number of remaining ions. (Bruce D. Smith, *The Emergence of Agriculture.* © Bruce D. Smith. Reprinted by permission of the author.)

AMS dating has revolutionized the dating of early agriculture in the Americas. For instance, researchers had used conventional carbon dating to date the first appearance of maize farming in Mexico's Tehuacán Valley to at least 5000 B.C. AMS dates on actual early cobs show that maize cultivation dates in the valley to no earlier than about 2700 B.C. Such agriculture dates to at least 5000 B.C. in the Veracruz lowlands near the Gulf of Mexico. Dates from individual cereal seeds have dated agriculture on the banks of the Euphrates River in Syria to about 10,000 B.C., centuries earlier than previously suspected.

The practical limits of radiocarbon dating are between 40,000 and 60,000 years. Researchers have tried detecting 14C atoms directly with a particle accelerator, a technique that would extend the limits of radiocarbon dating to as much as 100,000 years, although at present its limits, mainly because of contamination carried into soil by roots, are around 70,000 years.

When Arnold and Libby first developed radiocarbon dating they compared their 14C readings with dates from objects of known age, such as ancient Egyptian boats. These tests enabled them to claim that radiocarbon dates were accurate enough for archaeologists' purposes. But about 25 years later, just when archaeologists thought they at last had an accurate and reliable means for dating the past, some radiocarbon dates for dated tree rings of long-lived California bristlecone pines were published. They turned out to be consistently younger—for trees dating to before 1200 B.C. It turned out Libby had incorrectly assumed that the concentration of radiocarbon in the atmosphere has remained constant through time, so prehistoric samples, when they were alive, would contain the same amount of radiocarbon as living things today. But, in fact, changes in the strength of the earth's magnetic field and alterations in solar activity have considerably varied the concentration of radiocarbon in the atmosphere and in living things.

Fortunately, however, it is possible to correct 14C dates back to about 9000 B.C. by calibrating them with tree-ring chronologies, especially the long sequences for European oaks. Some idea of the changes in accuracy of 14C dating over the past 10,000 years generated from tree-ring calibrations can be gathered from Table 5.1 on page 104. Calibration of dates earlier than 9000 B.C. is still at an experimental stage. Recently scientists have used a new, highly accurate technique based on the decay of uranium into thorium to date fossil coral near Barbados in the Caribbean and in the South Pacific. They compared these dates to radiocarbon results and found that dates between 10,000 and 25,000 years ago have increasing margins of error, as much as 5,000 years in earlier millennia. Radiocarbon dates earlier than about 10,000 years ago must be treated as little more than approximations.

Despite its chronological and technical limitations, radiocarbon dating is of enormous significance. Some 14C samples have dated African hunter-gatherers to before 50,000 years ago and Paleo-Indian bison kills on the Great Plains to earlier than 11,000 B.C. They have provided chronologies for the origins of agriculture and civilization in the New World and the Old. Radiocarbon dates are a means for developing a truly global chronology that can equate major events such as the origins of literate civilizations in such widely separated areas as China and Peru. The prehistory of the world from some 40,000 years ago up to historic times is dated almost entirely by the radiocarbon method.

Obsidian Hydration

Every archaeologist dreams of a dating method that gives accurate ages for durable artifacts like stone tools and potsherds. **Obsidian hydration** has potential for this purpose. **Obsidian** is a natural glass formed by volcanic activity, often used by the ancients for sharp-edged tools, mirrors, and ornaments. A freshly exposed obsidian surface absorbs water from its surroundings, forming a measurable hydration layer that is invisible to the human eye. The thickness of the hydration layer can be used to develop absolute and

Tree-ring calibrations

Radiocarbon Age	Calibrated age in years A.D./B.C.
A.D. 1760	A.D. 1945
1505	1435
1000	1105
500	635
1	15
505 B.C.	767 B.C.
1007	1267
1507	1867
2007	2477
3005	3795
4005	4935
5005	5876
6050	7056
7001	8247
8007	9368
9062	9968

Calibrations based on Uranium/Thorium and AMS carbon 14 (Barbados)

AMS radiocarbon dates	Uranium Thorium calibration
7760 B.C.	9140 B.C.
8270	10,310
9320	11,150
10,250	12,285
13,220	16,300
14,410	17,050
15,280	18,660
23,920	28,280

Increasing differences after 25,000 B.C. (calibrated)

Calibrations based on tables in *Radiocarbon* 40 (3), 1998. It should be stressed that these calibrations are provisional, statistically based, and subject to modification, especially before 7,000 B.C.

Table 5.1 Changes in accuracy of 14C dating over the past 10,000 years generated from tree-ring calibrations.

relative chronologies for stone tools, but little is yet known about the effects of temperature changes and chemical compositions of soil on hydration. Obsidian hydration has been used successfully in widespread archaeological surveys around the Maya city at Copán, Honduras, to date isolated settlements.

Luminescence Dating

Luminescence dating, comprising **optical stimulated luminescence** (OSL) and **thermoluminescence** (TL), measures light emitted from baked clays, heated or burnt stone, and windblown sediments like sand. The former is used predominantly on sediments, while thermoluminescence helps date clays and burnt stone. Luminescence dating methods are based on the fact that every material on earth receives a low level of radiation from the radioactive elements in the environment. Exposure to radiation causes the electrons to separate from atoms. Many solid materials store these electrons, which accumulate steadily over time. When the solid is heated, the stored energy is released and emits light. The age of the sample comprises the length of time since the object was heated to a temperature higher than 3,500 degrees C.

OSL and TL have obvious applications for dating volcanic rocks and other geological formations, but they can also be applied to humanly heated objects such as clay vessels, heat-treated stone artifacts, or fired bricks.

Samples are taken by crumbling an object such as a potsherd, or by drilling tiny holes. The laboratory measures the natural TL of the object with an alpha radiation counter, the rate at which the sample has been obtaining radiation from the environment (by monitoring the location where it was found), and the amount of TL produced by known amounts of radiation. All of this assumes that the humanly manufactured object being tested has been heated to a sufficiently high temperature, which is not always the case. Unfortunately, many variables can affect the annual dose of radiation received by the sample, and moisture can alter the effects of radiation, so many people regard luminescence methods with suspicion.

Thermoluminescence is claimed to have an accuracy of about ± 7 percent and is most commonly used to date pottery or clay-fired objects between 50 and about 20,000 years old. TL dates have also been applied to burnt flint and other siliceous toolmaking materials found in Stone Age rockshelters and burials, such as Neanderthal graves in Israel dating to more than 40,000 years ago. A related dating method uses laser technology to date the emissions from quartz and feldspar grains in archaeological layers. OSL can date sites in the 100- to 100,000-year range by dating the sediments in which artifacts are found, and is claimed to date the first settlement of Australia to as early as 60,000 years ago—a controversial conclusion at best.

Although TL has been used to date such developments as the appearance of anatomically modern humans in southwestern Asia, most authorities agree that independent verification from radiocarbon or other approaches is advisable.

Electronic Spin Resonance

Electronic spin resonance (ESR) measures radiation-induced defects or the density of trapped electrons within a bone or shell sample without the need to heat them. This promising dating method is somewhat similar to TL and has the advantage of being nondestructive, being especially effective on tooth enamel, as well as bone, allowing investigators to date human fossil fragments up to about a million years old. ESR has important applications for the study of early human evolution and has been used to date Neanderthal teeth in southwestern Asia to about 100,000 years ago.

Uranium Series Dating

Uranium series dating measures the steady decay of uranium into various daughter elements inside any formation made up of calcium carbonates, such as limestone or cave stalactites. Because many early human groups made use of limestone caves and rockshelters, bones and artifacts embedded in calcium carbonate layers can sometimes be dated by this method, using techniques somewhat similar to those used in radiocarbon dating. Uranium series dating is most effective when applied to sites between 50,000 and 1 million years old.

Potassium-Argon Dating

Potassium-argon dating has provided general chronologies for earlier prehistory. Geologists use this method to date volcanic rocks as early as 4 to 5 billion years old and as recent as 100,000 years before the present. Potassium (K) is one of the most abundant elements in the earth's crust, present in nearly every mineral. In its natural form, potassium contains a small proportion of radioactive 40K atoms. For every 100 40K atoms that decay, 11 percent become 40Ar (Argon), an inactive gas that can easily escape from its present material by diffusion when lava and other molten rocks are formed. As volcanic rocks form by crystallization, the concentration of 40Ar drops to almost nothing, but the decay of 40K continues, and 11 percent of every 100 40K atoms become 40Ar. It is possible, therefore, using a spectrometer, to measure the concentration of 40Ar that has accumulated since the rock formed.

Many early archaeological sites, such as those at Olduvai Gorge, Tanzania, were formed during periods of intense volcanic activity. Dates have been determined for contemporary volcanic ashes, sometimes stratified above and below places where human tools and broken animal bones lie. Louis and Mary Leakey were able to determine potassium-argon dates for artifact and bone scatters at Olduvai, where early human fossils were found. The samples gave readings of about 1.75 million years. Even earlier dates have come from sites at *Hadar* in Ethiopia and Laetoli in Tanzania, both in East Africa, where volcanic materials associated with early human fragments have been dated by potassium-argon techniques to between 3 and 4.5 million years ago. Stone flakes and chopping tools have come from *Koobi Fora* in northern Kenya, dated to about 2.6 million years.

Potassium-argon dating is getting ever more accurate, and 1- to 4-million-year-old East African dates now have standard deviations in the 20,000- to 50,000-year range. Recent improvements in dating techniques have both reduced statistical errors and extended the range of potassium-argon dates into the past 100,000 years.

Fission Track Dating

Many minerals and natural glasses, such as obsidian, contain tiny quantities of uranium that undergo slow, spontaneous decay. The date of any mineral containing uranium can be obtained by measuring the amount of uranium in the sample, which is done by counting the fission tracks in the material—narrow trails of damage in the sample caused by fragmentation of massive energy-charged particles. The older the sample, the more tracks it possesses. Volcanic rocks are ideal for **fission track dating**, such as are commonplace at Olduvai Gorge and other early human sites. The volcanic level under the earliest hominin sites at Olduvai has been dated to 2.03 ± 02.8 million years ago, which agrees well with potassium-argon dates from the same location. This method is often used as a check on potassium-argon dates.

This array of absolute dating methods has developed a provisional chronology for the human past.

Discovery

Eruption at Akrotiri, Greece, 1967

Only rarely do archaeologists find sites associated with direct evidence of ancient climatic or natural phenomena that can be dated reasonably accurately. A half century ago, Greek archaeologist Spyridon Marinatos speculated that the flamboyant Minoan civilization of Crete was severely damaged by a huge volcanic eruption that blew the center of the island of Santorini (Thera), 62 miles (100 km) north into space, in about 1688 B.C. Few archaeologists agreed with his theory. Undeterred, Marinatos searched diligently for Minoan sites on Santorini, but he found that everything was buried under massive volcanic ash deposits. In 1967, he heard reports from farmers of masses of stones close underground in the fields around Akrotiri in the south of the island. So dense were the boulders that the farmers could not plow their land. Marinatos began digging into places where the ground had collapsed between the subterranean masonry and promptly discovered the Greek Pompeii, an island town of 3,500 years ago completely buried by pumice and ash when the volcano erupted (see Figure 5.13).

Akrotiri's houses are remarkably well preserved, their stone and timber walls often two stories high. Brilliant polychrome frescoes still adorn some of the rooms, depicting religious and military scenes, the island landscape, animals, and plants (see the chapter-opener photo on page 85). Food storage jars still stand in the basements of the houses. But there was no trace of the inhabitants, who had fled when ominous subterranean rumblings began. The imported Minoan pottery at Akrotiri is at least twenty to thirty years earlier than that from the latest levels of Cretan villages, proving that Marinatos was wrong. The Santorini eruption did not destroy Minoan civilization, whose palaces flourished less than 100 miles (160 km) away. A major earthquake about 200 years later contributed to the demise of the Minoan state.

Figure 5.13 Two-story houses perfectly preserved under volcanic ash at Akrotiri, Santorini Island, Aegean Sea, Greece.

SUMMARY

1. Space in archaeology is the exact location of an archaeological find in latitude, longitude, and depth, which together identify any point in space absolutely and uniquely.
2. The context of space has close links to ancient human behavior. Human behavior leaves patterns of artifacts in the archaeological record, which we study by spatial analysis. Archaeologists use this context by examining associations between artifacts and other evidence of human behavior.
3. Western archaeologists think of the human past as having a linear chronology, in contrast with many other societies that believe human existence is governed by cyclical time scales.
4. Archaeologists use two ways to date the past—relative and absolute chronology.
5. Relative chronology, the study of the chronological relationships among different sites, artifacts, occupation layers, and other features, is based on the principle of superposition. This principle, which originated in geology, states that the lower stratum is the earlier.
6. Seriation techniques allow archaeologists to place artifacts in relative chronologies; large-scale climatic changes during the Ice Age provide a chronological framework for earlier prehistory.
7. Absolute (or chronometric) chronology is the dating of the past in calendar years. Archaeologists use historical records and documents to date the past 5,000 years.
8. For earlier times, they employ three major techniques: (a) dendrochronology, tree-ring dating, uses the annual growth rates in oaks and other trees to date human societies in Europe, the American Southwest, and other areas back at least 8,000 years; (b) radiocarbon dating, the measurement of the decay of radiocarbon isotopes, allows the dating of sites as early as 40,000 years ago, with dates calibrated by tree rings or coral reefs extending back to about 15,000 years ago; and (c) potassium-argon dating, another isotopic dating method mainly used by geologists, uses volcanic rocks to date early Stone Age sites and the origins of humankind some 3 to 4 million years ago.

SIX

They Sought It Here, They Sought It There

Finding Archaeological Sites

Square Tower House cliff dwelling, Mesa Verde, Colorado.

CHAPTER OUTLINE

PREVIEW

How do you find archaeological sites? Chapter 6 describes the all-important process of archaeological research, then focuses on the accidental or deliberate finding of archaeological sites of all kinds. This is what is known as nonintrusive archaeology, archaeological survey both on the ground and using a wide variety of remote sensing methods. These include both photographs taken from aircraft and satellite imagery. We describe the recording of sites, including Geographic Information Systems, which allow researchers to look at site distributions in their changing environmental contexts. The chapter ends with a brief discussion of subsurface detection methods.

> *Archaeology is more than digging holes, counting potsherds, classifying arrowheads, and obtaining radiocarbon dates. We have to recognize the complexity of the human past in light of the fact that most of it is unknowable.*
>
> —Stephen Black and Kevin Jolly, *Archaeology by Design,* 2003

I'll never forget the first time I went out in the field looking for Stone Age sites. We were walking through a dry river valley, where river gravels showed through the stunted dry-season grass. My experienced companion walked with his eyes glued to the ground, picking up Stone Age scrapers without apparent effort. I moved at half his speed, puzzling over every piece, for I had not done this before. After half an hour we had hundreds of 100,000-year-old artifacts, collected from acres of gravel that had been sorted again and again by floodwaters. Artifacts from dozens of campsites had been mingled together in a hodgepodge of brown-colored artifacts and waste flakes. Suddenly, my companion bent down and picked up a broken flake. "That's the other half of a flake I collected in 1938," he declared. "Impossible," I replied. But he was right. When we got back to the museum, we opened the 1938 collection and the two pieces fitted together perfectly. It was a sobering lesson in the power and precision of an experienced archaeological eye. Since then, I have found many sites and artifacts on my own, but I am still in awe at my late colleague's incredible memory.

How do you know where to dig? How do you find sites? Many people are amazed at how archaeologists seem to have an uncanny ability to choose the right place for their excavations. Part of this ability is having a good eye for landscape, a penchant for putting yourself in the shoes of the people you are seeking, and, yes, just plain old-fashioned common sense. However, formal survey methods play an important role in archaeological fieldwork, especially today when many projects are carried out under fast-moving cultural resource management projects. This chapter explores the ways in which archaeologists discover and assess archaeological sites, a fundamental part of field research (see the Discovery box on page 111).

The Process of Archaeological Research

There was a time when archaeologists concentrated most of their efforts on excavating single sites. They would choose a promising location, excavate it, and study the recovered artifacts without worrying too much about the environmental setting or the broader context of their excavation. Today, archaeologists, whatever their theoretical

Discovery

The Sepulcher of the Maya Lord Pacal, Palenque, Mexico, 1949

Palenque is a Maya city, famous both for its architecture and for a long dynasty of talented lords, starting with Chan-Bahlum (Snake-Jaguar), who ascended to the throne on March 11, A.D. 431. The dynasty flourished for just under four hundred years, achieving the height of its power under the rule of Pacal (Shield) and his son in the seventh century. Pacal ruled for sixty-three years and turned Palenque into a major political force in the Maya lowlands. When he died, he was buried in an underground sepulcher beneath a pyramid and the celebrated Temple of the Inscriptions, built over fifteen years.

In 1949, Mexican archaeologist Alberto Ruz, convinced that a royal tomb lay beneath the pyramid, lifted a flagstone in the floor of the temple and cleared a rubble-filled stairway leading into the heart of the artificial mountain (Ruz, 1953). Five months of backbreaking work over two seasons cleared a stairway with forty-five steps, then a sharp U-turn, which led to another short twenty-one-step stairway and a corridor at the same level as the foot of the pyramid. After removing a stone and lime obstruction, Ruz came to a triangular doorway slab, guarded by six young sacrificial victims. He moved the stone enough to slip into an enormous rock-cut crypt with a procession of priests in stucco around the walls. A huge stone slab bearing intricate hieroglyphs filled the floor of the chamber (see Figure 6.1).

To lift the 5-ton stone, Ruz's workers felled a hardwood tree, lowered four sections of the trunk down the stairway, and then levered up the sarcophagus lid with car jacks and the timbers. Inside the sepulcher lay a tall man wearing jade and mother-of-pearl ornaments. He wore a jade mosaic mask with eyes of shell, each iris of obsidian. At the time of the excavation, no one could read Maya glyphs, so the identity of the ruler remained unknown. We now know it was Pacal. His carved sarcophagus lid commemorates his divine ancestry.

Figure 6.1 Drawing of the sarcophagus lid of the Maya lord Pacal the Great's tomb, Palenque, A.D. 683. The dead lord falls through fleshless jaws into the Underworld. Above him is the World Tree, with the bird-monster Wuqub 'Kaqix sitting on top of it. A band of celestial bodies and ancestral figures surrounds the scene. (Used with permission of Merle Greene Robertson, copyright 1973.)

perspective, think in the field in terms of interactions between humans and their natural environment, of sites in a landscape. In part because of the influence of cultural resource management, the focus has shifted away from excavation toward regional studies, studies with specific, problem-oriented perspectives, and also toward formal research design. In many cases, excavation is the strategy of last resort, for, as every archaeologist knows, to dig a site is to destroy a finite record of the past. But, whatever the type of field or laboratory work, archaeological research proceeds in the following general stages (see Figure 6.2 on page 112).

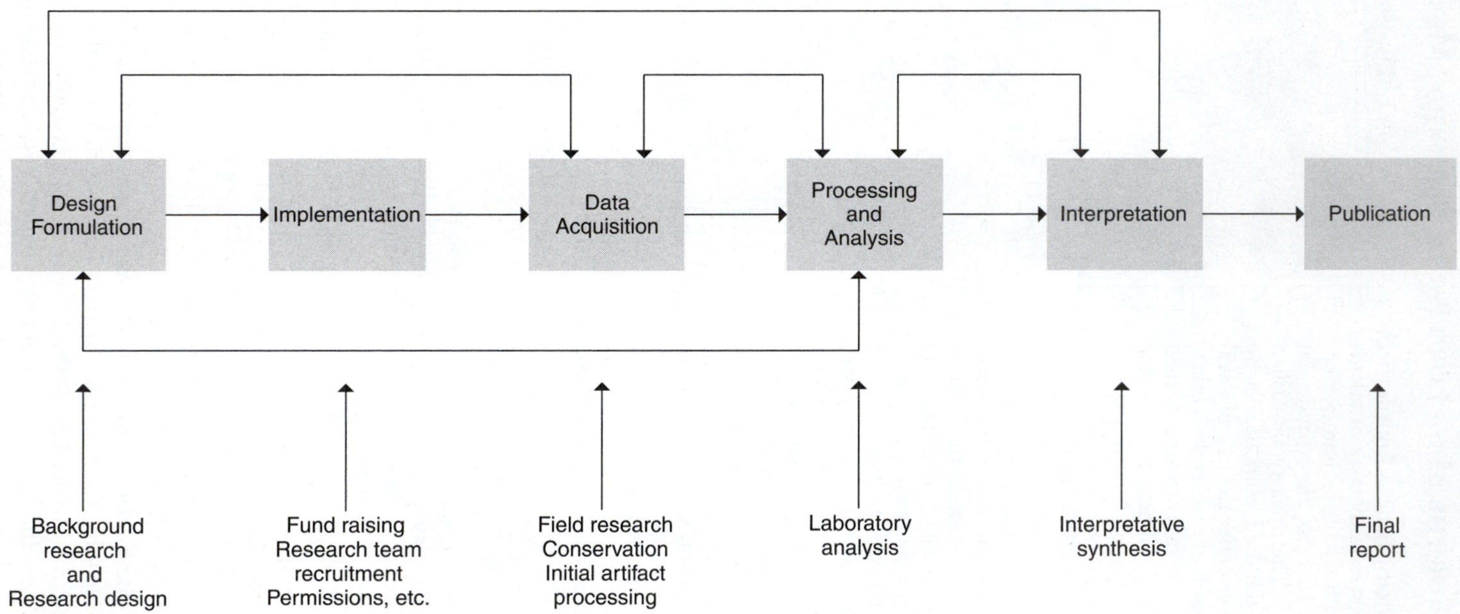

Figure 6.2 The process of archaeological research.

Design and Formulation

The problem is defined, its feasibility tested, and the entire background for the project is researched very carefully. This is the **research design,** which can take many forms. But all research designs have certain common elements:

- A context. The design should reflect a larger set of goals and fit into a larger body of archaeological knowledge. How does it contribute to the understanding of the archaeological record?
- Explicit and meaningful research questions to be answered, which match the scope of the project. These questions or hypotheses create the environment for linking your work to larger goals.
- Definitions of the data to be collected, and the methods to be used to collect it. This is a methodological overview, but one that's flexible enough to allow for changes on-site as the research unfolds.
- Information on how you will analyze your finds and report them. This plan has to be in place before any fieldwork starts, as such work is just as much part of research as survey or excavation.
- Accommodation to the "real world" that surrounds the research, be it a popular audience, a business client, or government policies. How are you going to present your work to the wider world? This aspect of the work is especially important in the CRM world. As Stephen Black and Kevin Jolly remark: "The CRM arena is everyday life itself, a world changing so fast that most of us feel like we can't keep up" (Black and Jolly, 2003: 4). How right they are!

All archaeological research begins with specific questions, questions that the researcher seeks to answer through a sequence of steps in archaeological research. Much depends on the nature of the research to be conducted. Some projects seek to answer large questions—for example: How and from where did Paleo-Indians on the northern Great Plains obtain toolmaking stone? Others are highly specific: What were the deep-sea fishing practices of the people living at a site on the south coast of Santa Cruz Island off the southern California coast in 1000 B.C.? In many cases, the formulated questions proceed from the broad to the narrow, allowing researchers to follow a logical sequence from one topic to the next. For example, an investigator on the deep-sea fishing site might hypothesize that dolphin fishing from planked canoes was the main deep-sea fishing activity. The accompanying statements could predict that dolphin bones will constitute over 75 percent of the fish remains in the site; bone fish hooks would be the dominant artifact (say, 65 percent). Many researchers content themselves with informal statements of expectations on which to base their investigations. For example: Paleo-Indian groups in such and such an area were 93 miles (149 km) from the nearest chert outcrop. This is where they are most likely to have obtained their toolmaking stone.

A research design is both academic and logistical. A flexible design divides the research process into specific stages, each of which, in turn, is carefully designed to carry out certain functions. Together they form a sequence of investigation that divides the flow chart into stages—not that the stages necessarily follow one upon the other in close order. Several may be carried out simultaneously. The design may or may not be a formal process, but it must be flexible and fluid enough to accommodate ever-changing circumstances in the field as well as individual needs. Many CRM research designs for small-scale projects like the investigation of a single building lot or a limited area of land are more or less standardized, but they are flexible enough to accommodate different circumstances. Either formally or informally, the research design spells out how the questions posed for the project will be investigated—by survey, by excavation of specific types at certain specified locations; what methods and specialized techniques will be used—in either very general terms or in specific detail. The logistics are directly related to the archaeological problem. What funds and equipment will be needed for the work? How many people will be involved? What specialized tests and permits will be needed? How will finds be curated when the work is over?

The finished research design for a purely academic project includes not only a definition of the research problem, but also a statement of specific goals, including sampling strategies to be used and specific hypotheses to be tested. It is also an accurate definition of the kinds of data the research team will be looking for to test its hypotheses. However, flexibility is essential if the research is not to be shackled too tightly. CRM projects are normally designed and carried out within tightly drawn boundaries, to ensure that they comply with legal requirements that the client, perhaps a developer or state roads department, has to fulfill—**compliance**. Some such projects have elaborate research designs. The one for the large-scale Federal Aid Interstate-270 Archaeological Mitigation project in southern Illinois in the 1980s revolved around no fewer than twelve basic questions and involved the processing of enormous amounts of data, much of it uncovered by using earthmoving machinery.

In a sense, a research design is like a flow chart, for it is created both to monitor the validity of research results and to maximize efficient use of money, people, and time.

Implementation

Fund-raising, an eternal problem for academic archaeologists; gaining permission for access to land and to excavate; acquiring equipment and a workforce—all of these are important ingredients of the implementation stage. CRM projects normally start with a competitive bidding process, have tightly drawn budgets, and are carried out on often precise timetables. Much of the planning work is effectively standardized, as is the costing, and the company or organization involved usually has a pool of equipment and archaeologists to do the work available at short notice.

Data Acquisition

Data acquisition is accomplished when field research takes place and can be a regional survey or a smaller-scale project, or an excavation.

Processing and Analysis

Archaeological finds come in many forms—as artifacts, food remains, houses, human skeletons, and so on. These finds are usually cleaned, identified, and cataloged in the field before being packed for transport to the laboratory. Once back from the field, these data—including not only finds, but the detailed notes, drawings, and other recorded data acquired in the field—are subjected to **analysis**. At this stage some specific materials, such as radiocarbon samples and pollen grains, are sent to specialists for analysis. Most laboratory analysis involves detailed artifact classification and study of animal bones and other food remains—the basis for the later interpretation of data (see Chapters 10 and 11). This is a particularly important stage of the work on CRM projects, where an inventory of sites, finds, and other information is a basic part of compliance.

Interpretation

At the stage of **interpretation**, everything is brought together into an interpretative synthesis to answer the research questions posed in the original design. Anthropological and historical models usually provide the most consistent interpretations of the archaeological record (see Chapter 4). Few CRM projects involve broad interpretative syntheses, as their terms of reference are confined to a highly specific area, which may literally be no larger than the right-of-way for an oil pipeline or a highway corridor.

Publication

In an ideal world, no research project is complete until the final results are published in a form accessible to other scholars. An unpublished site is effectively destroyed, not only by the excavations, but by the absence of any permanent record of the findings. Unfortunately, there is a huge backlog of unpublished excavations and surveys all over the world, something biblical archaeologist Hershel Shanks has called "archaeology's dirty little secret." Most academic archaeologists enjoy digging more than analysis and are under constant pressure to raise more money for fieldwork and new discovery. There is little money for publication. CRM contracts end with the completion of the final report on the project, usually a formal requirement of the contract. Relatively few of these are formally published, although many CRM archaeologists strive to bring their work to a wider scholarly audience.

Stages of Archaeological Fieldwork

Archaeological fieldwork has three stages, the first two of which are discussed in this chapter:

- *Finding Archaeological Sites.* The process of actually locating sites, which is either by accident or the result of deliberate **archaeological survey**.
- *Assessing the Sites.* Nonintrusive archaeology, which involves recording the location of sites, surface finds, and sometimes electronic subsurface detection.
- *Archaeological Excavation.* The investigation of the site by means of excavation (see Chapter 7).

Increasingly, excavation is a strategy of last resort. Many important projects focus on survey and site assessment using surface data, to preserve the archaeological record.

Accidental Discovery

Finding archaeological sites involves far more than merely locating a prehistoric settlement to dig. Some archaeological sites are so conspicuous that people have always known of their existence. The pyramids of Giza in Egypt have withstood the onslaught of tourists, treasure hunters, and quarriers for thousands of years (see Figure 2.2 on page 26). The Pyramid of the Sun at Teotihuacán, Mexico, is another easily visible archaeological site (see Figure 12.7 on page 244).

The eastern United States is dotted with hundreds of burial mounds and earthworks, which are easily distinguished from the surrounding countryside. One well-known early archaeologist simply hired a riverboat each summer and sailed along digging sites he saw on the riverbanks. Cemeteries may be marked by piles of stones, and the deep accumulations of occupation deposits at the mouths of rockshelters or caves or the huge piles of abandoned shells left by mollusk collectors are more readily located. Sites of this type are obviously simple to identify, and often have been known for centuries. For instance, in some parts of California, ancient shell **middens** (shell heaps) are recognizable at a considerable distance by their gray soil and the stunted grass growth on them.

Most archaeological sites are far less conspicuous. They may consist of little more than a scatter of pottery fragments or a few stone tools lying on the surface of the ground. Other settlements may be buried under several feet of soil, leaving few surface traces except when exposed by moving water, wind erosion, or burrowing animals. Finding archaeological sites depends on locating such telltale traces of human settlement. Once the sites have been found, they have to be recorded, and surface collections must be made at each locality to assemble a general impression of the activities of the people who lived there.

Accidental discoveries of sites, spectacular artifacts, or skeletons have revealed whole chapters of the past. Cowboy George McJunkin was searching for a lost cow near Folsom, New Mexico, in 1908, when he noticed some sun-bleached bones projecting from the soil of a dry gully. He pried loose a few bones and a stone spear point and took them home with him. They lay around the ranch house for 17 years before they came to the attention of Jesse Figgins, director of the Colorado Museum of Natural History. Figgins identified the extinct bison bones at once and wondered whether the owner of the stone spearhead had killed the animal. Excavations at Folsom revealed more stone points directly associated with bison bones, the first such find in North America. From this chance discovery came direct proof that humans had hunted extinct animals in North America soon after the Ice Age, as early as 10,000 years ago (see Figure 6.3).

The Cerén Maya village in El Salvador came to light when a bulldozer operator exposed a long-buried house mantled under feet of volcanic ash and completely invisible

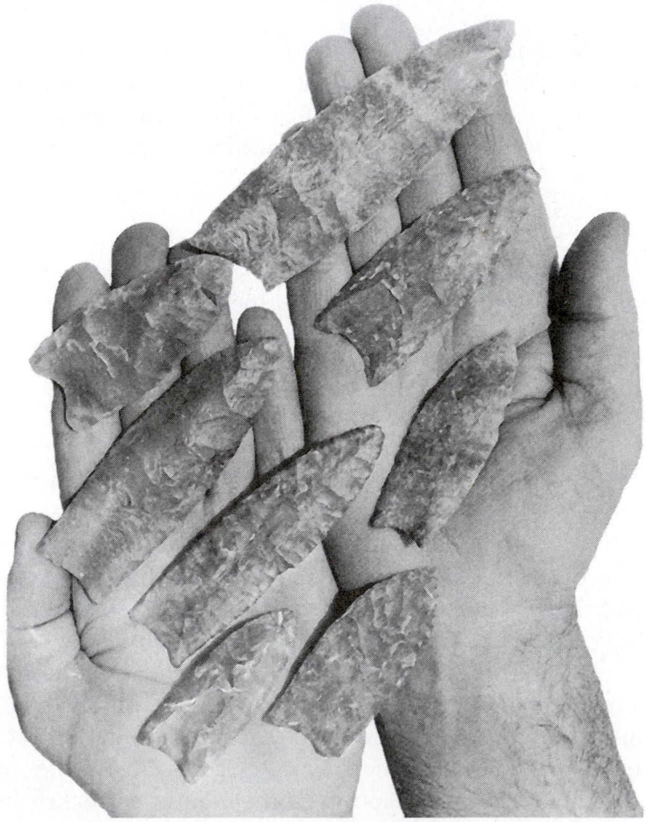

Figure 6.3 Paleo-Indian projectile points found in association with the bones of extinct bison on the Great Plains of North America.

from the surface. Some boys out hunting rabbits in 1940 found the magnificent Ice Age paintings in *Lascaux Cave* in southwestern France when their dog became trapped in an underground chamber entered through a rabbit hole.

Dramatic finds have resulted from despoiling of the environment. Deep plowing and freeway and dam construction have led to the uncovering—and damaging—of priceless sites. When Mexico City's metro (subway) was constructed under the modern city during the 1970s, the 28 miles (45 km) of tunnels yielded a wealth of archaeological material. Mexico City is built on the site of the Aztec capital of Tenochtitlán, overthrown by Hernán Cortés in 1521. Little remains of the Aztec city on the surface today, but the contractors for the metro recovered 40 tons of pottery, 380 burials, and even a small temple dedicated to the wind god Ehecatl-Quetzalcoatl. The temple is now preserved on its original site as part of the Piño Suarez station of the metro system. All of the tunneling operations were under the supervision of expert archaeologists, who were empowered to halt construction whenever an archaeological find was made.

Even more dramatic was the accidental rediscovery of the great Templo Mayor in the heart of Mexico City. Modern construction activity revealed the most sacred shrine of Aztec Tenochtitlán: the temples of the gods Huitzilopochtli and Tlaloc. Mexican archaeologist Eduardo Matos Moctezuma's excavations subsequently unearthed at least five successive temples and many rebuildings going back to as early as A.D. 1390, if not earlier (see Figure 6.4). The temple visited by Spanish conquistador Hernán Cortés had 114 steps and a drum so loud it could be heard 6 miles (10 km) away. The conquistadors pulled it down to build a Catholic cathedral nearby. The abandoned shrines were forgotten until the 1970s.

Nature itself sometimes uncovers sites for us, which are then located by a sharp-eyed archaeologist looking for natural exposures of likely geological strata. Olduvai Gorge is a great gash in the Serengeti Plains of northern Tanzania. An ancient earthquake eroded a deep gorge, exposing hundreds of feet of lake beds that had been buried long before. These buried lake deposits have yielded early tool and bone concentrations dating back at least 1.75 million years. They would never have been found without the assistance of an earthquake and subsequent erosion. The Olduvai area is but one of many examples from all over the world where nature has revealed the incredible bounty of the past.

Figure 6.4 A reconstruction of the central precinct of the Aztec capital, Tenochtitlán, with the great pyramid of the sun god Huitzilopochtli and the rain deity Tlaloc to the left.

Figure 6.5 Some of the 15,234 gold and silver coins from a late Roman hoard of the late 4th century A.D. The hoard, from Hoxne in eastern England, was buried in an iron-bound wooden box, and included expensive jewelry, silver tableware, including over 100 spoons and ladles. (Copyright: British Museum.)

The fields of the Western world have yielded many caches of buried weapons, coins, smith's tools, and sacrificial objects—valued treasures that were buried in times of stress by their owners. For whatever reason, the owners never returned to recover their valuables. Thousands of years later, a farmer comes across the hoard and, if a responsible citizen, reports the find to archaeological authorities. If not, yet another valuable fragment of the past is lost to science (see Figure 6.5).

Archaeological Survey

Archaeological survey means walking—a large-scale survey means lots of it, day after day, week after week, on carefully laid out transects that cross hill and dale. I always enjoy survey, for you develop a sense of the local landscape, meet all kinds of people, and get a unique impression of a place you might otherwise never encounter. And there is always the prospect of an important discovery. I have spent a month looking for Stone Age rockshelters in southwestern England and found no traces of human occupation whatsoever; returned from a week in southern Zambia with records of over 30 large mound villages; and walked in the Maya rain forest where you can see for only a few feet on either side. Survey is fascinating because no two days are alike and the rewards can be immense.

An archaeological survey can vary from spending an afternoon searching a city lot for traces of historical structures to doing a large-scale survey over several years of an entire river basin or drainage area. In all cases, the theoretical ideal is easily stated: to record all traces of ancient settlement in the area. But this ideal is impossible to achieve. Many sites leave no traces above ground. And no survey, however thorough and however sophisticated its remote sensing devices, will ever achieve the impossible dream of total coverage. The key to effective archaeological survey lies in carefully designing the research before one sets out and in using techniques to estimate the probable density of archaeological sites in the region.

Archaeological surveys are most effective in terrain where the vegetation is burned off or sparse enough for archaeologists to be able to see the ground. In lush vegetation areas such as those of the American South, only the most conspicuous earthworks will show up. And, of course, thousands of sites are buried under housing developments, parking lots, and artificial lakes, which have radically altered the landscape in many places.

A great deal depends on the intensity of the field survey. The most effective surveys are carried out on foot, where the archaeologist can locate the traces of artifacts, the gray organic soil eroding from a long-abandoned settlement, and the subtle colors of rich vegetation that reveal long-buried houses. Plowed fields may display revealing traces of ash, artifacts, or hut foundations. Scatters of broken bones, stone implements, potsherds, or other traces of prehistoric occupation are easily located in such furrowed soil. Observation is the key to finding archaeological sites and to studying the subtle relationships between prehistoric settlements and the landscape on which they flourished.

Archaeologists have many inconspicuous signs to guide them. Gray soil from a rodent burrow, a handful of humanly fractured stones in the walls of a desert arroyo, a blurred mark in a plowed field, a potsherd—these are the signs they seek. After a few days, you learn to spot the telltale gray earth sent up by burrowing animals from village sites from some distance off. And often, knowledgeable local inhabitants, especially landowners who have an intimate knowledge of their own acreage, provide information on possible sites.

There is far more to archaeological survey than merely walking the countryside, however. Such surveys can be of varying intensity. The least intensive survey is the most common: the investigator examining only conspicuous and accessible sites, those of great size and considerable fame. Heinrich Schliemann followed just this procedure when he located the site of ancient Troy at Hissarlik in Turkey in the 1870s. John Lloyd Stephens and Frederick Catherwood did the same when they visited Uxmal, Palenque, and other Maya sites in Mesoamerica in the early 1840s. Such superficial surveys barely scratch the archaeological surface.

A more intensive survey involves collecting as much information about as many sites as possible from local informants and landowners. Again, the sites located by this means are the larger and more conspicuous ones, and the survey is necessarily incomplete. But this approach is widely used throughout the world, especially in areas where archaeologists have never worked before.

Many more discoveries are made if archaeologists undertake a highly systematic survey of a relatively limited area. This type of survey involves not only comprehensive inquiries among local landowners, but actual systematic on-site checking of those reports. The footwork resulting from the checking of local reports may lead to more discoveries. But, again, the picture may be very incomplete, for the survey deals with known sites and does not cover the area systematically from one end to the other or establish the proportions of each type of site known to exist in the region.

The most intensive surveys have a party of archaeologists covering a whole area by walking all over it, often in straight lines, with a set distance between them. Such surveys are usually based on carefully formulated research designs. The investigators are careful to check that their site distributions reflect actual settlement patterns rather than where archaeologists walked.

Some such surveys have thrown light on rural life in ancient Greece by identifying the locations of individual farmsteads and small villages. Without resorting to expensive and time-consuming excavation, the research teams have used surface finds, such as pottery, to provide dating evidence for the sites, and have thus been able to show changing patterns of settlement from prehistory to the present day. At the same time, these surveys have found evidence for ancient Greek farming practices. One key discovery was the so-called halo of artifacts that surrounds many sites. Some ancient cities have haloes extending over several square miles. They result from intensive manuring—the carting out of animal dung, human excrement, and other organic wastes (including the accidental admixture of discarded pottery and other cultural material) and spreading them over the fields to increase fertility. Such an intensive agricultural practice is an indication of the high population density of many regions of Classical Greece. It was during this period, too, that extensive stone terraces were built on hillsides, again reflecting population growth and the need to increase agricultural productivity, in this case by creating new farmland.

What did the landscape of Classical Greece look like? A Stanford University research team carried out intensive field surveys in southern Greece of the southern Argolid at the eastern end of the Peloponnese. The researchers discovered several hundred archaeological sites of all periods and collected 45,000 ceramic pieces, mainly potsherds. Analysis of this huge body of material, coupled with study of soils and landscape, enabled them to chart changes in the settlement of the region from prehistory to the present day. The number of sites reached a peak during the fourth century B.C., when the area around the Classical town of *Halieis* became an important center of olive oil production, revealed by a combination of different kinds of evidence.

Rural settlements appear at this time on stony river plains and lower hill slopes, areas that give poor cereal yields but are ideal for olives. Olives were probably grown on terraces built on the hillsides, indicating a more labor-intensive use of the landscape. Further evidence for the production of olive oil comes from oil presses found both at rural farmsteads and at Halieis itself. At the same time, cereal growing continued on the fertile and water-retentive deeper soils.

The importance of olive oil production on the fourth-century Plain of Argos in southern Greece may well be linked to political events in neighboring regions, notably the destruction of Athenian olive groves by Spartan forces during the Peloponnesian War (431–404 B.C.). Olive trees take many years to mature, and Athens would have been dependent on imported supplies for several decades. The Plain of Argos is geographically close to Attica and would have been well placed to supply that need. Thus the southern Argolid survey provides an illustration of the intimate way in which rural fortunes may be linked to the politics of the wider world (see Figure 6.6).

Clearly, most archaeological surveys can record only a sample of the sites in the survey area, even if the declared objective is to plot the position of every prehistoric

Figure 6.6 Traditional olive press of a type used by Greek farmers right into the twentieth century. Donkeys turned the large stone of the press.

settlement. Such was the purpose of an ambitious survey of the Basin of Mexico, home of the Teotihuacán and Aztec civilizations of the past 2,000 years. The investigators managed to chronicle the changing settlement patterns in the basin since long before Teotihuacán rose to prominence after A.D. 100 right up to the Spanish Conquest and beyond. But they would be the first to admit that they have recovered only a fraction of the Basin's sites. For a start, most of the Aztec capital, Tenochtitlán, and its outlying suburbs lie under the foundations of Mexico City (see Figure 6.3 on page 116).

Sampling and Archaeological Survey

In the early days, archaeologists concentrated on conspicuous, easily found sites. Now, with so many sites endangered by all kinds of industrial development, they hurry to locate as many prehistoric locations as possible. Often, a survey is designed to make an inventory of archaeological sites in a specific area. When an area is to be deep-plowed or covered with houses, the burden of proof that archaeological sites do or do not exist in the endangered zone is the responsibility of the archaeologists. Time is often short and funds are very limited. The only way the archaeologists can estimate the extent of the site resource base is to survey selected areas in great detail, using formal sampling methods.

Sampling is the science of controlling and measuring the reliability of information through the theory of probability. Systematic and carefully controlled sampling of archaeological data is essential if we are to rely heavily, as we do, on statistical approaches in studying ancient adaptations to changing environmental conditions. Few modern archaeological surveys fail to make use of sampling, for many site distributions reflect the distribution of archaeologists rather than an unbiased sampling of the archaeological record. This bias applies particularly in vegetated areas like the eastern woodlands of North America and the Mesoamerican and Amazonian rain forests, where the cover is so thick that even new roads are in danger of being overgrown within weeks. Sampling ensures a statistically reliable basis of archaeological data from which we can make generalizations about our research data. Such generalizations are often estimates of probability, which means they have to be based on unbiased data.

Sampling in archaeological survey typically can involve **element sampling**, where one selects arbitrary grid samples randomly over a large area. This is useful for estimating the densities of archaeological sites over a research area. Alternatively, **cluster sampling** governs a survey made up of arbitrary survey units defined by area, a sample of which are examined for inventories of archaeological remains. Any given sampling unit may contain a cluster of elements, a sample of sites, artifacts, or features, in which each sampling unit is a collection (cluster) of elements. Thus statistical population is made up of a number of clusters, each with a specific number of elements, which determine cluster size. This approach is useful when, for example, you want to examine the properties of individual sites, not of arbitrary units in a grid covering a research area. What is the proportion of sites in Mexico's Valley of Oaxaca, with seashells dating to 1000 B.C.? What is the average site area of settlements within the sampling area, and so on?

Formal sampling provides a means for generalizing from the sample survey areas to larger regions. The reliability of these generalizations is tested by routine statistical procedures. This approach to archaeological survey, often called predictive modeling, is a powerful weapon to counter the destruction of archaeological sites by industrial activity.

Archaeologists cannot stop the destruction of every threatened site. The best they can hope for is a chance to make decisions on which sites in the archaeological resource base are to be preserved, which will be excavated before destruction, and which will fall to destruction in the name of progress. More and more archaeology in North America is such cultural resource management and results from efforts to conserve sites and to manage a diminishing resource base. CRM projects make intensive use of sampling surveys.

Remote Sensing

Today's archaeologists rely on technology and elaborate instrumentation to help them discover the past, especially on CRM projects. This is nondestructive archaeology—the analysis of archaeological phenomena without excavations or collecting of artifacts, both of which destroy the archaeological record. The major methods in this approach are generally labeled **remote sensing**. These techniques include aerial photography, various magnetic prospecting methods, and sidescan radar.

Aerial Photography

The building of today's inventories of archaeological sites would never have been possible without aerial survey techniques. Aerial photography gives an overhead view of the past. Sites can be photographed from many directions, at different times of day, and at various seasons. Numerous sites that left almost no surface traces have been discovered by analyzing aerial photographs. Many earthworks and other complex structures have been leveled by plows or erosion, but their original layout shows up clearly from the air (see Figure 6.7). The rising or setting sun can make large shadows, emphasizing the relief of almost vanished banks or ditches; the features of the site stand out in oblique light. Such phenomena are sometimes called shadow sites. I once had a chance to fly over southern England's chalk country two days after snow had mantled the rolling countryside. The ridges and hedgerows stood out sharply in the oblique light. So did the circular earthworks of Avebury, the standing stones casting long shadows in the chill winter sunlight.

Figure 6.7 Long-forgotten earthworks and burial mounds revealed by dark crop marks.

In some areas, it is possible to detect differences in soil color and in the richness of crop growth on a particular soil. Such marks are hard to detect on the surface but often show up clearly from the air. The growth and color of a crop are greatly determined by the amount of moisture the plant can derive from the soil and subsoil. If the soil depth has been increased by digging features such as pits and ditches, later filled in, or because additional earth has been heaped up to form artificial banks or mounds, the crops growing over such abandoned structures are high and well nourished. The opposite is also true, where soil has been removed and the infertile soil is near the surface, or where impenetrable surfaces such as paved streets are below ground level and the crops grow less thickly. Thus a dark **crop mark** can be taken for a ditch or pit, and a lighter line may define a more substantial structure. Time and time again, I've walked over a plowed field with an aerial photograph and had great difficulty spotting the crop mark on the ground. But they are there if you look closely enough, photograph in hand.

Much of the world has been photographed from about 24,000 feet (7,000 m) by military photographers. Such coverage has been put to use by archaeologists to survey remote areas such as the Virú Valley on Peru's north coast, where a team of archaeologists led by Gordon Willey plotted 315 sites on a master map of the valley. Many of the sites were stone buildings or agricultural terraces; others were refuse mounds that appeared as low hillocks on the photographs. By using aerial surveys, Willey saved days of survey time, for he was able to pinpoint many sites before going out in the field. When the settlements were visited, the fascinating story of shifting settlement patterns in Virú over thousands of years was made visible by a combination of foot survey and air photography.

Aerial remote-sensing devices of many types have become available in recent years to complement the valuable results of black-and-white photography. Infrared film, which has three layers sensitized to green, red, and infrared, detects reflected solar radiation at the near end of the electromagnetic spectrum, some of which is invisible to the naked eye. The different reflections from cultural and natural features are translated by the film into distinctive false colors. Vigorous grass growth on river plains shows up in bright red. Such red patterns have been used in the American Southwest to track shallow, subsurface water sources where springs were used by prehistoric peoples. The infrared data could lead the archaeologist to likely areas for previously undetected hunting camps and villages.

Aircraft and Satellite Imagery

In some areas, exuberant vegetation hampers archaeological surveys, especially in the Maya lowlands. For years, archaeologists have wondered how the Maya civilization managed to feed itself and have puzzled over the incompletely known distribution of its cities and ceremonial centers. Originally they believed the Maya population was supported by slash-and-burn cultivation, a *milpa* system still used today, in which people burn off and clear the forests, then cultivate the land for three or four years before leaving it fallow and moving on to virgin plots. The soils of the Maya lowlands, not particularly fertile, are vulnerable to soil erosion when cleared of vegetation and exposed to heavy rain. The Classic Maya population was far larger than such fields could support.

Chaco Canyon, New Mexico, was an important center of Ancestral Pueblo settlement a thousand years ago (see Figure 5.10 on page 100). Here, archaeologist Gwinn Vivian, mapped linear features that he thought were irrigation canals. When he dug into them, he found that they were deliberately leveled and carefully designed roadways. He mentioned his findings to Thomas Lyons, a geologist and together they examined aerial photographs of the canyon, including some taken by Lindbergh, which dated to before the time when grazing was permitted there. They soon found clear traces of a road system, commissioned more flights, and identified more than 186 miles (300 km) of road segments. When NASA flew over Chaco with a thermal infrared multispectral scanning (TIMS) device, they located a further 186 miles (300 km) of roads. TIMS measures the infrared thermal radiation given off by the ground, and is sensitive to even small differences. A computer converts the data from the camera into "false-color" images that map the terrain in terms of infrared radiation. The Chaco roads showed up as clear, tan lines against the surrounding red sand, and yet they are only up to 4 inches (10 cm) deep, their existence virtually unknown until remote sensing came along. A generation of archaeologists has puzzled over the Chaco road system, so far without success. Often, the roads are just short segments, which end in the middle of nowhere. Most segments are straight, others turn abruptly or are lined by low berms. We don't know whether they were incomplete, or merely symbolic depictions of sacred directions. They converge on Chaco, where rock-cut stairways lead down the precipitous cliffs.

The best-known source of aircraft-borne sensor imagery is Sideways Looking Airborne Radar (SLAR), which senses the terrain on either side of an aircraft's path, with the instrumentation tracking the radar pulse lines in the form of images whether or not clouds obscure the ground. A group of archaeologists, looking for a sensor system that would penetrate the dense forest cover of the Maya area, discovered an unexpected archaeological payoff in the imaging radar developed by NASA for spaceborne lunar sounders and in synthetic aperture radar. (The radar chosen for the Maya experiment was, in fact, developed for imaging the surface of the planet Venus.) On flights made over the Maya lowlands in 1978 and 1980, black-and-white and color infrared film were used to capture indications of archaeological sites and ancient landscape modifications. When the features discovered were plotted onto topographic maps, they revealed not only shadows of large mounds and buildings, but irregular grids of gray lines within swampy areas near known major sites. These lines were found to form ladder and lattice as well as curvilinear patterns that very closely matched conventional aerial views of known canal systems in the Valley of Mexico and the lowlands. Ground surveys revealed that the Maya grew large food surpluses using large-scale swamp agriculture, developing field systems that are nearly invisible on the ground today.

Archaeology has even gone into space. **Satellite sensor imagery** is used for both military and environmental monitoring. The best-known satellites are the LANDSAT series, which scan the earth with readers that detect the intensity of reflected light and infrared radiation from the earth's surface. The latest images pick up features only 90 feet (27 m) wide; the French SPOT satellites can work to within 60 feet (18 m). Computer-enhanced LANDSAT and SPOT images can be used to construct environmental cover maps of large survey regions that are a superb backdrop for both aerial and ground survey for archaeological resources. Recently, NASA's World-Wind satellite imagery and other government sources have become available on the Web, as has Google Earth, which, like World-Wind, provides dynamic imagery and a good search tool, a mosaic of photographic images laid over 3-D landscape models that provide a topographic backdrop. Unfortunately, only larger cities are covered at high resolution, such as would be useful for archaeology. Corona and Ikonos satellite imagery also hold promise (see Figure 6.8).

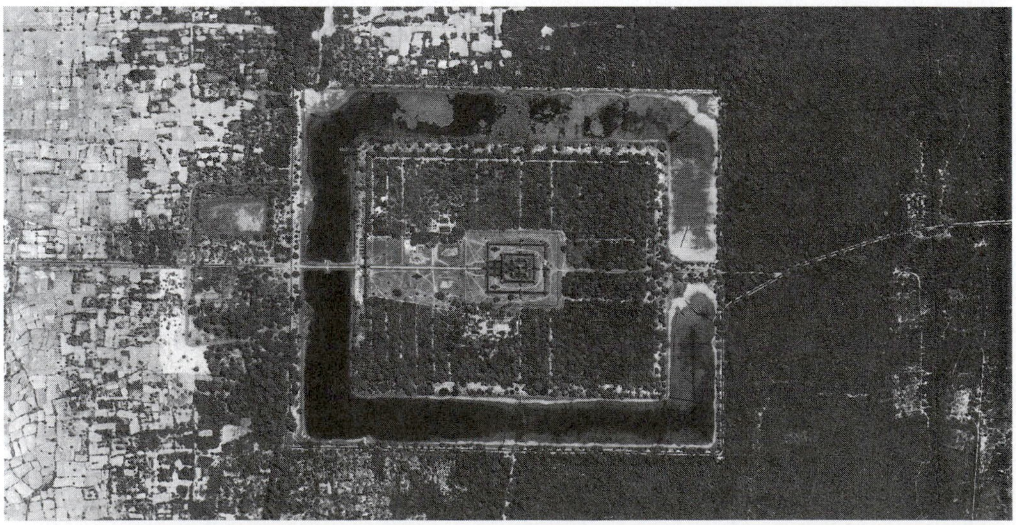

Figure 6.8 Satellite view of Angkor Wat, Cambodia.

The space shuttle *Columbia* used an imaging radar system to bounce radar signals off the surfaces of the world's major deserts in 1981. This experiment was designed to study the history of the earth's aridity, not archaeology, but identified ancient river courses in the limestone bedrock 5 feet (1.5 m) or more below the Sahara Desert surface. All remote sensing is useless unless checked on the ground, so a team of geologists, including archaeologist C. Vance Haynes of the University of Arizona, journeyed far into the desert to investigate the long-hidden watercourses. About the only people to work this terrain were the World War II British army and present-day Egyptian oil companies, the latter of which kindly arranged for a skip loader to be transported into the desert. To Haynes's astonishment, the skip-loader trenches yielded some 200,000-year-old stone axes, dramatic and unexpected proof that early Stone Age hunter-gatherers had lived in the heart of the Sahara when the landscape was more hospitable than it is today. The Haynes find is of cardinal importance, for African archaeologists now believe the Sahara was a vital catalyst in early human history that effectively sealed off archaic humans from the rest of the Old World. In later times, sub-Saharan Africa was isolated from the Mediterranean world until camel caravans opened up the desert in the first millennium A.D.

The latest remote sensing technology is Laser Altimetry, sometimes called **LIDAR** (Light detection and ranging), which is the optical equivalent of radar. This uses a laser range finder to measure height, which can yield accurate and dense digital models of topography, even the vertical structures of buildings, also trees, from the air. LIDAR provides astonishingly precise images of everything from standing ruins like pueblos to abandoned pithouse depressions and European medieval towns. It is still very expensive, but offers great promise for the future.

Radar imagery from space and other remote-sensing technologies are the high point of nonintrusive archaeology. They are at their best when combined with other remote-sensing data acquired from aerial photographs and such technologies as ground-penetrating radar.

Recording Archaeological Sites

Once sites have been identified, whether by field survey or satellite imagery, their location, features, and extent are carefully recorded. These data can be used to address various research questions or cultural resource management concerns. For example, studies of changing settlement distributions plotted against environmental data provide significant information on changing human exploitation of the landscape Thus, recording the precise global location of archaeological phenomena revealed by a survey is a high priority.

Information on site location can be recorded in a variety of ways. It is not enough just to record the precise latitude, longitude, and map grid reference. Special forms are used to record the location of the site, as well as information about surface features, the landowner, potential threats to the site, and so on. Every site in the United States is given a name and a number. Sites in Santa Barbara County, California, for example, are given the prefix CA-SBa- and are numbered sequentially. So many sites are now known in North America that most states and many large archaeological projects have set up computer data banks containing comprehensive information about site distributions and characteristics. Arkansas, for example, has a statewide computer bank that is in constant use for decisions on conservation and management.

Maps are a convenient way of storing large quantities of archaeological information. Traditionally, recording was done entirely by hand, but the increasing availability of a variety of computer mapping programs has facilitated both site recording and data storage. An important advance in recent years has been the advent of low-cost Global

Positioning Systems (GPS), which locate sites using satellite positioning systems. Handheld GPS units can be used in a variety of environmental settings and enable fieldworkers to locate sites within a few feet. They are especially advantageous in settings where roads and other identifiable features are limited, or where vegetation makes plotting sites on topographic maps challenging. With larger regional investigations, and extensive CRM projects, especially in the western United States, remote sensing and GPS are used to record and manage archaeological sites.

Geographic Information Systems (GIS)

Distribution maps have been part of archaeology for generations, but, in themselves, they are little more than clusters of dots on maps, perhaps with topography added. Many early maps reflected the distribution of archaeologists and their finds rather than the true density of sites across the landscape. **Geographic Information Systems (GIS)**, which appeared during the 1980s, has revolutionized the storage and display of cartographic data, including archaeological sites. Geographic Information Systems (GIS) are computer-aided systems for the collection, storage, retrieval, analysis, and presentation of spatial data of all kinds. GIS incorporates computer-aided mapping, computerized databases, and statistical packages, and is best thought of as a computer database with mapping capabilities. It also has the ability to generate new information based on the data within it.

You can now view archaeological sites in all kinds of geographic contexts simply by pressing a few computer keys—to the point that you can even sometimes look at sites against the topography and vegetation of the day. GIS comprises three elements: a powerful computer graphics program that draws the digital map, one or more external data bases linked to the items on the map, and a series of analytical tools that interpret and statistically analyze the stored data in graphic form. As a long term project, most U.S. states are putting their data bases of archaeological sites on GIS, using U.S. Geological Survey topographic maps, which are available in digital form.

I always think of GIS in terms of layers, the basic layer being the topographic map, to which you add layer after layer of information such as vegetation, water sources, archaeological sites, and so on—preparing a map that can display all kinds of different information, which can be changed at will. The metaphor is a base map, upon which you pile layers of tracing paper or transparent plastic that display different kinds of data. Instead, you use a georeferenced data base, where all the data, be it about soils or sites, is recorded using the same mapping system. Each data point has its own data base, where information such as artifact frequencies, unusual finds, and so on, are displayed, to say nothing of architectural features, storage pits, or contour lines. In short, the past is at your fingertips, and in such a format that you can ask questions of your map. How far away from a specific village were acorn-rich oaks to be found? What food resources and toolmaking materials lay within 3 miles (5 km) of the settlement? How far did people have to walk to reach the best soils for cultivating maize? You can even bring up the landscape in such a way that you can see the same view as the ancient inhabitants saw, an important strategic concern when you are afraid of raiders or surprise attacks from the sea. GIS does what archaeologists have done for generations—look at sites in the context of their environment—but it does it in a fraction of the time than it used to take, and with far greater sophistication and precision—once the data bases are constructed, an extremely lengthy process but one that makes sense when you are concerned with inventorying sites and predictive surveys.

From the archaeological perspective, GIS has the advantage of allowing the manipulation of large amounts of data, especially useful for solving complex settlement analysis problems at places like the Roman towns of *Pompeii,* Italy, and *Wroxeter,* England (for Wroxeter, see Chapter 12). Now the archaeologist can examine, for example, the environmental potential of areas where no sites have been found to assess the overall distribution of sites within the environment. CRM archaeologists make extensive use of GIS data in their work, which provide instant, and often comprehensive, information on environmental and archaeological data from regions large and small.

GIS also allows archaeologists to model different environmental scenarios and to study such problems as the ways in which different settlements controlled valuable land. British archaeologist Vincent Gaffney has recently produced a remarkable "virtual landscape" of Stonehenge at the various stages of its construction, which allows one both to "walk" the landscape and to reconstruct the sight lines from various features to the stone circles.

The Italian archaeologists responsible for Roman Pompeii, which was overwhelmed by an eruption of Vesuvius on August 24, A.D. 79, have used GIS technology to capture and interpret life in the town as it was 2,000 years ago, employing a computerized database of material excavated since 1862. They used an IBM computer to digitize archaeological maps and local terrain, to integrally link visual representations of the artifacts to both the detailed descriptions of each find from the city and to the locations in which they were found. The thousands of computerized pictures of specific artifacts are linked to the maps to provide detailed insights into individual houses, rooms, and walls, the places where the finds were excavated. This "Neapolis" system with its 50 gigabytes of detailed information about Pompeii can be used to study such topics as the relationships between lifestyle and distribution of wealth, the spread of fashions and trends, or to correlate fresco motifs on house walls from one end of the town to the other. In this instance, GIS is used to understand relationships not readily perceived by the human mind—the myriad interconnections that tie works of art, buildings, and individual artifacts to an entire culture and community.

The most comprehensive North American GIS project is the National Archaeological Data Base, an on-line system that now contains over 100,000 records of archaeological reports. Any archaeologist with a telephone line or on an electronic mail system can now access this archive, which also provides comprehensive site distribution from many states and background environmental information through the Geographic Resources Analysis Support System (GRASS), the GIS system used by the National Park Service (www.cast.uark.edu/other/nps/nadb).

Assessing Archaeological Sites

Assessing the significance of an archaeological site without excavation has become increasingly important as the catastrophic damage done to the archaeological record has hit crisis proportions. Thus, surface recording and assessment as well as subsurface detection methods have assumed great importance.

Site assessment involves several processes:

- Accurate mapping of the site and recording its precise geographic location. It is not enough just to record a site on a map, even if this is a GIS record with background environmental data. Special forms are used to record location, unusual features, and information on surface features, landowner, and so on. The site is given a name and number, and any potential threats to the resource are noted. This form is the basis for an entry in any pertinent computer database of archaeological sites.
- Surface collection of artifacts and other finds on the ground surface of the site—but this is not an invariable part of assessment.
- Subsurface investigation using electronic detection methods. These are used when the investigator suspects that significant features lie below the surface, both to acquire information and to form a basis for the research design.

Surface Collection

Controlled **surface collection** is a vital part of site assessment, for representative samples of artifacts from the modern ground surface can provide vital information on the age of the site and the various periods of occupation. For example, a pueblo site in the American Southwest might yield several forms of painted pottery, which, on the basis of stratigraphic observations elsewhere, can be placed in chronological order.

The same samples can sometimes be used to establish what activities took place on the site. A large sample of obsidian lumps and waste flakes might, for instance, be a clue that a quarry once flourished at the location. By plotting surface finds on a grid laid out over the site, the investigators can sometimes establish which areas of the site were most densely occupied and would be most productive for excavation. They may also reveal the presence of important structures below the surface.

Surface deposits can yield valuable information on artifact distributions and other phenomena lying underground. For this reason, surface collections form an important part of any archaeological survey, especially one that seeks to establish the limits of an ancient city, or different housing areas, such as was the case at Maya Copán or Roman Wroxeter.

Many archaeologists distrust surface collections, arguing that artifacts are easily destroyed on the surface and can be displaced from their original positions. But this viewpoint neglects a fundamental archaeological truth. All archaeological deposits, however deep, were once surface layers, subject to many of the same destructive processes as those outcropping on the surface today. In fact, with controlled surface collection involving random or some other sampling technique, present land surfaces can yield much valuable information on artifact distributions or other phenomena found underground, provided, of course, they have not been subjected to strip mining, deep plowing, or other catastrophic modifications.

With carefully controlled surface collection, and a clear understanding of the relationship between surface finds and those found below the ground, accurate site assessments are often possible. The large-scale survey of the hinterland of Copán relied heavily on surface collecting to identify sites large and small and to assess their significance. CRM surveys also rely heavily on surface collection.

Subsurface Detection Methods

All archaeologists dream of a new and revolutionary method that will enable them to find out what is underground without the labor of excavation! Thanks to radar and other electronic devices, modern technology shows promise of actually achieving this elusive goal. Ken Weeks and a team of fellow Egyptologists have embarked on a long-term project to map all of the royal tombs in Thebes's Valley of Kings. They have used a hot-air balloon, x-rays, and sonic detectors to map subterranean features and hidden chambers in royal tombs. The team recently discovered a long-lost tomb with many subterranean chambers built for the sons of the great New Kingdom pharaoh Rameses II.

Nonintrusive detection methods include the use of metal detectors, which have a bad name in the hands of treasure hunters but are an effective way of finding artifacts to depths of about 8 inches (20 cm) *in properly supervised hands*. **Resistivity surveys** use electric current transmitted through electrodes planted in the soil to detect subsurface structures like building foundations through their higher resistivity. Readings are taken across a grid laid out over the site when attempting to plot features like house foundations, pits, or stone walls. **Electromagnetic survey** is the opposite of resistivity, measuring the conductivity of features like walls, which is low, while the resistivity of the same structure is high. This method is faster, does not require electronic probes, and can be used to locate structures over large areas, such as was done at *Cahokia,* the great Mississippian ceremonial center near East St. Louis, Illinois.

Subsurface (ground-penetrating) radar has proved effective on a wide variety of sites, using a lower power antenna, but the data often requires expert interpretation. British archaeologist Vincent Gaffney used radar to plot the layout of much of the Roman town of Wroxeter in western England (see Figure 6.9).

Magnetometer surveys are also commonplace, using the fluxgate gradiometer, which provides magnetic readings as the surveyor walks along the grid lines across a site. The readings can be downloaded at the end of the session and provide a contour map of subsurface anomalies that may represent the results of human activity. Magnetometers have proved especially effective on sites with few surviving surface features, such as villages on the North American Plains.

Very often, researchers will combine several nonintrusive methods, as archaeologist Payson Sheets did at the Maya village of Cerén in El Salvador. The site was buried under up to 16 feet (5 m) of volcanic ash and was first located by a chance bulldozer cut. Obviously, it was not economical to bulldoze large areas, so Sheets turned to ground-penetrating radar, using an instrument developed for studying **permafrost** melting along the Alaskan oil pipeline. To eliminate all background vibration, he enlisted the services of an oxcart driver. The driver simply drove slowly and steadily along a carefully marked straight line. The subsurface stratigraphy was recorded on special paper and revealed strong reflectors, some of which turned out to be the clay surfaces of hut floors covered by ash (see Figure 6.10a on page 130).

Finally, Sheets used a resistivity survey meter to measure the variations in the resistance (resistivity) of the ground, hoping to locate stone walls or hard pavements. The three-dimensional software revealed interesting double-peaked anomalies, which, when tested with a drill rig, turned out to be large prehistoric structures (see Figure 6.10b on page 130).

A combination of geophysical methods provided an effective and economical way to locate subsurface features at Cerén—at a fraction of the cost that would have been incurred in bulldozing away acres of ashy overburden.

Nonintrusive archaeological survey is the most vital of all field research. Without adequate surveys and efforts at cultural resource management, the future of archaeology in some parts of the world, especially North America and western Europe, would be in grave doubt. There simply would be nothing left to explore.

Figure 6.9 Surface electronic survey in fields near the Roman city of Wroxeter, England.

Figure 6.10a Remote sensing at Cerén, El Salvador. Ground-penetrating radar slung behind an oxcart.

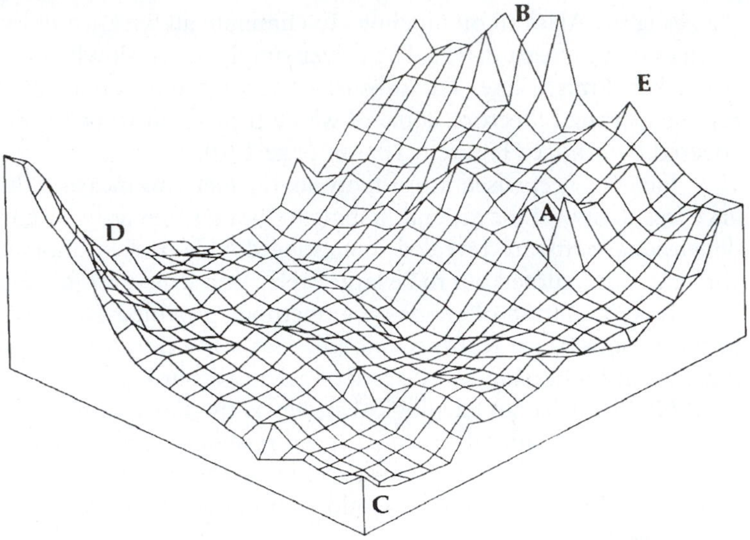

Figure 6.10b A three-dimensional computer plot of a resistivity survey at the Maya village at Cerén, El Salvador. The anomalies resulting from different electrical resistance show up as sharp peaks (A to E), of which A and B have been investigated and shown to be prehistoric structures.

SUMMARY

1. Archaeological fieldwork consists of finding, assessing, and excavating archaeological sites.
2. Many sites come to light by accident during construction work or other modern activity, or as a result of natural phenomena such as earthquakes.
3. Archaeological surveys locate and record sites within specific areas, using carefully formulated research designs, remote-sensing techniques such as aerial photography or even satellite imagery, and, above all, observation on foot on the ground.
4. Formal statistical sampling methods play an important role in survey work as a basis for estimating the site resource base in a specific region. They provide a statistically reliable basis of archaeological data for making generalizations about site distributions.
5. Increasingly, archaeologists record sites with computer-aided mapping methods known as Geographic Information Systems (GIS). GIS lets the researcher manipulate large amounts of data during complex analyses of ancient settlement patterns using sites and environmental and topographic data.
6. Site assessment involves mapping, surface collection, and subsurface investigation with electronic devices like ground-penetrating radar and resistivity meters. Such approaches were highly successful at the Cerén Maya village in El Salvador, where volcanic ash mantles an entire farming settlement.

SEVEN

Excavation

The ultimate in archaeological excavation. King Henry VIII's Privy Garden at Hampton Court, England, was restored after archaeological excavations located the outlines of flower beds and other features.

CHAPTER OUTLINE

PREVIEW

Excavation, once the primary activity of archaeologists, is now the strategy of last resort, because it destroys the archaeological record. Chapter 7 describes the process of archaeological excavation, various approaches to site testing and investigation, and the basics of recording and stratigraphic observation. We stress that there's no such thing as a standardized way of digging archaeological sites. Much of the chapter is devoted to summaries of some of the major challenges faced by excavators. We also discuss the ethical issues surrounding the excavation of human burials.

> *A mere hole in the ground, which of all sights is perhaps the least vivid and dramatic, is enough to grip their attention for hours at a time.*
>
> —P. G. Wodehouse, *A Damsel in Distress,* 1919

We all have dreams of digging into a mysterious, undisturbed tomb. Suddenly, you come across a sealed door. You break down the door and find yourself in an undisturbed, gold-strewn sepulcher that puts Tutankhamun's burial chamber to shame. But in reality, modern archaeological **excavation** is a precise, slow-moving process, working with trowels and brushes, often without a spectacular find, from one day to the next.

In this chapter we describe some of the basic principles of excavation and many excavation problems that archaeologists can encounter in the field. Realize, though, that each site presents distinctive challenges and requires modification of the basic principles enumerated here.

Planned Excavation: Research Design

The first principle of excavation is that digging is destructive. As archaeologist Kent Flannery once remarked, we are the only scientists who murder their informants (our sites) when we question them! The archaeological deposits so carefully examined during a dig are destroyed forever. Site contents are removed to a laboratory, permanently divorced from their context in time and space in the ground. And this is a radical difference from other disciplines: A chemist can readily re-create the conditions of a basic experiment, a biographer can return to the archives to reevaluate the complex events in a politician's life, but an archaeologist's archives are destroyed during the dig. All that remains from an excavation are the finds from the trenches, the unexcavated portions of the site, and the photographs, notes, and drawings that record the excavator's observations for posterity. One of the tragedies of archaeology is that much of the available archaeological data have been excavated under far from scientific conditions. Our archives of information are uneven at best. Increasingly, the ethics of archaeology research require absolutely minimal excavation consistent with acquiring essential scientific information.

The treasure hunter ravages a site in search of valuable finds and keeps no records. Archaeologists demolish sites as well, but with a difference: They create archives of archaeological information that document contexts for the objects they take back to the laboratory with them. Although they have destroyed the site forever, they have created a data bank of information in its place, the only archive their successors will be able to consult to check their results. Archaeologists have serious responsibilities: to record and

Discovery

The Princess of Khok Phanom Di, Thailand, 1984

Charles Higham of the University of Otago in New Zealand is one of the world's experts on the archaeology of southeastern Asia. Working closely with Thai archaeologists, he has made spectacular discoveries of early rice-farming villages and well-established Bronze Age settlements. In 1984, he began excavations at the large Khok Phanom Di mound on the floodplain of the Bang Pakong River. From a previous test excavation carried out by a Thai colleague, he knew that the occupation deposits were nearly 30 feet (9 m) deep, the mound resting on layers of shell midden debris. In the trial pit, Higham spotted "the hollow eye sockets of some prehistoric person," so he knew he would probably find burials (see Figure 7.1).

After digging through the uppermost levels, he found lighter, sandier soil about 3 feet (1 m) below the surface. He cleaned the surface of the deposit carefully and spotted the telltale outline of the dark filling of a grave. Soon the excavators uncovered a row of graves close to the foundation of a raised platform with a building on it. Their trowels traced the walls of beautifully polished black vessels, many of them decorated with curvilinear designs. Higham's excitement mounted as he uncovered fourteen burials. From the platform, "I could look down the row of skeletons and see the remains of men, women, and children, and even a tiny grave with the intertwined bones of two newly born infants, probably twins. It looked like a family group running through a couple or more generations" (Higham, 1994: 283).

The excavation penetrated downward into a large burial chamber, uncovering a pyramid of circular clay cylinders, once destined to become pots. When the pyramid was removed, the skeleton of a woman in her mid-thirties appeared, her wrist muscles well formed, probably from kneading clay. She had borne one or two children. Her chest was covered with tiny shell beads and a necklace of large, white I-shaped beads. Higham lifted the top half of the body in a single block of soil and dissected it in the laboratory, where he recovered no less than 120,787 shell beads, once sewn onto two ornate upper garments. The princess must have shimmered in the sunlight, her wealth and social position coming from her expertise at potmaking, evidenced by the burnished polishing pebbles found by her feet and the broken vessels covering her legs. Just 6 feet (2 m) away, Higham found another, identical grave covered by another heap of clay cylinders; this was the grave of an infant only fifteen months old. The child was adorned with the same decoration as that of her mother and lay with a tiny potmaking anvil, a smaller version of the anvils used by adults, by her side. Higham is convinced that this was the princess's daughter.

By the time the excavation finished six months later, Higham had recovered another 139 burials, representing seventeen to twenty generations of expert potters who had traded pots to obtain exotic shell ornaments. But none of them rivaled the splendor of the Princess of Khok Phanom Di.

Figure 7.1 Excavation at Khok Phanom Di. Thailand. The site yielded not only spectacular burials, but important evidence for early rice cultivation.

interpret the significance of the layers, houses, food remains, and artifacts in their sites, and to publish the results for posterity. Without accurate records and meaningful publication of results, an excavation is useless. Many CRM investigations in North America are now funded under contracts that require prompt reporting, even if only for limited circulation.

A generation ago, an archaeologist's first inclination was to dig sites to solve problems. Nowadays, there is increased awareness that excavation destroys irreplaceable evidence of the past, and we dig only when we must. Anyone who excavates without serious attention to record keeping and all of the other processes of excavation is committing vandalism of an unforgivable kind.

At the core of every modern archaeological excavation lies a sound research design, a design that very often has a regional rather than a specific site focus (see Chapter 6). The research design is developed to answer specific questions and to acquire maximum information with minimum disturbance of finite archaeological resources. It is, of course, a flexible, ever-changing plan, modified as hypotheses are tested, proved wrong, validated, or refined as a result of knowledge acquired in the ongoing excavation.

The design extends beyond the excavation itself. The end products of even a month's excavation on a moderately productive site are boxes upon boxes of potsherds, stone tools, animal bones, and other finds that have been cleaned, sorted, and bagged in the field. Rolls of drawings and stacks of computer disks hold valuable stratigraphic information. So do digital images, photographs, and hundreds of pages of field notes compiled by excavation staff as the long days of toil continue. At the same time, radiocarbon and soil samples are collected for later analysis. Freshwater shells and charcoal fragments are packed for shipment to specialist investigators. It takes months to analyze the notes and finds from even a small excavation. The dozens of boxes, hundreds of notebook pages, and megabytes of computer input contain a vast array of data that must be collated to reconstruct what happened at the site. It follows, then, that the excavation research design is constantly reevaluated to determine the future course of the dig and to monitor the long months of analysis and interpretation that follow. The days when a site was dug simply because it "looked good" are long gone.

The organization of even a moderate-sized excavation requires careful planning at the implementation stage of the research design. One classic example of such planning comes from the Midwest. Illinois archaeologists James Brown and Stuart Struever spent many field seasons in the 1970s excavating the *Koster* site in the lower Illinois River Valley. Here, at least 12 human occupations are represented at one site, the earliest of which dates to before 5100 B.C. Koster is a deep site, probably abandoned before A.D. 1000 after generations of Indians had settled at this favorable locality. It offered Brown and Struever a unique opportunity to examine the changing cultures of the inhabitants over more than 6,000 years. But the organizational problems were enormous. Koster is more than 30 feet (9 meters) deep, with each of the 12 cultural horizons separated from its neighbor by zones of sterile soil. Brown and Struever were fortunate in that they were able to treat each occupation level of this large site as an entirely separate digging operation.

The archaeologists had two options. One was to dig small test trenches and obtain samples of pottery and other finds from each stratigraphic level. But this approach, although cheaper and commonly used, was inadequate for the problems to be investigated at the Koster site. The excavators were interested in studying the origins of agriculture in the lower Illinois Valley. Brown and Struever therefore decided to excavate each living surface on a sufficiently large scale to study the activities that had taken place there. This procedure would enable them to examine minute economic changes. Thus the emphasis in the Koster excavations was on isolating the different settlement types that lay one on top of the other.

In developing the Koster research design, Brown and Struever needed to control a mass of complex variables that affected their data. They had to invent special procedures

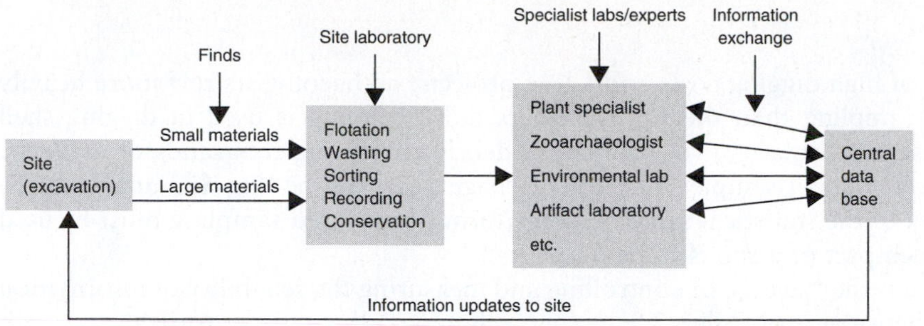

Figure 7.2 Flow chart of the organization of an archaeological excavation.

to ensure the statistical validity of their excavations. In order to acquire immediate feedback on the finds made during the excavations, they organized an elaborate data-processing system that sorted the animal bones, artifacts, vegetable remains, and other discoveries on location in the field. The tabulated information on each sorted find was then fed by remote access terminal to a computer many miles away. The excavators had instant access to the latest data from the dig. This system meant that the overall research design could be modified while an excavation was still in progress (see Figure 7.2).

The Koster site, although conducted a quarter century ago, is a classic example of academic research and elaborate research design that used complex computer technology. The dig employed dozens of people each field season. Most excavations, whether academic or CRM, operate on a far smaller scale, but the ultimate principles are the same: sound research design, very careful recording of all data, and scientifically controlled excavation. The Koster excavation was designed, like all good digs, to solve specific research problems formulated in the context of a sound research design.

Types of Excavation

Archaeological excavation is not digging by formula, but a carefully managed process that requires constant creative thinking. There are general methodologies for excavation, but the appropriate one varies from site to site and from moment to moment as an excavation proceeds. In a way, excavation is a process of negotiation that balances acquiring the maximum amount of information against potential destruction and the needs of contemporary society. Specific, yet flexible research designs are essential.

People commonly ask the same questions when they visit an excavation. How do you decide where to dig? What tools do you use? Why are your trenches in this configuration? How deep do you excavate? Every site differs in its complexity and special problems, but here are some general principles.

You can decide where to dig on a site by the simple, arbitrary choice of a spot that has yielded a large number of surface finds or one where traces of stone walls or other ancient structures can be seen above ground. When Richard Daugherty dug the Ozette whale-hunting site on the Washington coast, he began by digging through the place where the largest occupation sequence seemed to be. Why? He needed to obtain as complete a cultural sequence as possible. The logical way to do so was to dig through the deepest part of the site. There was, of course, no guarantee that his trench would penetrate to the earliest part of the whale hunters' site. But his choice was a practical way to start attacking the fundamental questions of when and for how long the whale hunters lived at Ozette. Similar decisions have been made at thousands of other sites all over the world.

Sampling

In these days of high digging costs and CRM projects, archaeologists rely more heavily on statistical sampling than their predecessors did. Sampling is used in digging shell heaps or dense accumulations of occupation debris containing thousands of artifacts. Obviously, only a small sample of a large garbage heap can be dug and analyzed. To ensure validity of the statistical samples, some form of unbiased sampling must be used to choose which part of a site is to be dug.

Sampling is the "science of controlling and measuring the reliability of information through the theory of probability." Sampling techniques allow us to ensure a statistically reliable basis of archaeological data from which we can make generalizations about our research data. Most archaeologists make use of **probabilistic sampling**, a means of relating small samples of data in mathematical ways to much larger populations. The classic example of this technique, commonly used in the disciplines of statistics and statistical theory, is the political opinion poll, testing national feelings from tiny samples, perhaps as few as 1,500 people. In archaeology, probabilistic sampling improves the likelihood that the conclusions reached from a survey or excavation on the basis of the samples are relatively reliable.

The use of formal sampling techniques in archaeology is still in an early stage. Simple **random sampling** is used when nothing is known ahead of excavation. It can be used, for example, when an archaeologist wishes to obtain an unbiased sample of artifacts from an ancient shell mound. One can arrive at this result by laying out a rectangular grid of squares on a site and then selecting the squares to be dug by using a table of random numbers. The excavated samples are thus chosen at random, rather than on the basis of surface finds or other considerations.

Stratified sampling, whereby the investigator uses previous knowledge of an area, such as its topographic variation, to structure further research, enables one to sample some selected units intensively, others less thoroughly.

Archaeological sampling, based as it is on descriptive and inferential statistics, is a complex subject. I urge you to consult the references at the back of this book.

Site Testing

In these days of subsurface radar technology and sophisticated geomorphological studies, site testing has become more sophisticated than it was even a few years ago. However, a number of testing approaches amplify such data or are used as stand-alone ways of deciding whether a site is worth further investigation or to establish its date, function, or type of occupation. Such methods are especially important on CRM projects.

Augurs and other forms of borers can be used to explore archaeological deposits—especially hydraulic corers, which provide column samples of subsurface layers and allow one to follow conspicuous or distinctive strata over considerable distances, even if they are buried far beneath the surface.

However, the **test pit** remains the most useful way of obtaining preliminary information on stratigraphy and culture history in advance of larger-scale excavation. Some test trenches are small control pits, dug carefully as a way of anticipating subsurface stratigraphy and occupation layers. Such excavations are reference points for planning an entire dig. More often, test pits are laid out in lines and over considerable distances to establish the extent of a site and the basic stratigraphy in different areas (see Figure 7.3 on page 137). Sometimes their locations are selected by statistical means, other times on the basis of surface finds or exposed features. Kent Flannery once called such trenches "telephone booths," an apt description of small cuttings placed to acquire highly specific information.

Figure 7.3 A line of test pits at Quirigua, a Maya ceremonial center, laid out at 49.2-foot (15-meter) intervals and aligned with the site grid.

Shovel pits are a variation on the test pit theme, usually used in surface survey to trace occupation deposits. They are little more than small holes dug with a shovel a few inches below the surface and are much used to establish the boundaries of shallow settlement sites and features.

Vertical Excavation

The layout of small digs is determined not only by surface features, density of surface finds, or sampling techniques, but by available funds as well. Most excavations are run on a shoestring, so small-scale operations have to be used to solve complex problems with minimal expenditure of time and money. Some of the world's most important sites have been excavated on a small scale by **vertical excavation**, digging limited areas for specific information on dating and stratigraphy (see Figure 7.4 on page 138). Vertical trenches can be used to obtain artifact samples, to establish sequences of ancient building construction or histories of complex earthworks, and to salvage sites threatened with destruction. The small trenches are often dug in areas where the deposits are likely to be of maximal thickness or where important structures may be found. Much vertical excavation consists of long cross sections cut across mounds, buildings, or other structures designed to establish their chronology and architectural sequence.

Vertical excavation comes into its own in small sites such as caves and rockshelters, where space is limited and the excavators have to cope with hidden boulders from ancient rock falls and other such obstructions. Sometimes the deposits spill out from the cave itself to the steep slope in front of the site, necessitating the use of a long, stepped vertical cutting, as was the case at the *Klasies River Cave* in South Africa, which records some of the earliest activities of *Homo sapiens* in tropical Africa. Vertical excavation is also important when investigating the banks and ditches of such sites as Roman forts or Iron Age encampments like *Maiden Castle* in Europe, and is widely used when investigating *Aden* and Hopewell burial mounds in North America.

Area, or Horizontal, Excavation

Large-scale excavations are normally used to uncover wider areas of a site. These **area excavations**, or **horizontal excavations**, used to uncover house plans and settlement layouts, are expensive (see Figure 7.5 on page 139). As a general rule, the only sites that are completely excavated are very small hunter-gatherer camps, isolated structures, and burial mounds. With larger settlements, all one can do is excavate several portions of the site in order to sample areas representative of the entire settlement. Again, modern archaeological ethics require minimal horizontal excavation consistent with the carefully controlled objectives of the investigation.

Figure 7.4 Vertical excavation on a British Iron Age hill fort and its fortifications in 1937: a classic example of Mortimer Wheeler's meticulous excavation methods, which were the foundation of modern excavation methods in Europe.

Area excavations expose large, open areas of ground to a depth of several feet. A complex network of walls, houses, or abandoned storage pits may lie within the site. Each of these ancient features relates to other structures, a relationship that must be carefully recorded if the site is to be interpreted correctly, as was the case at the Koster site. Horizontal excavation exposes large parts of a site, but the excavator is confronted with the problem of maintaining stratigraphic control from one side of the trench to the other. Many area excavations are organized on grid systems, which allow walls (often called balks) to be left between adjoining squares.

Horizontal excavation is highly effective with small hunter-gatherer sites, such as the artifact-and-bone scatters at Olduvai Gorge and other early human sites in East Africa, where the position of every stone flake and animal bone is recorded in place. Such an approach also works well with complex structures like Iroquois longhouses, which survive as complexes of decayed wooden postholes buried under a few inches of topsoil (see Figure 7.6 on page 139). Such structures were often expanded, rebuilt, or sited on top of another structure, resulting in a jigsaw of posthole patterns that can only be deciphered with a large area excavation. Perhaps the most remarkable horizontal excavations are those of historic gardens, among them King Henry VIII's private garden at Hampton Court by the River Thames in London (see the chapter-opener photo on page 131). Archaeologist Brian Dix located long-vanished flower beds, paths, and other features with a huge area excavation that exposed the entire buried garden, which was then reconstructed for modern visitors.

Large open area excavations require accurate recording over considerable distances, made much easier when the position of houses and finds can be recorded with a **total data station**, an electronic distance-measuring device with recording computer, which records data that can be downloaded into laptop computers at the end of the day's work.

Figure 7.5 An open plan, horizontal excavation on the Iron Age hill fort at Danebury, England. The Danebury research was carried out over many years, and the research designs were constantly modified.

Figure 7.6 Area excavation of an Iroquois longhouse near Onondaga, New York. The small stakes indicate positions of house wall posts; placement of hearth areas and support posts can be seen inside the walls. The Iroquois Nations dominated much of the North American Northeast in the centuries before Europeans arrived. Many settlements comprised close groupings of fortified longhouses.

Figure 7.7 Excavations under a high-rise building in the heart of the City of London show the complexities of modern urban archaeology.

Any form of horizontal excavation is expensive, even if earthmoving machinery is used to remove sterile overburden, but it provides a unique overall, horizontal view of human occupation or of entire human settlements obtainable in no other way.

There are numerous variations on the vertical and horizontal excavation theme, depending on the circumstances of the dig, the funding available, and the time available. In these days of tightly scheduled CRM excavations, a combination of excavation methods is used to acquire and record the maximum amount of information in the most cost-effective manner possible while maintaining high scientific standards. Some of the most complex excavations are conducted underground, such as those in London deep under high-rise buildings and in subway stations (see Figure 7.7).

Digging, Tools, and People

How do you do the digging? Much depends on the type of site you are excavating. A huge burial mound on the Ohio River may be more than 20 feet (6 meters) deep. Much of the sterile deposit covering the burial levels is removed with earthmoving machinery and picks and shovels. Earthmoving machinery in particular is now widely used on CRM excavations to save time, where its use has been brought to a fine art, involving minimal destruction. But as soon as the archaeologists reach layers in which finds are expected, they dig with meticulous care, removing each layer in turn, recording the exact position of their finds upon discovery. Smaller caves or cemeteries are excavated centimeter by centimeter. The earth surrounding the finds is passed through fine screens so that tiny beads, fish bones, and myriad small items can be found.

Excavation is in part a recording process, and accuracy is essential. The records will never be precise unless the dig is kept tidy at all times. The trench walls must always be straight. Why? So you can record the layers you are digging and follow them across the site. Surplus soil is dumped well away from the trenches so it does not cascade into the dig or have to be shifted when new areas are opened. The excavation is a laboratory and should be treated as such.

All archaeological digs are headed by a director, who is responsible both for organizing the excavation and for overseeing the specialists and diggers. Many larger academic and CRM digs involve a team of specialist experts who work alongside the excavators. When digging the famous Late Bronze Age site of about 1100 B.C. at *Flag Fen* in eastern England, archaeologist Francis Pryor worked with a timber expert, a paleontologist, soil scientists, experts on ancient metallurgy and mammal bones, even a specialist in prehistoric beetles. The only way to study this complex site was to develop a team approach that looked at the site in a broad environmental setting. A really large excavation in Mesopotamia or Mesoamerica can involve dozens of people—specialist archaeologists, a team of resident experts in other fields including an architect, graduate student trainees, and volunteer or paid workers who do much of the actual excavation. CRM projects involve closely knit teams of professional excavators and specialists who ensure compliance and proper recovery and interpretation of data.

In Chapter 15, we describe some of the ways in which you can obtain digging experience.

The traditional symbols of the archaeologist at work are the shovel and the triangular-bladed bricklayer's trowel. In fact, archaeologists use many other digging tools in their work. Earthmoving machinery, once despised, has become a necessity in these days of high costs and rapid-moving CRM excavation driven by contractors' deadlines. In the hands of an expert operator, a front loader or bulldozer or backhoe with toothless bucket are remarkably delicate implements for removing sterile soil and surprisingly thin slivers of overburden. On occasion, earthmoving equipment has been used to excavate sites doomed in the face of road construction. The right piece of equipment is capable of removing even thin arbitrary levels of a site with soft deposits, which are then passed through screens to recover the artifacts in them. Meanwhile, the archaeologists focus on hand excavation of important features.

Despite widespread use of mechanical earthmovers, most excavation still proceeds by hand. Picks, shovels, and long-handled spades carry the brunt of the heavy work. But the most common archaeological tool used in North America is the diamond-shaped trowel with straight edges and a sharp tip. With it, soil can be eased from a delicate specimen or an unusual discoloration in the soil can be scraped clean. Trowels are used for tracing delicate layers in walls, clearing small pits, and other exacting jobs. They are rarely out of the digger's hand.

Household brushes and paintbrushes often come in handy, the former for soft, dry sediments and for cleaning trenches, and the latter for freeing fragile objects from the soil. Even fine artists' brushes have their uses—cleaning beads, decaying ironwork, or fine bones. Enterprising archaeologists visit their dentists regularly, if only to obtain regular supplies of worn-out dental instruments, which make first-rate fine-digging tools! And so do 6-inch (15-centimeter) nails ground to different shapes. A set of fine screens for sifting soil for small finds, several notebooks and graph paper, tapes, plumb bobs, surveyors' levels, and a compass are just a few of the items that archaeologists need to record their excavations and process their finds. Increasingly, laptop computers, portable GPS units, and electronic recording equipment are part of the archaeologist's field kit because they provide fast, accurate ways of recording features, finds, and stratigraphy.

Recording

No dig is worth more than its records. Excavation notebooks provide a day-to-day record of each trench, of new layers and significant finds. Before any trench is measured out, the entire site is laid out on a grid of squares (see Figure 7.8a on page 142). Important finds, or details of a house or a storage pit, are measured on the site plan by simple three-dimensional measuring techniques or with an electronic recording instrument (see Figure 7.8b). It is information from your records, as well as the artifacts from the dig, that form the priceless archive of your excavation. If the records are incomplete, the dig is little better than a treasure hunt.

Stratigraphic Observation

The laws of superposition and association lie at the very core of archaeology, for they provide the context of archaeological finds in time and space. The layers of archaeological sites, be they natural or humanly created, form much quicker than geological levels, but they are subject to the same law of superposition. Thus the excavated stratigraphic profiles through an archaeological site represent a sequence of layers that have formed through time. Stratigraphic observation is the process of recording, studying, and evaluating stratified layers in archaeological sites, layers that were deposited horizontally, but are studied in the vertical (time) dimension.

Stratigraphic observation involves not only recording the layers, but confirming that they do, in fact, represent a sequence in time. Many factors can disturb stratified layers. For instance, rabbits can burrow through soft earth, or later occupants of a house may dig into underlying layers to construct storage pits, build foundations, or even bury the dead. This is where the law of association comes in, for the artifacts associated with stratified, undisturbed archaeological layers can then be placed in a relative chronology, and, if radiocarbon samples are dated from one or more layers, perhaps in an absolute one as well (see Figure 7.9 on page 143). Thus, accurate stratigraphic observation is the cornerstone of all excavation, for it provides the context for the studies of artifacts and human behavior that are the central goals of all excavation.

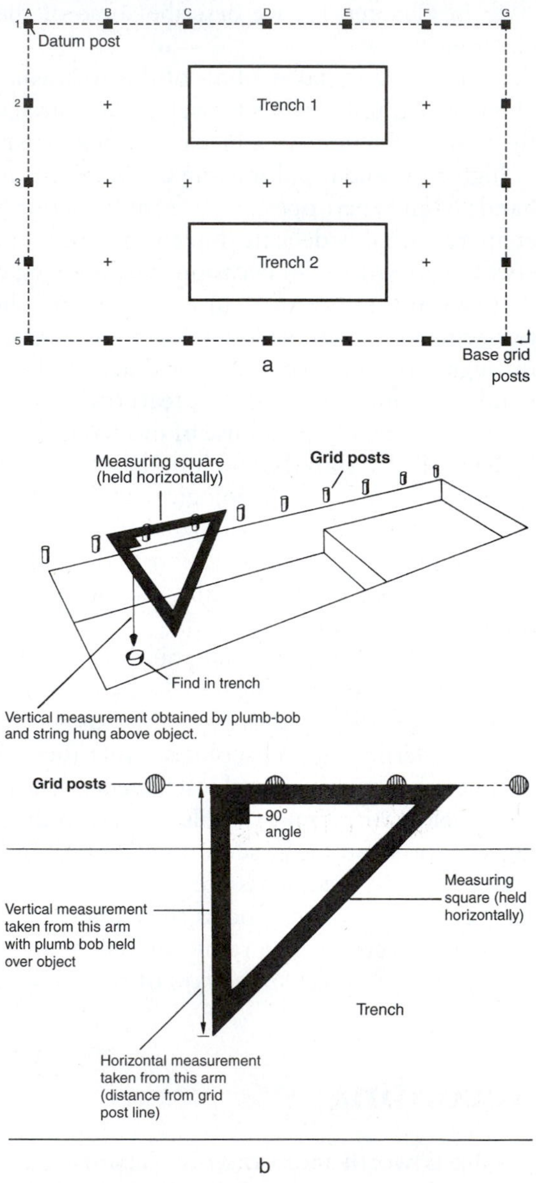

Figure 7.8 (a) Two trenches laid out with a grid. (b) Three-dimensional recording of the position of an object using the grid squares.

Reading a stratigraphic profile is an art, for you have not only to record the layers, but to interpret them as well, taking account of the natural formation processes as well as of human activities. This means watching for the subtle color changes resulting from the decay of adobe brick on pueblo sites; the thin lines of

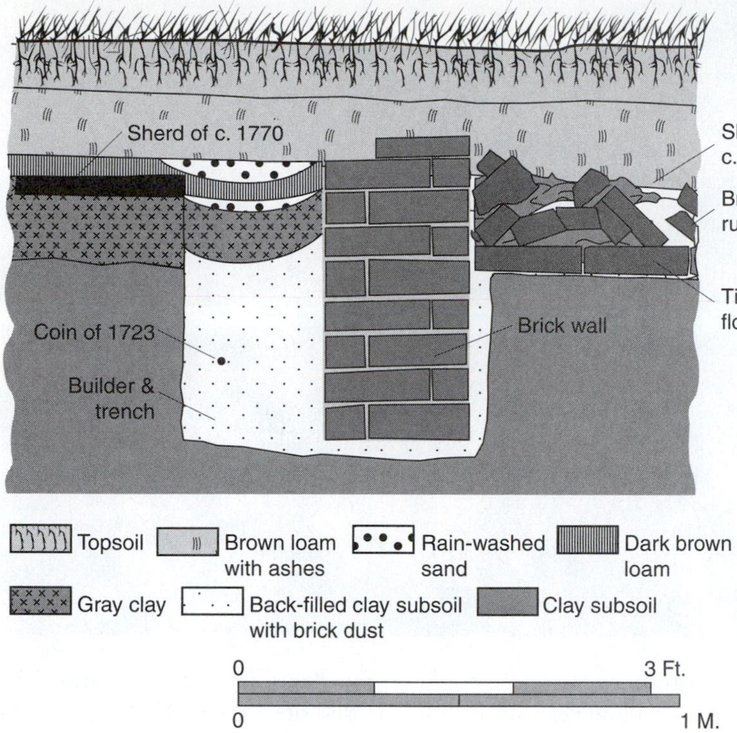

Figure 7.9 Dating the construction and the destruction of a building at *Colonial Williamsburg,* Virginia, by its associated artifacts. Judging from the coin of A.D. 1723, the builder's trench for the stone wall was dug no earlier than 1723, and the building fell into ruin before 1820.

hearths used for a short time, whose edges have spilled down a slight slope; and the loosely packed outline of a rabbit burrow used and abandoned many centuries ago. Often the changes are so subtle that they appear only as a slight color change or a minute difference in the texture of the soil. Only patience produces an accurate interpretation of a stratigraphic profile—looking at the trench wall in different lights, at dawn or in the oblique light of evening, wetting down dry strata with a fine water spray, even looking at the wall from below. All these tricks and many others help you interpret complex stratigraphic jigsaw puzzles, even on small sites.

Let us now turn from general principles to some specific excavation problems that will give you an insight into the multitude of challenges awaiting fieldworkers. As we indicated in Chapter 3, archaeological sites, in all shapes and sizes, are the basis for all field investigations. All contain traces of human activity in the form of artifacts, structures, and food remains. Archaeologists most commonly classify sites by their functions—that is to say, by the activities that took place within them. It is no coincidence that these various site categories present different excavation problems.

Excavation Problems

Open Campsites and Villages

Small sites, often little more than scatters of artifacts that were once places where specific tasks were performed, are probably the most common archaeological sites. However, the most obvious and most interesting locations are habitation sites, places where people have

Figure 7.10 Excavations on a hominin site at Bouri in Ethiopia's arid Afar Depression. The 2.5-million-year-old deposits at this site have yielded the world's earliest evidence for meat and marrow butchery with stone tools. A cranium of *Australopithecus garhi* was found nearby. The excavation was conducted with meticulous care, using brushes and small tools.

lived and carried out many activities. Hunter-gatherers have occupied temporary camps for short periods since the earliest millennia of prehistory. Where preservation conditions are good, archaeologists can sometimes identify such settlements, represented by concentrations of stone artifacts and broken animal bones, as well as the stone foundations of long-abandoned brush shelters. Such concentrations have been found in the Great Basin of the American West, in the arctic North, and also in sub-Saharan Africa.

Many hunter-gatherer camps are hard to identify from the surviving archaeological record (see Figure 7.10). The same is not true of later farming villages, which were usually occupied longer, resulting in the accumulation of considerable quantities of occupation debris as well as substantial house foundations. In about 9500 B.C., the inhabitants of the Abu Hureyra village in Syria's Euphrates Valley dwelt in a tiny settlement of square, mudbrick houses with courtyards, separated by narrow alleyways. The house foundations and numerous animal bones, as well as other artifacts, enabled excavator Andrew Moore to trace the extent and nature of the settlement. Iroquois farmers in the northeastern United States built substantial wood and bark longhouses, which were occupied over several generations and constantly modified (see Figure 7.6 on page 139). The decayed postholes from the walls provide an excellent record of Iroquois dwellings, often clustered in close juxtaposition in palisaded settlements.

Caves and Rockshelters

Cave people, complete with clubs, long hair, and brutish manners, are one of the popular stereotypes of newspaper cartoonists. Caves and convenient rocky overhangs did indeed serve as human dwellings from very early times, but were by no means the only home bases used by hunter-gatherers. The Late Ice Age Cro-Magnon people of southwestern France, famous for their rock art, occupied great rockshelters and caves in the deep river valleys of the Dordogne during the late Ice Age, between about 40,000 and 12,000 years ago. The *Danger* and *Hogup* caves in Utah reflect thousands of years of hunter-gatherer occupation. The dry environment of the desert preserved wood objects and basketry as well as minute details of economic life. And the dry caves of Tehuacán Valley in south-central Mexico provide part of the history of how maize cultivation developed in the New World.

Cave and rockshelter excavations are some of the hardest digs to carry out successfully (see Figure 7.11). The ground below cliff overhangs usually consists of ash and other debris piled up through successive human occupations. Sterile soils may interrupt this sequence of habitation, representing periods when the site was abandoned. Excavating such complicated sequences is slow and meticulous work. The trenches are usually restricted by the size of the shelter. Each hearth and small occupation layer has to be isolated from the others during excavation.

Many cave and rockshelter excavations deal purely with dating and stratigraphy, but others are more ambitious. When Hallam Movius dug the *Abri Pataud* rockshelter in southwestern France, he had to record at least six layers of human occupation dated to between 40,000 and 19,000 years ago, extending through more than 20 feet (6 meters) of stratified deposit. The site was excavated following a coordinated master plan that involved not only archaeologists but botanists, geologists, and other specialists as well. Movius was able to record minute changes in tool types as well as many details of the changing hunting and gathering practices of Abri Pataud's inhabitants.

Mound Sites

Occupation mounds (often called **tells** in southwestern Asia) are common in many parts of the world. Mound sites result when the same site is occupied for centuries, even thousands of years. Successive generations lived atop their predecessors' settlements. The

Figure 7.11 A meticulous excavation in Boomplaas cave, South Africa. Stone Age hunters visited the site for short periods over thousands of years. The excavators removed tiny layers of deposit, recording the positions of individual artifacts with the aid of a grid suspended from the cave roof.

Figure 7.12 Excavation of a city mound. Extensive trenching over many seasons into the ancient city of *Ashkelon* in Israel reveals structures in the Bronze Age levels.

result is a gradual accumulation of occupation debris, which, when excavated, provides a complicated picture of occupation levels. Even a small mound can cost a fortune to excavate, simply because the lowest levels are so deeply buried below the surface. A huge mound such as that of Ur in Mesopotamia, or even a relatively small mound like *Tepe Yahya* in Iran, can be sampled only by large trenches that cut into the sides of the mound in a series of great steps, or by very large-scale excavation indeed, using a combination of vertical and area trenches (see Figure 7.12).

There is far more to excavating an occupation mound than merely stripping off successive layers. So many natural and artificial processes, ranging from wind erosion to human activity, can change the stratigraphy of a site of this type that each presents a challenging new excavation problem.

Burial mounds, as opposed to occupation mounds, come in many configurations, ranging from conical tumuli to long communal sepulchers and elaborate tombs built for Siberian chiefs. These mounds, such as those used by Bronze Age people in Britain or the Hopewell folk of eastern North America, present complex excavation problems, often requiring total excavation. In many cases, the mounds were built in stages or the dead were buried in them at different times, long after the identity of the original occupants was forgotten. A generation ago, such mounds were often excavated completely, exposing the ancient land surface. Today, very carefully placed vertical trenches are most commonly used, with excavation being used only to answer specific questions. For example, at *Easton Down* near Avebury in England, archaeologist Alisdair Whittle excavated part of a communal burial mound to acquire pollen and mollusk samples that showed the mound had been erected on open grassland.

Earthworks and Forts

Many peoples—Iron Age peasants in western Europe, Maori warriors in New Zealand, Hopewell Indians in Ohio—built extensive earth fortifications to protect their settlements and sacred places. The Ohio earthworks enclose large areas of ground, but no one

Figure 7.13 The Iron Age hill fort at Maiden Castle, southern England; its extensive earthworks were excavated by Mortimer Wheeler.

knows exactly why such earthworks were undertaken. To excavate them would require both vertical excavation to record cross sections across the earthworks, and area investigation to uncover the layout of the structures built inside the earthworks. Such excavations were carried out on the great prehistoric fortress at Maiden Castle, England, many years ago. The massive earthworks of Maiden Castle were stormed by a Roman legion in A.D. 43. By careful excavation and use of historical data, the excavator Mortimer Wheeler was able to provide a blow-by-blow description of the battle for the fortress (see Figure 7.13).

> For a space, confusion and massacre dominated the scene. Men and women, young and old, were savagely cut down, before the legionaries were called to heel and the work of systematic destruction began. . . . That night when the fires of the legion shone out (we may imagine, in orderly lines across the valley), the survivors crept forth from their broken stronghold, and in the darkness buried their dead. (1943: 310)

Shell Middens

Shell middens—vast accumulations of abandoned shells, fish bones, and other food remains—are common in many coastal areas of the world. Remarkable results can be attained by studying these dense heaps, especially in reconstructing prehistoric diets (see Chapter 11). The excavation problem is twofold: first, to identify the stratified levels in the middens, and second, to obtain statistically reliable samples of food remains and artifacts from the deposits. Most shell midden digs use random sampling, described very briefly earlier, which employs vertical trenches or test pits. Some midden excavations unfold on a larger scale. We illustrate an example of a meticulous area excavation on a shell midden at *Galatea Bay* in New Zealand (see Figure 7.14 on page 148), where much information on ancient diet was found by using a carefully laid out grid of trenches. The excavation of a shell midden is mostly rather unspectacular, for the detailed statistical results come from laboratory analysis of artifacts rather than from actual digging. The Galatea Bay excavation provided detailed information on the

Figure 7.14 An exemplary area excavation of a shallow shell midden at Galatea Bay, New Zealand. This site was used in the second millennium A.D.

ways the inhabitants utilized different communities of shellfish, such as oysters of various sizes, through time.

Ceremonial and Other Specialist Sites

Some of the world's most famous archaeological sites are ceremonial centers, such as the pyramids of Giza in Egypt or the Maya ceremonial center at Copán, Honduras. Many ceremonial sites are enormous, and, like occupation mounds, present great difficulties for the excavator. Teotihuacán in the Valley of Mexico is, of course, far more than a ceremonial center. It was also a great city, which flourished from 200 B.C. to as late as A.D. 750. Discovering the true significance of the site has involved not only extensive area excavation designed to help reconstruct pyramids and major buildings, but sophisticated mapping and surface survey combined with small-scale excavation. René Millon and other archaeologists have mapped more than 12.5 square miles (20 square kilometers) of Teotihuacán in a survey program combined with excavation. Years of fieldwork have shown that the founders of the great city laid it out on a grid pattern that was followed for centuries. The Pyramids of the Sun and Moon were the original focus of the city, until an unknown but charismatic leader built a palace complex, marketplace, and temple to the Feathered Serpent god Quetzalcoatl in the so-called Cuidadela complex some distance away.

The Acropolis complex at Copán provided an extraordinary challenge to a team of American and Honduran excavators (see Figure 3.8 on page 62). Fortunately for science, the Copán River had exposed the layers of the temple complex. The diggers were able to tunnel into the center of the sacred buildings in an attempt to decipher the history of successive temples built at the same sacred location. No less than 2 miles (3.2 kilometers) of tunnels now burrow under the Acropolis. Tunneling offers a unique three-dimensional view of a building's history, aided in the case of Copán by deciphered Maya glyphs that record the history of the city's ruling dynasty. The excavators have managed to link individual temples buried in the heart of the Acropolis to different rulers between about A.D. 400 and 800.

Artifact patternings play a vital role in interpreting ceremonial centers, trading sites, quarries, and other specialized sites. Do these patterns reflect long-distance trading activity in, say, copper ornaments or seashells? Were marine stingray spines, which are present in ruins appearing to be shrines built hundreds of miles inland from the Gulf of Mexico, used for ritual bloodletting? Questions like these can be answered only by careful studies of spatial associations.

Burials and Cemeteries

The golden mask of the pharaoh Tutankhamun, the refrigerated bodies of Siberian horsemen and women from the Russian permafrost, desiccated mummies of humble folk from northern Chile: Human burials are the stereotypic finds of archaeology, reflecting humanity's abiding concern with the afterlife. The earliest human burials were left by Neanderthal peoples more than 70,000 years ago. Most human societies have paid careful attention to funerals and burials ever since. Burials have been deposited with simple or elaborate grave furniture designed to accompany the owner to the afterlife. People have buried their dead in isolated, shallow graves within their settlement, under hut floors, in special cemeteries, in caves, as cremated remains in jars, and in vast burial mounds. Some burials consist of the body alone; others lie with a few beads or a handful of clay pots. Royal personages were often buried in all their glory: *Shang* dynasty kings in China with their chariots; the rulers of early Ur, Mesopotamia, with their entire court; Maya nobles with their prize treasures; the Moche lords of Sipán in Peru in their full golden regalia. Sometimes, too, the remains of victims of natural catastrophes like earthquakes lie under the ruins of their houses (see Figure 7.15).

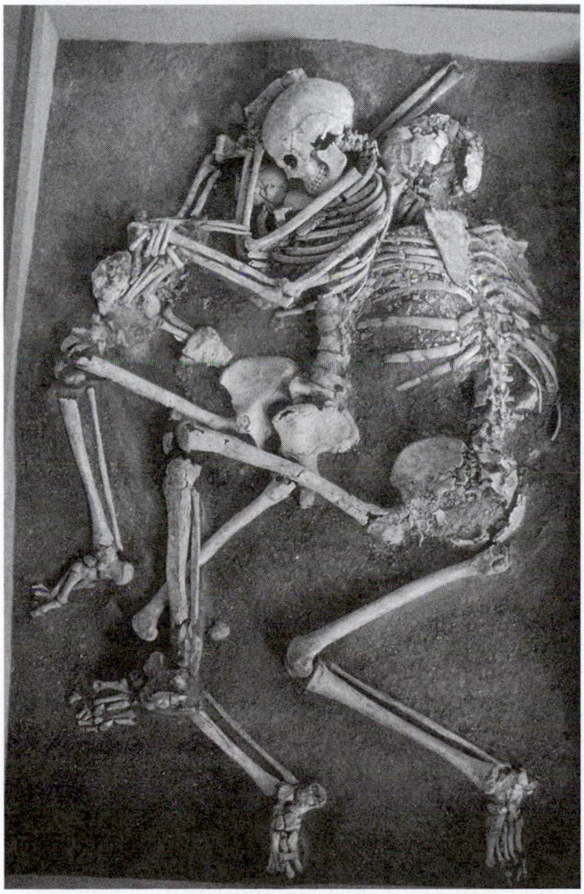

Figure 7.15 Involuntary burial. Earthquake victims at the Roman port of Kourion, Cyprus, killed in a giant temblor in A.D. 265. The family died while sleeping, the child clasped in the mother's arms.

By studying a group of burials from one cemetery, it may be possible to distinguish different social classes by the grave furniture buried with the remains. The common people may take nothing with them; merchants or priests may be buried with distinctive artifacts associated with their status in society. The Adena and Hopewell peoples of North America were much concerned with the afterlife during their heyday 2,000 years ago. From the distribution of the burials and cemeteries in their burial mounds, and from the cult objects and ornaments associated with the skeletons, it may be possible to gain some insights into the social organization of Adena and Hopewell societies (see Chapter 13). And, of course, burials are a fruitful source of information on personal ornamentation and appearance, too, for people were (and still are) often buried in the clothes and ornaments they wore in life. The physical characteristics of the skeletons themselves can provide valuable data on age, nutrition, sex, disease, and medicine.

French archaeologists led by Françoise Dunand have excavated more than 700 skeletons from a cemetery at *Duch,* a remote Egyptian village in the Libyan Desert west of the Nile River, occupied between 100 B.C. and A.D. 400. At least 5,000 people lived in the village during its heyday. The inhabitants of this obscure settlement are better known medically today than they were during their lifetimes. The excavators cleaned the skeletons in place, then x-rayed them with a portable machine hooked up to an on-site generator. They developed a clinical description of each body and took samples of hair, nails, and skin before placing the skeletons in well-protected tombs. This field research provided an extraordinary portrait of the Duch people. They were of Mediterranean physical type, slender and between 5 feet 1 inch and 5 feet 4 inches (1.55 and 1.62 meters) tall. They had pale skin and dark hair, like many ancient Egyptians, and an average life span of about thirty-eight years if they survived infancy. Many of them suffered from osteoarthritis and scoliosis as a result of hard agricultural labor and carrying heavy loads. More than two-thirds of the skeletons showed clear signs of having suffered from malnutrition at some point in their lives. Human skeletons and mummies are the dispassionate medical records of the past that reveal the consequences of years of inadequate diet and backbreaking work.

How do you excavate a burial? Whether digging a large cemetery or a lone burial, each skeleton and its associated grave, ornaments, and grave goods are considered a single excavation problem. Each burial is exposed as a unit that has both internal associations with its accompanying goods and external associations with other burials in the same and other levels. The first step is to identify the grave, either by locating a gravestone or a pile of stones, or from the grave outlines, which may appear as a discoloration in the surrounding soil. Once the grave outlines have been found, individual bones are exposed. The main outline of the burial is traced first. Then you uncover the fingers, toes, and other small bones. You leave the bones in place and take care not to displace any ornaments or grave furniture associated with them. Once the skeleton is exposed and fully cleaned where it lies, the layout of the burial and grave furniture is recorded by drawings and photographs before the skeleton is lifted bone by bone or encased in a cocoon of plaster of paris and metal strips (see Figure 7.15 on page 149).

Reburial and Repatriation

Burial excavation may seem very romantic. In reality it is not only technically demanding, but it raises important ethical questions as well. For years, archaeologists casually dug up Indian burials and other prehistoric graves all over the world, some of them even of people of known tribal or historical identity. Now both Australian Aborigines and Native Americans, among others, are objecting strenuously to excavation and destruction of ancient burial grounds—and with good reason. Why should their ancestors be dug up and displayed in museums, they argue? Many surviving communities retain strong emotional and religious ties with their ancestors, and excavation of their remains flies in the face of their religious beliefs. There are now demands for reburial of human remains stored in museums, especially of those that can be documented to have direct historical links with modern Native American groups.

The Native American Grave Protection and Repatriation Act (NAGPRA) of 1990 establishes two main requirements. First, all federal agencies and museums receiving federal funds are required to inventory their holdings of Native American human remains and associated funerary objects. They must also develop written summaries for religious objects not found in graves, sacred artifacts, and what are called "objects of cultural patrimony" that are in the collections they control. This inventorying process, which will take years to complete, also requires that agencies and museums establish, as best they can, whether their individual holdings have cultural affiliation, or, in the case of skeletons, lineal descendants with living Native American groups. If they do establish such relationships, they are required to notify the relevant Native American organization about the existence of the materials and to offer to repatriate them.

The second requirement protects all Native American graves and other cultural objects found within archaeological sites on federal and tribal land. This requirement encourages the in situ preservation of archaeological sites, or at least those parts of them that contain graves. It also requires anyone carrying out archaeological investigation on federal and tribal lands to consult with affiliated or potentially affiliated Native Americans concerning the treatment and disposition of any finds, whether made during formal investigations or by accident.

NAGPRA is having a profound effect on the way in which American archaeologists go about their business, for it mandates a level of consultation and concern for Native American rights that is far greater than has been the norm in the United States. This is quite apart from the scientific impact on the study of ancient Native American populations. The Native American Rights Fund estimates that as many as 600,000 Native American human skeletons may be in museums, historical societies, universities, and private collections. The signing of the 1990 act came after years of controversy that pitted, and still pits, Native Americans against scientists. The archaeologists and anthropologists point out that revolutionary new research techniques are beginning to yield a mine of new information about prehistoric North Americans. To rebury the database for such research would deprive science, and future generations of Americans, of a vital resource, they argue. Others, including some archaeologists, respond that this is an ethical and moral issue, and such considerations should outweigh any potential scientific gains. Native Americans feel deeply about repatriation for many complex reasons—if nothing else because they are concerned about preserving old traditions and values as a way of addressing current social ills.

Furious controversy sometimes surrounds newly discovered burials, like the recent case of a 9,000-year-old skeleton unearthed at *Kennewick,* Washington, where local Native American groups claimed ownership. This claim pitted them against the U.S. Army Corps of Engineers. The case ended up in litigation, with the courts finally allowing scientific study of the bones.

There will be no quick resolution of the repatriation issue, however promptly and sensitively archaeologists and their institutions respond to Native American concerns and comply with the provisions of the 1990 act. Only one thing is certain: No archaeologist in North America, and probably elsewhere, will be able to excavate a prehistoric or historic burial without the most careful and sensitive preparation. This involves working closely with native peoples in ways that archaeologists have not imagined until recently. Nothing but good can come of this.

SUMMARY

1. The process of archaeological research, including excavation, begins with the formulation of a comprehensive research design.
2. The design is then implemented; data are acquired in the field through excavation and then processed and analyzed in the laboratory.
3. Interpretation using anthropological and historical models is followed by final publication.
4. The research design is developed to answer specific questions and to acquire the maximum information with minimal disturbance of the finite archaeological record.
5. Excavation itself is a meticulous process of recording both finds and their context in time and space.
6. Vertical and test excavations are used to test and study stratigraphic sequences. Horizontal excavations uncover large areas of a site—for example, an entire Iroquois longhouse.
7. Stratigraphic recording is based on the principle of superposition, with care being taken to distinguish natural and humanly caused disturbances, such as animal burrows or garbage pits.
8. The chapter reviews the distinctive excavation problems associated with various types of archaeological sites, among them habitations, caves and rockshelters, burials, and shell middens.
9. Special problems surround human burials, which, in North America, are subject to stringent regulations surrounding their reburial and repatriation.

EIGHT

Archaeological Classification and Ancient Technologies

A Moche animal effigy adorned with gilded copper discs from Huaca de La Luna, Platform 1, Peru.

CHAPTER OUTLINE

PREVIEW

Chapter 8 is concerned with artifacts and ancient technologies. The classification of artifacts is a controversial subject, involving the use of statistical methods and a variety of different "types of types," including descriptive, functional, and stylistic types. At a larger scale, archaeologists rely on a hierarchy of archaeological units such as components and phases to order artifacts in time and space. After discussing the basics of the classification of artifacts, we review the major ancient technologies, from simple stone artifacts to elaborate iron objects and fine textiles.

> *Fieldwork has always been what defines archaeology in the popular imagination. . . . To most people, archaeologists are either working on a dig or writing a book about their exciting finds. The part in between the exciting discoveries and the published report receives little, if any, attention.*
>
> —Charles R. Ewen, *Artifacts,* 2003

Fresh air, modest (sometimes hectic) exercise, the potential for spectacular discoveries, a constant stream of challenging stratigraphic problems—nearly all archaeologists enjoy excavation or survey work most of all. They dread the moment of truth when they return to base with truckloads of stone tools or potsherds and confront an uncomfortable reality: Most of the work still lies ahead, and much of it is the routine work of sorting and artifact classification. I vividly remember once returning from the field with a 3-ton truckload of potsherds and animal bones from a densely occupied African village. We piled dozens of cartons in a corner of the laboratory. As I looked over the pile, I suddenly realized that I would hardly see the open air for months!

For all their wearing routine, the classification of artifacts and the study of ancient technology, discussed in this chapter, are both challenging and fascinating,

Back from the Field

The elaborate process of analysis and classification of finds of all kinds starts in the field alongside excavation—processing and organizing the finds so that they can be analyzed. These first stages in processing newly excavated archaeological finds are entirely routine (see Figure 8.1 on page 155). Most larger excavations maintain some form of field laboratory. It is here that the major site records are maintained, stratigraphic profile drawings are kept up to date, and radiocarbon samples and other special finds are packed for examination by specialists. A small team staffs the field laboratory. They ensure that all finds are cleaned, processed promptly, packed carefully, and labeled and recorded precisely. A successful laboratory operation allows the director of the excavation to evaluate the available data daily, even hourly. It is here, too, that basic conservation work is carried out: reassembling fragmented pots, hardening bones with chemicals, or stabilizing fragile objects. Computers play an important role in the field laboratory, for they are used to code vast quantities of information for later use.

The analysis continues back in the home laboratory, whether a short ceramic study for a small-scale CRM project or an enormous, years-long activity that results from a long-term survey or excavation. You need a good eye for detail, an orderly mind, and, above all, infinite patience. It takes weeks to sort and classify even a relatively small artifact collection.

Successful artifact analysis revolves around classification and typology, two fundamental archaeological skills.

Classification and Taxonomy

Our attitude toward life and our surroundings involves constant classification and sorting of massive quantities of data. Driving along the freeway this morning, I found myself unconsciously classifying the tide of automobiles on the road: luxury sedans, sport utility vehicles, pickups, vans. Then there were Chevrolets, Chryslers, Fords, Mercedes, and so on, all of them in different colors and model configurations. We never stop classifying artifacts, people, our surroundings. We classify types of eating utensils: knives, forks, and spoons—each type has a different use and is kept in a separate compartment in the drawer. In addition to classifying artifacts, lifestyles, and cultures, we make choices among them. If we are eating soup, we choose to use a spoon. Some people eat rice with a fork, some use chopsticks or their fingers, and others have decided that a spoon is more suitable. A variety of choices is available, but the final decision is often dictated by cultural custom rather than by functional pragmatism.

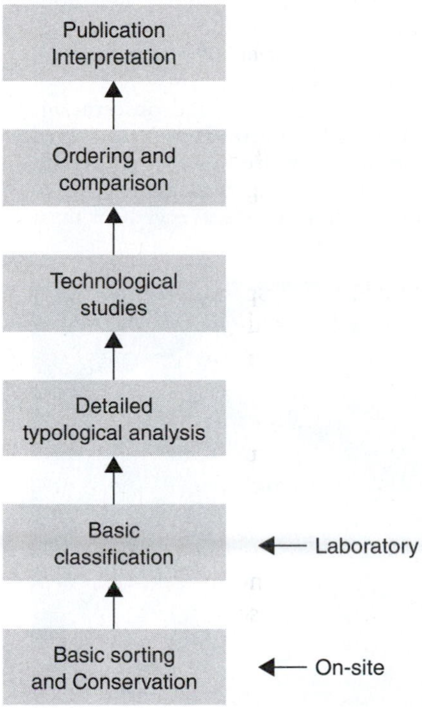

Figure 8.1 Classifying a potsherd collection. The basic stages of simple classification.

Everyone "classifies" because doing so is a requirement for abstract thought and language. Classification, in archaeology, is the process of dividing artifacts and other data into discrete types. Like the computer, however, classification should be a servant rather than a master. In archaeology, classification is a research tool, a means for creating data. All classifications used by archaeologists follow directly from the problems they are studying. Let us say that our excavator is studying changes in pottery designs over a 500-year period in the Southwest. The classification he or she uses will follow not only from what other people have done but also from the problems being studied. How and even what you classify stems directly from the research questions asked of the data.

Taxonomy is a system for classifying materials, objects, and phenomena used in many sciences, including archaeology. The taxonomies of biology, botany, geology, and some other disciplines are highly sophisticated systems that were mainly created in the nineteenth century and early in the twentieth. For example, biologists classify human beings within a hierarchy developed by Carolus Linnaeus in the eighteenth century. It begins with the kingdom Animalia, the phylum Chordata (animals with notochords and gill slits), the subphylum Vertebrata (animals with backbones), the class Mammalia, the subclass Eutheria, the order Primates, the suborder Hominoidea (apes and hominidae), the family Homininae, the genus *Homo,* the species *sapiens.* This hierarchy is gradually

Discovery

EARLY ANCESTOR: *AUSTRALOPITHECUS GARHI* IN ETHIOPIA, 2001

As scientists delve ever more deeply into the earliest chapters of human evolution, they find that changing primate behavior was a critical driving force in the emergence of toolmaking humans. The spectacular discoveries of recent years have shown that a great variety of hominin forms flourished on the East African savanna 2.5 million years ago. But when paleoanthropologist Tim White and his colleagues found *Australopithecus garhi,* they discovered a hominin with a remarkable mix of human and more ape-like features (see Figure 8.2). (The word *garhi* means "surprise" in the local Afar dialect.) The new find, believed to be about 3.2 million years old, has a primitive-looking projecting face and a small brain case but exceptionally large back teeth, a unique feature. Other fossilized bones at the same site show that *Australopithecus garhi* had long, human-like legs and stood about 4 feet 10 inches (1.47 m) tall. However, its forearms were still ape-like and long. These features place the new hominin find midway between the even more primitive, and older, *Australopithecus afarensis,* represented by paleoanthropologist Don Johanson's famous "Lucy," and the earliest known forms of true humans.

Adjacent to the hominin fossil site, a team of archaeologists found broken and crushed antelope and wild horse bones bearing cut marks and gouges, perhaps made by stone tools, although none were found at the site. The fossilized bones were crushed at the ends, as if hominins had used hammerstones to get at the marrow. Although this is not direct evidence that the hominins actually used stone tools and butchered the animals, it is certainly strong circumstantial evidence for such practices over 3 million years ago. Using stone tools to obtain meat and marrow could have been a major breakthrough in early hominin evolution, for such artifacts improved our remote ancestors' ability to feed themselves in a much wider range of settings. Regular access to highly nutritious foods such as bone marrow may have contributed to the evolution of larger hominin brain sizes.

Controlled experiments and observations on East Africa's Serengeti Plains have moved archaeologists away from early interpretations of our first ancestors as hunters. Most experts now believe they scavenged for meat from predator kills.

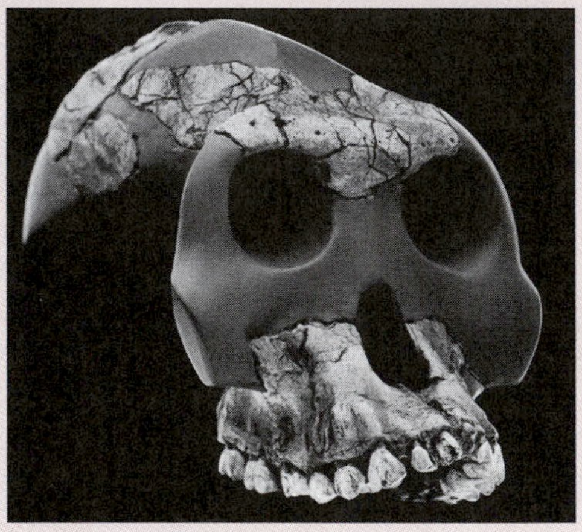

Figure 8.2 Australopithecus garhi.

refined until only *Homo sapiens* remains in its own taxonomic niche. It consists of a hierarchy of units. Each element in the hierarchy is defined and related to the others.

Archaeology has built its own taxonomy of specialist terminologies and concepts quite haphazardly. Archaeological taxonomies have three major objectives:

- *Organizing Data into Manageable Units.* This step is part of the preliminary data processing operation, and it commonly involves separating finds on the basis of raw material (stone, bone, and so on) or artifacts from food remains. This preliminary ordering allows much more detailed classification later on.
- *Describing Types.* By identifying the individual features (attributes) of hundreds of artifacts, or clusters of artifacts, the archaeologist can group them, by common attributes, into relatively few types. These **types** represent patterns of separate associations of attributes. Such types are economical ways of describing large numbers of artifacts. Which attributes are chosen depends on the purpose of the classification. Artifact types

(sometimes called archaeological types) are based on criteria set up by archaeologists as a convenient way of studying ancient toolkits and technology. They are a useful scientific device that provides a manageable way of classifying small and large collections of prehistoric tools and the by-products from manufacturing them.

- *Identifying Relationships between Types.* Describing types orders the relationships among artifacts. These stem, in part, from the use of a variety of raw materials, manufacturing techniques, and functions.

These three objectives are much used in culture-historical research. The advent of computers and statistical approaches to artifact classification have added a fourth objective:

- *Studying Assemblage Variability in the Archaeological Record.* These studies are often combined with ethnographic analogy or formal experiments with replicated technologies.

Archaeological classifications are artificial formulations based on criteria set up by archaeologists. These classificatory systems, however, do not necessarily coincide with those developed by the people who made the original artifacts.

Typology

Typology is a system of classification based on the construction of types. It is a search for patterns among either objects or the variables that define these objects, a search that has taken on added meaning and complexity as archaeologists have begun to use computer technology and sophisticated statistical methods.

Typology enables archaeologists to construct arbitrarily defined units of analysis that apply to two or more samples of artifacts, so that these samples can be compared objectively. These samples can come from different sites or from separate levels of the same site. Typology is classification to permit comparison, an opportunity to examine underlying patterns of human design and behavior. The value of typology is that it enables you to compare what has been found at two sites or in different levels of the same site. Typology, as James Deetz (1967: 111) puts it, has one main aim: "classification which permits comparison. . . . Such a comparison allows the archaeologist to align his assemblage with others in time and space." Let us look over the shoulders of a group of archaeologists as they sort through a large pile of potsherds, from one occupation level, on the laboratory table.

First the sherds are separated by decoration or lack of it, **paste**, **temper**, firing methods, and vessel shape (see Figure 8.3 on page 158). Once the undecorated or shapeless potsherds have been counted and weighed, they are put to one side, unless they have some special significance. Then the remaining sherds are examined individually and divided into types, according to the features they display. Some potsherds stand out because they enable one to distinguish different vessel functions—globular pots, shallow bowls, and so on, which provides one basis for type classification by function. Many sherds tell one little about vessel form or function, but they bear different painted designs, a basis for distinguishing different styles. The classifier piles them on the table by style of decoration: One pile consists of sherds painted with black designs; a second, red-painted fragments; a third, a group of plain sherds. Once the preliminary sort is completed, the archaeologists look over each pile in turn. They have already identified three broad types in the pottery collection. But when they examine the first pile more closely, they find that the black-painted sherds can be divided into several smaller groupings: one with square, black panels; another with diamond designs; and a third with black-dotted decoration. In the end, the researchers may identify three functional types and perhaps eight or nine stylistic types on the

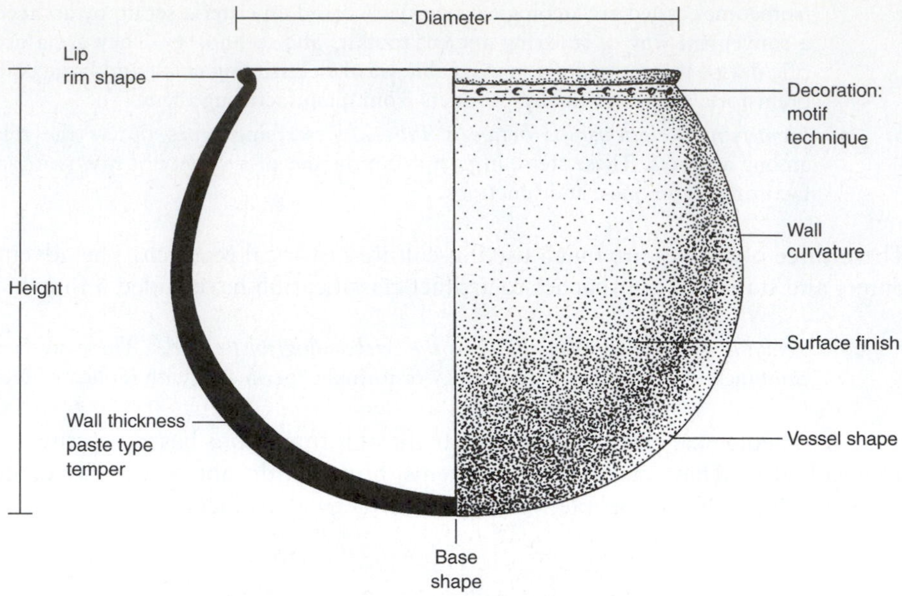

Figure 8.3 Some common attributes of a clay vessel. Specific attributes that could be listed for this pot are concave shoulder, dot and drag decoration, **mica** temper, round base, and thickness of wall at base.

basis of decoration and other stylistic features, each, perhaps, with several subtypes. The archaeologists study the collection in minute detail, identifying dozens, if not hundreds, of attributes, distinctive features of an artifact—for example, the thickness of a pot wall or a type of base-thinning on a stone projectile point. The features may be conspicuous or inconspicuous, stylistic or dimensional, or even based on chemical analyses. This is the process of typology, classifying artifacts so that one type can be compared with another. Obviously, the types from this one site can be compared with other arbitrary types found during laboratory sorting of collections from nearby sites.

Archaeological Types

For accurate and meaningful comparisons between artifacts to be made, rigorous definitions of analytical types are needed, to define not only the "norm" of the artifact type but also its approximate range of variation, at either end of which one type merges into one or two others. Conventional analytical definitions are usually couched in terms of one or more attributes that indicate how the artifact was made, the shape, the decoration, or some other distinctive feature. These definitions are set up following carefully defined technological differences, often bolstered by measurements or statistical clusterings of attributes. Most often, the average artifact, rather than the variation between individual examples, is the ultimate objective of the definition.

We all have strong opinions about how we classify artifacts, just as did the people who originally made them, for each has or had a distinctive role in society. Our immediate instinct is to look at and classify ancient artifacts from our own cultural standpoint. That is, of course, what prehistoric peoples did as well. The owners of the tools that archaeologists study classified them into groups for themselves, each one having a definite role in their society. We assign different roles in eating to a knife, a fork, and a spoon. Knives cut meat; steak knives are used for eating steaks. Likewise in ancient times: The stone arrowhead was employed in the chase; one type of missile head was used to hunt deer, another to shoot birds, and so on. The use of an artifact may be determined not only by convenience and practical considerations but also by custom or regulation. The light barbed spearheads used by some Australian hunting bands to catch fish are too fragile for dispatching a kangaroo; the special barbs permit the impaled fish to be lifted out of the water. Pots are made by women in most African and Native American societies, which practice division of labor by sex; each society has complicated customs, regulations, or taboos, which, functional considerations apart, categorize clay pots into different types with varying uses and rules in the culture (see Figure 8.4).

Furthermore, each society has its own conception of what a particular artifact should look like, whether it is a magnificent wooden helmet from the Pacific Northwest (see Figure 8.5 on page 160) or a simple acorn pounder from the southern California interior. Americans have generally preferred larger cars, Europeans small ones. These preferences

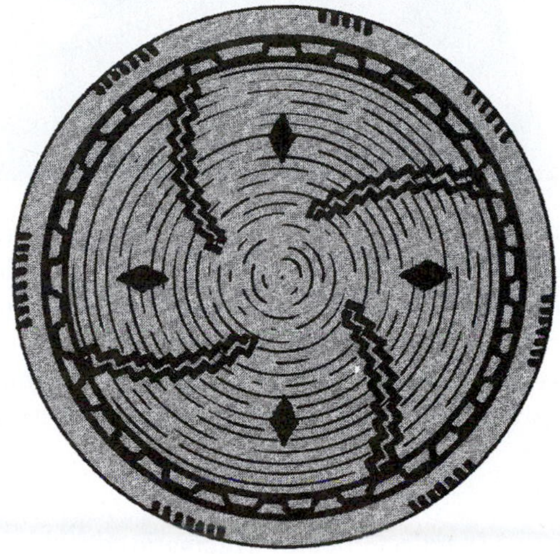

Figure 8.4 This Chumash parching tray is a good example of the difficulties of archaeological classification. This finely made basket was produced by the Chumash Indians of southern California by weaving plant fibers. The design was formed in the maker's mind by several factors, most important of which is the tremendous reservoir of learned cultural experience that the Chumash acquired, generation by generation, through the several thousand years they lived in southern California. The designs of their baskets are learned, and relate to the feeling that such and such a form and color are "correct" and traditionally acceptable. But there are more pragmatic and complex factors, too, including the flat, circular shape that enables the user to roast seeds by tossing them with red embers. Each attribute of the basket has a good reason for its presence—whether traditional, innovative, functional, or imposed by the technology used to make it. The band of decoration around the rim is a feature of the Chumash decorative tradition and occurs on most of their baskets. It has a rich red-brown color, from the species of reed used to make it. The step-like decoration was dictated by the sewing and weaving techniques, but the diamond pattern is unique and the innovative stamp of one weaver, which might or might not be adopted by other craftspeople in later generations. The problem for the archaeologist is to measure the variations in human artifacts, to establish the causes behind the directions of change, and to find what these variations can be used to measure. This fine parching tray is a warning that variations in human artifacts are both complex and subtle.

The Chumash hunter-gatherers occupied the Santa Barbara Channel region of southern California. So bountiful was the local terrestrial and marine environment that they were able to live in permanent villages, some housing as many as 1,000 people. They were ruled by chiefs and enjoyed a complex ritual and social life.

Figure 8.5 Tlingit carved wood helmet from the Northwest Coast, classified as a natural type when found in an archaeological context. This artifact would obviously be classified as a helmet from the perspective of our cultural experience. The Tlingit subsisted off foraging, sea mammal hunting, and fishing, and enjoyed one of the most complex hunter-gatherer societies on earth. (Height, 23 centimeters; width, 25 centimeters [9 inches, 10 inches].)

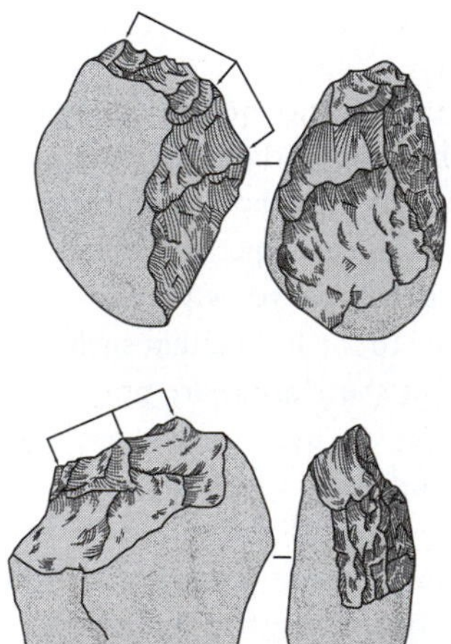

Figure 8.6 An Oldowan "chopping tool": A simplified picture of the process of making a jagged edge by flaking a cobble from both sides (*top*). A large disc-shaped Oldowan artifact in plain and side view (*bottom*).

reflect not only pragmatic considerations of road width and longer distances to travel in the New World but also differing attitudes toward traveling and, for many Americans, a preoccupation with prestige manifested in gold-leaf lettering and custom colors, hub caps, and style. The steering wheel is on the left, and the car is equipped with turn signals and seat belts by law. In other words, we know what we want and expect an automobile to look like, even though minor design details change—as do the length of women's skirts and the width of men's ties.

Archaeologists have a different problem. They have to devise archaeological types that are appropriate to the research problems they are tackling, an extremely difficult task. In archaeology, a type is a grouping of artifacts created for comparison with other groups. This grouping may or may not coincide with the actual tool types designated by the original makers. A good example of a type comes from the world-famous Olduvai Gorge site in East Africa, where Louis and Mary Leakey excavated a series of cache sites used by very early humans, *Homo habilis*. Mary Leakey studied the stone tools and grouped them in the **Oldowan tradition**, a tradition characterized by jagged-edged chopping tools and flakes (see Figure 8.6). She based her classifications on close examination of the artifacts, and the assumption that the first human toolkit was based on crude stone choppers soon became archaeological dogma.

Nicholas Toth of Indiana University has taken a radically different approach to classifying Oldowan artifacts. He has spent many hours not only studying and classifying the original artifacts, but also learning Oldowan technology for himself, replicating hundreds of artifacts made by *Homo habilis* 2 million years ago. His controlled experiments have suggested that *Homo habilis* was interested in the sharp-edged flakes they knocked off lumps of lava, for cutting and butchering the game meat they scavenged from predator kills. According to Toth, many of the "chopping tools" long thought to be the characteristic tools of *Homo habilis* were, in fact, just cores or the end product of knocking flakes off convenient lumps of lava. But the chances are that many were used as choppers as well as cores.

Controlled experiments like Toth's provide useful insights into how prehistoric peoples manufactured the tools they needed. Toth and other experts are now trying to study the telltale patterns of edge wear on the cutting edges of Oldowan flakes, for the polish, striations, and microflake scars left by working, for example, fresh bone as opposed to hide or wood are highly distinctive. With controlled experimentation and careful examination of edge wear, they hope to achieve a closer marriage between the ways in which the first humans used stone tools and the classifications devised by the archaeologist hundreds of thousands of years later (for more on experimental archaeology, see Chapter 9).

Everyone agrees that types are clusters of attributes or clusters of objects. Although patterns of attributes may be fairly easy to identify, how do archaeologists know what is a type and what is not? Controversy surrounds this issue. Should they try to reproduce the categories of pot that the makers themselves conceived? Or should they just go ahead and create "archaeological" types designed purely for analytical purposes? The archaeologist constructs typologies based on the reoccurrence of formal patterns of physical features of artifacts. Many of these formal types have restricted distributions in space and time, which suggest they represent distinctive "styles" of construction and/or tasks that were carried out in the culture to which they belong. For example, the so-called *Chavín* art style was widespread over much of coastal and highland Peru after 900 B.C. The jaguar, snake, and human forms of this art are highly characteristic and mark the spread of a distinctive iconography over a large area of the Andean region. Chavín art, and the characteristic styles associated with it, had a specific role in Peruvian society of the time (see Figure 8.7 on page 162).

The Concept of Types

Archaeological typology is based on the archaeologist's "concept of types," a subject of great controversy in archaeology. On a formal level, a type can be defined as a group or class of items that is internally cohesive and separated from other groups by one or more discontinuities. Archaeologists tend to use four "types of types" (descriptive, chronological, functional, and stylistic), which we describe briefly here; in practice they are rarely separated one from another, for experts tend to draw this kind of information from more general classifications of artifacts. Most researchers now argue that types are identified by combinations of attributes that distinguish and isolate one artifact type from another. In the final analysis, the idea is to organize data in such a way as to reveal continuities and breaks between groups of artifacts that display internal cohesion and are isolated from other such groups.

Attributes and Types of Types

Attributes are the physical characteristics used to distinguish one artifact from another. Every commonplace artifact we use has such attributes. The familiar glass beer mug has a curved handle that extends from near the lip to the base, often fluted sides, a straight, rounded rim, and dimensions that are set by the amount of beer it is intended to contain. It is manufactured of clear, relatively thick glass (the thickness can be defined by precise measurement). You can find numerous attributes in any human artifact, be it a diamond ring or a prehistoric pot. For example, a collection of 50 potsherds lying on a laboratory table may bear black-painted designs; 8 have red panels on the neck, 10 are shallow bowls, and so on. An individual potsherd may come from a vessel made of bright red clay that was mixed with powdered seashells so the clay would fire better. It may come from a pot with a thick rim made by applying a rolled circle of clay before firing, and a crisscross design cut into the wet clay with a sharp knife during manufacture. Each of the many individual features is an attribute, most of which are obvious enough. Only a critically selected few of these attributes, however, will be used in classifying the artifacts. (If all were used, then no classification would be possible: Each artifact would be an individual object identified by an infinite number of attributes.) Thus the archaeologist works with only those attributes considered most appropriate for the classificatory task at hand.

Figure 8.7 A Chavín carving on a pillar in the temple interior at Chavín de Huantar, Peru. This reconstruction makes the temple walls seem more regular and the background more open than they actually were. The distinctive motifs exhibit the style of Chavín art spread throughout highland and coastal Peru, marking an interval termed the Chavín "horizon" that cuts across many local sequences.

The selection of attributes and the entire process of archaeological classification involves many hours in the laboratory, working with large numbers of artifacts that are laid out on tables and examined individually. Today the archaeologist relies heavily on quantitative methods both for describing and comparing artifacts, and for recording and manipulating attribute data. A discussion of these approaches lies beyond the scope of this short book. Attribute-based classifications of artifacts are based on large numbers of attributes, selected by the classifier and usually coded on a computer. Statistical typologies are often derived from attribute clusters, the archaeologist using statistically derived attribute clusters as a way of dividing artifact collections into categories. This approach gives researchers an insight into the most important artifact clusters; however, many different criteria can affect such clustering. For example, a classification of bronze swords based on blade dimensions results in a very different clustering from one based on the sources and composition of the copper and tin used to fabricate them. Other quantitative approaches, outside the scope of this book, work with entire artifacts. They calculate the similarities between all possible pairs of objects in a collection to produce hierarchies of different artifact clusters.

Quantitative methods enable archaeologists to organize artifact data in intelligent, efficient, and replicable ways, allowing them to discern possible patterns that relate to past human behavior. These same techniques also allow them to evaluate the reliability of their inferences objectively and to make inferences about the interrelationships between different variables in attribute counts. As such, they are an invaluable aid to artifact classification.

You will encounter four general archaeological types that are in wide use in typological studies, as follows (see Figure 8.8 below and Figure 8.9 on page 164).

Descriptive types are the most elementary descriptions, based solely on the form of the artifact—physical or external properties. The descriptive type is used even when the use or cultural significance of the object or practice is known. For example, the excavations at *Snaketown* in southern Arizona revealed a "large basin-like depression," a mysterious feature that also turned up at other *Hohokam* sites in the Southwest. This descriptive type was subsequently proven to be a ball court, and so the noncommittal descriptive classification was abandoned in favor of a functional one that defined the structure's role in Hohokam culture.

Descriptive types are commonly used for artifacts and sites from early prehistory, when functional interpretations are impossible (see Figure 8.8).

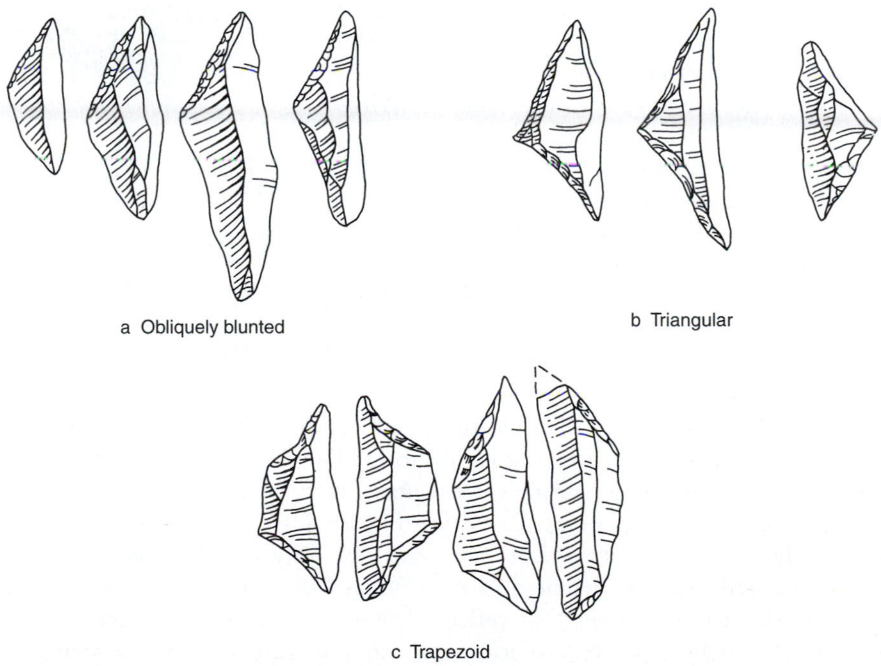

Figure 8.8 Eleven-thousand-year-old **Mesolithic** artifacts from Star Carr, England (shown actual size). You can classify these as follows: *descriptive type,* geometric small tools; *chronological type,* Mesolithic **microliths** (from the Greek "small stone"), Star Carr forms; *functional type,* microlithic arrowhead barbs. (From *Excavation at Star Carr* by Grahame Clark. Reprinted with the permission of Cambridge University Press.)

Chronological types are defined by form, but are time markers. They are types with chronological significance. Like descriptive types, they are part of a culture's inventory as reflected in the archaeological record, but are widely used to distinguish chronological differences. For example, in many parts of North America, *Clovis* and *Folsom* points were used for short periods of prehistoric time, the former in about 11,000 B.C. and the latter somewhat earlier (see Figure 6.3 on page 116). Projectile points have long been used as chronological markers in North American archaeology. Pottery is probably the most common form of chronological type, for the clay, decoration, and so on, change, and are shown to be significant historical indexes.

Chronological types are defined in terms of attributes that do show change over time (see Chapter 5). When the archaeologist compares artifacts known to be of different ages, certain attributes are observed to be different, so he or she uses them to define the types.

Functional types are based on cultural use or role rather than on outward form or chronological position. The same artifacts can be treated as functional or descriptive types. You can classify an assemblage in broad categories: "wood," "bone," "stone," and so on. But a functional classification can be adopted equally well: "weapons," "clothing," "food preparation," and so on.

Ideally, functional types should reflect the precise roles and functional classifications made by the members of the society from which they came. Needless to say, such an objective is virtually impossible to achieve because of incomplete preservation and lack of written records. Many artifacts—for example, the polished stone ax, the dagger, the bow and arrow, or the atlatl, the prehistoric throwing stick—were in use for thousands of years, indeed right into modern times. In many cases like these, it is easy to tell what an artifact was used for (see Figure 8.9). However, we have no means of visualizing the complex roles that some artifacts played in prehistoric society or of establishing the restrictions placed on their use by the society.

Figure 8.9 A functional type of artifact: A Scandinavian flint dagger, c. 4000 B.C.

Stylistic types are best exemplified by items such as dress, because style is often used to convey information by displaying it in public. The Aztecs of central Mexico lived in a ranked society where everyone's dress was carefully regulated by sumptuary laws—regulations governing dress codes (see Figure 8.10 on page 165). Thus a glance at the noble in the marketplace could reveal not only his rank but the number of prisoners he had taken in battle and many other subtle facts. Even the gods had their own regalia and costumes that reflected their roles in the pantheon.

Stylistic types can be expected, theoretically at any rate, to have a structure entirely different from that of functional ones. As such, they are not used often in archaeological classification, except when historical records are available. The approach is much debated.

Descriptions of different artifact types still remain a fundamental part of the archaeologist's work.

Figure 8.10 Aztec warriors wearing elaborate uniforms signifying different ranks, awarded according to the number of captives taken in battle. From the Aztec document known as the *Codex Mendoza*.

What Do Assemblages and Artifact Patternings Mean?

For generations, archaeologists studying culture history classified artifacts into assemblages, associations of tools that were thought to be contemporary. This approach assumed that human culture had evolved through the millennia. Thus artifact assemblages were merely traces of contemporary cultural "species" that extended far back into prehistory. This "organic" view of culture history saw assemblages of artifacts as distinct categories, like organic species, which did not modify their form from one context to the next. The organic approach assumed that a specific cultural tradition leads to only one characteristic type of industry in the archaeological record, an industry circumscribed in time and space. The organic view of the past is a highly organized scheme, rather like the medieval "chain of being" in early biology, where every living thing had its place in the general scheme of things.

American archaeologists have generally preferred a more "cultural" perspective, making considerable use of data on artifacts and other culture traits known to have been used by living societies in North America. The observation of these data has shown a strong correlation between the distributions of distinctive cultural forms and different environments. For example, plank houses and an elaborate canoe technology are characteristic of the peoples of the Pacific Northwest coast, where readily split cedar and other trees flourished in abundance. In contrast, desert peoples in the Great Basin lived in much more transitory settlements of brush shelters and houses using a highly portable toolkit that was adapted to a mobile desert lifeway. It is all very well to say that such correlations were true of historic times, but what about earlier prehistory? Can we say that artifact assemblages from the Great Basin dating to 5,000 years ago reflect similar adaptations, similar social groups? Were conditions different in the past from today—can modern artifact patternings be used as a basis for interpreting ancient behavior?

Some archaeologists, among them Lewis Binford, have attacked this problem by studying living hunter-gatherer societies. Binford spent time among the Nunamiut caribou hunters of northern Alaska. There he learned that the only way to understand a living society's subsistence and material culture is to conceive of all of their sites as part of a larger cultural system. The Nunamiut had residential sites and other kinds of sites used for specialized purposes. Thus, he argued, archaeologists have to identify the specific function of each site they examine, then fit the sites into a much larger, overall pattern of land use.

Archaeology's basic unit is the site; the artifacts in it are part of an assemblage pattern that reveals the different activities that took place there. If archaeologists want to understand the dynamics of cultural systems like that of the Nunamiut in the past, they have to study and interpret prehistoric living conditions, using such classificatory devices as typology, tool frequencies, and the relationships between tool debris and finished artifacts, as just some of their methods of doing so. Thus the role of classification in archaeology has shifted away from "organic" viewpoints that see artifacts and cultures as finite in time and space, to new means of problem-oriented classification that concentrate not only on individual tools, but on entire assemblages and their patternings.

However, the data for interpreting these patterns must finally come from sources other than stone tools or potsherds. In other words, classification alone is meaningless unless the classifications are interpreted in terms of other data. Here the study of contemporary societies—so-called middle-range research—is coming into its own (see Chapter 9). Artifact classifications are still carried out for the most part with approaches meant for reconstructing culture history, formulations of time and space that owed much to functional classifications of artifacts based on common sense. At the same time, however, explanatory frameworks based on theories of social change are providing new explanations of the past. They are designed to account for the structure and change that everyone can see in the archaeological record of the ages, phenomena that are far more dynamic and ever-changing than implied by the more rigid classifications of earlier scholars.

Units of Ordering

Recall from Chapter 5 that an assemblage is the diverse group of artifacts found together that reflects the shared activities of a community. This assemblage was found in a single site. Recall, too, that the site is the fundamental unit for all stratigraphic studies in archaeology. Units of ordering are universal in archaeology, but there are significant differences between those used in the Americas and in the Old World, which are glossed over here for space reasons. For example, Old World archaeologists refer to components as "industries" and to phases as "cultures." In general, Americanist terms are emphasized here (see Figure 8.11 on page 167).

Components and Phases

Many archaeological sites, such as the 8,000-year-old *Olsen-Chubbuck* bison kill site in Colorado, consist of a single assemblage of artifacts and a single component—another **archaeological unit**. A **component** is a physically bounded portion of a site that contains a distinct assemblage, which serves to distinguish the culture of the inhabitants of a particular level. Sites that were occupied many times, like Hogup Cave in Utah, visited repeatedly over a period of more than 9,000 years, contain many components, each of them distinguished by assemblages that separate them in time and space from other

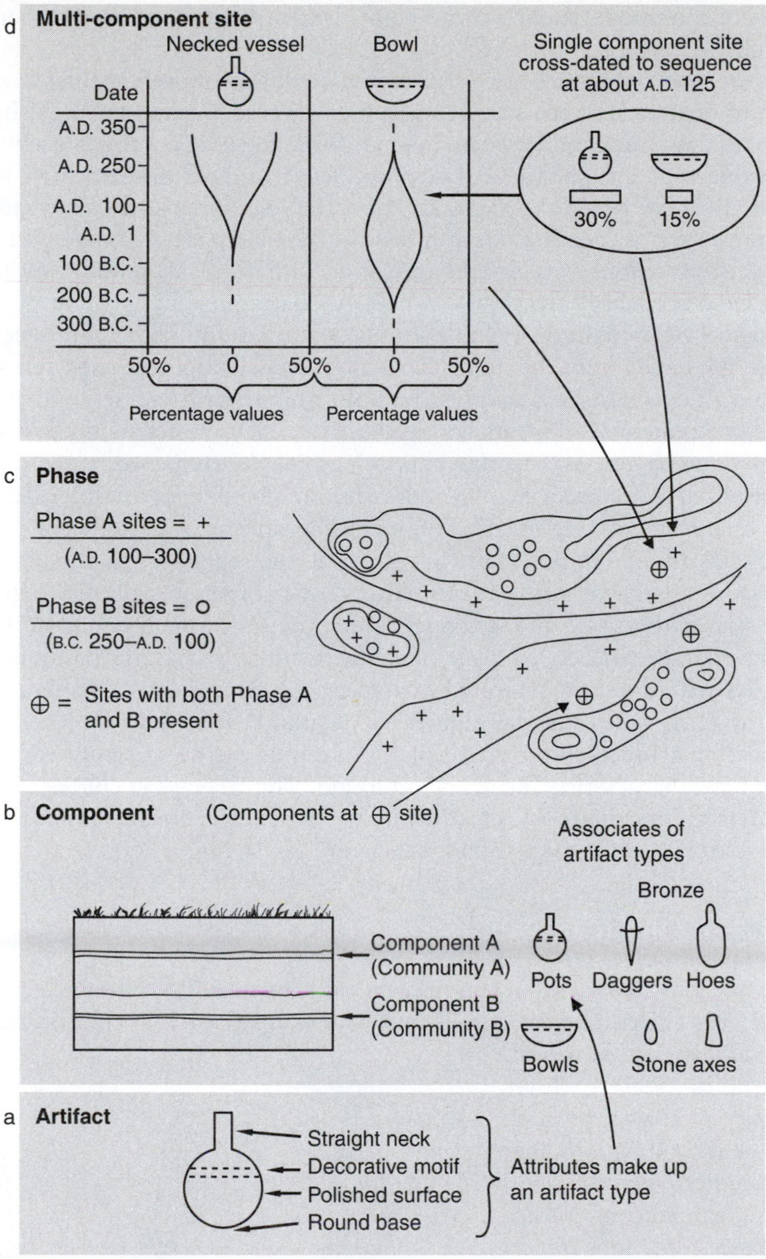

Figure 8.11 Archaeological units in use. (a) Patterns of attributes form an artifact type. (b) Cross section through a hypothetical archaeological site with two stratified components. The two components are radiocarbon dated to between 250 B.C. and A.D. 100 and between A.D. 100 and 350, respectively. Our artifact type is a diagnostic vessel in Component A, the later one. The total artifact content from the site is the assemblage. (c) Now the archaeologists have studied dozens of sites in their archaeological region, which consists of an estuary with an offshore island. Higher ground with pine forest overlooks the estuary. When they plotted site distributions, they found that the earlier, Phase B, sites were distributed on the higher ground, and the later components were established near the shore where shellfish were abundant. Only three sites contain both components, stratified one above the other. The two distributions are distinctive, both phases defined in space and time, forming a local sequence. (d) At the four two-component sites, the archaeologists seriated the pottery types and other artifacts and obtained distinctive battleship curves. Then they were able to fit other sites into the same sequence by cross-dating.

components at the same site. The social equivalent of the archaeologist's component is the community.

Once the research team's analysis is completed, they may find they have only one component to deal with. If the site was occupied several times, they might have two or three. How do they compare these components with those from other, nearby sites? And how do they develop a sequence of occupation levels and cultures for their local area?

When all of the artifact collections from the local area have been analyzed and classified to everyone's satisfaction, they are ordered in space and time with the aid of stratigraphic observations, seriation, cross-dating, and radiocarbon or tree-ring dates. In Chapter 5, we described both seriation and cross-dating techniques that place artifacts in chronological order with the help of battleship curves and dated components. Figure 5.7 on page 96 shows how the Tehuacán Valley archaeologists joined ten sites into a local sequence, a chronological ordering built up from several multicomponent sites and some single-component settlements within the area. They were also able to obtain some radiocarbon dates to give an accurate chronology for the sequence.

The research team discovered from distribution maps that two different dated components were repeated at settlements over a considerable area. These were so well dated and precisely distributed in time that two phases in the sequence could be identified.

A **phase** is a cultural unit represented by like components on different sites or at different levels of the same site, although always within a well-defined chronological bracket. The characteristic assemblage of artifacts of the phase may be found over hundreds of miles within the area covered by a local sequence. Many Old World archaeologists use the term *culture* in the same sense as phase. Both are concepts designed to assist in ordering artifacts in time and space. Phases or cultures usually are named after a key site where characteristic artifacts are found. The *Acheulian* culture, for example, is named after the northern French town of St. Acheul, where the stone hand axes so characteristic of this culture are found (see Figure 8.12).

Larger Archaeological Units

After many seasons' work, the research team may have studied several local sequences and may be able to describe their finds in a wide context such as that of the dozens of local sequences within the southwestern United States. Some characteristic art styles or artifacts, such as the Chavín art that flourished in Peru between 900 and 200 B.C., spread over considerable distances, perhaps representing the popularity of a new set of religious beliefs, which originated at *Chavín de Huantar* in the Andes mountain foothills (see Figure 8.7 on page 162).

Archaeologists sometimes use the term **horizon** to cover such phenomena, where a number of phases in neighboring areas contain rather general cultural patterns in common. The term **tradition** describes a lasting artifact type, assemblages of tools, architectural styles, economic

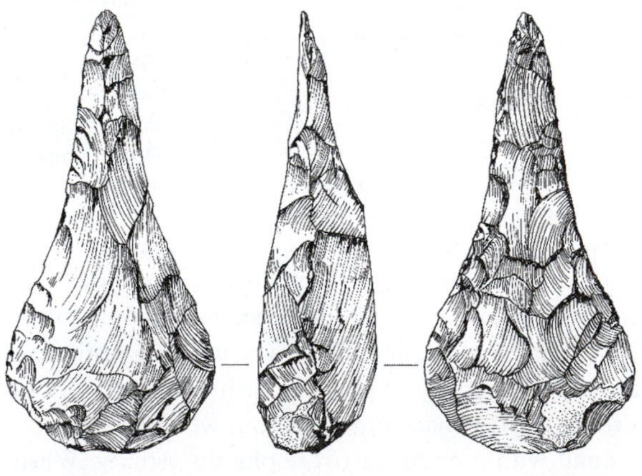

Figure 8.12 Three views of an Acheulian stone ax from Swanscombe on the River Thames, England. One-third full size. Acheulian hand axes were general-purpose artifacts used widely by archaic humans in Africa, Europe, and southern Asia from before a million years ago up to after 200,000 years ago.

practices, or art styles that last much longer than one phase or even the duration of a horizon. A single toolmaking tradition may continue in use while the many cultures that share it develop in entirely different ways. A good example of a tradition is the so-called Paleoarctic tradition of Alaska that originated at least as early as 9000 B.C. and lasted for several thousand years. Perhaps the most renowned larger archaeological units are those identified by the Danish archaeologist Christian Jurgensen Thomsen in 1816. His Stone Age, Bronze Age, and Iron Age technological labels (the so-called Three-Age System) are still in wide use.

Ancient Technologies

The artifacts that people have manufactured throughout their long history have enabled them to augment their limbs and extend their use of the environment. The technological achievements of humanity over the past two-and-a-half million years have been both impressive and terrifying. Today, we can land an astronaut on the moon, transplant human hearts, and build sophisticated computers. Yet, in the final analysis, our contemporary technologies have evolved in a direct, albeit branching, way from the first simple tools made by the earliest human beings. These evolving, and sometimes very durable, technologies have survived in the archaeological record and provide one of the primary sources of information on the past.

Stone, bone, clay, fiber, metal, shell, textiles, skin, hair, hide, and also wood were the main raw materials used by our forebears. Of these, metal ores require smelting, a technology that came into use in southwestern Asia about 5,000 years ago, and in the Americas within the past 2,000 years. Bone, fiber, and other organic materials like hide do not survive well, so it is no coincidence that stone and fired clay have attracted the most archaeological interest and provide the foundation for classification of many prehistoric cultures.

Stone

Stone tools were the earliest artifacts, little more than simple sharp-edged flakes struck off lava lumps by the simple expedient of knocking one stone against another. Over the ensuing millennia, people exploited almost every possibility afforded by rocks suitable for making tools of all kinds—axes, borers, choppers, knives, scrapers, and delicate spearheads. The manufacture of stone tools is a **reductive**, or **subtractive, technology**, for stone is acquired, then shaped by removing flakes until the desired form is achieved. Their making depends on the property of **conchoidal fracture**, characteristic of many crystalline rocks such as flint or obsidian. Such stone breaks in a predictable way when struck vertically, producing characteristic fracture patterns and **cores** or flakes, which allow an archaeologist to identify the rock as humanly modified, and as an artifact (see Figure 8.13 on page 170).

For millennia, people did little more than fracture a rock with another stone. Eventually, they began making tool flakes on both sides, like the Acheulian hand ax (see Figure 8.12 on page 168), eventually turning to bone, a softer hammer, to make thinner and better finished tools. After about 100,000 years ago, *Homo sapiens* used more sophisticated technologies that produced specialized artifacts such as spear points and scrapers designed for specific purposes. These technologies culminated in the use of punches to prepare dozens of fine parallel-sided **blades**—thin, often parallel-sided blanks used to make a wide variety of small tools such as chisel-shaped gravers for working bone and antler. The effect was somewhat like that of the Swiss army knife, in which a chassis with strong springs supports a variety of specialized tools such as knife

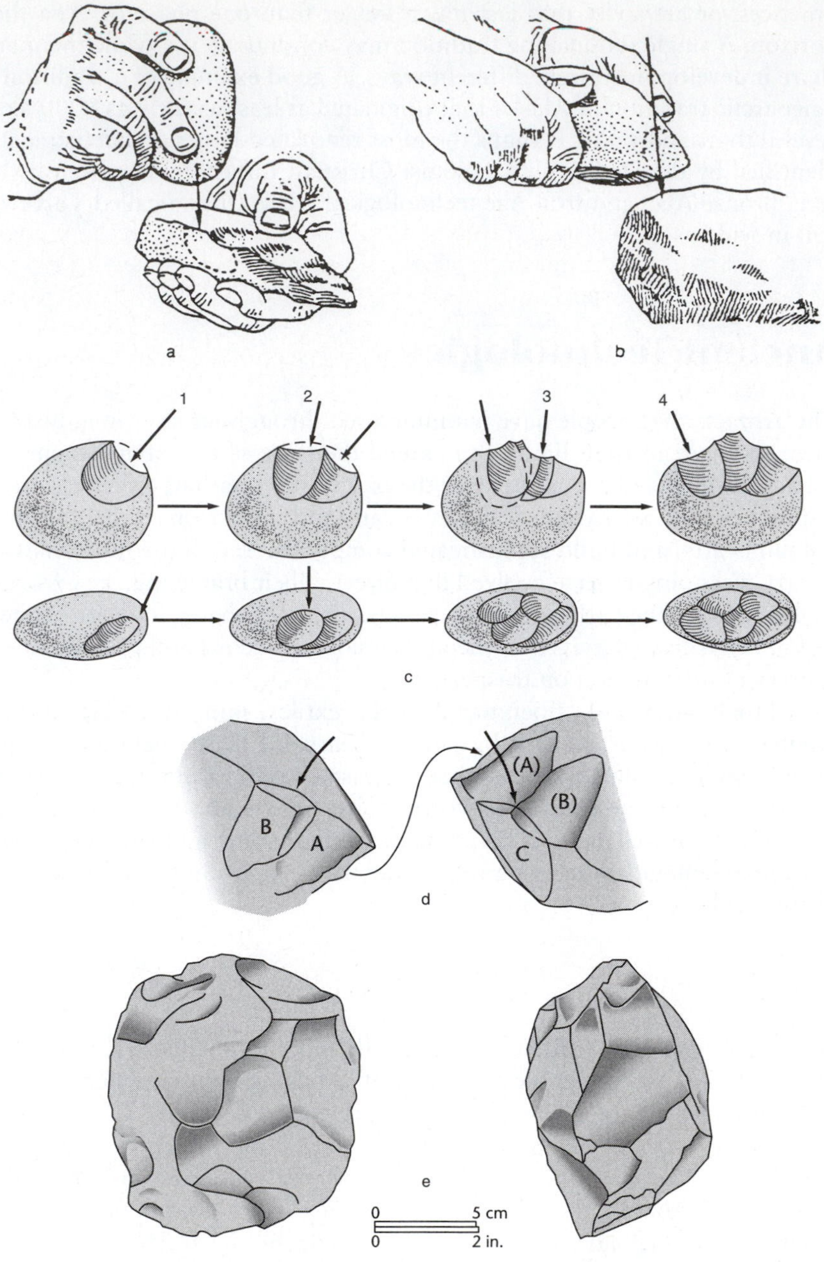

Figure 8.13 The earliest stoneworking techniques: (a) Using a hammerstone. (b) A variant on the hammerstone, striking a core against a stone block, the so-called anvil technique. (c) The earliest stone tools were made by a simple method. The top row shows the side view: First, two flakes were struck off (1 and 2); second, the stone was turned over and two more flakes were removed (3); third, a fifth flake completed the useful life of the core (4). The bottom row shows the process from above. (d) Making Oldowan bifaces. Top, a simplified picture of the process required for bifacial flaking. (e) A large Oldowan discoid-like artifact from Chesowanja, East Africa, in plain and side views. The stoneworker used this bifacial technique but did not fashion the biface along a long axis, as later humans did.

blades, corkscrews, or spikes. In the same way, a blade core produced blades, which in turn produced more specialized artifacts, some of which were then used to cut antler and other raw materials.

Later Stone Age peoples ground and polished stone when they needed a sharp and highly durable blade. They shaped the edges by rough flaking and then laboriously polished and ground them against a coarser rock, such as sandstone, to produce a sharp, tough working edge. Modern experiments have demonstrated the greater effectiveness of polished stone axes in felling forest trees, the toughened working edge taking longer to blunt than that of a flaked axe. Polished stone axes became important in many early farming societies, especially in Europe, Asia, Mesoamerica, and parts of temperate North America. They were used in New Guinea as early as 28,000 years ago and in Melanesia and Polynesia for the manufacture of canoes, which were essential for fishing and trade.

Some of the finest stoneworking dates from more recent times. The Predynastic Egyptians made superb ceremonial knives. Ancient Native Americans made delicate projectile points, shaping them with small billets of bone or antler and pressure techniques. By this time, many human societies produced diminutive stone artifacts designed as arrow barbs and used for other specialized purposes (see Figure 8.8 on page 163).

Expert stoneworkers still fashion artifacts to this day, especially gunflints for use in flintlock muskets. Gunflint manufacture was a flourishing industry in Britain and France into the twentieth century and is still practiced in Angola, Africa, where flintlock muskets are still in use for hunting. Lithic technology has a modern application as well. Obsidian flake and blade edges are so sharp that they are widely used by modern eye surgeons, on the grounds that such cutting tools are superior to modern steel!

It is all too easy to think of stone artifacts as merely lifeless objects, when, in fact, they once had a life of their own. Belgian archaeologist Daniel Cahen's reconstruction of stoneworking at the 9,000-year-old Meer site in northern Belgium, described at the beginning of Chapter 2, is a classic example of the "new" lithic analysis. He and colleague Lawrence Keeley combined edge-wear analysis with refitting to reconstruct a fascinating scenario. They used the evidence from three borers that were turned counterclockwise to show that a right-handed artisan walked away from the settlement, sat on a boulder, and made some tools, using some prepared blanks and cores he brought with him. Later a left-handed artisan came and sat next to him, bringing a previously prepared core, from which he proceeded to strike some blanks that he turned into tools.

For this reason, **lithic analysis**, the study of stone artifacts and technology, is based not only on the identification of attributes and types, but on actual reconstructions of the reductive technology used to make them. This requires **refitting** (**retrofitting**) of actual cores and waste flakes found in excavations, a painstaking task that can produce remarkable results, like identifying the work of individual stone workers, some of whom may be left-handed. Lithic experimentation, the actual replication of stone technologies, has long been part of experimental archaeology (see Chapter 9), and the study of the edge wear on long-discarded tools under microscopes combined with actual experiments has produced evidence for cutting hide, meat, and bone. Some artifacts have even produced trace elements of organic residues such as blood still clinging to the cutting edges of butchery tools.

Petrological analyses have been applied with great success to the rocks from which stone tools are made, especially ground stone axes in Europe. Petrology is the study of rocks (Greek *petros:* stone). A thin section of the ax is prepared and examined under a microscope. The minerals in the rock can then be identified and compared with samples from ancient quarry sites. British archaeologists have had remarkable success with this approach and have identified more than 20 sources of ax blade stone in Britain alone. Spectrographic analysis of distinctive trace elements in obsidian has yielded remarkable results in southwestern Asia and Mesoamerica, where this distinctive volcanic rock was traded widely from several quarry centers (see Chapter 12).

Lithic analysis is not just the study of artifacts; it is the understanding of what the implements mean in terms of human behavior.

Clay

From the earliest times, people used containers of all kinds, such as animal skins, bark trays, gourds, and ostrich eggshells. The invention of pottery seems to have coincided with the beginnings of more lasting settlement. Fired-clay receptacles have the advantage of being both durable and long-lived. We can assume that the first clay vessels were used for domestic purposes: for cooking, carrying water, and storing food. They soon assumed more specialized roles in salt making, in ceremonial activities, and as oil lamps and burial urns. In about 8000 B.C., the *Jomon* people of Japan started making baked clay containers, an innovation that took hold in southwestern Asia before 6000 B.C. and in the Americas after 2500 B.C.

Clay containers, or rather their broken fragments, have the advantage of being both durable and long-lived, which is why they are such an important part of the archaeological record. They served as water and storage containers, as cooking and drinking vessels. Their shape, style, and form have been the basis for thousands of archaeological analyses. Prehistoric artisans created their pieces individually, using the simplest of technology, but attaining astonishing skill in shaping and adorning their pots (see Figure 8.14). They selected their clay with great care, pounded it and prepared it to a fine consistency, then built up their pots in a variety of ways, most commonly by building up long coils of clay, or by using a mold, or, in later times in the Old World, by using a potter's wheel. The outside surface was smoothed with the hands, sometimes painted with

Figure 8.14 Hopi woman making pottery with clay coils, Oraibi Pueblo, Arizona, 1903.

a wet clay solution, then dried before being burnished, decorated, and fired in an open fire, or later in a kiln. As with other artifacts, the making of clay vessels was circumscribed by all manner of social and other variables, which are almost impossible to discern from conventional archaeological analysis. Such analyses focus on the form, function, style, and technology of the vessel. The latter includes studies of the fabric and clay paste, using such techniques as neutron activation analysis and x-ray diffraction to study what has been called "ceramic ecology," the interaction of resources, local knowledge, and style that led to finished clay vessels.

Some of the most remarkable ceramic research involves not the vessels themselves, but their contents. In 1988, German Egyptologist Günter Dreyer excavated the tomb of one of Egypt's first leaders at *Abydos* on the Middle Nile. Scorpion I lived in about 3150 B.C. His elaborate tomb contained four rooms stocked with at least 700 jars, which held a total of about 1,200 gallons (4,550 liters) of wine. Forty-seven of the jars contained wine pips, together with remains of sliced figs that were once suspended on strings in the wine, probably to sweeten it. The crusty residues adhering to the insides of the pots were analyzed with an infrared spectrometer and liquid chromatography, which revealed the remains of tartaric acids (found naturally in grapes), also of terebinth resin, which ancient vintners used to prevent wine from turning into vinegar. **Neutron activation analysis** of the jar clay yielded trace element clusters that were compared to a large database of samples from Egypt and the eastern Mediterranean. The database pointed to the southern hill country of Israel and Transjordan as the source of the vessels, an area where vine growing was well established in 3100 B.C. The wine probably traveled the Nile across an ancient trade route, "the Way of Horus," that linked southern Israel with Egypt via the Sinai Desert. By 3000 B.C., wine growing was well established in the Nile Deltas in northern Egypt, the source of the pharaoh Tutankhamun's wines 1,500 years later.

Metals and Metallurgy

"Hough!" "Hough!" The goatskin bellows emit a steady puffing noise as the African smith raises and lowers the bags with his hands, singing along the way. Every 20 minutes, another member of the team takes over as the master smith keeps a close eye on the clay furnace loaded with iron ore and charcoal. He adds charcoal, then more ore, then charcoal again. The smelt continues for seven hours until the master is satisfied. Then he rakes out the white-hot charcoal and recovers a lump of slag and smelted iron from the fire. All the preparation time and seven hours of arduous bellows work produced just enough iron to make one small hoe. In these days of mass-produced steel and all kinds of exotic metals, we forget just how much labor went into producing even a single iron tool. The development of metallurgy is one of humanity's great innovations, but it was certainly not a labor-saving invention.

Metals were familiar phenomena to ancient peoples in the form of rocks in their environment. Perhaps their color, luster, and weight made them attractive to use as ornaments. Eventually, people realized that native copper and other rocks could be formed into tools by a sequence of hammering and heating. But only eight metals—arsenic, copper, gold, iron, lead, mercury, tin, and silver—were worked before the eighteenth century A.D.

The earliest metal tools were made in southwestern Asia by 6000 B.C. by cold hammering copper into simple artifacts. Copper tools were commonplace by 4000 B.C., but the major revolution came after 3000 B.C. when smiths learned how to alloy the metal with arsenic, lead, or about 10 percent tin to produce tough-edged bronze tools and weapons. By 2500 B.C., practically every kind of metallurgical phenomenon except hardening of steel was known (see Figure 8.15 on page 174). The use of tin

Figure 8.15 A fine example of skilled metallurgy: A Celtic Iron Age helmet from the bed of the River Thames in London, 8.07 inches (20.5 centimeters) at the base. (Copyright The British Museum.)

alloying may have stimulated much trading activity, for the metal is relatively rare, especially in the eastern Mediterranean region. The *Uluburun* ship, described in Chapter 13, carried tin ingots, and 4,500 years ago, Chinese smiths were using clay molds to produce highly sophisticated three-legged cauldrons and other ceremonial vessels. Ironworking appeared in southwestern Asia in about 1500 B.C. and was in widespread use by 1000 B.C. Iron is a utilitarian and abundant metal ore, ideal for making farming tools and weapons. In contrast, few utilitarian metal objects were made in the Americas, where copper and gold were used predominantly for ornamentation and ritual purposes.

Gold played a vital part in prestige and ornament in many ancient societies. The pharaoh Tutankhamun is sometimes called the "Golden Pharaoh": His grave was rich in spectacular gold objects. The burials of Moche lords of A.D. 400 at Sipán, Peru, revealed the remarkable wealth of this desert civilization. One shroud-wrapped warrior-priest wore a pair of gold eyes, a gold nose, and a gold chin-and-neck visor; his head was lying on a gold, saucer-like headrest (see Figure 2.6 on page 35). Hundreds of minute gold and turquoise beads adorned this Lord of Sipán, who wore 16 gold disks as large as silver dollars on his chest. There were gold-and-feather headdresses and intricate ear ornaments, one of a warrior with a movable club.

The Aztecs and the Inka also were talented goldsmiths, whose magnificent products were shipped off to Europe and melted down for royal treasuries in the sixteenth century. Spanish conquistadors marveled at the Coricancha, the temple of the Sun god Inti in the Inka capital at Cuzco high in the Andes. The outside of the beautifully built stone temple was gilded with gold and silver, while inside lay a garden with golden clods of earth, golden maize, and golden herdsmen guarding golden llamas (see Figure 8.16 on page 175).

Figure 8.16 A silver long-haired Inka llama, which epitomizes late Andean artistry in sheet metal.

The analysis of metal artifacts again involves conventional classificatory techniques, but now relies heavily on technological researches. Again, spectrographic analyses provide clues as to the sources of raw materials. For example, we know that the copper ingots from the fourteenth-century B.C. Uluburun shipwreck off southern Turkey came from Cyprus (see Figure 13.14 on page 278). Chemical examination of copper and iron slags and of smelting furnaces can provide valuable information on ancient metallurgical processes. Archaeologists have sat alongside and watched as traditional smiths in Africa and elsewhere re-create ancient smelting and manufacturing techniques. They record furnace temperatures and other arcane details as a means of better understanding the techniques used in the remote past. The ultimate purpose of the technological analyses is to reconstruct the entire process of metal tool production from the mining of the ore to the production of the finished artifact.

Bone, Wood, Basketry, and Textiles

Bone and Antler. These materials were probably used from the beginnings of human history. The earliest artifacts apparently consisted of little more than fragments of fractured animal bone used for purposes that could not be fulfilled by wood or stone implements. The earliest standardized bone tools date from after about 100,000 years ago, but they assumed much greater levels of sophistication during the late Ice Age, when *Homo sapiens* used sharp-edged stone chisels to cut long splinters from antlers and turned them into spear points, harpoons, and fishing spears, as well as creating many specialized tools for foraging, fishing, and ceremonial purposes. They also used antler and bone as palettes for fine carvings and engravings of animals and geometric designs. The humble bone or ivory needle appeared about 25,000 years ago, a revolutionary artifact because it enabled humans to manufacture layered, tailored clothing, essential for colonizing the bitterly cold open plains of Europe and Eurasia with their nine-month winters.

Bone and ivory technology achieved great sophistication in the Bering Strait area of the far north, where a highly specialized sea-mammal-hunting toolkit came into use over 2,000 years ago. Elaborate typological studies have been made of the stylistic and functional changes in such diverse items as harpoons and the winged ivory objects fastened to the butts of harpoons. Other artifacts include picks made of walrus tusk and snow shovels and wedges of ivory and bone, as well as drills and domestic utensils.

Wood. Like bone, wood was used for human artifacts from the earliest times. Only occasionally do such artifacts survive, the earliest being a series of 400,000-year-old long wooden throwing spears from *Schoningen,* Germany, that would have been lethal

Figure 8.17 Cotton funerary textile from the Paracas Peninsula, Peru, perhaps depicting a shaman in trance.

against large game. The bogs and marshes of northern Europe have preserved entire wooden toolkits made by foraging families as early as 7000 B.C., including dugout canoes, fishing spears, traps, and spear points, and also wooden trackways across water-logged ground. The dry conditions of western North America have yielded rich finds of such artifacts as throwing sticks, and even duck decoys used to pursue waterfowl. Delicately made furniture survives in Pharaoh Tutankhamun's tomb.

The manufacture of wood tools involves such well-understood mechanical processes as cutting, whittling, scraping, planing, carving, and polishing. Fire was often used to harden sharpened spear points. Oil and paint imparted a fine sheen and appearance to all kinds of wood artifacts. Even more revealing are wood fragments from abandoned buildings, fortifications, and even track walkways. Microscopic analysis of wood fragments and charcoal can provide information on the wood types used to build houses, canoes, and other such objects. On very rare occasions, stone projectile heads and axes have been recovered in both waterlogged and dry conditions in which their wood handles and shafts have survived together with the thongs used to bind stone to wood.

Wood was probably the most important raw material available to our ancestors. The thousands upon thousands of ground stone axes in the archaeological record all once had wood handles (see Figure 11.1 on page 219). Wood was used for house building, fortifications, fuel, canoes, and containers. Most skilled woodworking societies used the simplest technology to produce both utilitarian and ceremonial objects. They used fire and the ringing of bark to fell trees, stone wedges to split logs, and shells and stones to scrape spear shafts.

Basketry and Textiles. Basket production is one of the oldest crafts. Basketry includes such items as containers, matting, bags, and a wide range of fiber objects. Textiles are found in many later, dry sites, and they are well preserved along the Peruvian coast. Some scholars believe that basketry and textiles are among the most sensitive artifacts for the archaeologist to work with, culturally speaking, on the grounds that people lived in much more intimate association with baskets and textiles than with clay vessels, stone tools, or houses. Furthermore, even small fragments of basketry and textiles display remarkable idiosyncrasies of individual manufacture. When preserved, baskets are amenable to the same kinds of functional and stylistic analyses as other artifacts.

The dry climate of the central Peruvian coast has preserved the wardrobes of *Paracas* nobles buried between 600 and 150 B.C. Paracas rulers wore mantles, tunics, ponchos, skirts, loincloths, and headpieces. These garments were embroidered with rows of brightly colored anthropomorphic, zoomorphic, and composite figures (see Figure 8.17 on page 176). Interpreting the iconographic patterns that appear on these ancient garments tells us something of Paracas religious and social customs. One of the important functions of a Paracas ruler was to mediate between people and the supernatural forces that influenced and determined life's events. Many of the rulers' garments were adorned with shaman figures, showing that the wearer had a special relationship with the supernatural.

People have accused archaeologists of being obsessed with the minute details of artifacts and technology to the exclusion of almost anything else. Doubtless there are such obsessives among us, but most researchers know that priceless information about people and human behavior lies behind even simple artifacts. We have only begun to tap the potential of multidisciplinary research into ancient technologies.

SUMMARY

1. Archaeologists rely heavily on formal classification systems in their analyses of artifacts.
2. Archaeology has its own taxonomy (classification system) for classifying artifacts and cultural units. This allows the organizing of data into manageable units and more detailed classification into artifact types using the individual features of artifacts, or clusters of tools.
3. Describing types provides a hierarchy that orders the relationships between artifacts and allows archaeologists to study assemblage variability in the archaeological record.
4. Typology is a system of archaeological classification based on the construction of types to permit comparisons from different levels and sites.
5. Types are distinguished by combinations of artifact features (attributes) that serve to distinguish one object from another.
6. Statistical methods play an important part in manipulating attribute clusters, and permit researchers to discern patterns that relate to past human behavior. They use descriptive types, chronological types, functional types, and stylistic types, defined in this chapter.
7. Archaeologists commonly use arbitrary archaeological units, such as components, phases (cultures), horizons, and traditions, also defined in this chapter, for studying larger cultural phenomena.
8. The chapter reviews major technologies of ancient times, including stone, wood, metal, and bone.

NINE

The Present and the Past

Maori war canoe drawn in 1769 by Captain James Cook's artist, Sydney Parkington.

CHAPTER OUTLINE

PREVIEW

Chapter 9 is concerned with the relationship between the archaeological record of the past, a static phenomenon, and the present. We discuss the complex site formation processes, which act on a site from the moment that it's abandoned. Preservation conditions, especially of inorganic finds such as wood and textiles, vary greatly under different conditions. We describe some notable finds that result from exceptionally cold, dry, and wet conditions, among them the tomb of the pharaoh Tutankhamun, and Tollund Man. A body of archaeological theory known as Middle Range Theory attempts to link the archaeological record with the present. We describe ethnographic analogy, ethnoarchaeology, and experimental archaeology, which are three approaches that seek to interpret the archaeological record of the past in the context of the present.

> *The archaeological record is contemporary. It exists with me today and any observation I make about it is a contemporary observation.*
>
> —Lewis R. Binford, *Working at Archaeology,* 1983

A tiny silk thread on an ancient Egyptian mummy of 1000 B.C., a perfectly preserved basket from a 500-year-old Indian village in the Pacific Northwest, and a deep-frozen horsewoman's grave from Siberia, where even horse trappings survive: These exceptional finds and many others show us just how much of the past has vanished in the soil. The archaeological record is tantalizingly incomplete, for what survives is but a fragment of what was once fabricated, built, and used.

I once discovered a series of stone tool scatters on the banks of the Victoria Nile River in northern Uganda. Thousands of tiny quartz chips and hundreds of discarded stone arrow barbs marked a site visited again and again by Stone Age hunter-gatherers over many millennia. Everything organic and perishable had vanished soon after the visitors departed, leaving only stone tools and the by-products of their manufacture for the archaeologist to study. There were no traces of the brush shelters where the people had slept; of their wooden spears, arrow shafts, and digging sticks; of the skin cloaks they had used to collect ripe nuts. Sun, rain, and wind, even trampling hippopotamuses feeding at night, had leached out the organic remains of human activity or trampled them into dust. A greater contrast to Austen Henry Layard's large-scale diggings at Nineveh in the 1840s is hard to imagine.

Most archaeological sites—the archaeological record—are far from spectacular, yet they can yield priceless information while the well-preserved finds grab the headlines. How, then, is this archaeological record formed? What humanly caused and natural factors affect the preservation of artifacts, food remains, and sites?

So far, we have discussed the basics of archaeology—culture, time and space, finding and excavating archaeological sites, and the analysis of artifacts and ancient technology. In Chapter 9, we cross a metaphorical bridge from data recovery to reconstruction of ancient lifeways, the study of people and their beliefs in the past, and to the interpretation and explanation of the archaeological record recovered from the ground. Before crossing to the other bank, we must look more closely at two issues we have so far left on one side: the nature and formation of the archaeological record, and the all-important factors that affect its preservation for us to study. We argue that the archaeological record

Discovery

Ancient Pacific Navigation

When British navigator Captain James Cook visited Tahiti in 1769, he puzzled over a question that has fascinated scholars ever since. How had the Tahitians colonized their remote homeland? How had humans with only simple canoes and no metals migrated across vast tracts of open ocean to settle on the remotest islands of the Pacific? Cook met an expert Tahitian navigator Tupaia and asked him how canoe navigators made their way from island to island out of sight of land. Tupaia explained how they used the sun as a compass by day and the moon and stars by night. When Cook marveled at the Polynesians' ability to sail against the prevailing winds for hundreds of miles, Tupaia pointed out that westerlies blew from November to January, and these were months when canoes could make good progress to windward. Tupaia carried a mental file of Polynesia in his head. Modern scholars believe that Tupaia could define an area bounded by the Marquesas in the northeast, the Tuamotus to the east, the Australs to the south, and the Cook Islands to the southwest. Even Fiji and Samoa to the west lay within his consciousness, an area as large as Australia or the United States.

Later explorers did not interview Tahitian navigators. Many scholars assumed that canoes blown accidentally far offshore colonized the Pacific Islands. But in 1965 English small-boat sailor David Lewis encountered aged canoe navigators in the Carolina Islands of Micronesia. He learned how the navigators used the zenith passages of key stars to navigate far from the land, using swell direction, waves reflected off distant land, even the flights of sea and land birds to make landfall on island archipelagos far from their departure point. They were also capable of returning to their homes safely, using the same signs of sea and sky. Lewis, determined to preserve a rapidly vanishing art, sailed his ocean-going, European-designed catamaran from Rarotonga in the Cook Islands to New Zealand using only a star map and a Polynesian navigator to help him. In the 1970s, Lewis apprenticed himself to the pilots of the Carolina Islands, learning how they made passages with the aid of sun, moon, stars, cloud and swell formations, even by watching passing birds.

In the late 1960s, anthropologist Ben Finney (1994) began long-term experiments with replicas of ancient Polynesian canoes. Finney's first replica was *Nalehia*, a 40-foot copy of a Hawaiian royal canoe. Tests in Hawaii's windy waters showed it could sail across the wind, so Finney planned a voyage from Hawaii to Tahiti and back. His second replica was built from a composite of canoe designs known throughout the Pacific Islands. *Hokule'a* is 62 feet (18.89 m) long, with double hulls and two crab-claw-shaped sails designed by Hawaiian Herb Kawainui Kane (see Figure 9.1). Finney, Satawal Island navigator Mau Piailug, and a mainly Hawaiian crew sailed *Hokule'a* from Hawaii to Tahiti and back in 1976. This journey was followed by a two-year voyage around the Pacific using only indigenous pilots. Thanks to the successful *Hokule'a* experiments, ancient Polynesian navigational skills have been preserved for posterity.

Figure 9.1 Pacific navigation. Landfalls on isolated islands depended on mountain peaks, signs that land was near, and wave patterns.

that comes down to us is a static phenomenon, very different from the dynamic human behavior that surrounds us today. As we shall see, controlled experiments with modern-day replicas of artifacts and observations of living people help us interpret the static archaeological record of the past (see the Discovery box on page 180).

The Archaeological Record Again

The discards of the past—food remains, structures, and artifacts—are of priceless value as a means of studying ancient human behavior. These material remains form the archaeological record, the archives used by archaeologists to study the past. The archaeological record comprises all kinds of archaeological finds, from the pyramids of Giza to an early human butchery site at Olduvai Gorge, Tanzania, occupied nearly 2 million years ago. California shell mounds, Ohio earthworks, Inka cemeteries—all are part of the archaeological record. So are isolated artifacts—the throne of Tutankhamun ("King Tut"), a wooden religious mask from a midwestern burial mound, and a Polynesian stone adze.

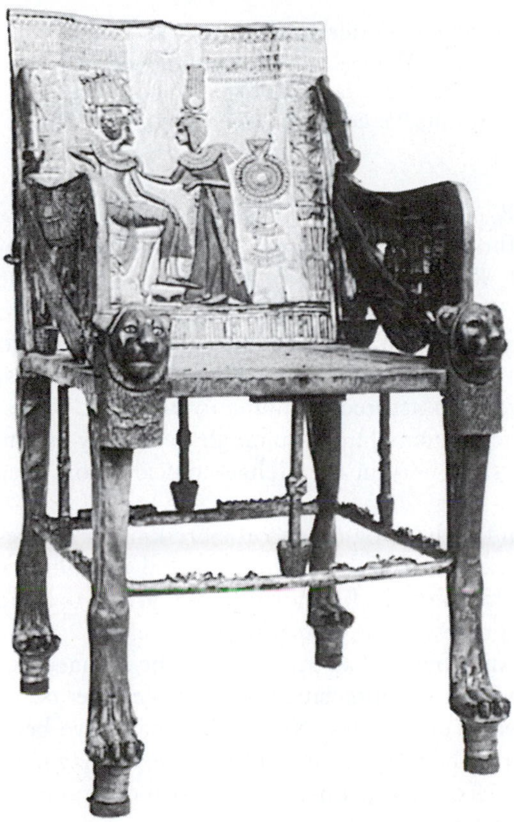

Figure 9.2 The throne of Egyptian pharaoh Tutankhamun, one of the many wood artifacts recovered from the richest royal sepulcher ever found. Tutankhamun died in his late teens in about 1323 B.C., having come to the throne in infancy. During his brief reign, the worship of the sun god Amun was restored at Thebes after a period of religious confusion. (Ashmolean Museum, Oxford, England, U.K.)

We seek to find out about prehistoric people from the traces of their activities. The carcass of a mammoth butchered 20,000 years ago is a mine of information on ancient hunting practices. Analysis of dried-out seeds or ancient human body feces found in archaeological sites tells us much about prehistoric diet. What we can find out about the past is severely limited, however, by the state of preservation of archaeological finds. Some substances, such as baked clay or stone, will survive indefinitely. But wood, bone, leather, and other organic materials soon vanish except under waterlogged, frozen, or exceptionally dry conditions. Everyone has heard of the remarkable tomb of Egyptian pharaoh Tutankhamun, whose astonishing treasure survived almost intact in the dry climate of the Nile Valley for more than 3,000 years (see Figure 9.2). This archaeological record is exceptionally complete and informative. We even know, from the bouquet of wildflowers laid on his inner coffin, that Tutankhamun's funeral took place in the spring.

But most archaeological sites are found where only a few durable materials survive. Constructing the past from these finds is a challenge, the sort of problem faced by the detective piecing together the circumstances of a crime from a few fragmentary clues. The analogy is close: Take two spark plugs, a fragment of a china cup, a needle, a grindstone, and a candlestick. Imagine someone from Patagonia digging them up in a thousand years' time and trying to tell you how the makers used the objects. This analysis is precisely what the archaeologist does in going about the work of being a special type of anthropologist. The data we amass from surface survey and excavation make up the archaeological record. As we have seen, the two basic units studied by archaeologists are sites and artifacts. These come down to us much modified by the ravages of centuries and millennia: the site-formation processes.

Site-Formation Processes

> The time machine, which has enchanted generations of readers and moviegoers, is a fictional artifact for transporting people through time. Although archaeologists would welcome a time machine, we are satisfied by the remarkable fact that objects made, used, and deposited in the past survive into the present. We need not go to the past, for it comes to us.

Archaeologist Michael Schiffer's point (1987: 3) is well taken, for the objects from the past that survive come down to us in two forms: either as historically documented artifacts—such as, for example, Orville and Wilbur Wright's first airplane—or in the archaeological record as abandoned artifacts like clay vessels or stone axes that are no longer part of a living society. The past in the form of artifacts does not come down to us unchanged, for complex processes have acted upon these objects, be they tools, dwellings, burials, food remains, or other manufactured or humanly modified items. Archaeologists not only have to study these artifacts but to untangle the many events and processes that contribute to the great variability in the archaeological record (see Figure 9.3 on page 183).

The factors that create the historic and archaeological records are known as **site-formation processes**. Site-formation processes are those agencies, natural or cultural, that have transformed the archaeological (or historical) record. There are two basic forms of site-formation processes: cultural processes and noncultural processes.

Cultural factors are those where human behavior has transformed the archaeological record. They can vary widely in their impact and intensity. For example, later occupants of a surface that was a hunter-gatherer camp in the Nile Valley may have been farmers and goat herders rather than hunters. The foundations of their houses may have cut deeply into underlying soil, and the hooves of their penned goats may have trampled on, and scattered, small stone artifacts lying on the surface.

People also reuse artifacts. To conserve prized tools and valuable raw materials, one may change the use of an artifact from a knife to a scraper or recycle a projectile point to another use. Sometimes prestigious or valuable objects become prized heirlooms passed down from generation to generation, or are buried with the dead—as soapstone pipes and other artifacts were with Hopewell kin leaders in the Midwest more than 2,000 years ago (see Figure 3.2 on page 52). Reuse, especially of such commodities as building materials, can become a potent factor in settlements that are occupied for longer periods of time, where people recycle old bricks and other materials for new dwellings. The wooden beams used in southwestern pueblos were recycled again and again, often generations, even centuries, after they were first cut. Then there is the dumping of trash. Whether underfoot or in secondary locations, trash heaps may form. These heaps often tend to cluster in specific locations that can be used for many generations, perhaps in a convenient, abandoned storage pit or an old dwelling. Disposal of the dead can also be viewed as another form of discard behavior.

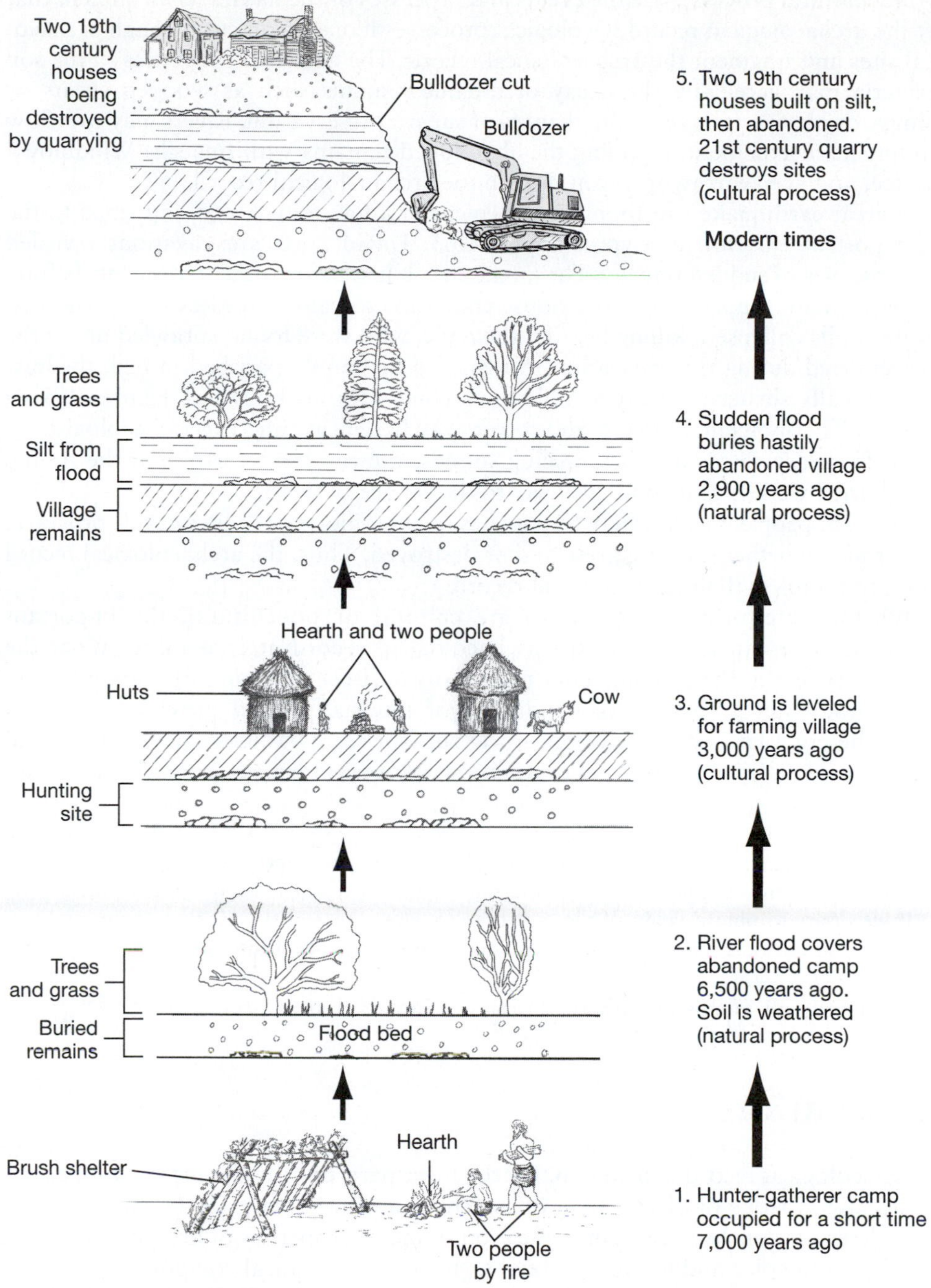

Figure 9.3 Site-formation processes.

It is a great mistake to think of any form of human discard behavior as random. The archaeologist must decipher the complicated behavioral processes—perhaps the logic, if you will—behind the accumulation of trash heaps, the disposal of the dead, and many other activities. In short, the archaeological record is not a safe place for artifacts, for myriad human activities can disturb them after deposition—plowing, mining, digging of foundations, land clearance, and even artillery bombardment, to say nothing of pothunting and site looting.

Noncultural processes are the events and processes of the natural environment that affect the archaeological record. Geological processes like erosion cut through archaeological sites and fragment the archaeological record. The chemical properties of the soil or bacteria may accelerate the decay of organic remains such as wooden spears or dwellings, or may even increase the chances of superb preservation. Rivers may overflow and inundate a settlement, mantling the abandoned remains with fine silt. Windblown sands, ice, and even earthworms can disturb the archaeological record.

A great earthquake can topple a settlement in a few minutes, as happened to the Roman port at *Kourion* in Cyprus in A.D. 365. David Soren's excavations revealed poignant scenes of sudden tragedy. The quake struck just before dawn. Moments before, a young girl had stepped out into a house courtyard to calm a restless mule. The surrounding walls collapsed, killing her and the mule, who were found sprawled under the debris removed during the excavation. A man and his family perished in bed, the husband frantically sheltering his wife and young child with his body (see Figure 7.15 on page 149). The moment of death and terror was frozen in time for archaeologists to uncover. It is easy to picture the crashing sounds, the rumbling earth, and the frantic cries of buried victims that soon give way to the silence of death.

In short, people decide where to put sites, but geomorphic (noncultural) processes can determine whether they are preserved or destroyed. Thus, the archaeological record is no more complete than the geological record.

Whether site-formation processes are cultural or noncultural, the important point is that one can never take the archaeological record at face value. What the archaeologist sees in the ground is not necessarily a direct reflection of human behavior. It is not enough to observe conditions of unusually good preservation or to describe the complex layers of a prehistoric rockshelter. One must also analyze and interpret the ways in which the archaeological record was formed. As Michael Schiffer put it (1987: 4):

> The real time machine, then, is the archaeological process: the principles and procedures that we as scientists apply to material traces in the historical and archaeological records. If we desire to obtain views of the past that are closer to reality . . . then we must build into our time machine a thorough understanding of formation processes.

A large component in this hypothetical time machine is that of preservation.

Preservation

The archaeological record is made up, for the most part, of only the most durable artifacts, usually in stone or clay. The environment is a hostile place for human artifacts, causing deterioration and drastic modification to many properties of artifacts, affecting everything from color and texture to weight, shape, and chemical composition.

The environmental agents of deterioration can be grouped into chemical, physical, and biological categories. Chemical agents are universal, for the atmosphere contains water and oxygen, which create many chemical reactions—for example, corrosion of some metals. Different water temperatures, irradiation of materials by sunlight, and atmospheric pollutants all cause chemical reactions. Buried objects are often subject to rapid chemical change, especially as a result of dampness. Soils also contain reactive compounds such as acids and bases, which contribute to deterioration—acid soils dissolve bones, for example. Many archaeological deposits are somewhat salty, a condition caused by salts derived from wood ash, urine, and the neutralization of acids and bases. Such saline conditions can retard some decay, but react severely with copper, iron, and silver.

Physical agents of deterioration such as water, wind, sunlight, and earth movement are also universal. Water is especially potent, for it can tumble artifacts on the shoreline, sometimes even fracturing them in ways that suggest human intervention. Rainwater can cascade off roofs and tunnel deep grooves into walls. Cycles of wetness followed by dryness can crack wood and cause rot, and melting and freezing ice cracks rocks and concrete. Physical agents operate on small and large scales alike. For example, the effects of the earthquake at Kourion on Cyprus in A.D. 365 not only flattened the small port but affected the landscape for miles around.

Living organisms are the main agents of biological decay. Bacteria occur almost everywhere and are usually the first to colonize dead organic matter and to begin the processes of decay. Fungi also occur widely and are especially destructive to wood and other plant matter, particularly in warm, damp climates. Beetles, ants, flies, and termites infest archaeological sites, especially middens and abandoned foods. Dogs, hyenas, and other such animals gnaw, chew, and scavenge bones and other organic materials from the surface of abandoned sites and game kills. The fragmentary animal bones scavenged by early hominins at Olduvai Gorge, Tanzania, bore clear signs of hyena teeth, for the predators had moved in on the abandoned hominin sites as soon as they departed.

Processes within the natural environment affect not only artifacts but the actual physical sites that form their context in time and space. Archaeologists who spend most of their time in the field are often known as "dirt archaeologists" because they are always working with one of the primary constituents of an archaeological site—the soil. The first human activity at any site takes place on a natural surface, on sediments sitting on underlying bedrock. Sometimes this sediment was weathered over a long time, and may contain pollen grains, plant remains, or other sources of environmental information. Some Stone Age and Bronze Age burial mounds in Europe were erected on undisturbed soils that contained forest pollen grains, giving a picture of the local environment at the time of construction. For example, these pollens tell us that a large burial mound near the famous stone circles at Avebury, England, was located on recently cleared forest land, close to cultivated fields. The original land surface under another nearby mound still bore the plow marks from recent cultivation (see Figure 9.4 on page 186).

After a site is abandoned, additional sediments usually accumulate on top of the archaeological remains—sediments accumulated by wind or water action, such as the windblown sands that accumulate in the rooms of Southwestern pueblos. The footsteps of humans and animals as well as burrowing animals, earthworms, wall flakings from overhanging cliffs, and the deteriorating elements of artifacts and structures contribute to the alteration of archaeological deposits. Stone Age rockshelters in southwestern France, for example, were occupied intermittently by hunter-gatherer groups between 15,000 and 50,000 years ago. Some of the larger ones contain densely packed layers of hearths, ash accumulations, boulders, and decaying structures. Untangling how these levels were formed is a complex process. Some of the larger rockshelters, like the famous *La Madeleine* shelter on the banks of the Vezère River, were occupied for months on end, especially when salmon were running or during spring and fall reindeer migrations. How does one distinguish longer-term occupation from repeated short visits on the basis of what remains in the deposits? A myriad of different environmental processes contribute to site formation and can transform the archaeological record in ways that can be mistaken for traces of human behavior.

The preservation of such fragile **organic materials** as bone, leather, skin, textiles, and wood depends on their physical environment. Soil and climatic conditions very strongly influence archaeological materials. The inorganic artifacts—stone, baked clay pots, mud bricks, gold, copper, and bronze—are preserved best. Much of the surviving archaeological record consists of such durable **inorganic materials** in the form of human tools (see Figure 8.12 on page 168).

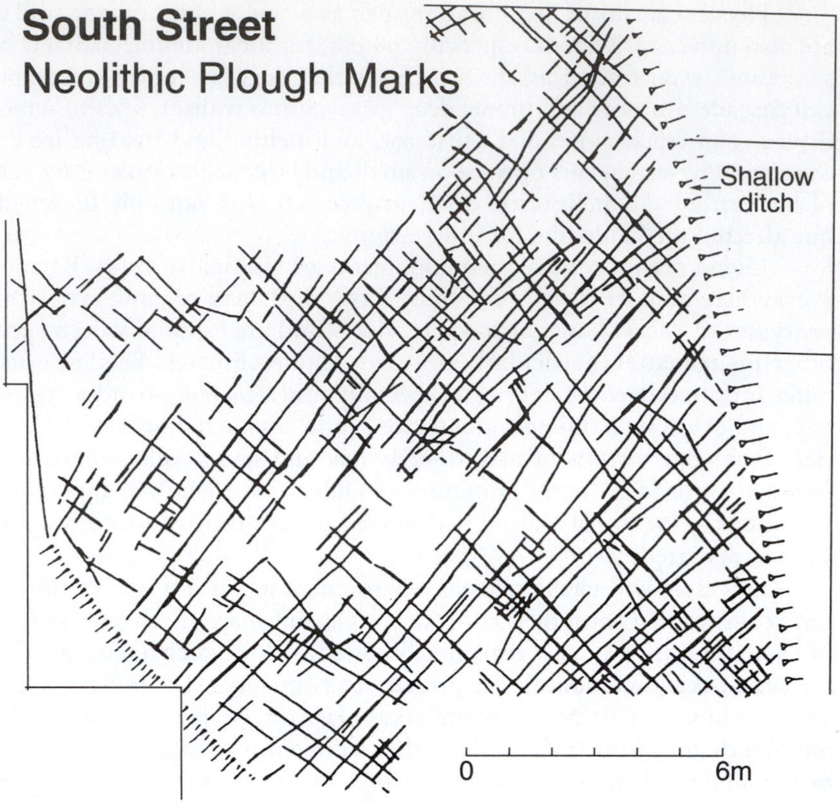

Figure 9.4 Plow marks on a cultivated field buried under a burial mound at South Street, Avebury, England.

Ancient peoples used many organic substances, materials that survive at relatively few locations. Bone and antler were commonly used by early hunter-gatherers, especially in Europe some 16,000 years ago. The desert peoples of western North America relied heavily on plant fibers and baskets for their material culture. Both hard and soft woods were used for digging sticks, bows and arrows, and other tools and weapons. Cotton textiles were much prized in coastal Peru 2,000 years ago. Nearly every human society collected wild vegetable foods for part of their livelihood. These and traces of broken animal bones and other food remains are sometimes found when preservation conditions are favorable.

Favorable Preservation Conditions

What are the most favorable conditions for preservation of archaeological finds? The fantastically rich tomb of the Egyptian pharaoh Tutankhamun, who died in 1323 B.C., yielded incredible finds, including his personal wooden furniture, much of his clothing, and the perishable ritual objects that accompanied the dead king to the next world (see Figure 9.2 on page 181). Tutankhamun's tomb is the only pharaoh's burial ever to be discovered intact, undisturbed by tomb robbers. The richness of the grave furniture came as a complete surprise and included not only his personal possessions, but his chariots, broken down in easily assembled parts. (In a recent study, French archaeologists have reconstructed the chariots and concluded they were drawn by small horses, even ponies.)

The Moche Lords of Sipán in northern coastal Peru were buried under an adobe clay platform in about A.D. 400. The dry conditions of the Peruvian desert preserved their lavishly adorned sepulchers, where three lords lay in graves stratified one above the other, each wearing their complete ceremonial regalia, including golden masks and elaborate gold and silver jewelry. We know from scenes painted on Moche pots that these were warrior-priests, who presided over warfare and ceremonies that involved the sacrifice of prisoners of war. In life, the lords would have glittered brightly in the sun when they appeared in public, in a dazzling display of political and spiritual power. They would have seemed like gods on earth (see Figure 2.6 on page 35).

Dry conditions like those of the Nile Valley have led to remarkable discoveries in the desert of the western United States as well, where caves in Utah and Nevada have yielded not only moccasins, sandals, bows and arrows, and other wood and fiber objects, but thousands of seeds, and even human excrement (**coprolites** or feces), which can be analyzed to give information on prehistoric diet (see Figure 9.5; see also Chapter 11).

Waterlogged, flooded sites also aid preservation. They can seal off organic finds in an oxygen-free atmosphere. Danish archaeologists have found prehistoric dugout canoes deep in ancient peat bogs, along with leather clothing, traps, and wood spears. Their most famous finds are the corpses of sacrificial victims buried in the bogs more than 2,000 years ago. We can gaze on the serene countenance of *Tollund Man*. His corpse is in such excellent condition that we know he had not eaten for at least 24 hours before his death, and that his last meal was a porridge of barley and wild grasses (see Figure 9.6 on page 188).

Richard Daugherty gained unusual insights into ancient whale hunting on the Northwest Coast of North America by digging a Makah Indian village at *Ozette*, Washington, long buried by sudden mud slides. The wet mud crushed cedar plank houses by the ocean, sealing their contents from the destructive effects of the atmosphere. The Ozette village was occupied for more than 2,000 years, right into the twentieth century. The buried houses provided a wealth of information about Makah life and artistic traditions of centuries ago. The thick mud preserved walls and beams, sleeping benches, and fine mats. Wood fishhooks, seal-oil bowls, cedar storage boxes,

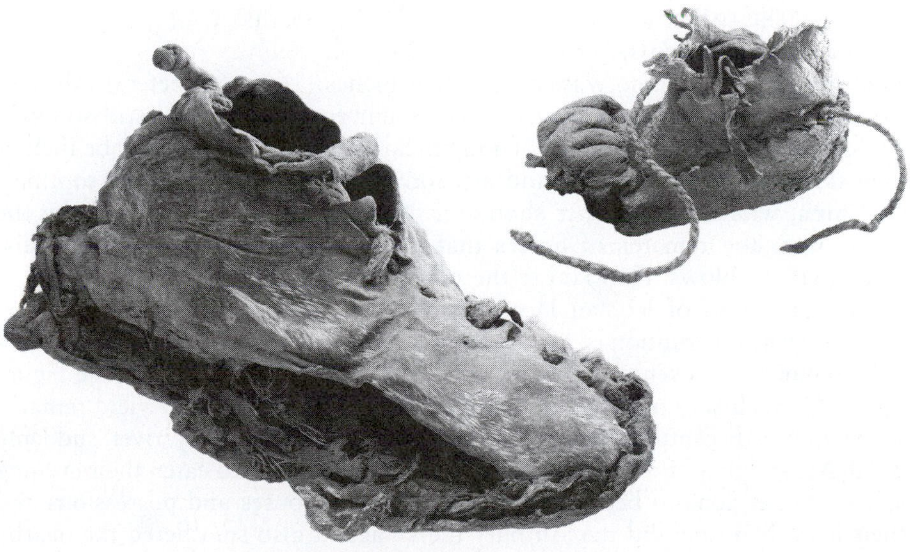

Figure 9.5 Perfectly preserved moccasins. The larger moccasin is from Hogup Cave, Utah (42B036) with catalog number FS47.7 and is a Fremont-style moccasin ca. 500 A.D. The smaller moccasin is from Promontory Cave, Utah (42B01) with catalog number 9764 and is a Puckered Toe child's moccasin ca. 1260 A.D. (Courtesy of Utah Museum of Natural History.)

and whaling harpoons were uncovered by using fine pressurized water jets to wash mud from the soft wood. The most remarkable find of all was a whale fin carved out of red cedar and inlaid with sea otter teeth, a unique ritual object without parallel in North America. Waterlogged conditions can also preserve complete field systems and trackways built across marshy ground. The celebrated Neolithic and Bronze Age trackways that survive in the peats of the low-lying Somerset Levels in southwestern England can be dated precisely by dendrochronology (see Figure 9.7 on page 189).

Figure 9.6 The head of Tollund Man, whose remarkably well-preserved corpse was discovered in the peat bogs of Denmark. He was probably a ritual sacrifice and is now preserved in the National Museum of Denmark, Copenhagen.

Fortunate is the archaeologist who finds a site with conditions as good as those at Ozette. They are very much the exception rather than the rule. Arctic cold and permafrost can literally refrigerate the past and preserve the minutest details of clothing, even skin tattoos. In 1993, Russian archaeologist Natalya Polosmak excavated an undisturbed burial chamber on the Ukok Plateau of southern Siberia, once home to ancient herders from the sixth to second centuries B.C. The chamber contained an ice-filled log coffin, which Polosmak thawed by pouring hot water onto it for days. The casket contained the body of a 25-year-old woman wearing an elaborate headdress. The woman, 5 feet 6 inches (168 centimeters) tall, had been laid to rest on her side, her strong hands crossed in front of her. The still-soft skin of one shoulder bore an intricate tattoo of a mythical creature. Her burial robe included a woolen skirt of horizontal white and maroon stripes and a yellow silk top, perhaps from China, which mantled her shoulders. A wood-handled mirror lay by the body. Nearby were the remains of horses that had been led to the graveside, dispatched with swift ax blows, then laid in the pit next to their mistress.

Everyone has heard of Roman Herculaneum and Pompeii—entire towns overwhelmed in A.D. 79 by an eruption of nearby Mount Vesuvius. The volcanic ash and lava buried both communities, even preserving the body casts of fleeing victims (see Figure 9.8 on page 189). Such sites are rare, but when they are discovered they yield remarkable finds. In the sixth century A.D., a volcanic eruption in a nearby river suddenly buried a small Maya village at Cerén in San Salvador. The people had eaten their evening meal, but had not yet gone to bed. They abandoned their houses and possessions and fled for their lives. Not only did the ash bury the village, it also smothered the nearby crops, burying corn, manioc, and agave plants as they stood in the fields. Payson Sheets and his research team have recovered entire dwellings and outhouses, and the artifacts within them, just as they were when abandoned. Each Cerén household had one building for eating, sleeping, and other activities, and a storehouse, a kitchen, and sometimes other structures (see Figure 9.9 on page 190).

Figure 9.7 A well-preserved Bronze Age trackway in the Somerset Levels, southwestern England.

Substantial thatched roofs projected far beyond the walls, providing not only covered walkways, but places for processing grain and for storage. Each household stored grain in clay vessels with tight lids, suspended some corn and chilis from the roof, and kept sharp knives in the rafters. The excavations have uncovered outlying maize fields where the plants were doubled over, with the ears still attached to the stalk, a "storage" technique still used in parts of Central America today. Judging from the mature maize plants, the eruption occurred at the end of the growing season, in August. Cerén provides an unusually complete look at life in a humble Maya settlement far removed from the great ceremonial centers where the elite lived.

However, as we have said, most archaeological sites yield only a fraction of the organic materials buried in them. The fortunate archaeologist may recover not only manufactured tools but some food remains as well—animal bones or a handful of shells, seeds, or other vegetable remnants—but only rarely does anything more survive. Obviously the picture one obtains of the inhabitants at such a site is incomplete

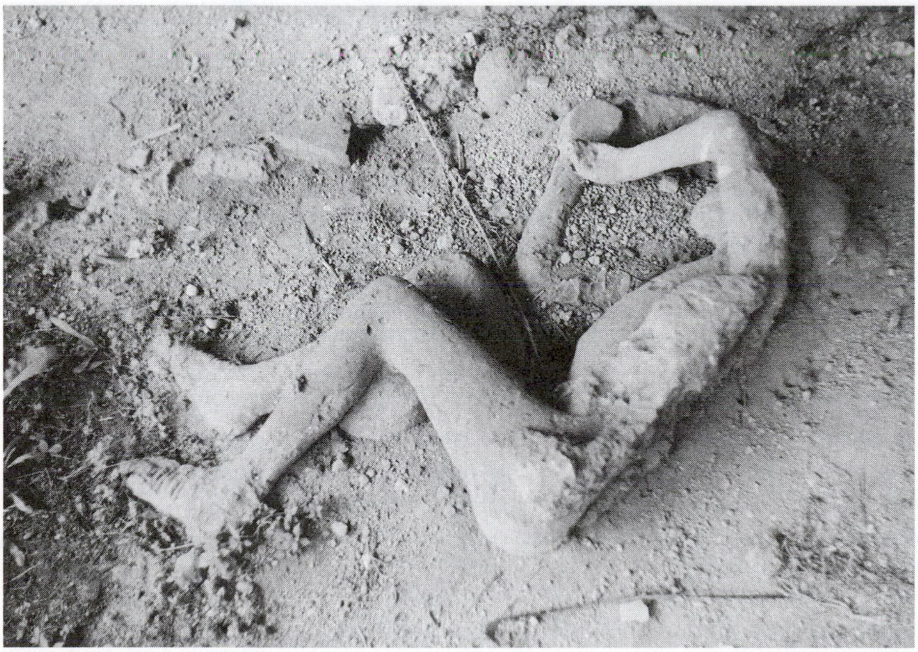

Figure 9.8 The body of a beggar smothered by volcanic ash outside the Nucerian gate at Pompeii, Italy.

Figure 9.9 Artist's reconstruction of the dwelling, workshop (right), and storehouse (left), Household 1, Cerén, El Salvador. (From *The Cerén Site*, 1st edition, by Payson Sheets. © 1992 Wadsworth, a part of Cengage Learning, Inc. Reproduced by permission. www.cengage.com/permissions.)

compared with that from Cerén or Ozette. This makes the problem of bridging the gap between past and present of the greatest importance.

Middle-Range Theory and the Archaeological Record

The archaeological record is static, whereas the present is ever-changing and dynamic. How, then, does one study the relationship between the static and dynamic, between the past and the present? This issue is of critical importance to archaeology, for most of our research is based on the assumption that because an artifact is used in a specific way, it was used in that way millennia before. This assumed relationship has two parts:

- The past is dead and knowable only through the present—by archaeologists studying it.
- Accurate knowledge of the present is essential to understanding the past.

Middle-range theory comprises methods, theories, and ideas that can be applied to any period and anywhere in the world to explain what we have discovered, excavated, or analyzed from the past. The general concept comes from sociology and describes a body of theory that is being formed as archaeologists try to bridge the gap between what actually happened in the past and the archaeological record of today. Lewis Binford and other archaeologists have searched for "Rosetta stones" that permit one to use observations of the static past to make statements about its long-vanished dynamics. They believe middle-range theory provides the conceptual tools for explaining artifact patternings and other material phenomena from the archaeological record.

Middle-range research is important to archaeology, whether one believes that this research is meant to specify the relationships between behavior and material remains or to understand the determinants of patterning and structural properties of the archaeological record. It is conducted by **ethnographic analogy**, by studying living societies (**ethnoarchaeology**), and/or by using historical documents or controlled experiments (**experimental archaeology**).

By no means do all archaeologists agree that the archaeological record holds no direct information on human behavior. Many argue that the relationship between human behavior and material culture in all times and places is what archaeology is all about. The controversy continues, but it is safe to say that ethnoarchaeology and experimental research, as well as analogy, have leading roles in today's research into the past.

The Living Past

We live in a world inhabited by an astonishing diversity of human societies. A century ago, many of them were still living in much the same way as their prehistoric ancestors. But the unchanging routine of planting and harvest, of life and death, of the seasons of game and vegetable foods, has withered in the face of Western exploration and industrial civilization. Today, few of these societies still enjoy their traditional lifeways. Many are extinct. The Tasmanians effectively vanished within 70 years of white settlement; the Indians of Terra del Fuego disappeared in the 1950s (see Figure 9.10). Ishi, one of the last California hunter-gatherers, managed to live in his home territory in the northern California foothills until 1911. He saw all of his companions wiped out by white settlers. The surviving Indian peoples of the Amazon region are rapidly fading away in the face of large-scale mining operations that are decimating their rain forest environment.

Anthropology has traditionally worked with non-Western societies and with peoples who have had to make far-reaching adjustments to encroaching industrial civilization. Anthropologists have followed the fates of these people as they have adjusted, often becoming impoverished minorities in large industrial cities. Since the nineteenth century, many of the societies once studied by anthropologists have, by their death or transformation, become part of the archaeological record. No longer living groups, they have left behind them surface scatters of artifacts and sites that are now the only chronicle of their societies other than early historical records, oral traditions, or anthropological studies of some generations ago. In short, they have become human cultures of the past.

For years, archaeologists talked about an "ethnographic present," a moment in time when a non-Western society first came in contact with Europeans, such as when Captain James Cook landed on Tahiti in the South Pacific in 1769. They tended to think of Tahitian culture, and other cultures for that matter, as frozen like time capsules, when, in fact, these cultures had changed continually for centuries, and still changed after European contact. There has never been an ethnographic present, but archaeologists have long recognized the value of records of such societies as a way of interpreting much older cultures. They approach the problem by using ethnographic analogy and ethnoarchaeology.

Figure 9.10 A group of Fuegian Indians.

Ethnographic Analogy

Early anthropologists collected vast quantities of information on traditional material culture of diverse societies all over the world. This material gave archaeologists a chance to compare still-living peoples and prehistoric peoples who had a basically similar technology. Thus, it was argued, the African San, Australian Aborigines, and other living hunter-gatherers who had no metals could be considered living representatives of prehistoric, stone-using hunter-gatherers. Under this approach, an archaeologist who dug a 20,000-year-old campsite in an arctic environment could turn to the Eskimo of today for comparative modern material. They believed that Eskimo and arctic Stone Age cultures bore remarkable similarities, on the grounds that they adapted to the same environment.

This type of reasoning was obviously simplistic because each human society, ancient or modern, has, or has had, its own distinctive adaptation to its environment, which helps shape all aspects of its culture in many ways. For example, some 15,000 years ago, the late Ice Age Magdalenian hunter-gatherers of southwestern France were expert reindeer hunters, whose sustenance relied heavily on the seasonal migrations of these animals. Similarly, modern subarctic hunter-gatherer groups in northern Canada live off migrating herds of caribou, a close relative of the reindeer. The late Ice Age environment of southwestern France and that of the Canadian subarctic are radically different, as are the technologies each group uses or used. It would be naive indeed to claim that the Magdalenians of 18,000 years ago were prehistoric examples of modern subarctic caribou hunters.

Archaeologists then began to make analogies with recent societies in new ways. They worked back from known, living peoples into earlier times. They began by digging sites of historically documented Indians and studying their contents, making full use of historical records to interpret their finds. Thus, photographs of Northwest Coast Indian homes taken in 1890 would be compared with excavated home foundations from comparatively recent times, say, A.D. 1500. If the features of both were the same, then it was reasonable to interpret the design of prehistoric houses from this model. The house would then be traced backward into prehistoric times in sites many centuries earlier than the historic settlements.

This method, very simply stated, is the basis on which archaeologists use ethnographic records to interpret prehistoric artifacts and sites. Considerable controversy surrounds such interpretations, for sophisticated research methods are needed if comparisons are to be made between modern artifact patternings and those found in prehistoric sites. For this reason many archaeologists believe that "living archaeology" (or ethnoarchaeology) is a more effective approach.

Living Archaeology (Ethnoarchaeology)

Much of the ethnographic material available to archaeologists was collected when anthropology was much less sophisticated than it is today. Very often ethnographers collected object after object or information on customs without recording detailed information on settlement layout or artifact patternings, the types of information that archaeologists now need so badly. One can hardly blame the pioneers, for they were out to record as much information about vanishing cultures as they could before it was too late, and subtle settlement details hardly seemed a high priority. Today, many of the settlements the anthropologists studied have themselves become archaeological sites. They are now virtually indistinguishable from prehistoric sites with their middens and crumbled hut foundations. They offer a unique opportunity to study the processes by which abandoned settlements turn into archaeological sites. Understanding these processes makes archaeological interpretation in general much easier, and so some archaeologists have gone out in the field to study "living archaeology" for themselves.

This form of living archaeology came into its own during the 1970s, with studies of both African San hunter-gatherers and Nunamiut caribou hunters in Alaska. More recent research has focused on such hunter-gatherer groups as the Hazda of northern Tanzania; on farming societies such as the Kalinga of the Philippines; and on several southwestern Asian groups. By living in, say, an Eskimo hunting camp and observing the activities of its occupants, the archaeologist hopes to record archaeologically observable patterns, knowing what activities brought them into existence. Sometimes historical documents can be used to amplify observations in the field. The earliest ethnoarchaeological work focused on specific artifact patternings and on studies of hunter-gatherer encampments that might provide ways of interpreting the very earliest human sites at Olduvai Gorge and elsewhere. But a major focus of later work has been to develop archaeological methods of inference that bridge the gap between past and present.

Many archaeologists regard ethnoarchaeology as simply a mass of observed data on human behavior from which they can draw up suitable hypotheses to compare with the finds from their excavations and laboratory analyses. This interpretation is totally wrong, for in fact ethnoarchaeological research deals with dynamic processes in the modern world.

The !Kung San

Anthropologist Richard Lee, who has spent many years studying the !Kung San of southern Africa, took archaeologist John Yellen with him on one of his expeditions. (The ! symbol denotes a click sound made with the tongue against the roof of the mouth.) Yellen spent many months studying the ways in which the San butchered animals and the fragmentary bones that resulted from butchery, cooking, and eating (see Figure 9.11). He drew plans of recently abandoned sites of known age, recorded the

Figure 9.11 Living archaeology: A !Kung San brush shelter and windbreak in the Kalahari Desert, southern Africa, recorded by archaeologist Francis Van Noten shortly after it was abandoned. (Professor F. L. Van Noten, Belgium).

positions of houses, hearths, and occupation debris, and talked to people who had lived there as a way of establishing precise population estimates and the social relationships of the inhabitants.

Yellen found that the San camps developed their layouts through conscious acts, such as building a shelter or a hearth, as well as through such casual deeds as discarding animal bones and debris from toolmaking. There were communal areas that everyone used and private family areas gathered around hearths. Some activity areas, such as places where women cracked nuts in the heat of the day, were simply located under a convenient shady tree. Yellen recorded that most food preparation took place in family areas. Most activities in San camps were related to individual families. Theoretically, therefore, one should be able to study the development of the family through time by studying changing artifact patternings. To do so in practice, of course, requires very comprehensive data and carefully formulated research designs.

Maya Metates

When archaeologist Brian Hayden was examining Maya stone tools of the post-Conquest colonial period near the Mexico-Guatemala border, he discovered that some present-day Mayan-speaking communities still made and used stone grinders and pounders—metates and manos—in the traditional way. Hayden designed a broad-based research project to examine the properties of the stone collected for tool manufacture, the efficiency of stone technology, and the evolution of the forms of stone tools as they were used and reused. He worked closely with a 50-year-old metate maker named Ramon Ramos Rosario. Hayden followed Rosario through the entire manufacturing process, from the selection of the material to the final surface smoothing of the artifact (see Figure 9.12). Time and motion studies showed that it took this expert 2.5 days to rough out and smooth a metate blank using only stone tools and 4.5 to 5.5 days to finish both a metate and a mano. Finally, Hayden examined the characteristics of the picks used to chip and peck the rock as if they were archaeological finds, combining these studies with use-wear analysis. Hayden seriated the picks on the basis of the intensity of edge-wear development and as a way of estimating the relative length of use of comparable tools. He compared his results to prehistoric artifacts and was able to show that many blunt-edged

Figure 9.12 Ramon Ramos Rosario making a stone metate.

Maya woodworking tools in archaeological sites were probably used by women to roughen used manos and metates.

The Hayden study demonstrates the power and potential of a many-sided approach to ethnoarchaeology, using data from the dynamic present to evaluate archaeological evidence from the static archaeological record.

Nunamiut Eskimos

In another instance, Lewis Binford's study of the Nunamiut caribou hunters of Alaska was designed to learn as much as possible about an Eskimo group's hunting practices. The Nunamiut depended heavily on meat, supplementing their flesh diet with the partially digested contents of caribou stomachs and about a cupful of vegetable foods a year. They relied extensively on stored food for eight and a half months a year, fresh meat being freely available for only about two months. Binford soon found that the Nunamiut food-procurement strategy was based on complicated decisions that involved not only the distribution of food at different seasons, but the storage potential of different animals and their parts, as well as the logistics of procurement, carrying, and storing meat. Was it easier to move people to the herds or to carry meat back to base? His research convinced him that the linkages between the facts of animal anatomy and the realities of lifeway strategies held the key to meaningful analysis of animal bones.

Binford studied the annual round of the Nunamiut, and also their butchery and storage strategies, developing indexes to measure utilization of different body parts. He also compared observations from modern kill sites to 42 archaeologically known locations that dated to earlier times. The Nunamiut research is valuable not only for the large body of empirical data it generated, but also because it showed just how locally confined any cultural adaptation is.

The Nunamiut research and other ethnoarchaeological projects serve as a cautionary tale, for they show that differences in artifacts and human behavior at different locations can result from entirely local considerations and not necessarily from cultural differences.

Tucson, Arizona: Modern Material Culture and Garbage

Although ethnoarchaeological investigations have tended to focus on hunter-gatherers, there are numerous instances of fascinating research on more complex societies, even our own. William Rathje's major long-term study of modern urban garbage in Tucson, Arizona, for example, is based on the latest archaeological methods and research designs. The project is designed to investigate the relationships between resource management, urban demography, and social and economic stratification in a modern context, where control data from interviews and other perspectives are available to amplify an archaeological study of a type that might be conducted at an ancient urban center. The Tucson garbage study has produced remarkable results, showing widely different patterns of resource management from one segment of the city's population to another, with the middle class being the most wasteful.

Experimental Archaeology

Archaeologists love experimenting with the past. One ardent early experimenter, Robert Ball of Dublin, Ireland, blew a prehistoric horn so hard that he produced a sound like a bellowing bull. Unfortunately, his heroic effort caused him to burst a blood vessel and die. Not all experimental archaeology is so risky, however. Archaeologists have been making stone implements, floating over oceans on rafts, and trying to re-create the past ever since the eighteenth century. Some of their achievements are remarkable.

Louis Leakey, the famous Stone Age archaeologist, not only dug early hominin sites, but also spent many years perfecting his skills as a stone toolmaker. He could shape a perfect prehistoric hand ax and skin an antelope with it in a few minutes—a favorite demonstration at conferences. One of the most remarkable experiments of all was Norwegian Thor Heyerdahl's *Kon-Tiki* expedition in 1947, in which he attempted to prove that Polynesia had been settled by adventurous Peruvians who had sailed balsa rafts across thousands of miles of ocean. Heyerdahl did succeed in reaching Polynesia in a balsa raft. His expedition merely proved, however, that long ocean voyages in Kon-Tiki rafts were possible. He did not prove that the Peruvians settled Polynesia.

People have cleared thick Danish woodland with stone axes and grown prehistoric crops in the American Southwest under conditions identical to those of centuries ago. The latter experiments lasted 17 years. Good crop yields were obtained in all but two years, when drought killed the young crops. Experiments in living the prehistoric lifestyle have proved popular, especially in Britain and Denmark, where television networks have financed long-term experiments with volunteer "prehistoric peoples." One British experiment centered on several families who were provided with crops and livestock and isolated in a reconstruction of an Iron Age village of about 200 B.C. They were left alone to survive for a year, the only concession being modern antibiotics and birth control pills. Such experiments are of questionable scientific value, but they do provide superficial insights into the realities of prehistoric life. More serious are controlled burnings of some faithful reconstructions of ancient houses, to show what structures would look like when reduced to ashes—as such dwellings are in many actual sites. British archaeologists have even built an entire experimental earthwork that they are digging up at regular intervals over 128 years. The resulting information on soil decay and artifact preservation will be invaluable for interpreting equivalent prehistoric sites.

Many recent experimenters have concentrated on replicating such phenomena as wear on the working edges of prehistoric stone tools. Lawrence Keeley and other researchers have examined stone artifacts such as Paleo-Indian points under high- and low-power microscopes. They are now able to distinguish between wear polishes associated with different materials, including wood, bone, and hide. This approach is now reliable enough to discern whether a tool was used to slice wood, cut up vegetables, or strip meat from bones. Sometimes, edge-wear studies can yield remarkable results, especially when combined with refitting—reassembling flakes with the parent core from which they were struck. These techniques enabled Daniel Cahen and Lawrence Keeley to identify the left-handed stoneworker at Meer, Belgium, mentioned in Chapter 8. By reassembling some of the stone flakes and cores, studying the wear patterns on tool-working edges, and examining distribution of stone fragments throughout the site, they were able to show that two people, one of them left-handed, had made some tools used to bore and shape fragments of bone.

In this, and in many other innovative projects, archaeologists are using the present to better understand the past, attempting to overcome the limitations imposed on us by the archaeological record and the formation processes that have affected it.

SUMMARY

1. The archaeological record is affected by complex site formation processes, such as human activities and soil chemistry.
2. Preservation conditions depend upon climate and oil conditions. Arid and very cold conditions, as well as waterlogged soils, offer the best opportunities for the preservation of organic remains such as corpses, soft tissue, textiles, and wood.
3. The archaeological record is static, whereas the present is ever-changing and dynamic.
4. Archaeologists assume that the past is dead and knowable only through the present, by archaeologists studying it. They use middle-range theory: methods, theories, and ideas that can be applied to any period and anywhere in the world to explain what they have discovered about the past.
5. This body of theory, derived from ethnographic analogy, ethnoarchaeology, the study of living cultural systems, and controlled experiments, is used to bridge the gap between what actually happened in the past and the archaeological record today.

TEN

Ancient Climate and Environment

Drilling an ice core atop the Quelccaya ice cap, Peru.

CHAPTER OUTLINE

PREVIEW

Human societies have adapted to changing environments and long- and short-term climate change since before the Ice Age began some 1.5 million years ago. In recent years, a revolution in the study of ancient climate change using deep-sea cores and ice cores, also tree-rings and pollen analysis, has made it possible to look at ancient human societies in the context of such changes on a much more detailed scale. Chapter 10 describes the major events of the Ice Age, then the Holocene, also the major climatological approaches for studying them. We discuss the impacts of El Niños and droughts on societies like the Moche of the Andes and the Ancestral Pueblo of the Southwest. The multidisciplinary science of geoarchaeology is of central importance in studying climatic change in the past.

. . . The Elysian Fields, where gold-haired Rhadamanthys waits, where life glides on in immortal ease for mortal man; no snow, no winter onslaught, never a downpour there but night and day the Ocean River sends up breezes singing winds of the West refreshing all mankind.

—Homer, *Odyssey* IV: 635–639

In 4500 B.C., a patch of woodland in northern England boasted mature oak, ash, and elm trees, interspersed with occasional patches of open grassland and swamp. In 3820 B.C., some foragers set fire to the forest, to encourage fresh green shoots for feeding deer. Birch and bracken now appeared. About 30 years passed before the landscape was cleared even more. Judging from numerous charcoal fragments, fire swept through the undergrowth, leaving fine ash to fertilize the soil. Now wheat pollen and that of a cultivation weed named *Plantago lanceolata* appeared. Fifty years of wheat farming ensued. These years saw only two fires, one after 6 years, the other 19 years after that. Then 70 years passed, during which agriculture ceased and the land stood vacant. Hazel, birch, and alder became more common and oak resurged as woodland rapidly gained ground. . . .

This scenario of brief clearance, slash-and-burn agriculture, then abandonment and regeneration was repeated at thousands of locations in ancient Europe in the early years of Stone Age farming. Over a few centuries, the natural environment of mixed oak forest was transformed beyond recognition by gardens and domesticated animals. Until a few years ago, we could only have guessed at these environmental changes. Today, fine-grained pollen analysis and other highly sophisticated methods allow the reconstruction of even short-lived climatic and environmental changes in the remote past.

Archaeology is unique in its ability to study culture change over very long periods of time. By the same token, it is a multidisciplinary science that also studies human interactions with the natural environment over centuries and millennia. Chapter 10 describes some of the ways archaeologists study long- and short-term environmental change from a multidisciplinary perspective (see the Discovery box on pages 200–201).

Discovery

Moche Human Sacrifice and El Niño, Huaca de la Luna, Peru, Sixth to Seventh Century A.D.

Human sacrifice was commonplace in pre-Columbian states, among them the Aztecs and the Inca. Early Spanish accounts of these societies abound with stories of people being burned alive, flayed, decapitated, or having their hearts ripped out. Archaeological evidence for such practices is fairly rare, which makes a dramatic find of a Moche sacrifice of 1400 years ago of unusual importance.

The Moche state controlled at least ten coastal valleys along the North Coast of what is now Peru during the mid-first millennium A.D. A small elite of fierce warrior priests built on the political and religious traditions of earlier Andean societies to create a complex, and very wealthy, society based on irrigation agriculture and far-flung trade with highland neighbors. The nobility, probably a network of princely families, ruled from imposing temple complexes based on adobe pyramids, built by thousands of commoners, who paid tribute to the state by compulsory labor, known in later centuries as *mi'ta*, an ancient Andean tradition. Much of what we know about Moche society comes not from written texts, but from their flamboyant visual culture, expressed in ceramics, metal artifacts, wooden sculptures, textiles, and wall paintings. A great deal of this visual culture is concerned with warfare, captured prisoners, and human sacrifice.

The greatest Moche center lay at the Huacas de Moche site, dominated by two huge pyramids named after the sun and moon. Huaca de la Luna, the Temple of the Moon, has been under continual investigation since 1991 by Peruvian archaeologists Santiago Uceda and Ricardo Morales (see Figure 10.9 on page 212). While excavating a plaza in a secluded area of the temple, Steve Bourget uncovered a precinct surrounded by high adobe walls, built in the sixth or seventh century A.D., where about seventy male warriors were sacrificed. Many of them were subsequently dismembered in the course of at least five different ritual events. After their sacrifice, the body parts of the victims were scattered around the ritual area, some of them accompanied by deliberately broken clay statuettes of named men, their bodies covered with elaborate symbols (see Figure 10.1). These were three-dimensional representations of individuals depicted in fine paintings.

What do these sacrifices mean? They may be ritual killings of prisoners of war, a frequent motif in Moche art, and one well documented by the burials of the Lords of Sipán, dating to about A.D. 400 (see Figure 3.5 on page 55). Bourget originally believed that the dead men were indeed casualties of a ritual battle, staged to placate the

Short-Term and Long-Term Climatic Change

Climatic change comes in many forms. The long cycles of cold and warm associated with the Ice Age occur on a millennial scale and have little more than long-term effects on human existence. For example, the existence of a low-lying land bridge between Siberia and Alaska during much of the late Ice Age may have allowed humans to forage their way from Asia into the Americas before 15,000 years ago, but the actual formation of the shelf that linked the two continents would have taken many centuries and human generations. Short-term climatic change, such as the floods or droughts caused by El Niño episodes or volcanic eruptions dumping ash into the atmosphere, are another matter. Memories of catastrophic famines and other events associated with such events would have endured for generations, for they had immediate impact on hundreds, if not thousands, of people. Through human history, people have developed strategies to deal with sudden climatic shifts bringing drought, hunger, or unexpected food shortages. Humans have always been brilliant opportunists, capable of improvising solutions to unexpected problems caused by environmental change. Thus environmental reconstruction and climatic change are two major concerns for archaeologists wherever they work.

Figure 10.1 Decapitated human sacrifice victims, Huaca de La Luna, Peru.

unknown forces that unleashed strong El Niños on Moche domains. But after further study, he realized that El Niños were, in fact, already fully integrated into Moche religion and ideology. The pectorals, bracelets, and other ornaments worn by the Sipán lords, and looted from other tombs, prominently depict exotic animals like the Peruvian eagle ray and swimming crabs that only arrived off the North Coast when the El Niño counter-current was flowing. The elite also wore depictions of local species affected by El Niño events such as octopuses, catfish, seabirds, and sea lions. The temple walls of Huaca de la Luna and other shrines also bear painted reliefs of animals associated with El Niños. Bourget theorizes that Moche rulers responded to the threat of El Niños by associating their authority with the awesome power of such events, which could transform the marine environment. When an El Niño event brought torrential rains that washed away entire irrigation systems and decimated the anchovy fisheries, the rulers used the occasion to reinforce their authority at times of crisis. They already wore the iconography of such events on their bodies, and caused it to be displayed on temples and on ritual vessels (see Figure 2.6 on page 35). Their authority came from their perceived unique relationship with the powers of the supernatural, reinforced by human sacrifice. So they used the immolation of the seventy sacrificial victims in this particular plaza, and probably in others, to reinforce their power and to maintain social solidarity in such times of crisis.

Long-Term Climatic Change: The Great Ice Age

About 1.8 million years ago, global cooling marked the beginning of the **Pleistocene** epoch, more popularly called the Great Ice Age. Together with the **Holocene,** which began about 15,000 years ago, it forms part of the **Quaternary** epoch. The Pleistocene was remarkable for dramatic swings in world climate. On numerous occasions during the Pleistocene, great ice sheets covered much of western Europe and North America, bringing arctic climate to vast areas of the Northern Hemisphere. Scientists have identified at least eight major glacial episodes over the past 780,000 years, alternating with shorter warm periods, when the world's climate was sometimes warmer than today. The general pattern is cyclical, with slow coolings culminating in a relatively short period of intense cold, followed by rapid warming. For 75 percent of the past three-quarters of a million years, the world's climate has been in transition from one extreme to another. We ourselves still live in the Ice Age, in a warm interglacial period. If the current scientific estimates are correct and humanly caused global warming does not interfere, we will probably begin to enter another cold phase in about 23,000 years.

No one knows exactly what causes the climatic fluctuations of the Ice Age, but they are connected with oscillations in the intensity of solar radiation and the trajectory of the earth around the sun. But such climatic changes are of great importance to archaeologists, for they form a long-term environmental backdrop for the early chapters of our past. Although almost no human beings lived on, or very close to, the great ice sheets that covered so much of the Northern Hemisphere, they did live in regions affected by geological phenomena associated with the ice sheets: coastal areas, lakes, and river floodplains. When human artifacts are found in direct association with Pleistocene geological features of this type, it is sometimes possible to tie in archaeological sites with the relative chronology of Pleistocene events derived from geological strata.

Deep-Sea Cores and Ice Cores

Our knowledge of Ice Age climatic change comes from many sources, including geological strata such as glacial deposits and ancient high beach levels, and fossil animal bones from environmentally sensitive mammals as large as elephants and as small as mice. Such approaches have long provided a crude outline of Ice Age glaciations. But in recent years the study of deep-sea and ice cores have revolutionized our understanding of the Pleistocene by providing long sequences of constantly changing Ice Age climate from deep below the ocean floor and the heart of the Greenland ice sheet.

The world's ocean floors are a priceless archive of ancient climatic change. Deep-sea cores produce long columns of ocean-floor sediments that include skeletons of small marine organisms that once lived close to the ocean's surface. These planktonic foraminifera (protozoa) consist largely of calcium carbonate. When alive, their minute skeletons absorb organic isotopes. The ratio of two of these isotopes—oxygen 16 and oxygen 18—varies as a result of evaporation. When evaporation is high, more of the lighter oxygen 16 is extracted from the ocean, leaving the plankton to be enriched by more of the heavier oxygen 18. When great ice sheets formed on land during glacial episodes, sea levels fell as moisture was drawn off for continental ice caps. During such periods, the world's oceans contained more oxygen 18 in proportion to oxygen 16, a ratio reflected in millions of foraminifera. A mass spectrometer is used to measure this ratio, which does not reflect ancient temperature changes but is merely a statement about the size of the oceans and about contemporary events on land.

One can confirm climatic fluctuations by using other lines of evidence as well, such as the changing frequencies of foraminifera and other groups of marine microfossils in the cores. By using statistical techniques, and assuming that relationships between different species and sea conditions have not changed, climatologists have been able to turn these frequencies into numerical estimates of sea surface temperatures and ocean salinity over the past few hundred thousand years and thus produce a climatic profile of much of the Ice Age (see Figure 10.2 on page 203). These events have been fixed at key points by radiocarbon dates (see Chapter 5) and by studies of paleomagnetism (ancient magnetism). The **Matuyama-Brunhes event**, a magnetic reversal of 780,000 years ago (when the world's magnetic field suddenly reversed), is a key stratigraphic marker, which can be identified both in sea cores and in volcanic strata ashore, where it can be dated precisely with potassium-argon samples.

Ice core studies are a comparatively recent development, but are now yielding increasingly accurate climatic portraits, especially of the later Ice Age and the past 10,000 years. They preserve records of annual snowfall going back far into the past. As the snow layers are buried deeper and deeper in a glacier, they are compressed into ice. The ice for winter and summer has different texture. Once researchers realized this, they were able to read ice cores like tree-ring samples, with very good resolution back for

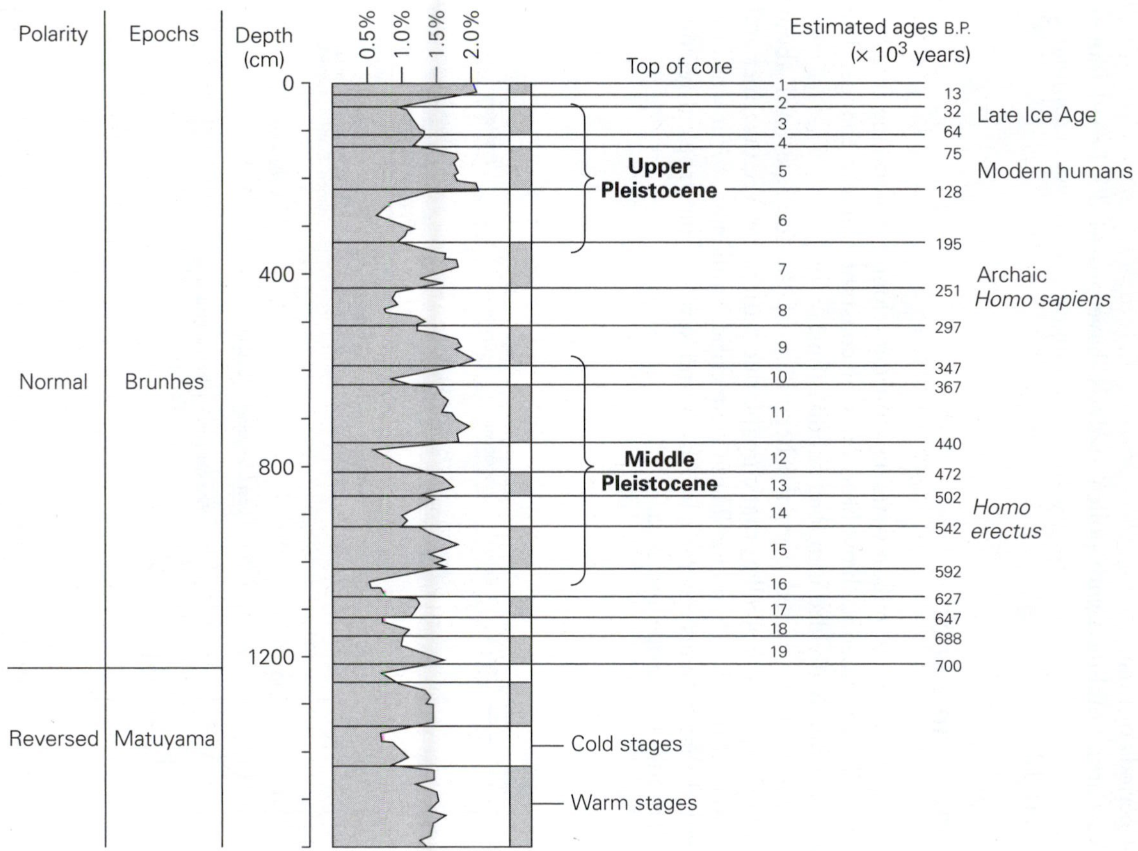

Figure 10.2 The deep-sea core that serves as the standard reference for the past 780,000 years comes from the Solomon Plateau in the southwestern Pacific Ocean. The Matuyama-Brunhes event occurs at a depth of 39.3 feet (11.9 meters). Above it a sawtooth-like curve identifies at least eight complete glacial and interglacial cycles.

12,000 years and improving accuracy back to 40,000 years. One ice core from Antarctica extends back over 400,000 years and shows that the past 10,000 years since the Ice Age have been some of the most climatically stable in human history. Ice cores have been especially useful for studying not so much the long-term fluctuations of Ice Age climatic change but the short-term episodes of warmer and colder conditions that occurred in the middle of glaciations, which had a profound effect on humanity. For example, scientists now suspect that there were bursts of human activity in late Ice Age western Europe about 35,000 and 25,000 years ago, when conditions were relatively warm for short periods of time.

Ice and sea cores, combined with pollen analysis, have provided a broad framework for the Pleistocene, which is in wide use by archaeologists and is worth summarizing here (see Figure 10.3).

The Pleistocene Framework

The Pleistocene began about 1.8 million years ago, during a long-term cooling trend in the world's oceans. These millennia have been ones of constant climatic change. The Pleistocene is conventionally divided into long subdivisions.

Lower Pleistocene times lasted from the beginning of the Ice Age until about 780,000 years ago. Deep-sea cores tell us that climatic fluctuations between warmer and colder regimens were still relatively minor. These were critical millennia, for it was during this long period that humans emerged in Africa and spread from tropical regions into temperate latitudes in Europe and Asia.

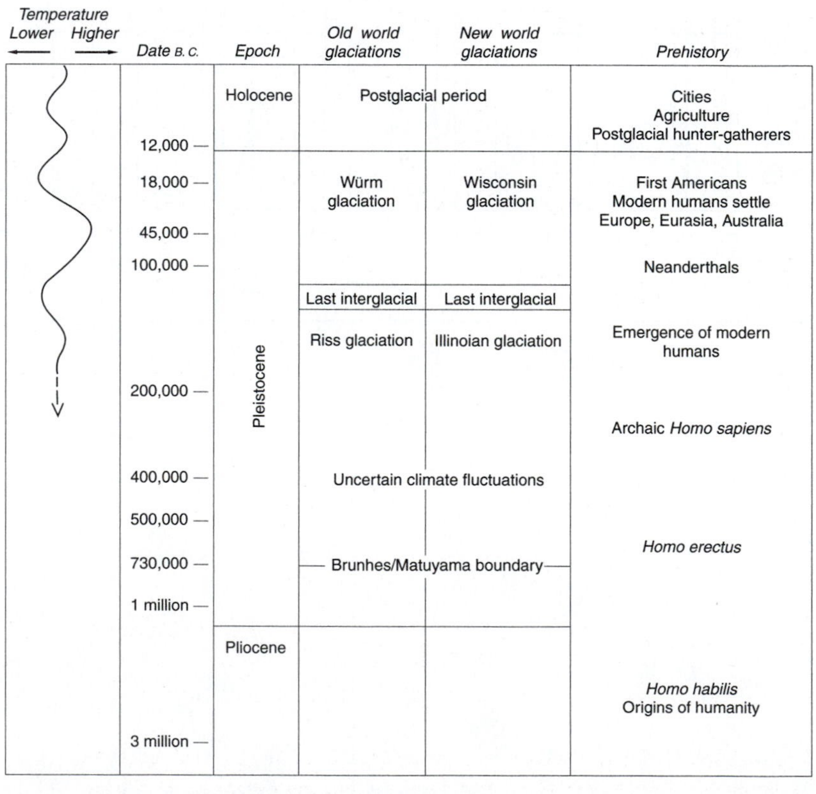

Figure 10.3 Provisional chronology and subdivisions of the Ice Age.

The *Middle Pleistocene* began with the Matuyama-Brunhes reversal in the earth's magnetic polarity about 780,000 years ago, a change that has been recognized geologically not only in deep-sea cores, but in volcanic rocks ashore, where it can be dated by potassium-argon samples.

Since then, there have been at least eight cold (glacial) and warm (interglacial) cycles, the last cycle ending about 12,000 years ago. (Strictly speaking, we are still in an interglacial today.) Typically, cold cycles have begun gradually, with vast continental ice sheets forming on land—in Scandinavia, on the Alps, and over the northern parts of North America (see Figure 10.4). These expanded ice sheets locked up enormous quantities of water, causing world sea levels to fall by several hundred feet during glacial episodes. The geography of the world changed dramatically, and large continental shelves were opened up for human settlement. When a warming trend began, deglaciation occurred very rapidly, and rising sea levels flooded low-lying coastal areas within a few millennia. During glacial periods, glaciers covered a full one-third of the earth's land surface, and during interglacials their extent was comparable to what it is today.

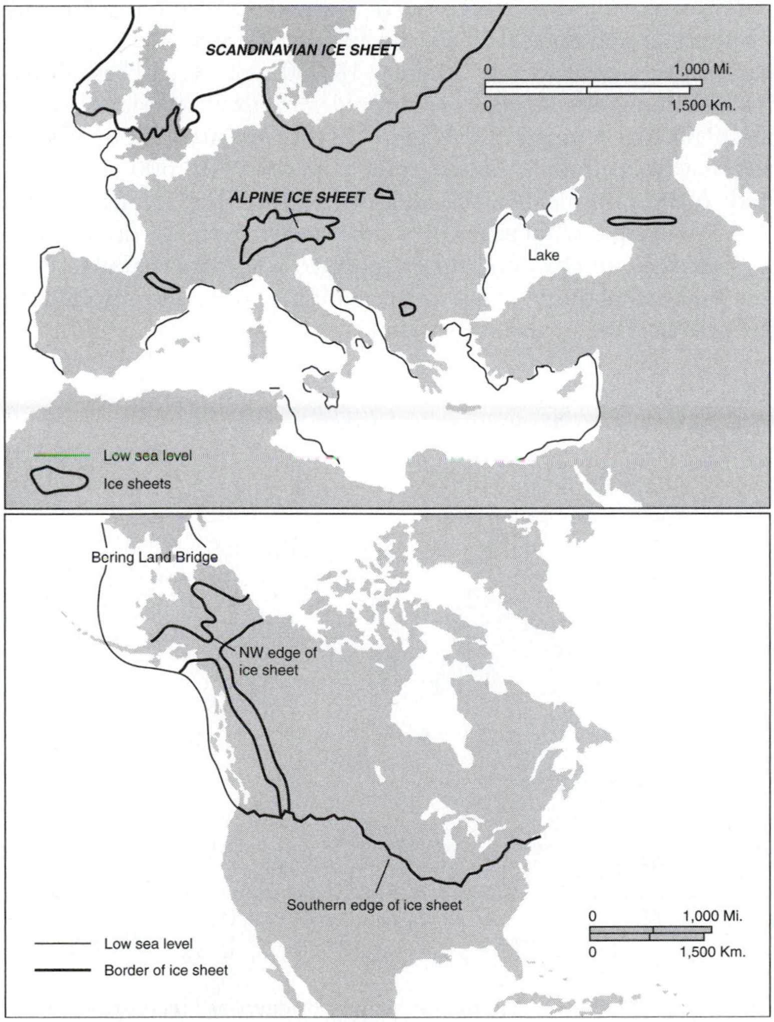

Figure 10.4 Distribution of major ice sheets in Europe and North America during the last Ice Age glaciation, and the extent of land exposed by low sea levels.

Throughout the past 730,000 years, vegetational changes have mirrored climatic fluctuations. During glacial episodes, treeless arctic steppe and tundra covered much of Europe and parts of North America, but gave way to temperate forest during interglacials. In the tropics, Africa's Sahara Desert may have supported grassland during interglacials, but ice and desert landscape expanded dramatically during dry, cold spells.

The *Upper Pleistocene* stage began about 128,000 years ago, with the beginning of the last interglacial. This period lasted until about 118,000 years ago, when a slow cooling trend brought full glacial conditions to Europe and North America. This Würm glaciation, named after a river in the Alps, lasted until about 15,000 years ago, when there was a rapid return to more temperate conditions.

The Würm glaciation was a period of constantly fluctuating climatic change, with several episodes of more temperate climate in northern latitudes (see Figure 10.2 on page 203). It served as the backdrop for some of the most important developments in human prehistory, notably the spread of anatomically modern *Homo sapiens* from the tropics to all parts of the Old World and into the Americas. Between about 25,000 and 15,000 years ago, northern Eurasia's climate was intensely cold, but highly variable. A series of brilliant Stone Age hunter-gatherer cultures evolved both on the open tundra of central Europe and Eurasia and in the sheltered river valleys of southwestern France and northern Spain, cultures famous for their fine antler and bone artifacts and exceptional artwork.

The world's geography was dramatically different 18,000 years ago. These differences had a major impact on human prehistory—one could walk from Siberia to Alaska across a flat, low-lying plain, the Bering Land Bridge (see Figure 10.5). This was the route by which humans first reached the Americas some time before 13,000 years ago.

Britain was joined to the Continent in the area of the English Channel and the southern North Sea. The low-lying coastal zones of Southeast Asia were far more extensive 15,000 years ago than they are now, and they supported a thriving population of Stone Age foragers. The fluctuating distributions of vegetational zones also affected the pattern of human settlement and the course of human history.

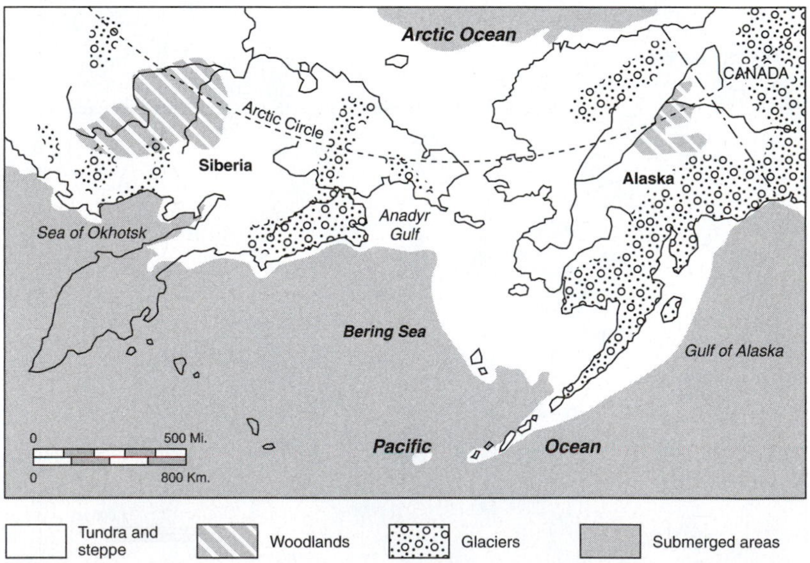

Figure 10.5 Map of the Bering Land Bridge, as reconstructed by multidisciplinary research. (From Jason W. Smith, *Foundations of Archaeology*, Glencoe Press, 1976. Reproduced by permission of Pearson Education, Inc.)

Pollen Analysis

As long ago as 1916, Swedish botanist Lennart von Post used fossil pollen grains from familiar trees like birches, oaks, and pines to develop a sequence of vegetation change for northern Europe after the Ice Age. He showed how arctic, treeless tundra gave way to birch forest, then mixed oak woodland in a dramatic sequence of change that survived in pollen samples from marshes and swamps all over Scandinavia. Since then, pollen analysis (palynology) has become a highly sophisticated way of studying both ancient environment and human impacts on natural vegetation.

The principle is simple. Large numbers of pollen grains are dispersed in the atmosphere and have remarkable preservative properties if deposited in an unaerated geological horizon. The pollen grains can be identified microscopically (see Figure 10.6) with great accuracy and used to reconstruct a picture of the vegetation, right down to humble grasses and weeds that grow near the spot where they are found.

Pollen analysis begins in the field. The botanist visits the excavation and collects a series of closely spaced pollen samples from the stratigraphic sections at the site. Back in the laboratory, the samples are examined under a very powerful microscope. The grains of each genus or species present are counted, and the resulting figures subjected to statistical analysis. These counts are then correlated with the stratigraphic layers of the excavation and data from natural vegetational sequences to provide a sequence of vegetational change for the site. Typically, this vegetational sequence lasts a few centuries or even millennia (see Figure 10.7 on page 208). It forms part of a much longer pollen sequence for the area that has been assembled from hundreds of samples from many different sites. In northern Europe, for example, botanists have worked out a complicated series of vegetational time zones that cover the past 12,000 years. By comparing the pollen sequences from individual sites with the overall chronology, they can give a relative date for the site.

Palynology has obvious applications to prehistory, for sites are often found in swampy deposits where pollen is preserved, especially fishing or fowling camps and settlements near water. Isolated artifacts, or even human corpses, such as that of Tollund Man, found in a Danish bog (see Figure 9.6 on page 188), have also been discovered in these deposits; pollen is sometimes obtained from small peat lumps adhering to crevices in such finds. Thus botanists can assign relative dates even to isolated finds that would otherwise remain undated.

Until recently, pollen analysts dealt in centuries. Now, thanks to much more refined methods and AMS radiocarbon dating, they can study even transitory episodes, such as the brief farming incident described at the beginning of this chapter. For example, dramatic falls in forest tree pollens at many locations in Europe chronicle the first

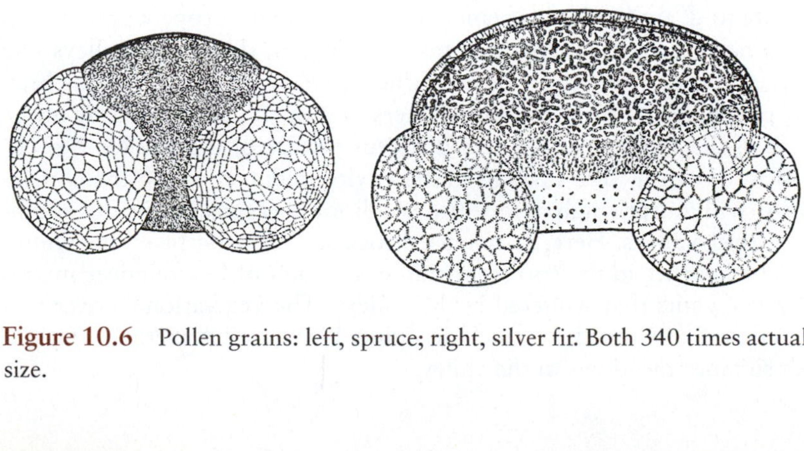

Figure 10.6 Pollen grains: left, spruce; right, silver fir. Both 340 times actual size.

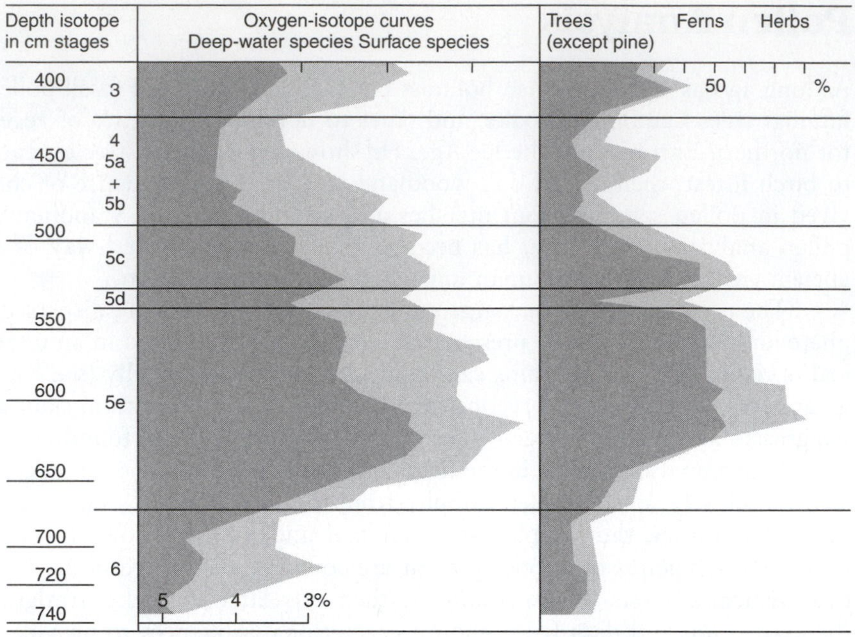

Figure 10.7 A long-term pollen sequence for the Ice Age from Spain (left) compared to oxygen-isotope curves taken from a deep-sea core in the nearby Bay of Biscay, showing the close correlation between the two.

clearance of farming cultures with almost decade-long accuracy—at a moment when characteristic cultivation weeds like *Plantago lanceolata,* already mentioned, appear for the first time. Southwestern archaeologists now have a regional pollen sequence that provides not only climatic information but also valuable facts about the functions of different pueblo rooms and different foods eaten by the inhabitants.

Identifying cultural activities from pollen sites can be extremely tricky, for the tiny grains can be transported to a site in many ways—by wind, water, rodents, even people bringing ripe fruit home. Sometimes, too, people use surface soil from neighboring areas, complete with its pollen content, to make a house floor. Some species like the sunflower have heavy pollen that can cling to ripe fruit. Such factors are likely to contaminate the pollen samples from many sites, unless one has other plant evidence, such as, say, squash rind or seeds, to confirm the palynological data.

Pollen analysis is providing new perceptions of Stone Age life at the height of the last glaciation in southwestern France, some 15,000 to 20,000 years ago (see Figure 10.7). This was, we are told, a period of extreme arctic cold, when Europe was in a deep freeze, people subsisting off arctic animals and taking refuge in deep river valleys like the Dordogne and the Vezère, where some of the earliest cave art in the world has been discovered. In fact, pollen grains from the rockshelters and open camps used by Stone Age hunter-gatherers of this period paint a very different picture of the late Ice Age climate in this area. It is a portrait of a favored arctic environment in which the climate fluctuated constantly, with surprisingly temperate conditions, especially on the south-facing slopes of deep river valleys. Here, people used rock shelters that faced the winter sun, where snow melted earlier in the spring, within easy reach of key reindeer migration routes and of arctic game that wintered in the valleys. The vegetational cover was not treeless, as is commonly assumed, but included pine, birch, and sometimes deciduous trees, with lush summer meadows in the valley.

The late Ice Age was a period of continual, and often dramatic, short- and long-term climatic change. Some of these changes lasted millennia, bringing intervals of near-modern conditions to temperate Europe interspersed with much colder winters. Other cold and warm snaps extended over a few centuries, causing human populations to adapt to dramatically new conditions. Just as today, there were much shorter climatic episodes, which endured for a year or more, bringing unusually warm summers, floods, droughts, and other short-term events.

Short-Term Climatic Change: The Holocene

The last prolonged Ice Age glaciation ended about 15,000 years ago, when North American and European ice sheets retreated and the world entered a period of pronounced global warming. Then the great glaciers retreated, sea levels rose from 300 feet (91 meters) below today's levels to near-modern heights, and vegetation patterns throughout the world changed considerably. Thus dawned the Holocene period (Greek *holos:* recent), which saw massive global warming, sudden cold snaps, and periods of warmer climate than today, with the appearance of both food production and civilization, and eventually of the Industrial Revolution. Many people believe this warming has been continuous and is reflected in the record warm temperatures of today. In fact, the world's climate has fluctuated just as dramatically as it did during the late Ice Age. Recent research is revolutionizing our knowledge of these changes, which started new chapters in human history, overthrew civilizations, and caused widespread disruption. (It should be stressed that the Holocene is a purely arbitrary scientific term, used to distinguish post–Ice Age times. We are, in fact, in a warmer interval of the Pleistocene, and, one day, the earth will become colder again—subject, of course, to the effects of humanly caused global warming.)

We can identify Holocene climatic changes from ice cores, sedimentary records in caves, tree rings, and pollen samples, with a chronological resolution that improves every year as analytical methods become ever more refined.

Centuries-Long Changes: The Younger Dryas and the Black Sea

At least three major cold snaps have cooled global temperatures over the past 11,000 years. The last of these was the so-called Little Ice Age, which lasted from about A.D. 1300 to 1850. The earlier two of these cold intervals had major effects on the course of human history, which we can now assess thanks to new deep-sea core, ice core, and pollen researches.

The *Younger Dryas* lasted from 11,000 to 10,000 B.C. For some still-little-understood reason, global warming ceased abruptly, perhaps as a result of sudden changes in the warm water circulation in the Atlantic Ocean. Within a century or so, Europe again shivered under near–Ice Age conditions as forests retreated and widespread drought affected areas like southwestern Asia. This catastrophic drought after centuries of ample rainfall may have been a major factor in the appearance of agriculture and animal domestication in areas like the Euphrates and Jordan River valleys, where dense forager populations had long subsisted off abundant food resources. What happened next has been documented by botanist Gordon Hillman with plant remains at the Abu Hureyra site (see Chapter 11). When the drought came, nut harvest yields plummeted, game populations crashed, and wild cereal grasses were unable to support a dense human population. So the foragers turned to cultivation to supplement their food supplies. Within a few generations, they became full-time farmers. The Younger Dryas–induced drought was not the only cause of agriculture, but the sudden climate change was of great importance.

The Black Sea was an enormous freshwater lake (often called the Euxine Lake) isolated from the Mediterranean by a huge natural earthen levee in the Bosphorus Valley between Turkey and Bulgaria during the early Holocene. Four centuries of colder conditions and drought again settled over Europe and southwestern Asia between 6200 and 5800 B.C. Many farmers abandoned long-established villages and settled near the great lake and other permanent water sources. Deep-sea cores and pollen diagrams chronicle what happened next as the climate warmed up again after 5800 B.C. Sea levels resumed their inexorable rise toward modern high levels. Salt Mediterranean waters climbed ever higher on the Bosphorus levee. Then, in about 5500 B.C., the rising water breached the barrier. Torrents of salt water cascaded into the Euxine Lake 500 feet (152 meters) below. Within weeks, the great waterfall had carved a deep gully and formed the narrow strait that now links the Black Sea to the Mediterranean. The former lake not only became a brackish ocean, but rose sharply, flooding hundreds of agricultural settlements on its shores, perhaps with great loss of life. This long-forgotten event has recently been reconstructed from deep-sea cores taken in the Mediterranean, also in the Black Sea, which chronicle not only the cold snap and drought, but the sudden change in the now-drowned lake.

The Black Sea discoveries are so new that archaeologists still have to assess their full consequences. The flooding of the huge lake does coincide with the spread of farmers across temperate Europe from the Balkans. Some experts believe the environmental catastrophe and the spread of farming were connected, as people fled their once-fertile homelands.

Short-Term Climatic Change: El Niño

We look back at the past through obscure mirrors, which become increasingly easy to use as we approach recent times. Our knowledge of Ice Age climatic change is necessarily on a grand scale, for, until recently, even ice cores did not attain the year-by-year resolution needed to track short-term shifts. Yet such sudden changes are the most important of all to human populations, who have to adjust constantly to unusual weather conditions—to droughts and floods, to unusual heat and cold. The Younger Dryas and Black Sea drought and flood are centuries-long events that are short by geological and early prehistoric standards. We are only now beginning to understand their profound impact on ancient societies. As research into these and other centuries-long events has intensified, more scholars have payed increasing attention to violent year-long episodes such as monsoon failures, volcanic eruptions, and, most important of all, El Niños.

Identifying ancient short-term climatic change requires extremely precise and sophisticated environmental and climatic evidence, much of it obtained from ice cores, pollen diagrams, and tree rings. Ice cores, in particular, are revolutionizing our knowledge of ancient climatic shifts, for they are now achieving a resolution of five years or less, which really allows the study of drought cycles and major El Niño events of the past.

El Niños like those in 1982–1983 and 1997–1998 grabbed world headlines, and with good reason. Billions of dollars of damage came from drought and flood. California enjoyed record rains, Australia and northeast Brazil suffered through brutal drought, enormous wildfires devastated rain forests in Southeast Asia and Mexico. Once thought to be a purely local phenomenon off the Peruvian coast, El Niños are now known to be global events that ripple across the entire tropics as a result of a breakdown in the atmospheric and ocean circulation in the western Pacific. From the archaeologist's point of view, El Niños are of compelling interest, for they had drastic effects on many early civilizations living in normally dry environments, where flooding could wipe out years of irrigation agriculture in hours. Humanity was not that vulnerable to El Niños until people settled in permanent villages, then cities, when the realities of farming and growing population densities made it harder for them to move away from drought or flood (see Figure 10.8).

The Moche Civilization

A classic example of such vulnerability comes from the north coast of Peru, where the Moche civilization flourished around A.D. 400, ruled by powerful, authoritarian warrior-priests, who ruled from great pyramid centers (see Figure 10.9 on page 212; see also Figure 2.6 on page 35). The Moche survived in one of the driest environments on earth by using elaborate irrigation schemes to harness spring runoff from the Andes in coastal river valleys. Everything depended on ample mountain floodwaters. When drought occurred, the Moche suffered.

The Quelccaya ice cap in the Cordillera Occidental of the southern Peruvian highlands lies in the same zone of seasonal rainfall as the mountains above Moche country. Two ice cores drilled in the summit of the ice cap in 1983 provide a record of variations in rainfall over 1,500 years, and, indirectly, an impression of the amount of runoff that would have reached lowland river valleys during cycles of wet and dry years (see chapter-opener photo on page 198). In the southern highlands, El Niño episodes have been tied to intense short-term droughts in the region, also on the nearby *altiplano,* the high-altitude plains around Lake Titicaca. The appearance of such drought events in the ice cores may reflect strong El Niño episodes in the remote past. However, it is more productive to look at long-term dry and wet cycles.

The two ice cores, 508 and 537 feet (155 and 164 meters) long, each yielded clear layering and annual dust layers that reflected the yearly cycle of wet and dry seasons, the latter bringing dust particles from the arid lands to the west to the high Andes, accurate to within about twenty years. The cores show clear indications of long-term rainfall variations. A short drought occurred between A.D. 534 and 540. Then, between A.D. 563 and 594, a three-decade drought cycle settled over the mountains and lowlands, with annual rainfall as much as 30 percent below normal. Abundant rainfall resumed in 602, giving way to another drought between A.D. 636 and 645.

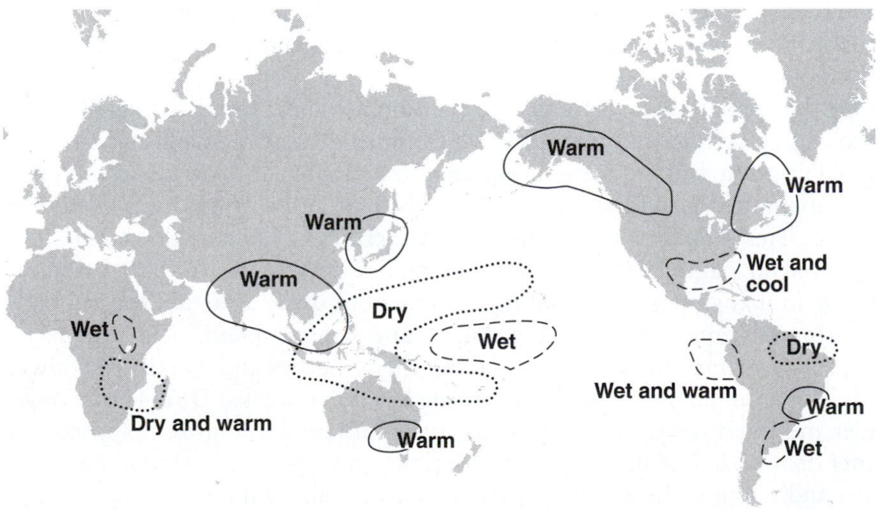

Figure 10.8 The worldwide effects of a strong El Niño, reconstructed on the basis of the 1982–1983 event. We can assume that generally similar effects were experienced over the past 5,000 years.

Figure 10.9 The Moche pyramid known as *Huaca del Sol,* capital of powerful Moche lords in the fifth century A.D. The pyramid was extensively damaged by powerful El Niño events.

The 30-year drought of A.D. 563 to 594 drastically reduced the amount of runoff reaching coastal communities. The effect of a 25 or 30 percent reduction in the water supply would be catastrophic, especially on farmers near the coast, well downstream from the mountains. Moche society apparently prospered until the mid-sixth-century's severe drought cycle. As the drought intensified, the diminished runoff barely watered the rich farming land far downstream. Miles of laboriously maintained irrigation canals remained dry. Blowing sand cascaded into empty ditches. By the third or fourth year, as the drought lowered the water table far below normal, thousands of acres of farmland received so weak a river flow that unflushed salt accumulated in the soil. Crops withered. Fortunately, the coastal fisheries still provided ample fish meal—until a strong El Niño came along without warning, bringing warmer waters and torrential rains to the desert and mountains.

We do not know the exact years during the long drought when strong El Niños struck, but we can be certain that they did. We can also be sure they hit at a moment when Moche civilization was in crisis, grain supplies running low, irrigation systems sadly depleted, malnutrition widespread, and confidence in the rulers' divine powers much diminished. This was the time of the human sacrifices at Huaca de la Luna (see the Discovery box on pages 200–201). The warmer waters of the El Niño reduced anchovy harvests in many places, decimating a staple both of the coastal diet and highland trade. Torrential rains swamped the Andes and coastal plain. The arid rivers became raging torrents, carrying everything before them. Levees and canals overflowed and collapsed. The arduous labors of years vanished in a few weeks. Dozens of villages vanished under mud and debris as the farmers' cane and adobe houses collapsed and their occupants drowned. The floods polluted springs and streams, overwhelmed sanitation systems, and stripped thousands of acres of fertile soil. As the water receded and the rivers went down, typhoid and other epidemics swept through the valleys, wiping out entire communities and eroding fertile soils. Infant mortality soared.

The Moches' elaborate irrigation systems created an artificial landscape that supported dense farming populations in the midst of one of the driest deserts on earth, where farming would be impossible without technological ingenuity. The farmers were well aware of the hazards of droughts and El Niños, but technology and irrigation could not guarantee the survival of a highly centralized society driven as much by ideology as by pragmatic concerns. There were limits to the climatic shifts Moche civilization could absorb. Ultimately, the Moche ran out of options and their civilization collapsed.

We do not know how long El Niños have oscillated across the globe, but they have descended on Peru for at least 5,000 years. A new generation of climatic researches from ice cores and other data show that short-term climatic shifts played a far more important role in the fate of early civilizations than once realized.

Tree Rings: Studying Southwestern Drought

Many ancient societies lived in environments with unpredictable rainfall, where agriculture was, at best, a chancy enterprise. The ancient peoples of the southwestern United States farmed their semiarid environment with brilliant skill for more than 3,000 years, developing an extraordinary expertise at water management and plant breeding. One central philosophy of modern-day Pueblo Indian groups encompasses movement—the notion that people have to move to escape drought and survive. Until recently, archaeologists did not fully appreciate the importance of movement in southwestern life and were at a loss to explain the sudden dispersal of the Ancestral Pueblo people of Chaco Canyon and the Four Corners region in the twelfth and thirteenth centuries A.D. New climatic studies have shown that climate played an important role in the dispersal.

Dendrochronologies for the Ancestral Pueblo are now accurate to within a year, giving us the most precise time scale for any early human society anywhere. In recent years, the Laboratory of Tree-Ring Research at the University of Arizona has undertaken a massive dendroclimatic study that has yielded a reconstruction of relative climatic variability in the Southwest from A.D. 680 to 1970. The same scientists, headed by Jeffrey Dean, are now producing the first quantitative reconstructions of annual and seasonal rainfall, also of temperature, drought, and stream flow for the region. Such research involves not only tree-ring sequences but intricate mathematical expressions of the relationships between tree growth and such variables as rainfall, temperature, and crop yields. These calculations yield statistical estimations of the fluctuations in these variables on an annual and seasonal basis.

By using a spatial grid of 27 long tree-ring sequences from throughout the Southwest, Dean and his colleagues have compiled maps that plot the different station values and their fluctuations like contour maps, one for each decade. This enables them to study such phenomena as the progress of what Dean sometimes calls the "Great Drought" of A.D. 1276 to 1299 from northwest to southeast across the region. In 1276, the beginnings of the drought appear as negative standard deviations from average rainfall in the northwest while the remainder of the region enjoys above-average rainfall. During the next ten years, very dry conditions expand over the entire Southwest before improved rainfall arrives after 1299. This form of mapping allows close correlation of vacated large and small pueblos with short-term climatic fluctuations (see Figure 10.10 on page 214).

When the research team looked at the entire period from A.D. 966 to 1988, they found that the tree-ring stations in the northwestern region accounted for no less than 60 percent of the rainfall variance. In contrast, stations in the southeastern part of the Southwest accounted for only 10 percent. This general configuration, which persisted for centuries, coincides with the modern distribution of seasonal rainfall in the Southwest: predictable summer rainfall dominates the southeastern areas, while the northwest receives both winter and summer precipitation. Winter rains are much more uncertain. When the scientists examined this general rainfall pattern at 100-year intervals from 539 to 1988, they observed that it persisted most of the time, even though the boundary between the two zones moved backward and forward slightly.

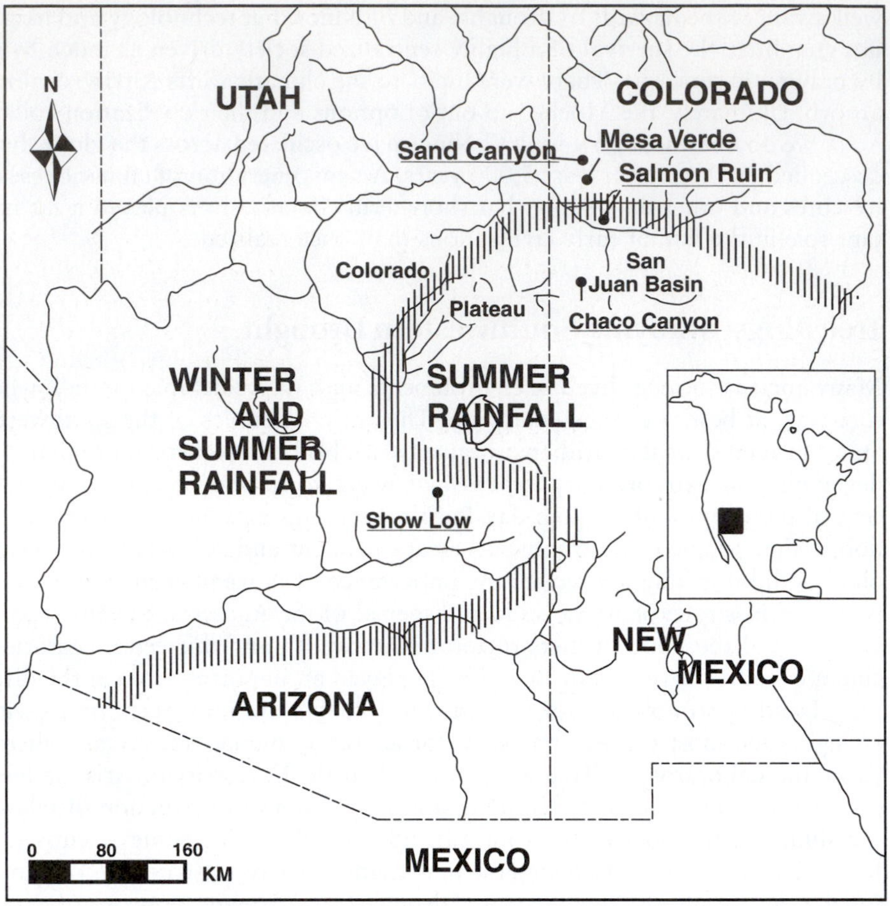

Figure 10.10 The climatic regimens of the American Southwest, showing the general configuration of rainfall across the region reconstructed with tree rings. The northwestern area receives both summer and winter rainfall, the southeastern area only predictable summer rainfall.

But this long-term pattern broke down completely from A.D. 1250 to 1450, when a totally aberrant pattern prevailed in the northwest. The southeast remained stable, but there was major disruption elsewhere. For nearly two centuries, the relatively simple long-term pattern of summer and winter rains gave way to complex, unpredictable precipitation and severe droughts, especially on the Colorado Plateau. The change to an unstable pattern would have had a severe impact on Ancestral Pueblo farmers, especially as it coincided with the Great Drought of A.D. 1250 to 1299.

Why did this breakdown occur? Dean divides the relationship between climatic change and human behavior into three broad categories. Certain obvious stable elements in the Ancestral Pueblo environment have not changed over the past 2,000 years, such as bedrock geology and climate type. Then there are low-frequency environmental changes—those that occur on cycles longer than a human generation of 25 years. Few people witnessed these changes during their lifetimes. Changes in hydrological conditions such as cycles of erosion and deposition along stream courses, fluctuations in water table levels in river floodplains, and changes in plant distributions transcend generations, but they could affect the environment drastically, especially in drought cycles.

Shorter-term, high-frequency changes were readily apparent to every Ancestral Pueblo person: year-to-year rainfall shifts, decade-long drought cycles, seasonal changes, and so on. Over the centuries, they were probably barely aware of long-term change, for the present generation and their ancestors enjoyed the same basic adaptation, which one could call a form of "stability." Cycles of drought, unusually heavy rains, and other high-frequency changes required temporary and flexible adjustments, such as farming more land, relying more heavily on wild plant foods, and, above all, movement across the terrain.

Such strategies worked well for centuries, as long as the Ancestral Pueblo people farmed their land at well below its carrying capacity. When the population increased to near carrying capacity, however, as it did at Chaco Canyon in the twelfth century, people became increasingly vulnerable to brief events like El Niños or droughts, which could stretch the supportive capacity of a local environment within months, even weeks. Their vulnerability was even more extreme when long-term changes—such as a half century or more of much drier conditions—descended on farming land already pushed to its carrying limits. Under these circumstances, a year-long drought or torrential rains could quickly destroy a local population's ability to support itself. So the people dispersed into other areas, where there was ample soil and better water supplies. Climate change and drought did not, of course, cause the Ancestral Pueblo dispersal by themselves, for other significant political and social factors came into play. Without question, however, the Ancestral Pueblo people dispersed from Mesa Verde and Chaco Canyon in part because drought forced them to do so. Unlike the Moche in distant Peru, they had the flexibility to move away.

The coming decades will see a revolution in our understanding of ancient environments and short-term climatic change as scientists acquire a closer knowledge both of climates in the past and of the still little-known forces that drive the global weather machine. Like our predecessors, we still live in the Ice Age, which, some estimates calculate, will bring renewed glacial conditions in about 23,000 years' time. So it is hardly surprising that, like our forebears, we have had to adjust to constant short-term climatic changes. And, as humanly induced global warming accelerates, these changes may become more frequent and violent, spelling danger for an overpopulated world.

Geoarchaeology

Sediments and soils contain a record of climate change, for climate helps drive geomorphic and landscape changes on earth. **Geoarchaeology**, the study of archaeology using the methods and concepts of the earth sciences, plays a major role in reconstructing ancient environments and landscapes. This is a far wider enterprise than geology and involves at least four major approaches:

- Geochemical, electromagnetic, and other remote sensing devices to locate sites and environmental features (see Chapter 6).
- Studies of site-formation processes and of the spatial contexts of archaeological sites (see Chapters 5 and 9), a process that includes distinguishing humanly caused phenomena from natural features.
- Reconstructing the ancient landscape by a variety of paleogeographic and biological methods, including pollen analysis.
- Relative and chronometric dating of sites and their geological contexts.

Geoarchaeology plays a major role in the study of early Egyptian and Mesopotamian civilizations. Both lay in fertile lands transected by great rivers. The annual inundations of the Nile brought silt to the floodplain from far upstream, fertilizing the fields. In drought years, when the flood failed, crops failed and people went hungry. In about 2180 B.C., the Nile experienced poor floods for generations. The pharaohs were powerless and Egypt fell apart into its nine provinces, each ruled by powerful warlords. More than a century passed before powerful leaders from Upper Egypt reunited the kingdom. The pharaohs learned their lesson and invested heavily in centralized storage and irrigation. In Mesopotamia, Sumerian cities were at the mercy of flood and drought, especially when high floods caused river courses to change or when sluggish waters failed, leading to a rapid rise in the salinity of the soil and much lower crop yields.

On a smaller scale, people are geomorphic agents, just like the wind. Accidentally or deliberately, they carry inorganic and organic materials to their homes. They remove rubbish, make tools, build houses, abandon tools. These mineral and organic materials are subjected to all manner of mechanical and biochemical processes while people live on a site and after they abandon it. The controlling geomorphic system at a site, whatever its size, is made up not only of natural elements but of a vital cultural component as well. The geoarchaeologist is involved with archaeological investigations from the very beginning, and deals not only with formation of sites and with the changes they underwent during occupation but also with what happened to them after abandonment.

In the field, the geoarchaeologist is part of the multidisciplinary research team, recording stratigraphic profiles within the excavation and in special pits close by to obtain information on soil sediment sequences. At the same time, he or she takes soil samples for pollen and sediment analyses and relates the site to its landscape by topographic survey. Working closely with survey archaeologists, geoarchaeologists locate sites and other cultural features on the natural landscape using aerial photographs, satellite images, and even geophysical prospecting on individual sites. As part of this process, they examine dozens of natural geological exposures, where they study the stratigraphic and sedimentary history of the entire region as a wider context for the sites found within it. The ultimate objective is to identify not only the microenvironment of the site but also that of the region as a whole—to establish ecological and spatial frameworks for the socioeconomic and settlement patterns that are revealed by archaeological excavations and surveys.

SUMMARY

1. The study of long- and short-term climatic and environmental change is of vital importance to archaeologists concerned with human societies' changing relationships with their surroundings.
2. This chapter describes ways of studying such changes. Deep-sea cores and ice drillings provide us with a broad framework of climatic change during the Pleistocene (Ice Age) that chronicles at least eight glacial periods during the past 780,000 years.
3. The Pleistocene itself is divided into three broad subdivisions, the last of which coincides with the spread of modern humans across the world from Africa. The Holocene covers postglacial times and witnessed not only global warming, but at least three short periods of much colder conditions.
4. The Younger Dryas brought drought and cold conditions and may have helped trigger agriculture in southwestern Asia.
5. The catastrophic flooding of the Black Sea lake in about 5500 B.C. by salt water from the Mediterranean caused major population movements in Europe.
6. Short-term events such as El Niños and droughts in the southwestern United States are studied with the aid of ice cores, geological observations, and tree rings—methods achieving increasing precision.
7. We are now beginning to realize that short-term climatic change played a vital role in the rise and fall of many human societies.
8. Geoarchaeology is a multidisciplinary approach to the study of human adaptations that reconstructs ancient landscapes using such techniques as remote sensing and paleographic and biological methods such as pollen analysis.

ELEVEN

Come Tell Me How You Lived

Dogon women grinding grain, Mali, West Africa.

CHAPTER OUTLINE

PREVIEW

Chapter 11 discusses the ways in which archaeologists reconstruct ancient subsistence. To establish entire ancient diets is often near-impossible, except when isotopic analysis on bones can be used, or human coprolites are available. We describe zooarchaeology, the study of animal bones, the identification of animals, the study of butchering methods, and comparing different assemblages. Next, we turn to botanical remains and flotation methods, before briefly surveying ways of studying birds, fish, and mollusks. We also assess ways in which rock art can throw light on ancient subsistence.

> *There was a noise, and behold a shaking, and the bones came together, bone to his bone. And when I behold, lo, the sinews and the flesh came up upon them, and the skin covered them above, but there was no breath in them.*
>
> —*Ezekiel* 37:7–8

How did ancient peoples make their living? The old stereotype of Stone Age hunters pursuing large game animals like saber-toothed tigers and living off orgies of frenzied meat consumption vanished generations ago. We now know that plant foods and fish were vital components in many ancient diets, and ancestral Native Americans had an astounding knowledge of potentially cultivable native plants. Reconstructing ancient subsistence is a painstaking process, involving days of analysis of animal bones broken into tiny fragments and highly specialized research into tiny plant seeds recovered with sophisticated sampling machines.

In some ways, studying ancient subsistence is archaeological detective work at its best. Astoundingly detailed information about prehistoric foraging and agriculture can come from the tiniest of clues, such as fish scales and seed impressions in clay pots. But, as always, these triumphs of detection form part of a larger concern, a search for answers to fundamental questions. For example, when studying prehistoric subsistence the archaeologist seeks to answer many fundamental questions, among them the role of domestic animals in a mixed farming economy. How important was fishing to a shellfish-oriented population living by the ocean? Was a site occupied seasonally while the inhabitants concentrated on, say, bird snaring to the exclusion of all other subsistence activities? What agricultural systems were used? How was the land cultivated? In this chapter we review some of the ways we seek the answers to these and related subsistence questions (see the Discovery box on pages 220–221).

Evidence for Subsistence

The archaeological evidence for prehistoric subsistence consists of artifacts and food remains. How much survives depends, of course, on preservation conditions on the site. All too often the evidence for ancient diet is incomplete. Stone axes or iron hoe blades may give an indication of hunting or agriculture, but they hardly yield the kind of detail archaeologists need. Many artifacts used in the chase or for agriculture were made from such perishable materials as bone, wood, and fiber (see Figure 11.1 on page 219).

Food remains survive very unevenly. The bones and teeth of larger mammals are the most common subsistence data, but careful excavation often reveals remains of such small animals as birds, fish, and frogs as well as invertebrates, such as beetles. Plant remains are very perishable and usually are underrepresented, despite the development of sophisticated field recovery methods.

Ancient Diet

The ultimate aim in studying prehistoric food remains is not only to establish how people obtained their food but to reconstruct their actual diet. An overall picture of prehistoric diet requires, of course, constructing a comprehensive list of food resources available to the people within that particular environment and then answering questions such as these: What proportion of the diet was meat? How diverse were dietary sources? Did the principal diet sources change from season to season? Was food stored? Were some foods more desirable than others? These and many other questions can be answered only from composite pictures of prehistoric diet reconstructed from many sources of evidence.

Figure 11.1 Ground stone axes, one with a wooden handle, from Ireland.

Occasionally, however, it is possible to gain insights into actual meals consumed thousands of years ago. The stomach of Tollund Man, whose body was buried and preserved in a Danish peat bog, contained the remains of finely ground porridge made from barley, linseed, and several wild grasses (see Figure 9.6 on page 188). No meat was found in his belly. The Ice Man from the European Alps, described in Chapter 13, consumed meat, unleavened bread, and an herb for his last meal (see Figure 13.4 on page 263). However, his bones showed clear signs of malnutrition from famines in his ninth, fifteenth, and sixteenth years. Ancient digestive tracts also yield informative waste products. Human excrement (coprolites or feces) found in dry caves in the United States and Mexico has been analyzed microscopically. The inhabitants of *Lovelock Cave* in the central Nevada desert were eating bulrush and cattail seeds, as well as Lahontan chub from the waters of nearby Humboldt Lake. These fish were eaten raw or roasted over a fire. One coprolite contained the remains of at least 51 chub, calculated by a fish expert to represent a total fish weight of 3.5 pounds (1.6 kilograms). The same people were eating adult and baby birds, as well as water tiger beetles. Human feces from Texas caves near the mouth of the Pecos River have been subjected to pollen analyses so precise that the investigators established the sites to have been occupied regularly during the spring and summer months for 1,300 years between 800 B.C. and A.D. 550.

Although coprolite studies are a promising source of dietary information, the food remains from most sites are far too incomplete to allow more than a very general impression of diet. Research using the ratio between two stable carbon isotopes—12C and 13C in animal tissue—has enabled scientists to establish the diet of prehistoric

Discovery

THE GÖBEKLI TEPE CARVINGS, TURKEY, 1994

German archaeologist Klaus Schmidt discovered the large Göbekli Tepe mound in southeastern Turkey during an archaeological survey in 1994. He knew at once that it was a site that dated from the very earliest centuries of agriculture from the stone artifacts scattered on the surface, around 9600 B.C. At the same time, he picked up dozens of smashed limestone slabs, many of them carefully shaped.

Göbekli Tepe lies atop a large hill overlooking the surrounding plains. It's a conspicuous landmark, but turned out to be a site whose occupants were still hunting and gathering, and were not farming at all. But they built a series of unique and evocative shrines and erected large decorated pillars, which Schmidt calls megaliths. Most were T-shaped monolithic pillars, standing several feet high and weighing as much as 10 tons. The limestone came from nearby quarries. One, abandoned there, was nearly 23 feet (7 m) long and weighed an estimated 50 tons.

Many of the pillars bear pairs of arms and hands in low relief, as if they were stylized depictions of people, the horizontal part of the T representing the head (see Figure 11.2). Some bear carvings of lions, foxes, wild boars and oxen, even birds, spiders, and insects. Bones of most of these creatures come from the village middens. The pillars themselves formed circular or oval enclosures, as many as twelve of them separated by stone benches. Two pillars of the finest quality and greater size lay in the center of each enclosure.

Fortunately for Schmidt, later farmers dumped refuse into the enclosures and buried them before they could be disturbed. Schmidt has excavated four so far, but a geomagnetic survey has revealed traces of at least twenty more containing more than 200 pillars.

What are we to make of Göbekli Tepe? A prodigious amount of labor created the pillars and enclosures, but there are no signs that the site was ever an inhabited settlement. There are no dwellings, no courtyards, and little domestic refuse. Göbekli Tepe was a shrine, a place that must have been known to villagers living over a wide area, who could see the mound from a long way away. Nearby lies Nevali Çori, another settlement that Schmidt had excavated earlier. But Nevali Çori was a place where people lived for a considerable period, where there was a small shrine with T-shaped megaliths and carvings of humans and animals. Schmidt believes that the inhabitants of this and other settlements visited Göbekli Tepe on a seasonal basis, when they quarried and carved megaliths and erected them in sacred enclosures. Once one structure was completed, they would infill it and build another. He also believes that the enclosures were built not for the living, but for the dead. So far, the excavators have found no traces of burials, but they may lie behind the enclosure walls or beneath the stone benches. This would account for the progressive abandonment and building of the shrines.

populations as they switched from wild foods to a predominantly maize diet. Carbon is metabolized in plants through two major pathways: C4 and C3. The plants that make up the diet of animals have distinct C13 values. Maize, for example, is a C4 plant. In contrast, most indigenous temperate flora in North America is composed of C3 varieties. Thus a population that shifts its diet from wild vegetable foods to maize also will experience a shift in dietary isotopic values. Because C13 and C12 values do not change after death, researchers can study archaeological carbon from food remains, humus, and skeletal remains to gain insight into ancient diet.

For example, a detailed bone chemistry analysis of adult burials from *Grasshopper Pueblo* in east-central Arizona shows the great potential of this approach. Joseph Ezzo was able to show that between A.D. 1275 and 1325, males had greater access to meat and cultivated plants, and females had greater access to wild plants. Between 1325 and 1400, both men and women ate virtually the same diet, one in which meat and wild plant foods were less important. This may have resulted from a combination of social and environmental factors: increased population, drought cycles, and use of marginal

a

b

Figure 11.2 Göbekli Tepe, Turkey: (a) A large subterranean building showing the tops of two central T-shaped monoliths and two others embedded in the dry stone walls at the edge of the building, where a bench is emerging from the excavations. (b) A T-shaped monolith from the site, with low-relief sculpture.

Tiny hunter-gatherer communities produce relatively small food surpluses. It would have been difficult for them to muster the large numbers of people to build shrines and erect monoliths to commemorate their ancestors. Perhaps agriculture in this region began when hard-pressed hunter-gatherer bands looked for new ways to feed people as they fulfilled their ritual obligation to the dead. One logical way to do this would have been by increasing the supply of wild plant foods by sowing them to supplement the food supply. If Schmidt is correct in this assumption, then it may be that human beliefs and social systems changed before economic life, when ritual observances and obligations to ancestors and clan figures became overwhelmingly important to hunter-gatherer societies. After all, everyone was familiar with the germination of wild plants. Why not then plant them deliberately?

farming land, which compelled the Grasshopper people to live on agricultural products. The people responded to food stress by increasing storage capacity, reducing household size, and eventually by moving away.

The stable carbon isotope method has been used to study the diet of prehistoric Northwest Coast populations in British Columbia. Forty-eight samples from prehistoric human skeletons from 15 sites along the coast revealed a dietary reliance of about 90 percent on marine sources, a figure much higher than crude ethnographic estimates. The same data suggest that there has been little dietary change along the British Columbia coast for the past 5,000 years, which is hardly surprising, given the rich maritime resources of the shoreline.

Recent research has focused on nitrogen isotopes that allow researchers to distinguish between marine and freshwater and terrestrial food sources, an approach of importance when investigating changeovers from more land-based diets to marine ones, an important issue in ancient California. Trace element analysis of such materials as strontium and zinc in bones and other organic materials tells us much about ancient diet. Nearer to modern times, a sample of President George Washington's hair has revealed a diet of wheat, beans, and much corn. The sample also revealed a strong but not overwhelming signal from meats, while Washington also ate some seafood. His diet was roughly in the middle of a chart compiled from dietary surveys of 10,000 modern-day University of Virginia students. Isotopic tests also allow research into child weaning practices, dietary changes over the life of an individual, even mobility from one area to another, identified by studying the bone chemistry of burials in royal graves and cemeteries (sacrificial victims, for example, could come from a different area).

Animal Bones

Broken animal bones can tell us a great deal about ancient hunting, herd management, and butchery practices. One can identify mammal species from their skeletal remains. Unfortunately, however, most animal bones found in archaeological sites are highly fragmentary. Until recently, researchers assumed they were in such small fragments because the inhabitants slashed to ribbons every carcass they butchered. But research on modern predator kills and controlled experiments on butchered animals, mainly in Africa, have shown that a great many complex and little-understood forces act on bones found in archaeological sites long after they are dropped where archaeologists find them. Weathering as bones decay in the open air, compaction of the sediments in which they are buried, chemistry of the soil, even treading by animals can break up bones and help determine which parts of the body survive and which do not. Add to these accidents the butchering activities of the prehistoric inhabitants, and you have an archaeological jigsaw puzzle to piece together (see Figure 11.3 on page 223).

Generally speaking, the older the archaeological site, the more daunting it is to study postdepositional forces. The problem is particularly confusing at locations such as Olduvai Gorge or Koobi Fora in East Africa, where hominins chewed and cut bones more than 2 million years ago—and probably scavenged their meat from predator kills as well. On more recent sites, one finds that people often utilized the carcasses they butchered to the maximum. Every piece of usable meat was stripped from the bones of even the smallest animals or from the larger mammal portions brought back to the settlement. Sinews were made into thongs. Skins became clothing, containers, or even part of a shelter. Even the entrails were eaten. The hunters smashed the bones themselves to get at the marrow or for manufacture into arrowheads or other tools. Animal bones were fragmented by many domestic activities, quite apart from trampling underfoot and scavenging by dogs and carnivores. Thus one has the formidable task of identifying from tiny, discarded fragments the animal that was hunted or kept by the site's inhabitants and the role the animal played in the economy, diet, and culture of the community.

Faunal Analysis (Zooarchaeology)

Most animal bone collections consist of thousands of scattered fragments from all parts of a site. Occasionally, however, a kill site, perhaps from prehistoric bison kills on the Great Plains or the big game slaughtered by Stone Age hunters in East Africa, provides a chance to reconstruct the hunters' activities in more detail. Apart from such unusual finds, most collections have to be sorted out in the laboratory simply to give a general impression of hunting and stock-raising techniques at the site. The goal of zooarchaeology—the study of animal bones found in the archaeological record—is to reconstruct the environment and behavior of ancient peoples as thoroughly as animal remains allow. But the study of such bones is complicated by the natural and humanly induced processes that operate on organic remains as they lie on or in the ground. The study of this transition by animal remains from the biosphere is known as **taphonomy**.

Taphonomy involves two related forms of research: observing recently dead carcasses as they are gradually transformed into fossils, and studying fossil remains with the knowledge gained from these observations. The crux of the zooarchaeologists' difficulty is their subject: a collection of animal bones, the part of the fossil assemblage that is actually excavated or collected. This fossil assemblage in turn consists of the body parts that survive in the archaeological record, an assemblage very different from the

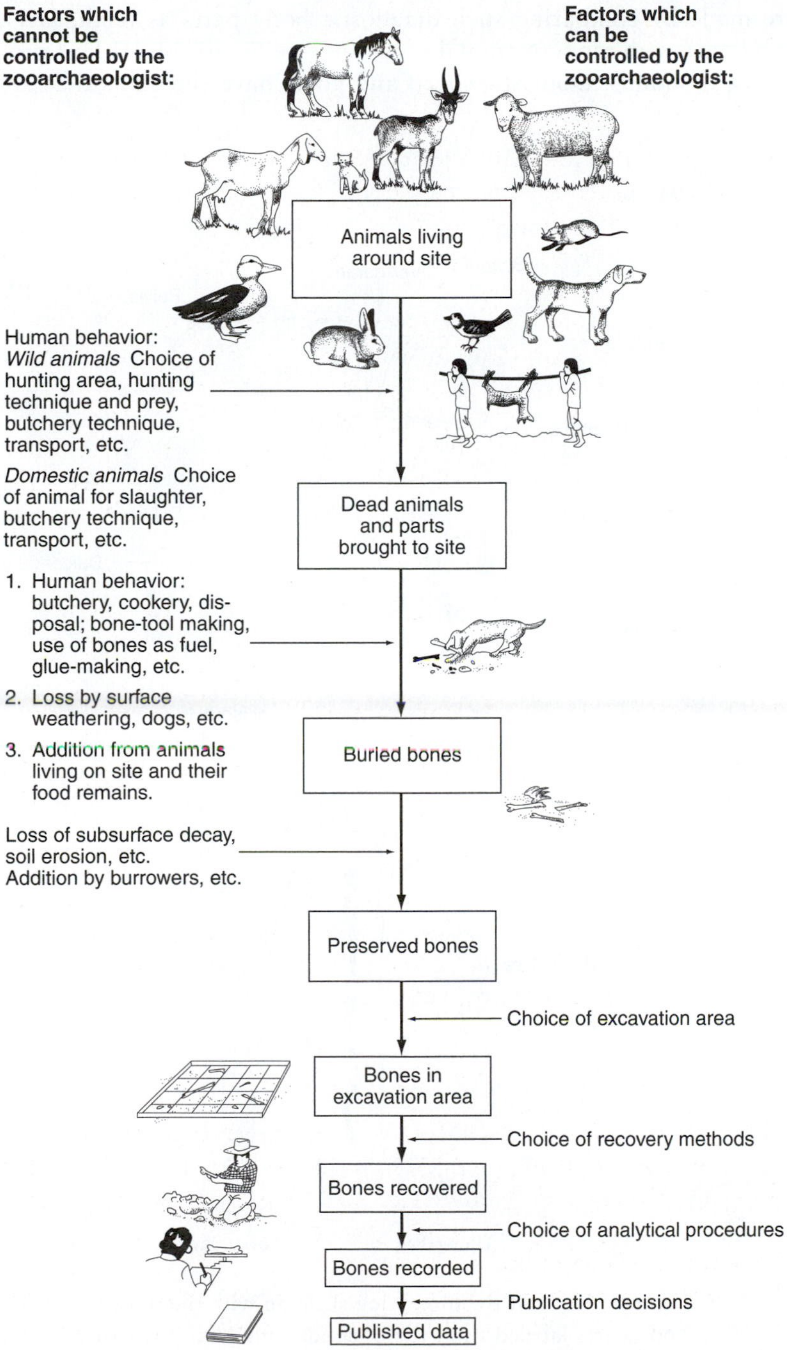

Figure 11.3 Some of the factors that affect animal bones found in archaeological sites. On the left are factors over which the archaeologist has no control; on the right, those that can be controlled.

original community of live animals that once populated the natural environment in their "natural" proportions. Animal bone analysis involves two fundamental problems: first, estimating the characteristics of a fossil assemblage from a collected sample, a statistical problem; and second, inferring what the original bone assemblage was like before it became a fossil, a taphonomic problem (see Figure 11.3 on page 223).

Researchers begin by isolating the diagnostic fragments. Often only a few bones are identifiable to the species level. One 3,000-year-old Central African hunter-gatherer settlement yielded only 2,128 identifiable fragments out of 195,415 bones! The actual identifications are made by comparing such diagnostic body parts as teeth, jaws, horns, and some limb bones with modern animal skeletons (see Figure 11.4). This procedure is not as easy as it sounds. Domestic sheep and goats have skeletons that are

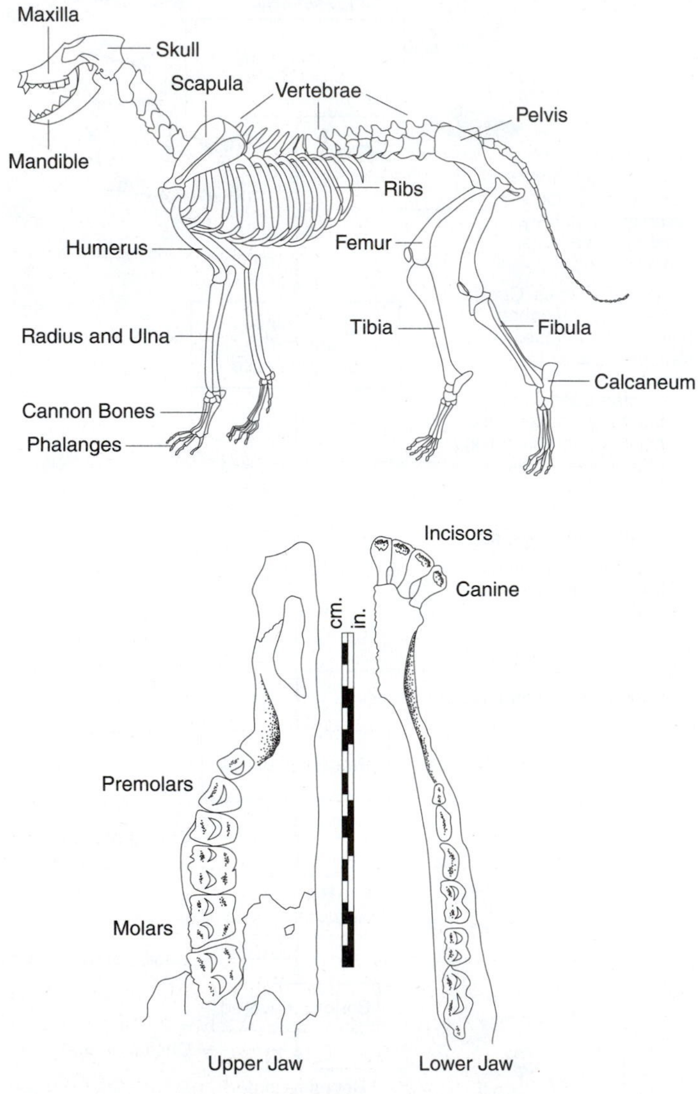

Figure 11.4 At the top, a dog skeleton with the most important body parts labeled from the bone identification point of view. At the bottom, a domestic ox jaw seen from below (upper jaw) and above (lower jaw). Notice the characteristic cusp patterns of molars and premolars that grow as the beast gets older.

almost identical to those of their wild ancestors; the bones of the domestic ox closely resemble those of the African buffalo; and so on. But accurate identifications are vital, for they provide answers to many questions. Are both domestic and wild animals present? If so, what are the proportions of each group? Were the inhabitants concentrating on one species to the exclusion of all others? Are any now-extinct species present?

Comparing Bone Assemblages

Having identified the animals present, how do you compare the proportions of different species from one site with those from another? The work is fraught with difficulty because it is almost impossible to infer the once-living population from the surviving bones.

Zooarchaeologists therefore apply two measures of specimen abundance to study the relative abundance of species:

- *The Number of Identified Specimens (NISP)* is a count of the number of identifiable bones or bone fragments present that can be identified as to animal. This count has obvious disadvantages because it is easy to overestimate one species at the expense of another, especially if its bones are cut into small fragments. The NISP has some limited use in conjunction with the Minimum Number of Individuals (MNI).
- *The Minimum Number of Individuals (MNI),* a count of the number of individuals necessary to account for all of the identifiable bones. This count is based on careful inventories of individual body parts (e.g., jaws). The MNI is a much more accurate estimate of the number of animals present in a collection. For example, Joe Ben Wheat used the thousands of bison skulls from the Olsen-Chubbuck bison kill to estimate that the hunters killed no fewer than 190 animals.

Using these two counts together brackets the actual number of animals present in a bone sample, but the figure is still only an approximation, even when used with sophisticated computer programs.

Species Abundance and Cultural Change

Climatic change rather than human culture was probably responsible for most long-term shifts in abundance of animal species during the great Ice Age. Some changes in the abundance of animals in bone collections, however, must reflect human activity—changes in the way in which people exploited animals.

Zooarchaeologist Richard Klein has studied two coastal caves in South Africa—Klasies River and *Nelson's Bay*—to document such changes. The Klasies River cave on the Cape coast was occupied by Middle Stone Age hunters from about 130,000 to about 70,000 years ago, during a period of progressively colder climate. The people took seals, penguins, and shellfish and lived off the eland, a large antelope. The nearby Nelson's Bay cave was occupied by Late Stone Age people, after 20,000 years ago. These people took not only dangerous or elusive land mammals such as the Cape buffalo, but birds and fish, both quarries requiring some skill to hunt or take successfully.

Did these changes between the two sites reflect cultural change or climatic differences? Were eland more abundant in earlier times, or just easier to hunt? Klein examined the toolkits from each cave and found that Middle Stone Age artifacts were large spear points and scrapers, but the later Nelson's Bay people used bows, arrows, and an elaborate toolkit of small, more specialized tools. This more specialized toolkit allowed the Nelson's Bay groups to hunt more dangerous and tricky quarry with great success. Therefore, eland were less common prey later not because of climatic change but because other animals were hunted, too. Then, too, in later times the population was larger. Klein suggests the growth from his examination of the limpet and tortoise shells from both sites. The Nelson's Bay specimens are smaller, as if these creatures were allowed to grow larger in earlier millennia when fewer people were there to exploit them.

Game Animals

A collection of game animals yields a wealth of information about the great variety of mammals that ancient hunters killed with astonishingly simple weapons. North American Paleo-Indian bands used game drives, spears, and other weapons to hunt herds of now-extinct big game. Twenty thousand years ago, big-game hunters on the banks of the Dnieper and Don rivers in western Russia cooperated in pursuing mammoth and other arctic mammals. They cached supplies of game meat to tide them over the long, bitterly cold winters, which lasted more than eight months.

When the identified game animal bones are counted, one species may appear to dominate. Some hunters concentrate on one or a few species, whether from economic necessity, convenience, or cultural preference. They may take hundreds of bison in fall, when they are fat from summer forage, and kill the minimum in spring, when the animals are in poor condition after the harsh months. Even with these differences taken into account, the figures can be misleading, for many societies restrict the hunting of particular animals. Others forbid males or females to eat certain species, although other species may be consumed by everyone. The !Kung San of the Kalahari today have complicated personal and age- or sex-specific taboos to regulate their eating habits. No one may eat all of the 29 game animals regularly taken by the San. Indeed, no two individuals have the same set of taboos. Such complicated restrictions are repeated with innumerable variations in other hunter-gatherer societies. The simple dietary figure of, say, 40 percent white-tailed deer and 20 percent wild geese may, in fact, reflect much more complex behavioral variables than mere concentration on two species.

Domesticated Animals

Domestic animal bones present even more difficulties. Owners can affect their herds and flocks in many ways—by selective breeding to improve meat yields or to increase wool production, and by regulating the ages at which they slaughter surplus males and old animals. All domesticated animals originated from wild species with an inclination to be sociable, a characteristic that aided close association with humans.

Animal domestication may have begun when a growing human population needed a regular food supply to support a greater density of people per square mile. Wild animals lack many characteristics valuable in their domestic relatives. Wild sheep have hairy coats, but their wool is unsuitable for spinning. The ancestors of oxen and domestic goats produced milk for their young but not enough for human consumption. People have selectively bred wild animals for long periods to enhance special characteristics. Often the resulting domestic animals can no longer survive in the wild.

The history of domestic animals must be written from fragmentary animal bones found in sites occupied by prehistoric farmers. The difference between domestic and wild animal bones is often so small that it may be next to impossible to tell the two apart. From a single jaw, no one can tell a domestic sheep or goat from a wild one. Archaeologists have to work with large numbers of animals, studying changing body sizes and bone characteristics as the animals undergo selective breeding. Early southwest Asian domestic sheep are smaller and display less variation in size than their wild relatives. Even then, it is, according to the Scriptures, "difficult to tell the sheep from the goats."

Ancient Butchery

Prehistoric peoples hunted game animals for food and used their hides for garments and tents, and their stomachs for bags. Domesticated animals provided meat and were used for plowing, for riding, or for their milk. Establishing such practices from fragmentary animal bones is difficult, involving close study of both the age of slaughtered animals and the ways in which they were butchered.

Just as with comparing different assemblages, the problem is turning figures and percentages into meaningful interpretations of human behavior. Research such as Lewis Binford's studies of Alaskan caribou hunters has provided valuable information for such approaches (see Chapter 9).

Determining the sex and age of an animal may provide a way of studying the hunting or stock-raising habits of those who slaughtered it. Many mammal species vary considerably in size and build between male and female. With species such as the North American bison, researchers can often distinguish male from female by bone sizes, but the determination is much more difficult with animals where the size difference is less.

Teeth and the **epiphyses** (joints) at the end of limb bones are most commonly used to establish the ages of prehistoric animals. In almost all mammals, the epiphyses fuse to the limb bones at adulthood, so one can immediately establish two categories of animals: immature and fully grown. Teeth and complete jaws are a more accurate way of establishing animal age. Teeth provide an almost continuous guide to the age of an animal from birth to old age. With complete jaws one can study immature teeth as they erupt. Large numbers of them enable archaeologists to count with some accuracy the proportions of immature and very old animals with heavily worn teeth.

Richard Klein has used the height of tooth crowns to study the age of mammals taken by Stone Age hunters at the Klasies River and Nelson's Bay caves in South Africa. He has identified two "mortality distributions" that apply to prehistoric and living animal populations.

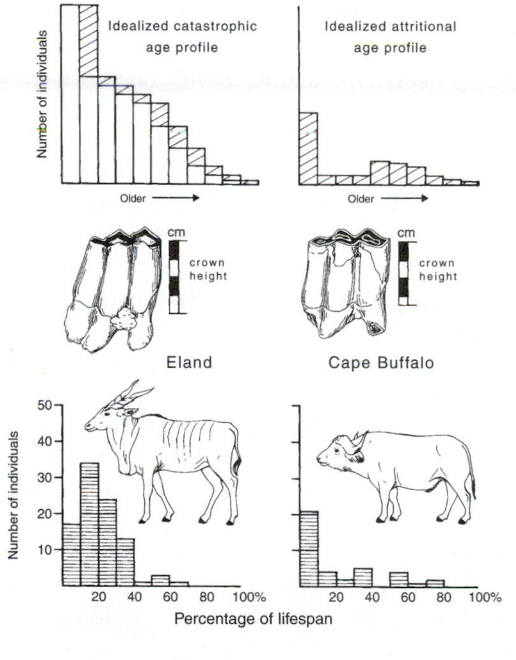

Figure 11.5 Idealized mortality data based on molar crowns of two common South African mammals, the eland and the Cape buffalo. Left, idealized catastrophic age profile. Right, idealized attritional age profile (for explanation, see text).

A **catastrophic age profile** is stable in size and structure and has progressively fewer older individuals. This is the normal distribution for living antelope populations (see Figure 11.5). If a group of hunters drives a herd over a cliff, you will find a distribution like this, for they are not being discriminating in their hunting.

An **attritional age profile** shows underrepresentation of prime-age animals relative to their abundance in living populations, but young and old are overrepresented. This profile is thought to result from scavenging or simple spear hunting.

The eland tooth profiles at both Klasies River and Nelson's Bay were close to the catastrophic profile, and so Klein argued that they were hunted in mass game drives. In contrast, the more formidable Cape buffalo displayed an attritional profile, as if the hunters had preyed on immature and old beasts over long periods.

These interpretations are fine at a general level, but it is much harder to draw more specific conclusions. Lewis Binford's Nunamiut caribou hunters from Alaska direct much of their hunting activities toward obtaining meat for winter consumption. In the fall, they pursue caribou calves to obtain clothing. The heads and tongues of these young animals provide meat for the people who process the skins.

The fragmentary bones in an occupation level are the end product of the killing, cutting up, and consumption of domestic or wild animals. To understand the butchery process, the articulation of animal bones must be examined in the levels where they are found, or a close study made of fragmentary pieces. Rarely is an entire kill site preserved, like the famed Olsen-Chubbuck bison kill in Colorado, where at least 190 bison were driven to their deaths, then dismembered, more than 8,000 years ago. Archaeologist Joe Ben Wheat showed that for several days the hunters camped by their prey as they dismembered the uppermost bison in the confused heap of dead animals before them. When they had eaten their fill and dried enough meat to last them a month or more, they simply walked away and left the rotting carcasses. Archaeologists found the articulated and butchered skeletons thousands of years later.

Bone analyses also reveal that many ancient hunters were selective in the chase. For example, John Speth's excavations at *Garnsey,* New Mexico, on the southern plains, reveal that ancient Plains hunters were expert observers of their prey. In about A.D. 1550, a group of hunters visited a gully where they knew bison would congregate in late March or April. Instead of just killing every animal on sight, they tended to concentrate on the males. Speth believes this was because males are in better condition in spring, and their bone marrow has a higher fat content. Hunters everywhere prefer fatter meat, for it is an important source of energy and essential fatty acids. In spring, such flesh was hard to come by, for the bison herds were recovering from the lean winter months. So the hunters selected male bison at Garnsey, consuming only the choicest parts of the carcass with the highest fat content.

Interpreting butchery techniques is a complicated matter, for many variables affect the way in which the carcass is dismembered. Toughness of hide, available tools, size and portability of the animal, and potential use for skins and horn are a few of the variables. The only way to interpret body parts in this context is by understanding in detail the cultural system that generated them. For instance, herders, finding a constant surplus of males beyond their breeding requirements, may castrate some of these animals and then use them for riding and for dragging carts or plows. But even with some insights into the cultural system and excellent bone preservation, it is frequently hard to interpret the meaning of butchering techniques.

So many factors affect the counts of identified bones from any collection of animal remains that one must interpret the fragments in the context of artifact patterns, site-formation processes, and all other sources of data potentially bearing on the behavior of the people who killed the animals.

Plant Remains

Gathering and agriculture are almost invariably underrepresented in most sites because the tiny seeds and other vegetable remnants that result from such activities as food storage, grinding, and harvesting are among the most fragile of all archaeological remains. Except for occasional burned seeds found in hearths or storage pits, the vegetable remains from human feces, and grain impressions in clay pot walls, much evidence for prehistoric gathering and agriculture comes from dry sites, where preservation conditions are almost perfect (see Figure 11.6). However, the development of sophisticated **flotation** techniques in recent years has enabled archaeologists to recover large samples of tiny plant remains from settlements in every kind of environment imaginable, including moist environments like those at Koster in Illinois.

a

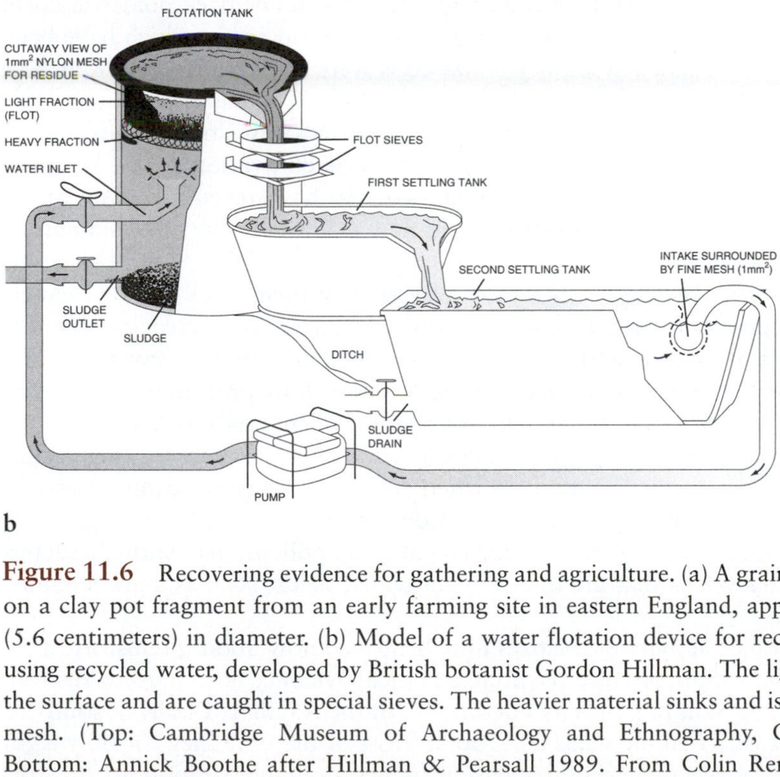

b

Figure 11.6 Recovering evidence for gathering and agriculture. (a) A grain impression preserved on a clay pot fragment from an early farming site in eastern England, approximately 2.2 inches (5.6 centimeters) in diameter. (b) Model of a water flotation device for recovering plant remains using recycled water, developed by British botanist Gordon Hillman. The lightest remains float to the surface and are caught in special sieves. The heavier material sinks and is trapped in light nylon mesh. (Top: Cambridge Museum of Archaeology and Ethnography, Cambridge University. Bottom: Annick Boothe after Hillman & Pearsall 1989. From Colin Renfrew and Paul Bahn, *Archaeology: Theories, Methods, and Practice*, published by Thames and Hudson, Inc., New York, 2001. Reprinted by permission.)

Flotation methods are used both in the field and in the laboratory. With this technique, water or chemicals are used to free tiny seeds from the soil (see Figure 11.6b on page 229). The freshly excavated earth is poured into a container and sinks slowly to the bottom while the light seeds float to the surface. Some botanists prefer to collect soil samples in the field, then process them in the laboratory, where they can work with samples that have not been screened or treated in any other way, giving them a random sample for statistical purposes. Armed with statistical samples of plant remains, **paleobotanists**, experts on ancient plants, can not only determine what people ate and used, but can trace the beginnings of domestication of native plants. Sometimes plant remains can give clues as to the uses of different structures by establishing the abundance of different seeds around them, or even establish what seasons of the year a site was occupied; but such analyses are very difficult and in their infancy.

Flotation methods have revolutionized the study of plant remains, for they provide large seed samples that can be studied with statistical methods. At the *Ali Kosh* mound in Iran, Kent Flannery and Frank Hole thought that plant remains were scarce. Then they used flotation methods and recovered 40,000 seeds from the trenches. In recent years, botanists have obtained literally pints of seed samples from the early farming village at Abu Hureyra in Syria—samples so complete that botanist Gordon Hillman has been able to chronicle major shifts in plant-gathering preferences over more than 3,000 years. When Abu Hureyra was a small foraging settlement before 10,000 B.C., the people relied heavily on acorns and other nut crops in nearby forests. But as the forests retreated in the face of dry conditions, the people turned to wild cereal grasses, which they soon domesticated to provide extra food supplies.

Much of our knowledge of early major food crops such as wheat, barley, and maize has come from dry caves. Richard MacNeish assembled a continuous sequence of human occupation in the Tehuacán Valley in Mexico for the period from 10,000 years ago to the Spanish Conquest. He dug more than a dozen open sites and caves, all so dry that they yielded 80,000 wild plant remains and 25,000 specimens of domestic corn. MacNeish was able to identify diminutive maize cobs in several caves, which have been AMS dated to about 2700 B.C. These early maize cobs were no more than 0.78 inch (2 centimeters) long, but later ones were far larger. Unfortunately, MacNeish was unable to identify the original wild ancestor of Tehuacán maize, now known to be a native grass still growing in Mexico today—teosinte. The earliest maize cultivation in the Americas currently dates to the sixth and fifth millennia B.C.—on the basis of pollen grains at the San Andrés site in lowland Veracruz, Mexico, and new evidence from the Panamanian rainforest, dating to about 5000 B.C.

Farmers modify the landscape around them by grazing their herds and by clearing forests. Simple, shifting cultivation techniques required new garden acreage every season. Each time cultivation required more cleared woodland, drastic environmental changes were triggered. Few people have ever tried to assess how profoundly early agricultural economies affected the world environment. Pollen analysis has provided remarkable evidence of how early farmers cleared natural environments for their fields. Many European marshes chronicle a moment when dense oak forest suddenly gives way to an open landscape in which grass pollens predominate. The sudden change often coincides with the appearance of domesticated cereal grain pollens, also with characteristic but inconspicuous weeds that are found in cultivated fields, such as a grass named *Plantago lanceolata*.

This early clearance activity dramatizes how little we know about prehistoric agriculture and gathering, simply because the archaeological evidence is so hard to recover. For example, the !Kung San, present-day inhabitants of the Kalahari Desert in southern Africa, know of at least 85 edible seeds and roots. Most of the time they eat only eight of these. The rest of the vegetable resource base provides a reliable cushion for this foraging population in times when key vegetable foods are scarce. Such people have a buffer against famine that many farmers with their cleared lands, much higher population densities, and crops that rely on regular rainfall rarely enjoy. Is a farming life really to be preferred? A few studies of the skeletons of early farming populations show how malnutrition due to food shortages was commonplace in many areas.

Birds, Fish, and Mollusks

Bird bones, although very informative, are often neglected at the expense of larger mammal remains. As long ago as 1926, Hildegarde Howard studied a large bird bone collection from an Indian shell midden on the eastern shores of San Francisco Bay. The inhabitants had hunted many waterbirds, especially cormorants, ducks, and geese. When Howard looked more closely at the bones, she found that all of the geese were migrant winter visitors that frequent the Bay Area between January and April. Nearly all the cormorants were immature specimens, birds about 5 to 6 weeks old. What time of the year had the Indians occupied the site, she wondered. Howard consulted present-day records pertaining to when cormorants hatch and used these to estimate what time of year the earlier inhabitants must have eaten the young cormorants. Based on these records, she estimated the cormorants had been killed about June 28. She then determined that the Indians must have lived there once in the winter and a second time in the early summer.

Fishing, like bird hunting, became more important as people began to specialize in different lifeways and adapt to highly specific environments. Evidence for fishing comes from both artifacts and fragile fish bones, which, when they survive, can be identified with considerable accuracy. Freshwater and ocean fish may be caught with nets or with basket-like fish traps. Indians who lived on the site of modern Boston in about 2500 B.C. built a dam of vertical stakes and brush. When the Atlantic tides rose, fish were directed into gaps in the dam and trapped in huge numbers. Barbed fish spears and fishhooks are relatively common finds in some archaeological sites, but such artifacts tell us little about the weight of fishing in prehistoric subsistence. Did the people fish all year or only when salmon were running? Did they concentrate on coastal species or venture far offshore in large canoes? Such questions can be answered only by examining the fish bones themselves.

The Chumash Indians of southern California were remarkably skillful fishermen, who went far offshore in plank canoes to fish with hook and line, basket, net, and harpoon. It was no surprise when the fish bones found on archaeological sites at Century Ranch, Los Angeles, included not only the bones of such shallow-water fish as the leopard shark and California halibut, but the remains of albacore, ocean skipjack, and large rockfish, species that occur in deep water and can only be caught there. Early Spanish accounts speak of more than 10,000 Indians living in the Santa Barbara area of California alone, a large population indeed. Archaeology has shown that this maritime population was able to exploit a very broad spectrum of marine resources, but despite this abundance there were occasional famines.

Fishing, with its relatively predictable food resources and high protein potential, allows much more sedentary settlement than other forms of hunting and gathering. The Northwest Coast Indians enjoyed a very rich maritime culture based on ocean fishing and salmon runs that enabled large numbers of people to live in one area for long periods and to build permanent dwellings.

Shellfish from seashore, lake, or river supplied a good portion of the prehistoric diet for many thousands of years. Freshwater mollusks were important both to California Indians and to prehistoric people living in the southeastern United States. Most mollusks have limited food value, and so great quantities are needed to feed even a few people. One estimate for 100 people's mollusk needs for a month runs as high as

3 tons. In all probability, mollusks were more a supplemental food at set times of the year than a staple. They were simply too much effort to collect in sufficient quantity.

Even sporadic collecting led to rapidly accumulating piles of shells (shell middens) at strategic points on lake or ocean shores, near rocky outcrops or tidal pools where mollusks were commonly found. Shell midden excavations in California and elsewhere have yielded thousands of shells, which are counted, identified, and also measured to check for size changes. When Claude Warren sampled a shell midden near San Diego, California, he found five major species of shellfish commonly exploited by the inhabitants. The earliest shellfish collectors concentrated on the bay mussel and oysters, both of which flourish on rocky shores. But by 4000 B.C., the lagoon by the shell middens had so silted up that mud-loving scallops and Venus shells were now collected, for the earlier species were unable to flourish in the new, sandy environment. Soon afterward, however, the lagoon became clogged and the shellfish collectors moved away, never to return. Their abandoned seashells told the story of the changing environment around the sites.

Both freshwater and saltwater shells were widely used as ornaments in prehistoric times. Gulf Coast shells were bartered over enormous distances of the southeastern and midwestern United States to peoples who had never seen the ocean. Sometimes such ornaments could assume incredible prestige value. When nineteenth-century explorer David Livingstone visited Chief Shinte in central Africa in 1855, he found him wearing two seashells that had come over 994 miles (1,590 kilometers) inland from the distant East African coast. The chief told him that two such shells would buy a slave; five would buy a large ivory elephant tusk. Small wonder that enterprising merchants were trading china replicas of these shells in central Africa half a century later.

Rock Art

Sometimes prehistoric rock art gives vivid insight into subsistence activities of long ago, such as hunts and fishing expeditions. Hunter-gatherers and fishing cultures have left behind paintings of their daily life on the walls of caves and rockshelters. In recent years, South African archaeologist David Lewis-Williams and others have used oral traditions and nineteenth-century ethnographies to develop interpretations of some of the rituals depicted in the paintings. However, the art also has a valuable role to play in the interpretation of subsistence activities. Careful examination of these paintings can take us back centuries and millennia to the time when people were killing the animals whose bones lie in occupation deposits under the observer's feet. Many details of weapons, domestic equipment, and hunting and fishing methods can be discerned in these vivid scenes.

The Stone Age paintings of southern Africa have long been known not only for their representations of important symbolic rituals in hunter-gatherer life, but also for their depictions of life in prehistoric times. At *Tsoelike River* rockshelter in Lesotho, southern Africa, paintings show fishermen assembled in their boats (see Figure 11.7 on page 233). They have cornered a shoal of fish that are swimming around in confusion. Some boats have lines that seem to be anchors. The fishermen are busy spearing their quarry. Another famed scene depicts a peacefully grazing herd of ostriches. Among them lurks a hunter wearing an ostrich skin, his legs and bow protruding beneath the belly of the apparently harmless bird. One can only wonder if his hunt was successful.

The artists painted big-game hunts, honey collectors, women gathering fruit, cattle raids, even red-coated British soldiers. Scenes like these take us back to hot days when a small group of hunters pursued their wounded quarry until it weakened and collapsed. The hunters, having stalked their prey for hours, relax in the shade as they watch

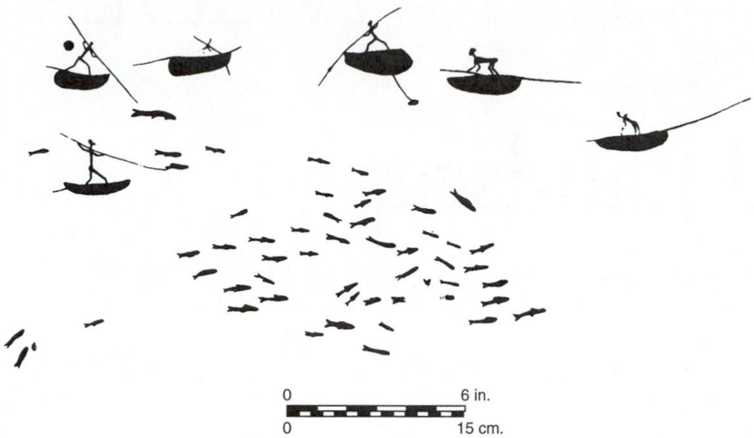

Figure 11.7 The fishing scene from Tsoelike rockshelter, Lesotho, southern Africa.

its death throes. Then they settle down to butcher the dead animal before carrying the meat and skin home to be shared with their group. Few artifacts survive from scenes such as these, but the objective of reconstructing ancient subsistence patterns is to re-create, from the few patterned traces that have survived in the soil, just such long days in the sun.

SUMMARY

1. Archaeological evidence for subsistence comes from artifacts and food remains, with animal bones forming the most common source of information.
2. Reconstructing entire diets is much harder, for the proportions of different foods in the diet have to be established. Bog corpses, human feces, and stable carbon isotope analysis provide invaluable information on ancient diets.
3. Fragmentary animal bones broken up for food (zooarchaeology) provide information on hunting and herding, requiring careful analysis of the minimum numbers of species present and counts of the minimum number of individuals.
4. Zooarchaeology can sometimes provide information on hunting preferences, butchery, seasonal occupation of camps, and on early domesticated animals and animal husbandry.
5. Wild and domesticated plant remains can be studied in carbonized seed form, or as imprints on clay pot walls, but flotation methods provide larger statistical samples for analyses of changing foraging and farming practices. AMS radiocarbon dating lets researchers date individual seeds or cobs, providing new information on the origins of food production.
6. Birds, fish remains, and shellfish are invaluable sources on seasonal occupation and intensive foraging in many parts of the world.

TWELVE

Settlement and Landscape

The earthworks of Avebury, England.

CHAPTER OUTLINE

PREVIEW

Chapter 12 moves away from the study of individual sites, artifacts, and food remains into changing ancient settlement patterns. We examine the hierarchy of human settlement from individual sites to entire regions and discuss some of the methods used to study them, including Geographic Information Systems. Landscapes are distinct from settlement patterns, for they are humanly perceived and change constantly through time. We discuss ways in which archaeologists study sacred and secular landscapes in a search for the intangible beliefs of ancient societies.

The earth is not just a series of dramatically poised topographic features that incite the wonder of man or beckon for exploitation, but is rather a living, breathing entity in an inanimate universe. The land with its water, plants, and animals is a spiritual creation put into motion by the gods in their wisdom. These elements are here to help, teach and protect through an integrated system of beliefs that spell out man's relationship to man, nature, and the supernatural. To ignore these teachings is to ignore the purpose of life, the meaning of existence.

—Robert McPherson, *Sacred Land, Sacred View: Navajo Perceptions of the Four Quarters Region,* 1992

"I am my own aborigine," Irish archaeologist Seamus Caulfield once commented. We were standing on the forbidding limestone cliffs of County Mayo in northwestern Ireland, gazing at the rolling bogland of Céide Fields. Caulfield grew up in nearby Belderigg, a hamlet of small houses surrounded by ancient field walls built and rebuilt over thousands of years. As a small boy, he went barefoot for six months of the year, feeling underfoot the texture of narrow pathways, marshlands, and small fields. Years later, Seamus Caulfield still has a tactile relationship with his home community and with the farmland that once sustained it, the kind of close relationship with environment and landscape once enjoyed by preindustrial societies all over the globe. He calls these familiar farmlands his "landscape of memory." Thanks to archaeology, Caulfield has traced his ancestry back on this land to a long-forgotten Stone Age field system built before 3000 B.C.

Caulfield inherited a passion for archaeology from his schoolteacher father, who had discovered stone walls deep under the peat that mantles the local landscape. In 1983, he began to map the buried stone walls at nearby Céide Fields. First, he tried using aerial photographs to identify the field systems, but the peat covered everything. Then he turned to the low-tech tools of his youth, a 6-foot-long (2-m-long) iron T-bar and a special spade used for cutting peat sods. Caulfield and his students laid out lines across the hills and ran transects of probes at 1-foot (0.3-m) intervals across the bogland. The peat was much shallower where the buried stone walls lay. Soon, hundreds of bamboo poles marked walls and fields.

Season after season, Caulfield returned to Céide Fields until he had mapped more than 4 square miles (6.4 sq. km) of intact farming landscape, undisturbed since 2400 B.C. (see Figure 12.1 on page 236). With the help of geologists and palynologists, Caulfield showed that the warmer and wetter climate after the Ice Age brought pine forests to the area. Tree rings tell us that the forest suddenly vanished in 2800 B.C.,

Figure 12.1 Céide Fields, County Mayo, Ireland. (Photo © Dept. of Environment, Heritage and Local Government, Ireland.)

opening up grassland ideal for cattle grazing. For nearly five hundred years, small groups of farmers separated their pastures with low stone walls, dividing the land into a patchwork of lines, rectangles, and squares. Each family lived in a small thatched round house set within a stone enclosure amidst a mosaic of constantly changing fields modified over successive generations.

After five centuries, the damp climate defeated the farmers. Wet bog, with its mosses, heathers, and moor grass, spread inexorably across the hills. The grasslands vanished, the cattle herders retreated inland, and the boundary walls disappeared under peat. County Mayo was a peaceful part of Ireland. No Roman armies or social catastrophes disrupted life at Céide Fields, ensuring a high level of cultural continuity in this corner of Ireland. Seamus Caulfield's family has lived at Belderigg for generations. Thanks to his research, he feels he can safely claim himself as an "aborigine," a distant descendant of the local farmers of some two hundred generations ago.

The Céide Fields project is a classic example of settlement archaeology, the topic of this chapter—the ways in which archaeologists study households, communities, and ancient cultural landscapes. The next two chapters widen our focus away from single sites and artifacts to the broader compass of ancient societies and the ways in which they interacted with one another. This chapter examines ways in which archaeologists study ancient settlement patterns and landscapes; Chapter 13 discusses interactions, between individuals and groups, forensics, and ancient trade.

The toolkits and food remains found in archaeological sites reflect their inhabitants' material culture and subsistence activities. Hunter-gatherers tend to have portable toolkits, manufactured for the most part from organic materials that do not survive well in archaeological sites (see Figure 9.11 on page 193). Many of their sites are temporary camps. Rarely can the archaeologist look at the patterning of artifacts and food remains in such camps, for many are gone forever. But the more sedentary farmer settles much longer in one spot and is confronted with much more elaborate annual tasks. The farmer has to store each year's food surplus, too, an activity that immediately adds complexity to a farming settlement. Substantial houses, storage pits, cemeteries, threshing floors, cattle enclosures—all of these can be elements in even a small farming village.

Archaeologists study patterning in such structures as houses and storage pits just as thoroughly as they study artifacts and food remains. They also analyze distributions in time and space of different communities and relationships between them. These activities are classified as **settlement archaeology**, which reveals the many ways in which individual communities relate to one another—through trade, religious beliefs, and social ties, among others. Settlement archaeology research requires a combination of common sense and careful mapping and surveying combined with fine-grained excavation, and, often, high-technology science.

Settlement Patterns

Settlement archaeology is part of the analysis of human interactions with, and adaptations to, the natural and social environment. The houses and villages of a prehistoric society, like the artifacts and food residues beside their hearths, are part of the settlement pattern. This pattern involves relationships among people who decided—for practical, political, economic, ideological, and social reasons—to place their houses, settlements, and religious structures where they did. Settlement archaeology also allows us to examine the relationships among different communities and trading networks, as well as ways in which people exploited both their environment and social organization. By studying settlement patterns, we have a chance to examine the intangible factors that caused culture change in ancient times.

For instance, the Chumash Indians of southern California lived on the islands and shores of the Santa Barbara Channel, where natural ocean upwelling nourished one of the richest inshore fisheries on earth. Seven hundred years ago, this rich bounty of marine resources allowed the Chumash to live in densely populated, permanent settlements with as many as 1,000 inhabitants. The most important of these villages clustered at sheltered spots on the coast with good canoe landings, kelp fisheries close offshore, and sea mammal rookeries within easy reach. If you find a series of coastal Chumash settlements in sheltered positions that protected them from the southeastern storms of winter, you can reasonably assume there were sound, practical reasons behind the site distribution. Within the village itself, we know that a complex variety of social, economic, and even personal factors dictated the layout of houses in relation to one another.

At another level, an entire village or city may reflect a society's view of their world and the cosmos. The ancient Mesoamericans placed great emphasis on lavish public ceremonies set in the heart of large ceremonial centers. Fifteen hundred years ago, great lowland Maya cities like Copán and Tikal were replicas in stone and stucco of the layered Mesoamerican spiritual world of the heavens, the living world, and the underworld (see Figure 3.8 on page 62). Their pyramids were sacred mountains, the doorways of the temples atop them the sacred openings by which the ruler, as intermediary with the spiritual world, traveled to the Otherworld up and down the *Wacah Chan,* the symbolic World Tree that connected the layers of the Maya universe. A thousand years later, the vast plaza of the Aztec capital, Tenochtitlán, stood at the center of the ancient Mexican world. When Spaniard Hernán Cortes and his conquistadors climbed to the summit of the great temple of the sun god Huitzilopochtli and the rain god Tlaloc in 1519, they stood at the axis of the Aztec universe. The four quarters of the Aztec world radiated from a temple so sacred that pyramid after pyramid rose at the same location (see Figure 6.4 on page 117).

The relationship between an individual and the landscape can be as complex as that of an entire society. A central African farmer once showed me his land, a patchwork of small gardens, some intensely cultivated, others lying fallow as the soil regenerated after years of use. I saw just land until he pointed out the subtle signs of regenerating soil, different kinds of grasses to be eaten by his cattle in the weeks ahead, the flowering nut trees that would come into harvest at the end of the wet season. The landscape came alive, a quilt of gardens, plants, and animals protected by his ancestors, who were now the spiritual guardians of the land. My friend's relationship to his surroundings was a "landscape of memory," built from generations of his own and his predecessors' experience.

Settlement archaeology is about these many layers of dynamic relationships, some of which are nearly impossible to discern without the careful use of analogy with living societies. For working purposes, many archaeologists divide these layers of relationship into a loose hierarchy of three general levels—households, communities, and distribution of communities (see Figure 12.2).

Households

The eruption came as a sudden rumble that shook the Maya village at the end of the day 1,400 years ago, just as everyone was finishing their evening meal. An underground fissure less than a mile away had erupted with little warning. Clouds of ash and gases darkened the sky. The villagers fled for their lives, leaving their dirty dishes behind them. Within a few days, the tiny hamlet and its surrounding fields lay under 15 feet (4.6 meters) of ash.

About 1,400 years later, a bulldozer operator leveling the ground for grain silos accidentally uncovered the corner of a thatched hut mantled in ash. The Maya village at Cerén, El Salvador, is an extraordinary archaeological treasure, a prehistoric settlement

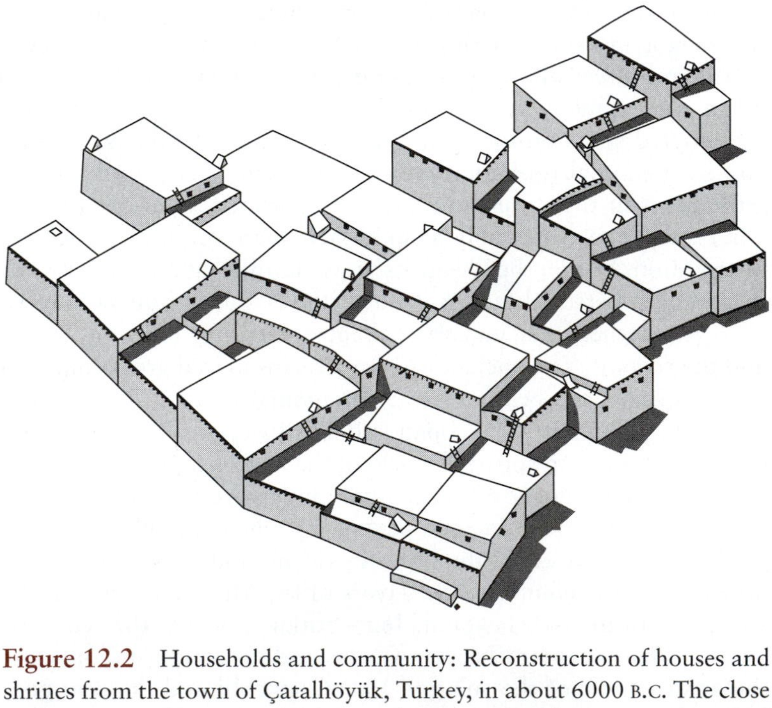

Figure 12.2 Households and community: Reconstruction of houses and shrines from the town of Çatalhöyük, Turkey, in about 6000 B.C. The close juxtaposition of houses provided insulation against climatic extremes and protection against enemies. Çatalhöyük, an important farming center, owed much of its importance to trade in fine-grained obsidian, which was mined nearby. In its heyday, it was one of the largest human settlements in the world.

frozen in time (see Figure 9.9 on page 190). Archaeologist Payson Sheets has plotted the contents of entire Cerén houses. One household lived in a complex of four buildings: a kitchen, a workshop, a storehouse, and a residence where the inhabitants socialized, ate, and slept. Sheets and his colleagues found grindstones still standing on forked sticks that elevated them above the ground, even a well-tended garden near the storehouse with three species of medicinal herbs, each plant standing in its own mound of soil. A nearby field held ridges of young maize plants 8 to 15 inches (20 to 38 centimeters) high, typical August growth in this environment.

The Cerén excavations reveal humble Maya households going about their daily business, their artifacts preserving by chance the one moment in the day when men, women, and children were all together for the evening meal. Archaeological sites like Cerén are archives of human interactions, where patterns of artifacts, food remains, and other material finds provide vital information on ancient human behavior. Few sites have the exceptional preservation found at Cerén, but many contain informative patternings of artifacts that reflect activities of all kinds.

When Kent Flannery and his students excavated farming villages in the Valley of Oaxaca, Mexico, dating to between 1350 and 850 B.C., they not only uncovered and recorded the one-room, thatched, pole-and-mud houses, but plotted the associated artifact patterns as well. They carefully distinguished between the house with its contents and the cluster of household storage pits, graves, and garbage heaps that lay nearby. The researchers plotted household features very carefully and identified areas where special activities took place from the specialist toolkits—for bead making and obsidian toolmaking—associated with them (see Figure 12.3 on page 240). Every household obtained, processed, and stored food, although the types of food consumed by each varied. Some Oaxacan households also spent much time making stone tools or ornaments. These specialist activities presumably supplied the needs of the community as a whole. In this Mexican example, and in all studies of individual structures, the artifacts and activities associated with them are just as important to the archaeologist as the design and layout of the structure itself.

We should never forget that households are chronicles of human interactions, communities even more so. Archaeological sites, whether small hunting camps, humble farming villages, or vast cities, are archives of human interaction. People lived and died in these places. They grew up, got married, had children, quarreled with neighbors. These daily interactions, between men and women, rich and poor, traders and their customers, slaves and masters, come down to us in the form of distinctive artifact patternings and community settlement patterns. The anonymous testimony of artifacts from individual houses, from neighborhoods, palaces, and temples, reveals the full, and often unsuspected, diversity of ancient human communities (see Figure 12.4 on page 241).

Households require slow-moving area excavation, so that the exact position of every artifact, features such as hearths or pits, and the tiniest of food remains like seeds and broken animal bones can be recorded electronically and photographically before anything is lifted from the dwelling. Sometimes, I've managed to identify the activities of different individuals while still excavating the house floor: stoneworking activity surviving as a scatter of stone tools and the waste flakes and cores used to make them; butchering of a rabbit by a cluster of broken bones. More often, however, the database in the laboratory computer is the best source of information, allowing you, for example, to call up the position of every potsherd of a certain style, or all ox forelimb bones. It is then that you discern unexpected associations, subtle signposts to long-forgotten domestic activities, or even of children playing. Short of a burial or a house belonging to a known historical individual, this is about as close as you can get in archaeology to individuals as opposed to households. This type of excavation is invaluable when studying male and female roles, or the cultural diversity of a household revealed by distinctive artifacts.

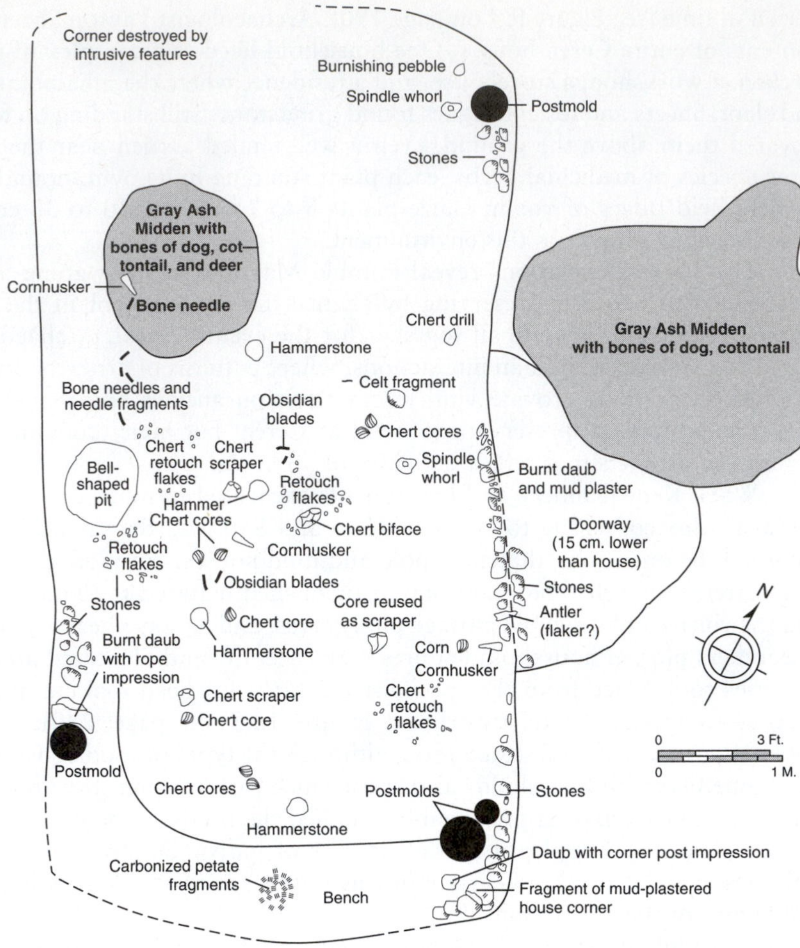

Figure 12.3 Plan of a house at Tierra Largas, Valley of Oaxaca, Mexico, from around 900 B.C., with selected artifacts plotted on the floor.

Like a shipwreck on the seabed, a well-excavated ancient house can be a sealed capsule of a moment in the past, which can be read by an expert like a book (see the Discovery box on pages 242–243).

Communities

Every household member interacts with other members of the household and with individuals in other households within the **community**. And entire households interact with other households as well. Once we begin to look at a community of households, new complexities enter the picture. The first is permanency of settlement, which is affected primarily by the realities of subsistence and ecology. How long San forager camps in Africa's Kalahari Desert are occupied is determined by availability of water, game, and vegetable foods near the site; the camp moves at regular intervals. In contrast, the farmers of Çatalhöyük, a Turkish farming settlement of 6000 B.C., lived in the same crowded village of mud houses separated by narrow alleys for many centuries, because they were anchored to their nearby fields (see Figure 12.2 on page 238).

In such small communities, family and kin ties were of overwhelming importance, affecting the layout of houses, household compounds, and groups of dwellings. By

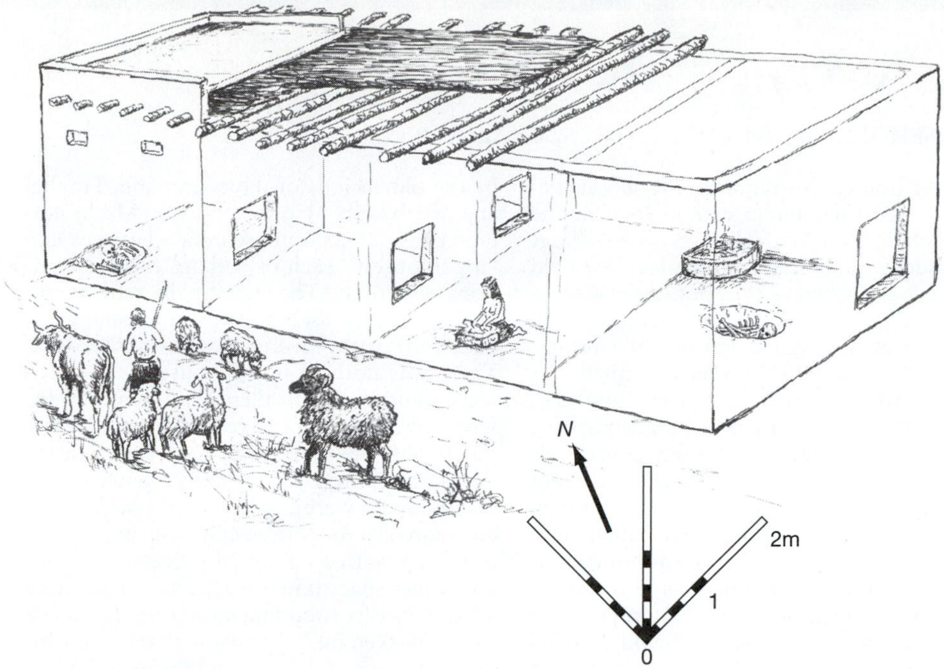

Figure 12.4 Isometric reconstruction of a house at Abu Hureyra, Syria, occupied by a family engaged in cereal agriculture and goat herding. Note the burials under the house floor. c. 7500 B.C. (From *Village on the Euphrates* by Andrew M. T. Moore, copyright © 1999 by Oxford University Press, Inc. Used by permission of Oxford University Press, Inc.)

mapping and analyzing artifact patterns and house inventories, you can sometimes find traces of different residential clusters within a single community. Kent Flannery and a University of Michigan research team used such data plots to find at least four residential wards (*barrios*) within the rapidly growing village of *San José Mogote*, which flourished in Mexico's Valley of Oaxaca after 1350 B.C. A trash-filled erosion gully separated each cluster of square thatched houses from its neighbors.

Small communities, like cities, are never static entities. People's children grow up, marry, and start new households nearby. Houses burn down or collapse, so new dwellings take their place. As often happened with Iroquois villages in the American Northeast, a settlement would outgrow its fortifications, then erect an extended palisade to protect new longhouses (see Figure 7.6 on page 139). The study of an ancient community is a study of constant interactions between individuals, **household groups**, and members of the settlement discerned through the careful study of **activity areas** (places where individuals carried out specific tasks like food preparation) and artifact patternings.

The behaviors and interactions of people living in much larger communities like cities are also reflected in artifact patternings and in the settlement pattern of the city as a whole. Whereas economic and environmental realities often affect the siting of a smaller community, more complex factors such as religious authority come into play with ancient cities. For example, the city of *Eridu* in southern Iraq was the largest human settlement on earth in 4000 B.C. Eridu lay close to the Euphrates River, with easy access to the wider world of the Persian Gulf. Perhaps 5,000 people clustered in the crowded precincts of the city, which at first was little more than an agglomeration of villages of close kin or specialist artisans living close to one another for mutual protection and economic interest. They lived in the shadow of the great mudbrick ziggurat temple mound of the god Enlil, a veritable artificial mountain that reached toward the wide heavens

Discovery

HOUSEHOLDS AT MARKI, CYPRUS, C. 2200 B.C.

Studying households requires not only meticulous excavation, but a careful look at the social changes behind changes in dwellings and, indeed, in entire communities. Few field projects have achieved this, but recent discoveries on Cyprus in the eastern Mediterranean area step in the right direction. The Bronze Age village at *Marki* was occupied for between 500 and 600 years after 2400 B.C. During these five or six centuries, the village grew from a community of a few households into a much larger 15-acre (6-ha) settlement with narrow alleys, before declining and then being abandoned. The maximum population was about 400 people. Marki was both a self-sufficient farming community and a copper mining settlement, exploiting outcrops in the nearby Troodos Mountains. David Frankel and Jennifer Webb (2006) have excavated about 21,500 sq. feet (6,555 sq. m) of the settlement, which enabled them to study the changing ways in which the inhabitants used the space available to them (see Figure 12.5).

The excavators identified 33 compounds, which they consider separate households. Some were in use for centuries, others for shorter periods of time. Most of the compounds were rectangular courtyards with small, enclosed rooms built of mudbrick on stone foundations. The rooms had plaster wall benches, hearths, clay ovens; narrow alleys linked the houses. Most of the compounds were remodeled and renovated, partly because mudbrick buildings decay relatively fast. Typically, the builders would tear down the mudbrick walls, and rebuild on the existing foundations, which were constrained by the dimensions of the compound. Frankel and Webb were able to subdivide Marki into nine phases, each representing what they call "a palimpsest" each of perhaps three generations of activity. Throughout the settlement's history, each household lived in a rectangular courtyard with covered rooms at the back. There was nothing in the houses or the artifacts associated with them that hinted at different wealth levels between households. The inhabitants never followed a master plan for the community over many generations. Compounds were added haphazardly and cumulatively. As time went on, the population increased, with a continual process of negotiation over space under way. The village, once a hamlet of freestanding structures, became a tightly packed built up area with relatively little open space and limited access to individual compounds.

The cycles of rebuilding and renovation of dwellings occupied over long periods of time clearly suggests that houses were inherited by each generation from its predecessor, remaining occupied by well-established families. Two compounds in particular maintained their boundaries for three or four centuries and may have exercised considerable authority as a result. One of them even maintained an offshoot household, which was interconnected to it for several generations before becoming larger and finally becoming a separate compound.

While many details of the negotiations that accompanied the enlargement or subdivision of household spaces will always elude us, some general trends are notable. There was a move

above (see Figure 12.6 on page 244). Eridu's temple was the highest point in the flat countryside for many miles around, a symbol of an intensely sacred place favored by the gods. Compelling political and religious factors helped determine the site of Eridu, the chosen city of Enlil. Like many other ancient cities, this oldest of human cities was a symbolic center of the universe, the holiest place on earth.

The largest community settlement pattern ever investigated systematically is that of Teotihuacán, Mexico, where René Millon has mapped dozens of residential compounds, a market, and vast ceremonial structures (see Figure 12.7 on page 244). He even found special quarters where foreigners from Oaxaca and lowland Veracruz on the Gulf of Mexico—revealed by their distinctive architecture and pottery—lived for centuries in an alien city. Millon sought the answers to many questions. What social classes existed in the city? What specialist crafts were practiced and where? How many people lived at Teotihuacán at different periods? The only way to answer such questions was to map

Figure 12.5 House compounds at Marki, Cyprus.

toward greater privacy, both within compounds and houses, reflected by the full enclosure of compounds, also the eventual separation of sets of compounds from one another.

During the earliest generations of the settlement, the inner rooms of compounds faced into a minimally enclosed courtyard in which a wide range of activities took place. This implies a high degree of social and economic cooperation between individual households in a tiny community of about 40 people. Within a century or so of first settlement, self-contained households came into being, now secure enough to survive as individual economic units. By this time, population increases and larger families may have led to each maintaining its own dwellings and land. But the one adjoining compound suggests that there was an increasing emphasis on extended family relationships.

Marki reflects the kinds of profound economic and social changes that can be identified through careful excavation of individual households within a small community. After generations of constant interaction between everyone in the community, a more impersonal village developed, where people tended to live in enclosed compounds and knew well only the people in their own neighborhoods. Simultaneously, new mechanisms for social control may have developed at Marki, which involved such intangibles as ties of kin and obligations between members of extended families. We will never know.

the entire city and make comprehensive surface collections and test excavations to give an overall picture of the total settlement pattern.

Thanks to the mapping project data, we know that teeming neighborhoods of single-story, flat-roofed, rectangular apartment compounds complete with courtyards and passageways lay beyond the enormous ceremonial precincts of the city. Narrow alleyways and streets about 12 feet (3.7 meters) wide separated each compound from its neighbors. Each housed between 20 and 100 people, perhaps members of the same kin group. Judging from artifact patternings, some sheltered skilled artisans, families of obsidian and shell ornament makers, weavers, and potters.

What was life like inside Teotihuacán's anonymous apartment compounds (*barrios*)? Mexican archaeologist Linda Manzanilla has investigated one such complex close to the northwest edge of Teotihuacán, searching for traces of different activities within the complex. The stucco floors in the apartments and courtyards had been swept

Figure 12.6 A reconstruction of the ziggurat temple at Eridu, Iraq.

Figure 12.7 Pyramid of the Sun, Teotihuacán, Valley of Mexico. The pyramid and other structures at Teotihuacán formed the core of a vast prehistoric city. The great mass of the pyramid was designed as part of a setting for grandiose public ceremonies, which were a common feature of Mesoamerican religious beliefs. Teotihuacán was a city conceived on a grand scale, its ceremonial precincts designed to give the visitor a sense of the power of the gods and the forces of the spiritual world.

clean, so Manzanilla and her colleagues used chemical analyses of the floor deposits to search for human activities. She developed a mosaic of different chemical readings, such as high phosphate readings where garbage had rotted, and dense concentrations of carbonate from lime (used in the preparation of both tortillas and stucco) that indicated cooking or building activity. Manzanilla's chemical plans of the compound are accurate enough to pinpoint the locations of cooking fires and eating places where the inhabitants consumed such animals as deer, rabbits, and turkeys. She was able to identify three families totaling about 30 people who lived in three separate apartments within this community inside a much larger community. Each apartment had specific areas for sleeping, eating, religious activities, and funeral rites.

Teotihuacán's barrios have revealed intense interactions between people who knew one another well, and between these tight-knit communities and the wider universe of the city itself. Walking along one of the cleared streets, you can imagine passing down the same defile 1,500 years earlier, each side bounded by a bare, stuccoed compound wall. Occasionally, a door opens onto the street, offering a view of a shady courtyard, of pots and textiles drying in the sun. The street would have been a cacophony of smells and sounds—wood smoke, dogs barking, the monotonous scratch of maize grinders, the soft voices of women weaving, the passing scent of incense.

Distribution of Communities

No human being has ever lived in complete isolation, for even the smallest hunter-gatherer family group has at least fleeting contacts with neighboring bands at certain times of the year. But as human societies become more complex and settlements more lasting, intercommunity relationships become much more complicated. Different settlements depend more and more on one another for essential raw materials (such as salt or copper ore) and for specialist products (stone knives, religious ornaments, and the like). Growing villages might split into two settlements that, although separated in space, still maintain close ties of kinship. Human settlement patterns are not just site dots on maps. They are complex and constantly changing networks of human interaction, of trade, religion, and social ties, of differing adaptations to local environmental challenges.

For years, the study of community distributions depended on large-scale archaeological surveys that combined aerial photographs with months of systematic foot survey on the ground. Such studies began with the development of a classification of archaeological sites in a region. Each of these site types has a relationship to others, the total distribution of all site types making up a settlement pattern. Each site type is defined by the characteristic structures, artifact patterns, food remains, and small finds therein. These definitions provide us with a way to organize the sites into a hierarchy of successive levels of settlements (see Figure 12.8 on page 246). For instance, the Maya city of Copán was a major ritual and trade center, the seat of an important kingdom. A hierarchy of secondary centers, small towns, villages, and tiny hamlets lay throughout the city's territory, each dependent on the others, and each with a well-defined position in the hypothetical pyramid of human settlement. Trading and the payment of tribute played a major role in linking the different layers of this and other settlement hierarchies in the ancient world. So did the availability of food and other resources within the immediate vicinity of a settlement. Eric Higgs of Cambridge University developed a method known as **site catchment analysis**, which inventories resources within different radiuses of sites, an effective way of defining where people obtained food and other commodities (see Figure 12.9 on page 247).

William Sanders and a large research team from Pennsylvania State University surveyed the entire Valley of Mexico, center of the Aztec civilization, in the 1970s. They compiled distribution maps of every known archaeological site and plotted them against comprehensive environmental data, with dramatic results. Sanders showed how the population of the Basin ebbed and flowed over many centuries, with the rise and fall of the great city of Teotihuacán in the first millennium A.D. The most dramatic changes came some centuries later when the growing Aztec capital, Tenochtitlán, achieved overwhelming dominance. By the end of the fifteenth century A.D., the imperial capital housed at least 200,000 people, living in dense residential areas now buried under the concrete jungle of Mexico City (see Figure 6.4 on page 117). The concentration of sites nearby was such that Sanders estimated at least 400,000 city and country dwellers occupied a 230-square-mile (368-square-kilometer) zone of foothills, plains, and lake bed areas near the capital. He calculated that about a million people lived within the confines of the Basin of Mexico at the time. Tenochtitlán was a magnet to outlying populations. Its very presence skewed the entire settlement pattern of the Basin. So many people lived there that the Aztecs farmed every local environment in the region, to ensure there was enough food to go around.

Tenochtitlán stood at the center of an organized landscape, created by ambitious rulers who thought nothing of creating about 25,000 acres (10,000 hectares) of highly productive swamp gardens in the southern part of the Basin alone. Over less than two centuries, the local settlement pattern changed from a patchwork of small states and major centers to a highly centralized agricultural landscape capable of meeting the basic food needs of at least half a million people.

Few settlement patterns show such dramatic changes as those in the Basin of Mexico. Sanders was a pioneer in combining environmental and archaeological data in settlement archaeology, but his project was unsophisticated by the standards of some of today's projects, which rely on high technology to integrate field surveys with a wide variety of spatial data.

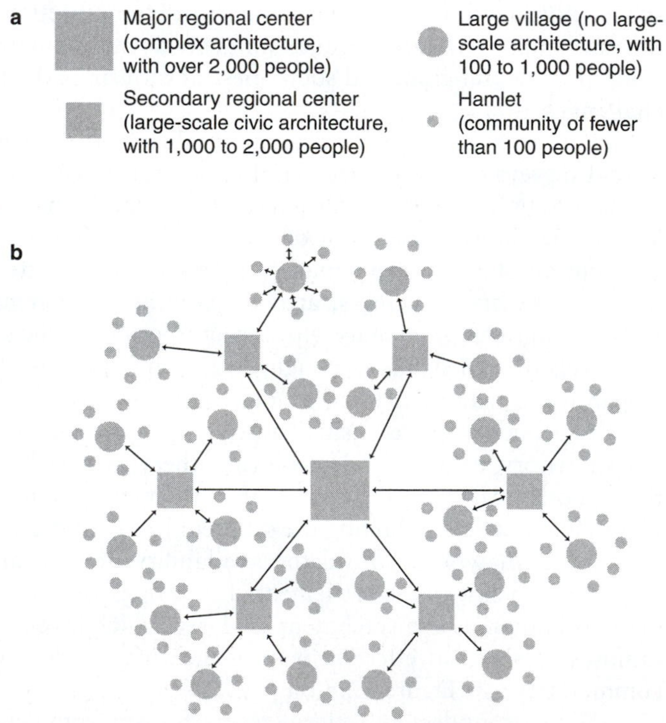

Figure 12.8 A site hierarchy in Mesoamerica. (a) Simplified hierarchy of site types. (b) Hypothetical site hierarchy on the ground, with the major regional center serving secondary centers spaced at regular intervals. These in turn serve larger villages and their networks of hamlets.

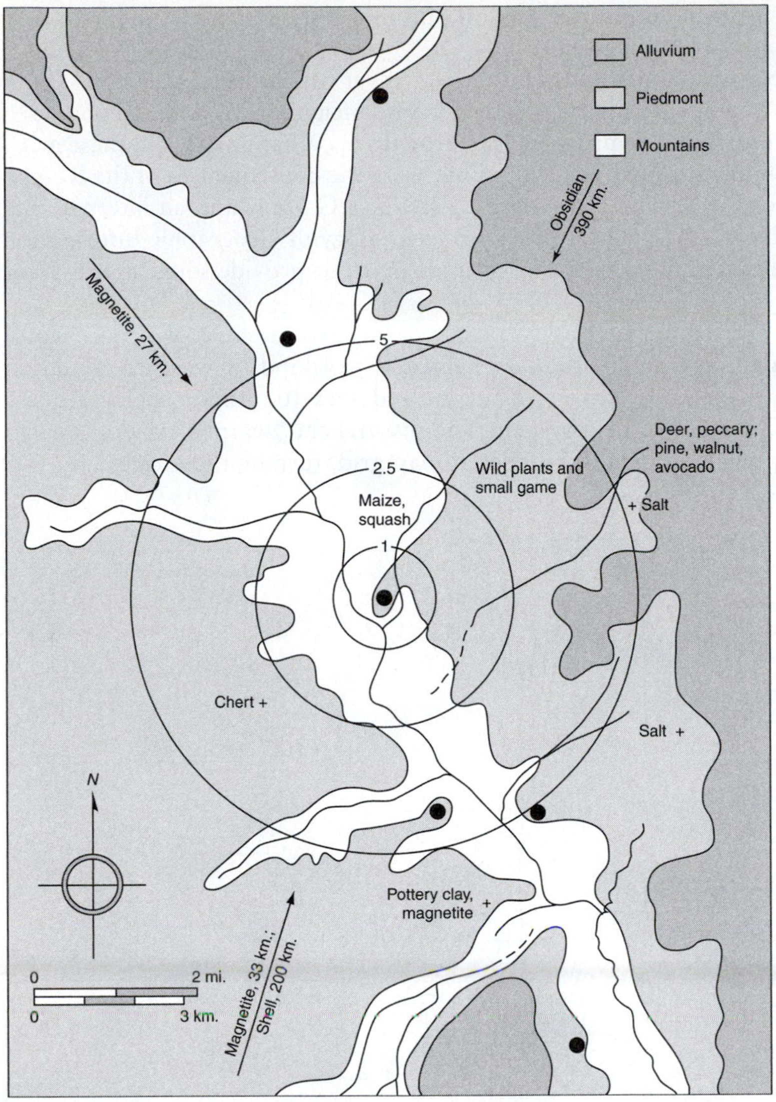

Figure 12.9 A simple example of site catchment analysis, not using GIS, from the Valley of Oaxaca, Mexico. The inhabitants of this farming village, occupied between 1150 and 850 B.C., obtained their basic agricultural needs within a radius of less than 1.5 miles (2.4 kilometers). Common minerals and seasonal plant foods were found within the 3-mile (5-kilometer) circle, game meat and construction materials within a 9-mile (14.4-kilometer) radius. (Radii in kilometers.)

Geographic Information Systems and Roman Wroxeter, England

Virconium Cornoviorum, the Roman town at present-day Wroxeter near Shrewsbury in west-central England, was the fourth largest urban center in Roman Britain. Wroxeter started as a legionary camp in A.D. 60, then became a town 30 years later, flourishing until the fifth or sixth century. Most Roman towns lie under modern cities like London or York. Fortunately for archaeologists, much of Wroxeter is in open country. For more than a century, generations of excavators investigated the major public buildings and commercial zone of the town. They used aerial photographs and surface collections of potsherds and other artifacts to plot the general outlines of the settlement and to develop a detailed chronology of its buildings.

However, these simple approaches could not answer fundamental questions about the history of a once-strategic military gateway into neighboring and unconquered Wales. Many Roman forts and camps lie close to the town. What impact did these army encampments have on the rural population? What were the consequences of the Roman conquest on local Iron Age farmers? Archaeologist Vince Gaffney and an international team of researchers have combined the powerful technology of Geographic Information Systems (GIS) with aerial photographs and ground survey to provide some answers (for GIS, see Chapter 6).

The Wroxeter archaeologists could draw on a massive archive of aerial photographs of the surrounding countryside, taken under every kind of weather condition imaginable over more than half a century. They located over 40 farming enclosures and the remains of a once-extensive field system. The researchers "warped" digital images of the aerial photographs onto Britain's national map grid, turning the images into GIS

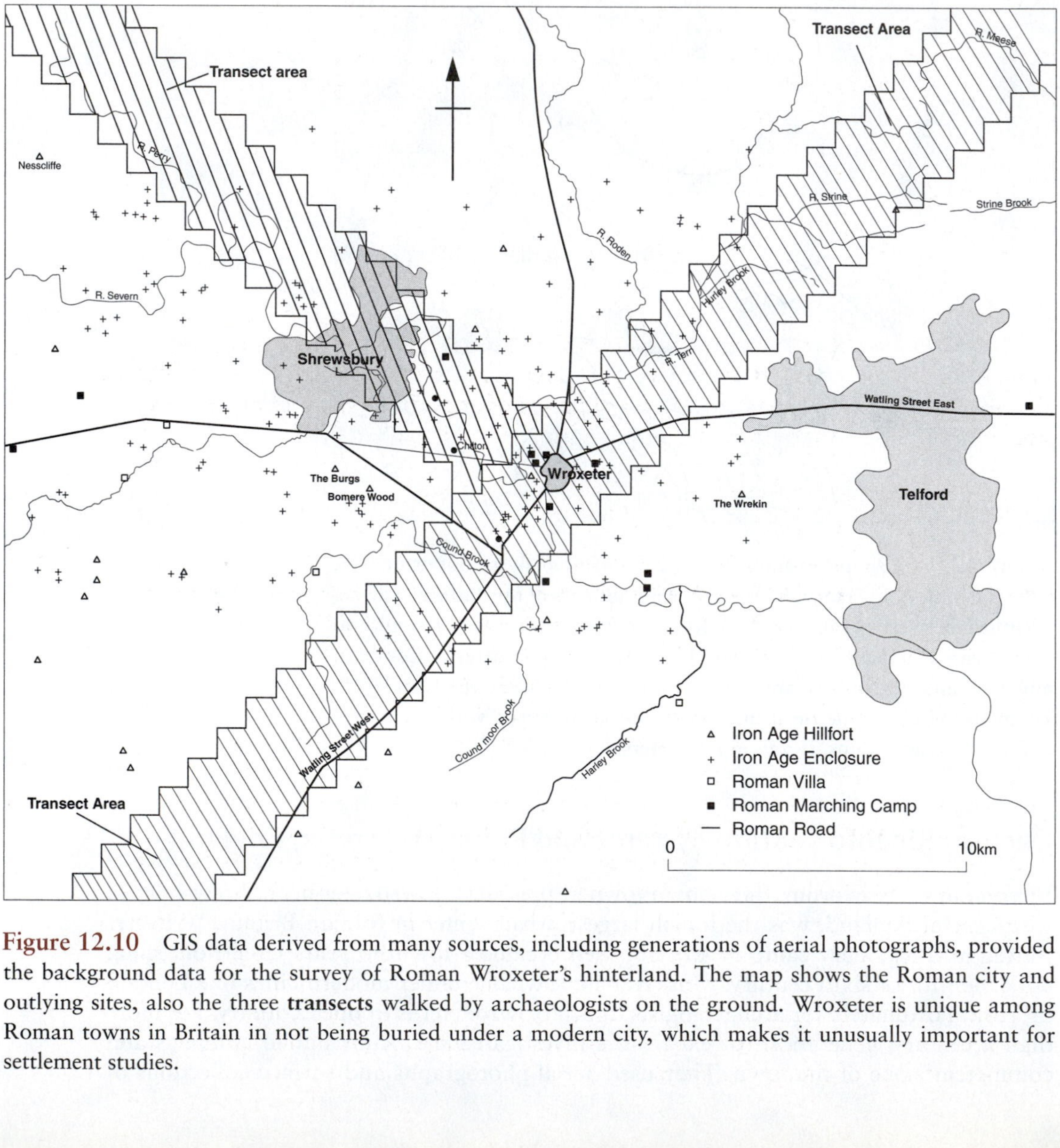

Figure 12.10 GIS data derived from many sources, including generations of aerial photographs, provided the background data for the survey of Roman Wroxeter's hinterland. The map shows the Roman city and outlying sites, also the three **transects** walked by archaeologists on the ground. Wroxeter is unique among Roman towns in Britain in not being buried under a modern city, which makes it unusually important for settlement studies.

maps so accurate a field-worker can measure and interpret such features as the Roman street grid at Wroxeter itself with margins of error as small as 3 feet (a meter). (See Figure 12.10 on page 248.)

The Wroxeter project is unusual in that the archaeologists working on the ground have the ability to manipulate all available archaeological data on the screen before they go into the field. The field workers rely heavily on volunteers, who are recording the Roman town's topography by taking measurements every 33 feet (10 meters). A magnetometer survey combined with ground-penetrating radar has revealed hitherto unknown buildings on the edge of the town. For generations, experts on Roman Britain had called Wroxeter a carefully planned "garden city," with parks and open spaces. GIS and remote sensing have revealed a less well-organized community with uncontrolled expansion at its margins as it drew people from the surrounding countryside.

The Wroxeter data is so complete that you can even explore the dynamic, ever-changing settlement pattern on the Web (www.archant.bham.ac.uk/brifan/research/wh/Base.htm). Your computer leads you through three-dimensional images of a long-vanished Roman town. Within a few years, Wroxeter's archaeologists will be able to answer questions about changing patterns of supply and demand. By assuming that the town was the economic hub of the surrounding area, they will be able to show how mass-produced pottery from remote sites flowed through the region along an existing infrastructure of roads, tracks, and rivers, accessible through the GIS database.

Population

Settlement patterns across a landscape evolve in response to three broad variables: environmental change, interactions between people, and shifts in population density. Of these three, population is the hardest to study.

Population growth was not a major factor in human history until after the Ice Age, which ended about 15,000 years ago. No question, however, that growing population densities were a major factor in the development of agriculture in southwestern Asia in about 10,000 B.C., and in the appearance of the first cities and civilizations about 7,000 years later. In the case of farming, much drier conditions, diminished supplies of wild plant foods, and many more mouths to feed turned many hunter-gatherer groups in the Jordan Valley and modern-day Syria into sedentary farmers within a few centuries.

Unfortunately, estimating population densities is often little more than guesswork. Despite attempts to develop censuses from house counts and refuse accumulation, most population estimates are at best rough approximations. For instance, one estimate places the population of Britain in 11,000 B.C. at about 10,000 people; another places the average population of early states in southern Iraq at about 17,000.

Nevertheless, changing population distributions are of great importance, for there is a clear cause-and-effect relationship between population and the potential carrying capacity and productivity of agricultural land. As populations grow, goes one popular argument, people try to collect or produce more food, perhaps by developing highly efficient ways of fishing or hunting, or by turning to agriculture. Like the ancient Egyptians, farmers may face the challenge by developing large-scale irrigation systems capable of producing several crops a year and feeding many more people.

Population, then, is a critical variable in settlement archaeology, as William Sanders and his colleagues showed, with the rapid growth of the Aztec capital in the Basin of Mexico. Although Sanders's population estimates were little more than informed guesses, he was able to show a dramatic rise over several centuries. Such general trends are of great interest, for they enable us to monitor large-scale processes like the rise or fall of an entire civilization.

The Archaeology of Landscapes

The word **landscape** defies easy definition, but everyone agrees that landscapes are created by humans. A landscape is like a piece of sculpture, which changes in response to the artist's hands. Perceptions of the landscape change constantly, even in fair weather and foul. Places on the landscape are laden with meaning. Caves can be conduits to the underworld, places where shamans passed in trance into the supernatural realm. Cloud-shrouded mountain peaks can be abodes of gods and mythic heroes. The Nile was sacred to the Egyptians; the city of Teotihuacán was built on a long-term master plan oriented toward the cardinal directions, each of which had their own gods, even their own colors. Even today, some societies hold certain trees sacred, attribute supernatural qualities to fire and water, and assign benign and evil qualities to different winds. These are intangible qualities, which change with the generations and vanish utterly when a site is abandoned or a society goes into eclipse. Even then, the **landscape of memory** continues to change as new people arrive, fresh settlements spread across the landscape, or the plow replaces the digging stick, the automobile the horse-and-cart.

The Ceíde Fields in northwestern Ireland described at the beginning of this chapter is a vivid example of a changing landscape. The ancient Stone Age landscape is not all there is, for the surrounding countryside bears ample traces of much later occupation, including abandoned farms from the era of the Irish potato famine of 1845-1848 that killed tens of thousands of people. The archaeologist Seamus Caulfield was born in a small village in the heart of this landscape, and has vivid memories of the changes in its own lifetime and in that of his parents and grandparents—his own landscape of memory.

We've come to think about the "archaeology of landscape" as opposed to settlement distributions. Some mention of this new avenue of archaeological inquiry is important at this juncture because it ties in with two major topics in Chapter 13: human interactions and the archaeology of the intangible. In archaeological terms, the landscape around Maya Copán or Stone Age Avebury in southern England has changed ever since humans first settled in both areas. Both landscapes have changed radically within the past century, quite apart from preceding centuries and millennia of different uses. Our challenge is to reconstruct the landscape as its various users saw it—what is often called their "landscape of memory."

Archaeologists study landscapes in many ways: with ecologically based systems approaches, with technology-laden methods that involve GIS and satellite data, or, at the other extreme, in almost literary fashion, describing such phenomena as eighteenth-century gardens or French markets (see Figure 12.11 on page 251). A new generation of settlement research is turning to landscape geography as a means of studying actual ancient landscapes, where symbolic relationships to the environment as well as ecology play important roles.

Many archaeologists engaged in landscape research think in terms of three dimensions of organizing landscape:

1. Physical characteristics and properties
2. Historical transformations over time
3. People's physical and symbolic relationships with their environments

Landscape analysis is a form of historical ecology, where changing landscapes over long time periods serve as cultural records. Landscapes are symbols of cultural stability that preserve enduring meanings over time. As such, they are as much a cultural record as an individual site and an artifact, and, when considered as a way in which people organize their relationship with the social world, a potentially vital source of information on ideology and cultural intangibles. Much of this research is informed by ethnographic and historical records.

Remote sensing has a powerful role to play in research into cultural landscapes. William Paca was one of the signors of the Declaration of Independence and a Governor of Maryland. During a five-year research project on his Wye Hall Plantation on Maryland's Eastern Shore, James Harmon, Mark Leone, and their colleagues mapped the largely intact terrace system, formal garden, and work areas such as slave yards (The house burnt down in 1870 and is not original.) Paca and others of his contemporaries deliberately manipulated the environment to create cultural landscapes defined in part by sight lines. The research team acquired LIDAR data on a day when the trees were leafless to maximize views of the ground, then used data processing algorithms to process the raw data. (For LIDAR, see Chapter 6.) They emerged with a contour map of a massive bowl-shaped landscape with terraces built by basket loads of soil carried by Paca's 100 slaves (see Figure 12.12 on page 252). The images and excavation revealed three terraces and two slopes, also eight garden beds on the upper terrace, laid out in pairs. All the beds were set at a 15-degree angle to forms diverging sight lines that focused on the distant water view. A combination of GIS, LIDAR, and conventional survey and excavation revealed a cultural landscape that had been largely forgotten. The same approach is now being applied to other great estates in Maryland.

Sacred Landscapes: Mirrors of the Intangible

We are *Homo sapiens,* capable of subtlety, of passing on knowledge and ideas through the medium of language. We have consciousness and self-awareness and are capable of foresight. We can express ourselves, show emotions, and we have a unique capacity for symbolic and spiritual thought. This quality allows us to define the boundaries of existence, and to conceptualize the relationship between the individual, the group, and the cosmos—the intangible.

Figure 12.11 Landscaping as a statement of power. William Paca, a prominent eighteenth-century Annapolis, Maryland, colonist, designed his garden with carefully arranged perspectives and terraces to give visitors and passersby a sense of power and prestige.

With spiritual beliefs and the cosmos, we enter the world of intangible human behavior. Archaeologists study the material remains of the past, which provide but a dim reflection of ancient spiritual beliefs. Obviously, some important sites were of religious significance. The Pyramid of the Sun at Teotihuacán is one, Stonehenge is another. Sacred places and the mythic landscapes associated with them, played a vital role in all societies. They were settings for rituals that ensured the continuity of cultural traditions, places where the word of the

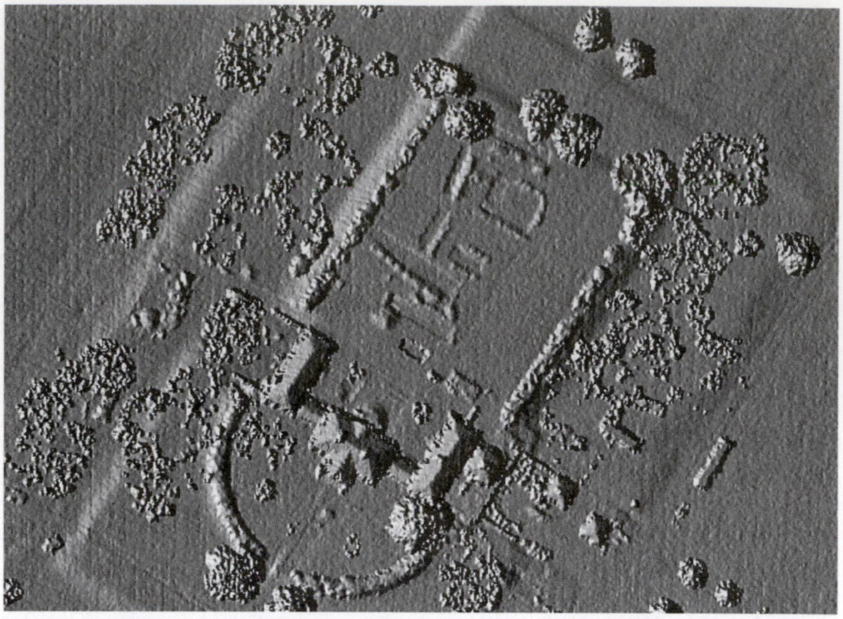

Figure 12.12 A LIDAR image of the great house of William Paca called Wye Hall and the surrounding platforms, which were the setting for the 1790s garden designed by Luke O'Dio for William Paca and built by his slaves. The image was the first version and shows the tops of trees, as well as the house, terraces, and excavated trenches.

gods rang out in familiar chants passed from one generation to the next. Sacred mountains such as the Hindu Mount Meru, the Greeks' Olympus, or the Lakota Indians' Black Hills often served as cosmic axes. Maya lords built great ceremonial centers as symbolic representations of their world of sacred mountains, caves, trees, and lakes. To demolish a sacred place was to destroy the essence of human existence itself. In 1521, Spanish conquistador Hernán Cortés razed the Aztec capital Tenochtitlán in the Valley of Mexico, knowing its temples and plazas replicated a cherished and all-encompassing supernatural world

In most ancient societies, the material and spiritual worlds formed a continuum, with no boundary between them. An "external" landscape on the earth was also an "internal" landscape of the mind, or a "landscape of memory," where colors, jagged peaks, streams, groves of trees, cardinal directions, and other phenomena had spiritual associations and their places in local mythology. The study of ancient landscapes provides unexpected and often rewarding insights into the ancient intangible.

Sacred places like the Pyramids of Giza, Stonehenge, or Maya Tikal lay in the hearts of much wider cultural landscapes, defined by generations of experience with supernatural qualities. The stone circles at Avebury in southern Britain formed part of a much larger sacred landscape, defined not only by natural landmarks but also by burial mounds, sacred avenues delineated by stone uprights, and structures where the bodies of the dead were exposed before burial in communal tombs (see chapter-opener photo on page 234). In recent years, teams of archaeologists have been gradually reconstructing this long-vanished, fragmentary landscape with survey and excavation that reveal its gradual evolution over many centuries.

Maeshowe and the Stones of Stenness

A classic example of a sacred landscape has emerged from cutting-edge research in the Orkney Islands, off northern Scotland. Two stone circles, the Stones of Stenness and the Ring of Brodgar, also a burial mound known as Maeshowe, lie at the heart of the landscape.

The Stones of Stenness are a towering circle of monoliths encircled by a large rock-cut ditch with a single entrance and an outer bank. In the center lay a stone hearth. The nearby *Ring of Brodgar* is much larger, and, if completed, would have had more than 60 standing stones and two opposed entrances surrounded by a ditch 9 feet (3 meters) deep and 148 feet (45 meters) across. *Maeshowe* is what is called a **passage grave**, where a long entrance passage leads to a massive central chamber with three raised side rooms. Four stone monoliths stand inside the chamber, not structural elements but apparently of symbolic importance. This communal grave lay inside a wall and a ditch that, when flooded, gave an impression of an island within a larger landscape. Maeshowe was a place of the dead, separated from the living world by its ditch and bank.

In 1983, archaeologist Colin Richards began a field survey to locate Stone Age farming settlements. The survey yielded surface scatters at several locations, including one on level ground close to Maeshowe and the Stones of Stenness. Five years of excavation at this Barnhouse site revealed a farming village, radiocarbon dated to around 3100 to 2900 B.C.—a group of freestanding houses each about 16 feet (5 meters) across, roofed with turf and looking somewhat like low mounds. As the village developed, it acquired a concentric layout, with one group of dwellings surrounding an open central area, a second group on the periphery.

One structure, on the western side of the settlement, was much larger, about 42 feet (12.8 meters) long and 32 feet (10 meters) wide, more than twice the size of surrounding huts. A smaller house faced it across a narrow, paved passage, the doorways facing one another, as if there was a relationship between the two. The interior was quite unlike that of the dwellings, comprising six large recesses formed by corner buttresses, with two masonry piers that effectively divided the building into two symmetrical halves, each with a central fireplace. Someone entering the building did so on the east side, so that the western portion was the "deepest" space within it. The sophisticated masonry used in the interior recalls that of Maeshowe. Thus, the structure may be associated with both the living and the dead, lying as it does on the western side of the settlement, toward sunset.

Subsequently, the inhabitants built a large square building at the western edge of the now abandoned village, surrounding it with a raised clay platform and a stone enclosure wall. It is as if the entire character of the settlement changed, as the building rose on the site of a large hearth, replaced with another one inside the new structure. At the same time, the stones from the original hearth were lifted and moved to form a central hearth in the middle of the Stones of Stenness.

The moving of the hearth stones highlights the importance of ritual in everyday life at Barnhouse, with all kinds of ceremonies, private and public, marking the passage of the seasons and peoples' individual lives. This village, and others still undiscovered, saw themselves as part of a constantly changing landscape. During the life of the settlement, the construction of Maeshowe and the two stone circles changed perceptions of the countryside in a process that Colin Richards and his colleagues call "monumental choreography."

A sense of order, of ritual arrangement, pervaded village life. You see it in the early circular houses, with their cruciform interiors dominated by a stone "dresser," right and left recesses, and a hearth. (An example can be seen at the reconstructed,

Figure 12.13 A reconstructed hut interior at Skara Brae, Orkney Islands. Note the stone dresser.

nearby village of Skara Brae (see Figure 12.13). The hearth, probably always lit, kept human existence going with life-maintaining fire. Richards and his colleagues believe the house architecture was a partial representation of the inhabitants' abstract beliefs and concepts of order.

During the 400-year occupation of Barnhouse, the Stones of Stenness rose 656 feet (200 meters) southeast of the village. Here, again, there is the same sense of order: a central hearth, just as in the houses, two standing stones in the center (removed at some point), and the entire monument surrounded by a wall, this time a ditch and bank. So the general principles of spatial organization occur, even if the Stones of Stenness fulfilled a very different ceremonial role, presumably involving rituals and privileged knowledge, and a carefully perceived order of the world (see Figure 12.14).

Stenness and Brodgar with their massive standing uprights create an awesome reaction in the visitor's mind. They are permanent, conspicuous places set in the midst of the landscape. No question, the builders created them as durable structures, destined to last far beyond their lifetimes—which they have done. Their construction

Figure 12.14 The Stones of Stenness, Orkney Islands.

Figure 12.15 Maeshowe, Orkney Islands, the mound aligned with the gap between two hills.

involved numerous people cooperating in the quarrying, hauling, and erection of the stone uprights, also complex social pacts that involved both individual and group prestige, and strong ties of obligation between families, kin groups, and entire communities.

The grassy mound of Maeshowe lies in full view a half mile (1 km) southeast of the village on slightly raised ground, constructed on the site of an earlier farming village, perhaps signifying a relationship between the living and the dead, the past and the present (see Figure 12.15). The passage faces the southwest, the rays of the setting sun at the midwinter solstice illuminating the interior of the central chamber. Then the interior returns to darkness; the sun begins its return journey and again the interior is illuminated in a process of symbolic rebirth shared with the ancestors. Thus, Maeshowe marked a fixed moment in the annual cycle of the agricultural year, the beginning of regeneration. The passage grave mound bears a close relationship to the nearby hill of Hoy, which dominates the landscape. Richards and his colleagues believe Maeshowe, the residence of the ancestors, was built to resemble the earth with its rock covered with soil, situated midway between the humanly inhabited world and the nether regions.

Thus, from 3300 B.C. onward, Barnhouse acted as a focal point for an entire landscape of a passage grave, stone circles (henges), and standing stones, all erected over a 400-year period. Village architecture and the great monuments are closely related, so much so that the one is an extension of the other, just as the builders intended—a dramatic example of the continuity of human life from the living world into the realm of the dead, the ancestors, who were as much part of the cyclical world of the seasons, of planting and harvest, of life and death, as their successors.

The Stones of Stenness and the Ring of Brodgar lie on opposing promontories that separate two lochs. In turn, a natural bowl of hills surrounds them, so that both monuments appear to be surrounded by water, yet encircled by hills. If you stand inside them, you have the impression of a circular landscape, where you can follow concentric rings out from the stone circle, to the ditch (filled with water for much of the year), to the bank, and then the surrounding water and encircling hills. Visitors to the interior of the henges would walk across a narrow causeway, as if it were crossing water into a place where standing stones imitated the surrounding topography of the hills overlooking the villages and lives of the local people.

The ritual landscape formalized the social landscapes of daily life. The stone circles and Maeshowe are the surviving elements of what were once the contexts for colorful, elaborate ceremonies that involved adornment, ceremonial clothing, perhaps dancing and chanting. Such rituals would have briefly transformed the qualities of the monuments. But for most of the year, sheep would have grazed quietly among the stones. This spectacular monumental landscape resulted from cosmology, a way of understanding and viewing the world that came through the realities of human existence in a small village on the shore of a freshwater lake.

SUMMARY

1. Many factors determine settlement patterns, including environment, economic practices, and technological skills.
2. Settlement archaeology is part of the study of human interactions with, and adaptations to, the natural and social environment.
3. The following are the three basic levels of human settlement: the single building, the arrangement of such buildings in the community, and the distribution of such communities against the landscape.
4. Both site catchment analysis and GIS play important roles in studying the relationships between hierarchies of different sites located in ancient landscapes.

THIRTEEN

The Archaeology of People

An artist's reconstruction of the Amesbury archer, c. 2470 B.C.

CHAPTER OUTLINE

PREVIEW

In the final analysis, archaeology is the study of people and their relationships with one another. Chapter 13 examines ways in which archaeologists study individuals and groups, a process that relies heavily on bioarchaeology, the study of human remains. Bioarchaeologists can tell us the sex and age of ancient people and provide information on their illnesses and injuries. However, the study of groups involves such issues as social ranking, ethnicity, and social inequality, using artifacts, settlement patterns, and also human remains. The study of gender in ancient societies has assumed importance in recent years, and is also discussed here. The chapter ends with a discussion of trade and exchange, also of religion and ideology, both of which flourish within often elaborate social contexts.

Sad fragility of human things! How many centuries and thousands of generations have passed away, of which history, probably, will never tell us anything. . . . How many distinguished [people]—artists, sovereigns, and warriors—whose names were worthy of immortality, are now forgotten, laid to rest under the thick dust which covers these tombs!

—Henri Mouhot, *Travels in the Central Parts of Siam,* 1872

"The murmur and hum of their voices could be heard more than a league [three miles] away. . . ." Conquistador Bernal Díaz marveled at the great market in the heart of the Aztec capital, Tenochtitlán, in 1519. The Spaniards wandered among throngs of buyers and sellers, at least 20,000 of whom flocked to the marketplace daily. They were impressed by the orderliness of the stalls and their cleanliness. Every kind of merchandise had a separate quarter. Dealers in gold, silver, semiprecious stones, feathers, and other exotics sold goods brought from every corner of the Aztec empire. You could buy capes, chocolate, dogs, foodstuffs of every kind, even ice from high on the slopes of the mountains. A dozen judges sat in shifts in a large hall, presiding over the orderliness of the market. Inspectors wandered through the crowds checking for price gouging or false measures. A standardized pricing system was based on staple commodities such as cacao beans, cotton cloths, and small T-shaped pieces of copper. Tenochtitlán's market was the hub of a vast pre-Columbian empire held together by force, trade, and tribute. But this panoply depended on interactions between people.

For all the hi-tech wizardry of today's archaeology, we must never forget that archaeologists study people, not just artifacts, food remains, and culture change. This chapter, "The Archaeology of People," uses artifacts, forensics, and other material remains to look behind the facades of ancient societies, at the complex interactions between groups and individuals that are at the very heart of all human societies.

Studying the Deceased: Bioarchaeology

Individuals like the the Ice Man reveal the power of **bioarchaeology**, the multidisciplinary study of ancient human remains, as a way of understanding the people of the past and their behavior. (Genetics and DNA are described briefly in Chapter 4. Here we focus

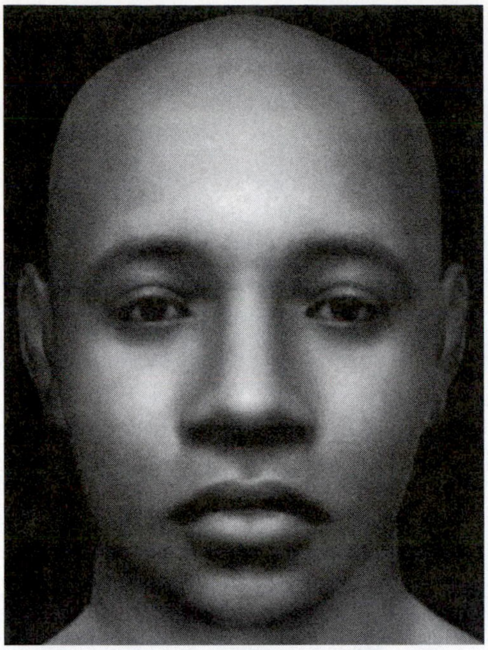

Figure 13.1 Once Robin Richards has completed his work, it's up to special-effects artists to breathe life into the pharaoh, adding eye color, eyebrows, and skin tone to the face. This digital image of Tutankhamun was the world's first facial reconstruction of the Boy King and was created for the BAFTA-nominated film "Who Killed Tutankhamun?" made by Atlantic Productions. (Copyright Atlantic Productions Ltd.)

on bone studies.) Think of it as ancient forensics; indeed **forensic archaeology** has become a useful tool for modern-day detectives, some of whom have been trained by archaeologists, dealing with human remains. Archaeologists have been called in to excavate mass graves in Kosovo and in Iraq, where their expertise with cemeteries is extremely useful. Teams of excavators have also investigated MIA crash sites in Vietnam and even investigated an Alabama cemetery where graves had been illegally disturbed for new burials since 1858. As an offshoot of such work, Richard Gould of Brown University has formed disaster response teams, who work to recover human remains and other evidence from such sites as the World Trade Center and a Providence, Rhode Island, nightclub destroyed by a catastrophic fire.

Facial reconstructions have proved a popular, if controversial, part of bioarchaeology. By using modern medical techniques used in facial and plastic surgery, it's possible to establish, at least approximately, what the pharaoh Tutankhamun looked like (see Figure 13.1), or the appearance of a savagely injured medieval soldier. However, facial reconstructions are only a small part of the bioarchaeological story.

Sex and Age

Bones provide telltale information on the cause of death, nutrition, diseases and chronic medical conditions including parasites, and diet, also nutrition (see Figure 13.2 on page 260). While individual skeletons can yield valuable information, a sample population from a cemetery is the biological anthropologist's dream, for then one can study overall health, life expectancy, infant mortality, and even differences in diet within a contemporary population. For example, Nikola Koepke and Joerg Baten studied 2938 female and 6539 male skeletons from Europe dating to the past 2,000 years. They found that females tended to vary more than males, but stature varied with population density and social inequality, also climate and gender inequality. On the other side of the world, Maya commoners were shorter than nobles, almost certainly a result of dietary differences.

Malnutrition, Stress, and Work-Related Injuries

The Ice Man suffered through several periods of malnutrition during his lifetime, identified both on his body as telltale **Harris Lines** found at the end of limb bones. Chumash Indian dead from southern California display not only Harris Lines, but other medical conditions, among them series of irregular lines on their tooth enamel, a sign of childhood malnutrition. Some skeletons also have the characteristic pitting and thickening of the eye sockets, a condition known as cribra orbitalia resulting from anemia and parasitic infections.

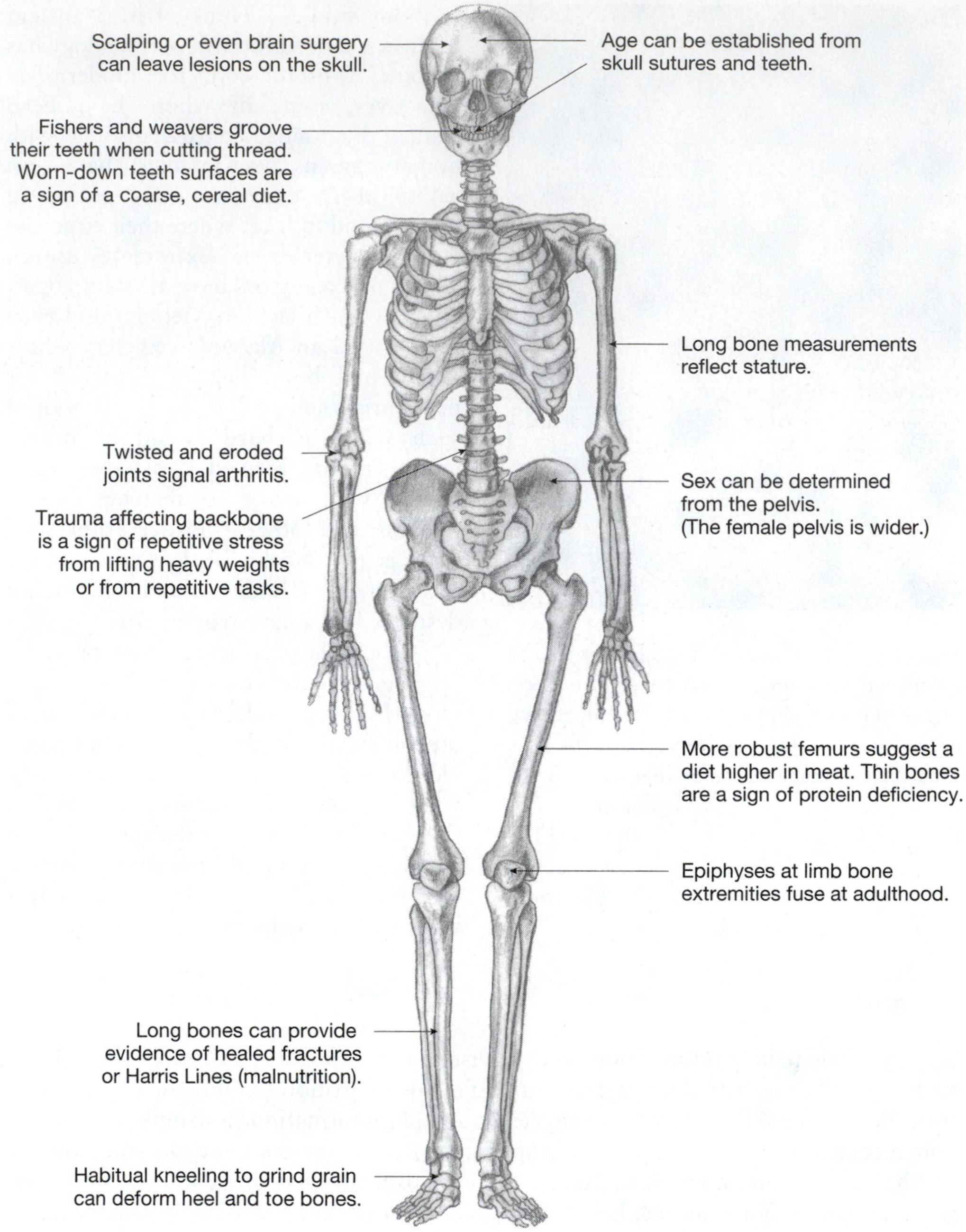

Figure 13.2 Some categories of information that can be gleaned from human remains.

Quite apart from medical pathologies, there are occupational injuries, too, many of them resulting from repetitive tasks. Medieval fishers in Europe display spine deformations that result from years of hefting heavy nets. Many of the 87 adults from the early farming village at Abu Hureyra, Syria, displayed enlarged neck vertebrae resulting from carrying heavy loads on their heads, as many subsistence farmers do to this day. As we will see below, many of the young and adult Abu Hureyra women had collapsed vertebrae and arthritic big toes resulting from years of grinding grain on their knees. The repetitive back-and-fro movement played havoc with their spines. King Henry VIII's flagship *Mary Rose*, which sank off Portsmouth, England in 1545, carried 415 people. Over half of them were archers, armed with heavy yew wood long bows, each with a massive draw weight of 150 lbs (68 kg). Firing long bows was an arduous task, requiring the archer to push the bow away from his body to release the arrow, usually with his left shoulder. Almost 20 percent of the individuals among the *Mary Rose* skeletons display a characteristic deformity of the left shoulder resulting from the strain of manipulating heavy bows, a condition known as "Little League Elbow," first identified among youthful baseball players in Southern California.

Violence

Paleopathology, the study of medical conditions and injuries on people of the past, does not often reveal specific causes of the death, except in the cases of fatal wounds inflicted by weapons of all kinds. Violence abounds in archaeological sites, right back to Stone Age times. Some wounds result from hunting injuries, commonplace, for example, among Neanderthal males of 50,000 years ago, whose simple spears required them to close with even large animals at close quarters. Egyptian hunter-gatherers of 12,000 years ago include numerous arrow injuries, perhaps resulting from conflict over precious food resources in an ever-more crowded world. Chumash Indian cemeteries of A.D. 1100 have yielded casualties buried with arrowheads in their corpses.

Few paleopathological studies rival the savagery revealed by the bones of the dead from the Battle of Towton in northern England, fought in A.D. 1461, one of the few mass graves from a major battle ever discovered. The engagement lasted 10 hours and is said to have been the bloodiest conflict ever fought on English soil, a hand-to-hand battle with no quarter given on either side. As many as 28,000 soldiers perished; local rivers ran red with blood; corpses were scattered over a swathe of countryside 6 miles (9.6 km) long. A 1996 excavation yielded a sample of the casualties—males between sixteen and fifty years old. Most of the skeletons from the grave had perished from savage blows or cuts to the head (see Figure 13.3). One skull displayed at least eight blade wounds resulting from close combat, death coming from a lethal blow to the back of the head. Other crania displayed traumatic injuries made by cross-bow bolts, arrowheads, and war hammers. Most limb wounds were confined to the forearms, received when parrying blows from assailants. The Towton skeletons provide a frightening portrait of the fear, vengeance, hatred and bloodlust of medieval warfare.

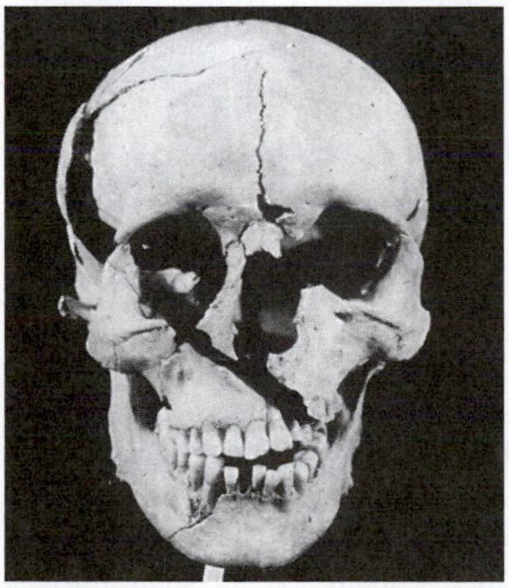

Figure 13.3 The brutality of medieval warfare. A Towton soldier's skull with a fatal sword gash.

Cannibalism, the consumption of human flesh, horrifies us, but has been part of human societies since Neanderthal times, perhaps even earlier. It's very difficult to study it dispassionately, or to document more than butchery of human remains. Biological anthropologist Tim White, an authority on early hominins, applied the same research methods to a human bone deposit from Mancos Pueblo in the American Southwest. He found that the human remains had been split, cut up, and the marrow extracted exactly as it had been from animal bones in the same garbage heap. Despite White' meticulous analysis, we do not know if actual consumption of human flesh took place. If it did, was it for symbolic, ritual purposes, or was it an attempt to supplement a diet of maize, beans, and game meat during a period of persistent

Discovery

The Ice Man of the Alps, c. 2400 B.C.

In September 1991, German mountaineers Helmut and Erika Simon made their way around a narrow gully at 10,530 feet (3,210 meters) near Hauslabjoch in the Italian Alps. Erika suddenly spotted a brown object projecting from the ice and glacial meltwater in the bottom of the gully. At first she thought it was merely a doll, but she soon identified the skull, back, and shoulders of a man with his face lying in water. She had stumbled across the casualty of a 5,000-year-old mountain accident.

The first police on the scene also assumed the man was a climbing victim. A unique archaeological find became corpse number 91/619 on the local coroner's dissection table. Within days, the authorities realized the body was very old and called in archaeologist Konrad Spindler of the University of Innsbruck, Austria. Local archaeologists organized a dig at the site, which was already under 2 feet (0.6 meters) of snow. They used a steam blower and a hair dryer to recover parts of a grass cloak, leaves, tufts of grass, and wood fragments. By the end of the excavation, they had established that the man, now nicknamed "Ötzi the Ice Man," had deposited his ax, bow, and backpack on a sheltered ledge. He had been in a fight some time before.

The Innsbruck University research team used the latest archaeological and medical science to conserve and study the forty-seven-year-old man. Within a few weeks, five AMS radiocarbon tests dated Ötzi's body to between 3350 and 3150 B.C. Biological anthropologists estimated his height as about 5 feet 2 inches (1.6 meters) and took DNA samples that showed his genetic makeup to be similar to that of today's Europeans. Ötzi's last meal consisted of meat, some herbs, and unleavened bread, probably consumed in the spring. He suffered from parasites. Smoke inhaled while living in small dwellings with open hearths had blackened his lungs as badly as those of a modern-day smoker. Ötzi had endured prolonged malnutrition in his ninth, fifteenth, and sixteenth years. His hands and fingernails were scarred from constant manual labor. He had groups of tattoos—mostly parallel vertical lines—on his lower back, left calf, and right ankle.

On his last day alive, Ötzi wore a leather belt that held up a loincloth. Suspenders led from the belt to a pair of fur leggings. He wore an outer coat of alternating stripes of black and brown animal skin, and an outer cape of twisted grass just like those that were still being worn in the Alps a century ago. Ötzi's bearskin cap fastened below his chin with a snap. On his feet he wore bearskin and deerskin shoes filled with grass held in place by a string "sock" (see Figure 13.4).

Ötzi was a self-sufficient man on the move. He carried a leather backpack on a wooden frame, a flint dagger, a copper-bladed ax with a wooden handle, and a yew longbow and skin quiver filled with 14 arrows. His equipment included dry fungus and iron pyrite for fire lighting and spare arrowheads.

Today, Ötzi lives in a special freezer that replicates glacial conditions. Scientists are still

hunger and drought? Cannibalism will always remain an enigma of the past, for the motives for consuming human flesh are always complex, and often profoundly secret.

Strontium and People's Lives

Strontium enters the food chain from eroded rocks and provides geological signatures, which are preserved in tooth enamel of both animals and humans. Once the signatures are known, then it is possible to identify the place of birth of the tooth's owner, which may or may not be the same location as where the person died.

Strontium has the potential to write people's life stories, but there is a long way to go before there is a sufficient archive of strontium signatures to allow anything more than provisional insights into ancient lives. The Ban Chiang cemetery in northeast Thailand contains ten phases of human burials grouped in three periods between 2100 B.C. and A.D. 200. But did these people live their lives in one place? A sample of burials provided strontium, carbon, and oxygen isotopes from second and third

Figure 13.4 A reconstruction of Ötzi the Ice Man wearing a grass cloak and carrying his weapons.

puzzling over why he was so high in the mountains. A few wheat seeds lodged in his fur garments tell us he had recently been in a farming village. Some wild seeds come from a valley south of the Alps, as if he had climbed from the Italian side. Was he a shepherd caught out at high altitude? Had he fled to the mountains to escape a family feud, or was he simply hunting wild goats? Recently, computerized tomography revealed a flint arrowhead lodged in his thorax, which had been fired from his left side, smashed his shoulder blade and lodged close to his left lung. Ötzi had also parried a dagger attack with his hands. He probably survived no longer than a few hours after that. Why he was wounded by an arrow remains, of course, a complete mystery.

Fleeing from his enemies and badly weakened, he lay down on his left side, his head on a boulder, perhaps taking shelter from rapidly deteriorating weather in the small gully. Judging from his relaxed limbs, he passed out and froze to death a few hours later. For 5,000 years, Ötzi's body lay in the gully, which protected his corpse as a glacier flowed overhead.

Ötzi the Ice Man is the earliest European to have survived as an identifiable individual, one of the few people of the past to come down to us so well preserved that we know almost more about him than he knew himself—his injuries, his diseases, his parasites. This remarkable discovery comes as something of a jolt, because in Ötzi we come face to face with a once-living person, who laughed and cried, worked and played, loved and hated, and interacted with others.

molars. At Ban Chiang, there were striking differences between the men and women. The males displayed considerable variation, while the women tended to remain constant. The researchers believe that this pattern reflects a society that was matrilocal, where the women stayed in one place, while the men were often absent on hunting expeditions or married into sedentary settlements inherited through the female line. Apart from group dynamics, strontium research offers fascinating insights into individual life histories.

Individuals

The Ice Man is a rarity. Few individuals survive from the remote past, except as desiccated mummies like those from Egypt, Mongolia, and Peru, or as frozen or waterlogged corpses, such as those of Tollund Man (see Figure 9.6 on page 188) or refrigerated arctic families preserved in permafrost. We know, for example, from his mummy that the

Egyptian pharaoh Rameses II was 5 feet 8 inches tall (1.7 m) and that he suffered from arthritis, dental abscesses, and poor circulation (see Figure 13.5). Thanks to bioarchaeology and modern medical science, we now possess remarkably accurate portraits of some ancient lives.

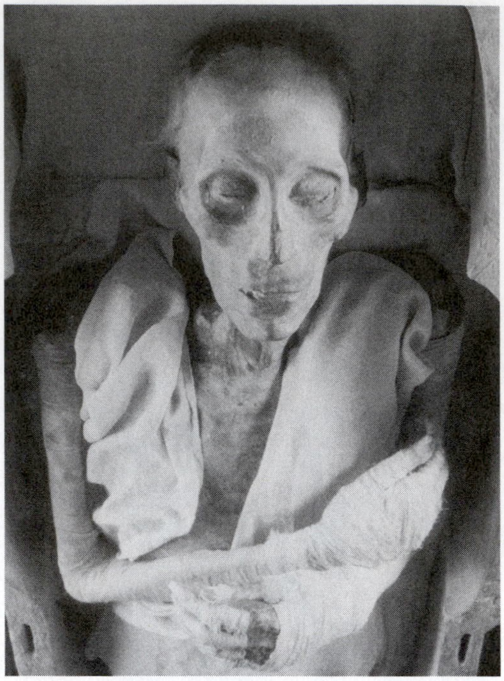

Figure 13.5 The mummy of Egyptian pharaoh Rameses II (1279–1212 B.C.).

A classic example of a life story is the so-called Amesbury archer, who was buried in about 2470 B.C., 3 miles (4.8 km) from Stonehenge in southern England (see the chapter-opener photo on page 257). The strongly built 35- to 45-year-old man wore a cloak fastened with a bone pin. He lay on his left side with his legs bent and his head facing north. He had suffered from an abscess in his jaw and had had a serious accident a few years before his death that ripped off his left kneecap. As a result, he walked with a straight foot, which swung out to his left. He also suffered from a bone infection that caused him constant pain. All the organic materials like bow staves and clothing had long vanished, but we can make intelligent guesses as to his clothing and possessions on the basis of what survives.

Another grave lay close by, dug at the same time as the archer's, containing the skeleton of a man between 25 and 30 years old. The two men displayed the same unusual bone structure in the foot—a heel bone with a joint with one of the upper tarsal bones in the foot itself. This strongly suggests that they were relatives.

Oxygen isotope analysis of the archer's teeth provided a startling clue as to his homeland. The oxygen isotope ratio of the water you drink depends on the source of the water, the distance from the coast, and the altitude, latitude, and local temperature of the rainfall. Drinking water in warmer climates has more heavy isotopes than that from colder environments. Thus, the scientist can compare the isotope ratios of ancient teeth with those from modern drinking water samples and find out where the people lived. The oxygen isotope record of the Amesbury archer's teeth showed that he had spent his youth in a colder climate than southern Britain—in the Swiss Alps. In contrast, the younger man in the second grave had a lighter oxygen isotope ratio in his wisdom teeth, as if he had spent his late teens in central England or northeast Scotland. The Amesbury archer is proof that people traveled long distances at this early time, far more than was hitherto suspected.

Groups

The relationships between individuals, their own households, communities, and society at large express themselves in all manner of tangible and intangible ways. There are relationships between people and communities that are expressed by gift exchanges, as well as through kin ties and reciprocal obligation, also through trade. Then there are the issues of division of labor and of ever-changing roles of men and women from one generation to the next. Many such relationships are intangible, in the sense that they cannot be identified readily in the archaeological record, except in indirect ways.

As individuals, we all live in constant contact with other people: family members, kin, fellow community members, and people from many different groups. Our lives are ones of interaction and constant negotiation with others, hedged in by kin rules, personal relationships, and social distinctions between individuals. Archaeologists study three important phenomena that reflect such interactions: social ranking; relationships between individuals, households, communities, and the wider society; and social diversity (ethnicity).

Social Ranking

Rare and unusual artifacts, be they exotic seashells, gold necklaces, or obsidian mirrors, have been signs of rank for thousands of years, proclaiming the status of those who own or wear them. Generally speaking, the more complex the society, the more great wealth, such as hoards of buried gold ornaments or fine drinking vessels, was concentrated in a few hands. Wealth and power became synonymous: Witness the elaborate palaces and public buildings of Mycenaean rulers in Greece or the richly decorated Sumerian temples in Mesopotamia.

As was the case with great Maya ceremonial centers like Tikal and Palenque in Mesoamerica, many such structures were built as important symbolic statements of political, social, and religious power. Copán, for example, is a symbolic model of the Maya spiritual world, complete with sacred mountains, trees, and caves (see Figure 3.8 on page 62). The temple of the sun god Amun at Karnak, Egypt, was a powerful statement of divine kingship, adorned with paintings and statues of great pharaohs and of the gods. Accompanying hieroglyphs and small details of royal costume provide constant symbolic reminders of royal power and divine-given authority (see Figure 13.6).

Figure 13.6 The scribe god Thoth makes an offering at Karnak, Thebes, Egypt. Such depictions of Egyptian gods were designed to validate the divine authority of the king.

Figure 13.7 The Avenue of the Dead at Teotihuacán, Mexico

Evidence of social ranking can sometimes be inferred from buildings and community layout. Teotihuacán shows every sign of having been an elaborately planned city, with special precincts for markets and craftspeople, and the houses of the leading priests and nobles near the Avenue of the Dead, which bisected the city (see Figure 13.7). In instances like this, it is easy enough to identify the houses belonging to each class in the society, both by their architecture and by the distinctive artifacts found in them.

Human burials are the most important source of information about prehistoric social organization and ranking. For instance, the Egyptian pharaoh Khufu expended vast resources on building his pyramid and mortuary temple at Giza (see Figure 2.2 on page 26). Thousands of laborers moved more than 2.3 million limestone blocks weighing from 2.5 to 15 tons to build his pyramid during his 23-year reign. Sometimes the differing status of burials may indicate that a society was rigidly ranked. The royal burials at Ur and their accompanying cemetery of commoners are one example (see Chapter 1). Iron Age chieftains in central Europe went to their deaths surrounded by elaborate possessions (see Figure 13.8 on page 267).

Sometimes the distinctions were more subtle. At *Ban Na Di* in Thailand, Charles Higham and Rachanie Thosarat excavated a cemetery dating to between 700 and 400 B.C., where the skeletons were laid out in rows. They dug two areas, each containing human remains. The men, women, and children in each area were accompanied by the same kinds of local pots, but those in the more northwesterly part of the cemetery lay with stone, bronze, and shell bracelets, and many more shell disc beads than those elsewhere. Cattle figurines and complete forelimbs of what must have been sacrificial beasts came from five of the more richly decorated interments. Then as now, cattle must have been a symbol of wealth. One 5-year-old child lay under a crocodile skin shroud—only the bony plates for the body survived over the body. A nearby woman wore a large bone pendant fashioned from a crocodile skull. Higham and Thosarat speculate that the people in the richer part of the cemetery were associated with a crocodile totem group. They believe that one segment of Ban Na Di society had greater access to exotic goods, perhaps as a result of enjoying higher social status in the community. The distinctions in

Figure 13.8 A bronze couch on which the body of a 40-year-old chieftain lay, from the richly adorned Iron Age burial at *Hochdorf,* Germany, dating to about 550 B.C. Made of six riveted metal sheets, the bed is supported by bronze human figurines mounted on wheels. The chieftain wore gold shoes, a gold neck ring, and gold bracelets, as well as brooches of the same material—in all, 1 pound (half a kilogram) of gold—wealth acquired from control of trade with the Mediterranean world to the south. He lay in an oak burial chamber under a large earthen mound.

wealth are not great, but sufficient to hint at a higher status, perhaps membership in the senior line of descent from founding ancestors.

Ethnicity and Social Inequality

Archaeology offers unique perspectives on ethnic diversity, what is sometimes called "the archaeology of inequality": the ways in which people have exercised economic and social power over others.

Elites have used many tactics to exercise power over others—everything from gentle persuasion to divine kingship, precedent, economic monopolies, and naked force. Perhaps most important of all are the ideologies of domination. The ancient Maya lords built great ceremonial centers with towering pyramids and vast plazas that were symbolic models of the Maya universe. It was here that the ruler went into a shamanistic trance, communicating with the gods and ancestors in lavish public ceremonies. Everything validated the complex relationship between the living and the dead, between ruler and commoner, displayed in lavish, pointed metaphors that confirmed the divine power of the supreme lords.

Political and social power are extremely heterogeneous phenomena that are exercised in many forms. From the archaeologist's point of view, what is fascinating is using material objects like pottery to study how people negotiated their social positions and resisted the submergence of their own culture. Artifacts offer a unique way of examining the history of the many communities that kept no written records but expressed their diverse feelings and cultures through the specific artifacts and commodities they purchased and used.

The classic studies of such resistance are from the southern United States, where the earliest Africans to reach North America brought their own notions of religion, ritual, and supernatural power to their new homes. "The guinea negroes had sometimes a small inclosure for their god house," wrote one Florida plantation owner in 1839. Historical records rarely refer to such shrines, but archaeologists have found blue beads and other charms at many slave sites in the North American Southeast. Black African slaves arrived in North America with cultural values and a worldview radically different from that of their masters. Slave plantations were part of much wider and very complex networks that linked planters to other planters, planters to slaves, and slaves to slaves on other plantations. Despite oppressive conditions, African Americans maintained their own beliefs and culture, which they melded over the generations with new ideas and material innovations from their new environment. They believed that their culture, their way of living, everything from cuisine to belief systems, was the best way.

African spiritual beliefs in all their variety were highly flexible and were often responses to outside influences, whether political, religious, or economic. Thus, existing spiritual beliefs adapted readily to the new American environment, adopting new artifacts or modifying existing ones over the generations. For example, archaeologists working at Thomas Jefferson's Monticello estate in Virginia have recovered crystals, pierced coins, and other ritual artifacts from Mulberry Row, where his slaves resided.

Traditional practitioners were operating in a hostile environment, so they were careful to disguise their activities. At the Levi Jordan cotton and sugar plantation in south Texas, archaeologists Kenneth Brown and Doreen Cooper excavated a cabin occupied by an African-American healer magician. The cabin yielded animal bones, iron spikes, and other artifacts that were part of the paraphernalia of a traditional West African healer. To the African-American workers on the plantation, these objects had a symbolic meaning that was not revealed to outsiders. It was for this reason that none of the healer's tools of trade bore any telltale symbolic decoration that might reveal their true purpose. And at the eighteenth-century New Salem plantation in New England, Gerald Sawyer has found clusters of African-American burials surrounding a Christian cemetery, complete with engraved headstones and quartz fragments placed next to them, a known African-American ritual practice.

African Americans were disfranchised from white people in their own villages and slave quarters to the point that their masters and mistresses may well have been more like parts of their environment than key players in their social lives. In South Carolina and Georgia, slaves even spoke a distinctive African-American language. Children growing up in this culture used material objects like earthen bowls that were made by members of this culture and heard stories of magic and religious chants that were important ways of establishing African-American identity, of maintaining ideological power and molding values. Although many slaves may not have resisted their inferior, white-bestowed social status on a day-to-day basis, they ignored European-American culture in favor of their own and rejected an ideology that rationalized their enslavement.

Leland Ferguson has documented this resistance in South Carolina, where, in 1740, blacks outnumbered whites by almost two to one, and one-half of that majority was African born. Here, as elsewhere along the South Atlantic coast, African women arrived with a knowledge of pot making that they used to fashion domestic wares in their new homes. Their distinctive unglazed earthenware products occur in slave quarters, on plantations, and in cities (see Figure 13.9 on page 269). Once considered Native American pots that had been traded to slaves, these "Colono wares" were the product of complex demographic and cultural forces that resulted from interactions between blacks and whites, and between both of them and Native Americans. Ferguson found that what he calls the "container environment" of South Carolina consisted of wood, basketry, and earthenware manufactures broadly similar to those of the slaves' African homeland. Ferguson believes that African-American eating habits were much the same as those of West Africa and radically different from those of the European Americans around them. Colono ware is remarkably similar over a large area, made by people living in an ethnic environment where reciprocal relationships with one another were of vital importance, and where there were strong ties to ancestral African culture. It was, says Ferguson, an unconscious resistance to slavery and the plantation system. The

Figure 13.9 Colono ware vessel.

development of southern culture, he concludes, was a long process of quasi-political negotiation. It is exciting that we can use archaeology to look at the early stages of this complex process of negotiation from both sides.

Another fascinating chronicle of ethnic resistance comes from an archaeological investigation of the route taken by a small group of northern Cheyenne when they broke out of Fort Robinson, Nebraska, on January 9, 1879. They fought a running battle with the garrison, across the White River, up some bluffs, and into open country, where it took the military 11 days to capture them. This much is beyond controversy, but the route that the Cheyenne took out of the river valley is disputed. According to military accounts, the escaping party moved up an exposed sandstone ridge to reach the bluffs. This exposed route was illogical, indeed foolhardy, for there was a full moon. Cheyenne oral traditions insist on another route to the bluffs through a well-protected drainage that offered excellent cover from pursuing riflemen. Archaeologists from the University of South Dakota Archaeology Laboratory investigated the escape routes with the collaboration of local Cheyenne representatives. They used random shovel testing and metal detectors to search for spent bullets in three areas—two drainages and the exposed ridge mentioned in military accounts. The survey recovered no bullets from the exposed ridge, but did find them in the drainages, thereby confirming the oral account of the Cheyenne Outbreak.

This may seem like a footnote to modern history, but it is important to remember that the Outbreak has become a classic story of the American West in white eyes, immortalized by John Ford's movie *Cheyenne Autumn*. This film tells the story from the victors' perspective, and it is a form of moral tale of the Old West. Now oral tradition and archaeology have shattered part of the myth, telling the story from the Indian perspective in circumstances where science has helped fashion a mosaic of the recent past that is the historical truth rather than a myth.

The most compelling studies of ethnic minorities and their resistance to social domination come, at present, from the United States, from historical sites where written records amplify the archaeological record in important ways. As so often happens, methodology developed on historical sites will ultimately be applied to prehistoric situations. What, for example, was the lifeway of slaves and workers in ancient Egypt? We know from excavations in workers' quarters at the pyramids of Giza that many laborers lived harsh lives, suffered from malnutrition, and had very short life expectancies. Such excavations raise many questions about the relationships between the rulers and the ruled. Archaeology, with its rich potential for studying the mundane and the trivial, the minutest details of daily life, is an unrivaled tool for the dispassionate study of social inequality and ethnicity.

Gender

For more than two-and-a-half million years, men and women have interacted, negotiated with one another, and shared the responsibilities of life and survival. Yet archaeologists have paid little attention to the study of gender and changing interactions between the sexes in the past. In part, this is because of a lack of interest in the subject, but also because the archaeological record has been seen as anonymous, and archaeologists have been more concerned with explaining general processes of culture change than with the archaeology of individual people. Only recently have archaeologists turned their attention to the complex issue of gender and gender relations, a promising avenue of new research.

Gender is not the same as sex, which refers to the biological male or female. Gender is socially and culturally constructed. Gender roles and relations acquire meaning in culturally and historically meaningful ways; therefore, gender is a vital part of human social relations and a central issue in the study of ancient human societies.

The expression of gender varies and has always varied, from society to society and through time. Some archaeologists, like Margaret Conkey and Joan Gero, write of "engendering archaeology," an attempt to reclaim men and women in nonsexist ways in the past. This goes much further than merely demonstrating that pots were made by women and stone projectile points by men, or trying to identify women's activities in the archaeological record. The archaeology of gender deals with the ideology of gender, with roles and gender relations—the ways in which gender intersects with all aspects of human social life. How are roles and social relationships constructed? What contributions did men and women make to ancient societies? An engendered archaeology uses a wide diversity of archaeological methods and approaches to find out how gender "works" in ancient societies, to unravel its cultural meanings.

The most promising approaches use science to study male/female roles. The Abu Hureyra farming village in Syria is one of the earliest known agricultural settlements in the world (see Figure 12.4 on page 241). In about 10,000 B.C., the inhabitants switched from hunting and foraging to growing cereal crops. For hours on end, the Abu Hureyra women would labor on their knees, grinding grain for the evening meal, as the monotonous scraping sound echoed through the settlement. Biological anthropologist Theya Molleson studied the many skeletons found under the Abu Hureyra houses and soon found out that the people were remarkably healthy, except for bone deformities caused by arduous and repetitive tasks. Then she noticed that some adolescents had enlarged portions on their neck vertebrae, the result of carrying heavy loads. She also identified many knee bones with bone extensions on their articular surfaces, the result of repeated kneeling for long periods of time. Many female skeletons also had stressed low back vertebrae, enlarged toe joints, and gross arthritic conditions of the big toe.

Molleson was puzzled by these deformities, until one of her colleagues visited Egypt and noticed that kneeling supplicants on the walls of ancient temples always had their toes curled forward. The only activity at Abu Hureyra that could produce the same effect was kneeling in front of the stone grinding querns found set into the house floors. Intrigued, Molleson now reconstructed the grinding process. The grinder put grain on the quern and gripped the grinding stone with both hands. He or she then knelt with the toes bent, pushing the stone forward, arms turning inward as the stone reached the end of the quern. At the end of the stroke, the upper body was almost parallel to the floor. Repeated every day, such a back-and-forth movement would cause backbone damage identical to those on the skeletons, also placing bending stress on the knee and hip joints, and eventually causing arthritic conditions in the toes—conditions found in the Abu Hureyra bones. Molleson is virtually certain that women and girls suffered repetitive-stress injuries because they shouldered the laborious task of preparing food.

The Engendered Past

To engender the past means to focus not only on major material achievements like metallurgy or pot making, or on ancient environments, but also on interpersonal relations and the social dynamics of everyday activity. These are the activities that take up most of people's daily lives—hunting, gardening, preparing meals, building houses, and so on. But gender also impacts on trade, craft specialization, state formation, religion, and ritual—to mention only a few major human activities.

Gender research in archaeology is concerned not just with women, but with people as individuals and their contributions to society. Archaeologist Elizabeth Brumfiel has studied Aztec women, who were expert weavers. Indeed, weaving was a fundamental skill for an Aztec noblewoman (see Figure 13.10). However, she points out that to characterize them merely as weavers ignores the vital links between weaving, child rearing, and cooking (to mention only a few women's tasks) and the wider society in which the women lived. For instance, the population of the Valley of Mexico increased tenfold during the four centuries before the conquest, a striking testimony to the success of the Aztec household economy. Women wove textiles and the capes that were the badges of social status in Aztec society. Their woven products were vital to the enormous tribute system on which Aztec civilization depended. Cotton mantles even served as a form of currency. Cloth was a primary way of organizing the ebb and flow of goods and services that sustained the state.

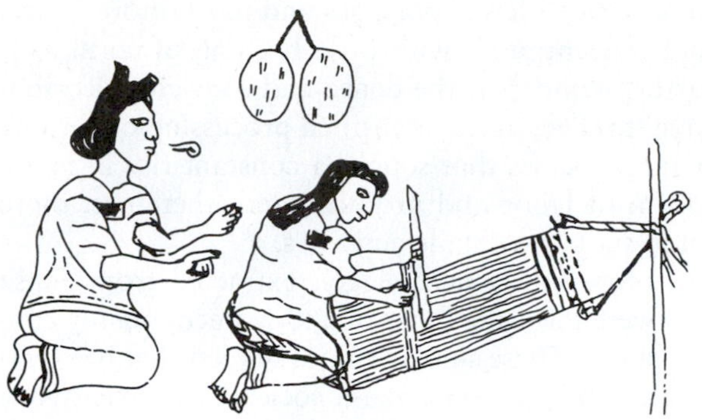

Figure 13.10 An Aztec woman teaches her daughter how to weave. From the *Codex Mendoza,* one of the few surviving Aztec codices.

Brumfiel shows that the Aztec household and the roles of women were much more varied than those attributed to them by early Spanish observers. Furthermore, the skills of cooking and weaving were important political tools, ways of maintaining social and political control. Thus, she argues, the idealization of these skills in both Aztec folklore and schooling developed because women were makers of both valuable goods and of people. It was they who assured the continuity of Aztec kin groups. More simplistic views of Aztec life mask the dynamic and highly adaptive role that women played in this remarkable civilization.

Gender studies are often based on extrapolations from ethnoarchaeological and ethnological data. The Sausa are maize and potato farmers who live in highland Peru's northern Mantaro Valley. Before the Inka took control in about A.D. 1460, the Sausa lived in local population groups of several thousand people. Their conquerors, anxious to increase maize production, dispersed them into small village settlements. Archaeologist Christine Hastorf was interested in the changing social dynamics resulting from the Inka conquest. How did women's social position change as a result of the new conditions? She approached this question by using two different avenues—the distribution of food remains in excavated settlements compared with those in modern house compounds, and dietary evidence obtained by stable isotope analyses of male and female skeletons from ancient Sausa villages.

In Andean households, women are responsible for food preparation and storage. Hastorf studied the relationship between the distribution of plant remains in dwellings and compounds, and the behavior of men and women in that household. For example, in households with male heads, she found the most diverse plant forms in kitchen areas, and fewer crop seeds elsewhere in the compound where other activities took place. In contrast, a household with a female head had concentrations of crop seeds not only in the kitchen area but on the patio, as if there were different constraints acting on the preparation and consumption of food.

Next, Hastorf plotted the distribution of crop seeds in pre-Hispanic compounds. The pre-Inka structures date from a time when maize was less common and of great sacred value. The inhabitants of every dwelling used and consumed a wide range of plant foods, including maize, potatoes, and many legumes. Maize occurred mostly in patio areas. It was here, argues Hastorf, that communal activities such as beer making took place, beer being a commodity that was a vital part of ritual, social, and political meetings. A later Inka-period compound yielded fewer potatoes and much more maize. Here the processing of corn was more concentrated, with little burning of corn, as if more of it was consumed as beer. Hastorf wonders if the dense and restricted distribution of maize in the later compound might reflect more intensified processing of corn by women. They were now living under Inka policies that sought a constant rise in maize production, regular taxation in the form of labor and produce, and, therefore, more restricted, intensified roles for women in support of male activities.

Hastorf also studied the stable isotopes in bone collagen extracted from Sausa skeletons. She found that pre-Inka diets were the same for men and women, mainly consisting of quinoa and tubers, with some maize. These similar values suggest that beer was shared between men and women. Then the Inka entered Sausa society. The twenty-one skeletons (twelve males, nine females) from these centuries reveal a higher consumption of maize, but half of the male diets were much richer in maize than those of the women. Hastorf believes this reflects changed social conditions under Inka rule. The women were processing much more maize into beer, which was consumed not by everyone but by a relatively small proportion of the males in the community. The dietary differences reflect a changed political climate in which the Sausa, once small groups, were now incorporated into a larger political sphere, which depended on men becoming involved in far more gatherings, rituals, and obligatory tasks, when beer was consumed. The women worked harder, but their position outside the home was more restricted under the Inka regime.

As the Hastorf example shows, gender research will be a marriage between modern high-tech science and good old-fashioned archaeological observation. This will give us the potential to go far beyond the material, to probe the subjective and the gender driven, even, as Hastorf demonstrates, the ways in which men and women adapt to changing circumstances. This kind of meticulous research with its concerns for the changing dynamics of ancient society offers great promise for the future.

Wider Society: Prestate and State Societies

Human society has changed dramatically since the first appearance of modern humans in Africa more than 100,000 years ago. Much effort has gone into deciphering the complexities of ancient social organization, the most successful approaches being those that use broad evolutionary frameworks. These provide a general outline for tracing human social organization from the first simple family structures of the earliest humans to the highly complex state-organized societies of the early civilizations.

All theories of human prehistory are based on the premise that human societies have changed over long periods of time and that the general trend throughout prehistory has been toward a greater complexity of human culture and social institutions. This does not mean, of course, that all human societies have evolved in a linear, ladder-like way, as Victorian anthropologists once believed. Cultural change has proceeded, and still proceeds, in many directions. If there is a general trend over time, it is toward increasing social and political complexity.

Furthermore, this trend toward greater complexity has manifested itself in remarkably similar ways in terms of political and social organization. Many archaeologists take this broad similarity into account by grouping early human societies into two broad, arbitrary categories: prestate societies and state-organized societies.

Prestate societies are small-scale societies based on the community, band, or village. They vary greatly in their degree of political integration and can be divided into three groupings, which are, however, only gross generalizations.

Bands are autonomous and self-sufficient groups that usually consist of only a few families. They are egalitarian, with leadership coming from experience and the personal qualities of particular individuals rather than from inherited or acquired political power.

Tribes are egalitarian-like bands, but with more social and cultural organizations. They have developed kin-based social mechanisms to accommodate their more sedentary lifestyle, to redistribute food, and to organize some communal services. Some more complex hunter-gatherer societies—for example, the North American Pacific Northwest Coast groups—can be classified as tribes, although most were associated with village farming.

Chiefdoms are societies headed by individuals with unusual ritual, political, or entrepreneurial skills and are often hard to distinguish from tribes. Society is still kin based, but more hierarchical, with power concentrated in the hands of powerful kin leaders responsible for the redistribution of resources. Chiefdoms tend to have higher population densities and to display signs of social ranking, reflected in more elaborate material possessions for leading individuals. Chiefdoms vary greatly in their elaborateness, but reached a high level of sophistication in Hawaii, Tahiti, and among the Mississippian people of the U.S. Midwest and South after A.D. 1000.

Many researchers now question the general utility of the band-tribe-chiefdom classification, on the grounds that it is too rigid and of limited application. At a general level, prestate societies are remarkable for their small-scale social and political organization, although the degree of complexity can vary dramatically, from a few families to an elaborate chiefdom extending over an entire Pacific island.

State-organized societies (civilizations) operate on a large scale, with centralized social and political organizations, class stratification, and intensive agriculture. They have complex political structures, many permanent government institutions, and are based on notions of social inequality, the assumption that privilege will reside in the hands of a few individuals. State-organized societies are synonymous with the early urban civilizations—those of the Sumerians, ancient Egyptians, Maya, and others—that were governed by supreme rulers with absolute powers. These preindustrial civilizations, founded on social inequality and maintained by the labor of thousands, were the precursors of the industrial civilizations of later history.

The absolute power of Egyptian pharaohs or Maya lords came from their perceived supernatural powers, which were embedded in compelling, often recited ideologies. Pyramids, plazas, and temples provided the settings for lavish public ceremonies, where the ruler would appear before his subjects as drums played, chants were sung, and incense rose into the sky. Sacred places were the settings where civilization was validated. They provide one way for archaeologists to decipher the religious beliefs of our forebears.

Interaction: Trade and Exchange

Human interactions involving trade and exchange are among the most complex and durable of all relationships. Few human societies have been self-sufficient. Hunter-gatherers like American Paleo-Indians and Late Ice Age Europeans exchanged tool making stone and sea shells over long distances. Once food production replaced hunting and gathering, human needs were more complex. People needed access to a much wider range of raw materials and finished artifacts, which they obtained by trading with neighbors. For this reason, trade has been defined as the "mutually appropriative movement of goods between hands." To which one can also add ideas passed over long distances. Trade always involves two elements: the goods and commodities being exchanged and the people doing the exchanging. Any form of trading activity involves some form of social system that provides the people-to-people relationships within which the trade flourishes.

Trade appears in the archaeological record in the form of exotic objects discovered in sites far from their point of origin. For instance, the Indians of the Lake Superior region obtained copper from natural outcrops near the lake. They traded the precious metal over thousands of miles, as far away as Ohio. In California, Mesoamerica, and southwestern Asia, one well-known trade commodity was obsidian—fine volcanic glass widely prized for making knives, ornaments, and mirrors (see Figure 13.11).

Types of Trade

Gift giving is a common medium of exchange and trade in societies that are relatively self-supporting. The exchange of gifts is designed primarily to reinforce a social relationship, both with an individual and of a group as a whole. The gifts serve as gestures that place obligations on both parties. This form of trade is common in New Guinea and the Pacific

Figure 13.11 Obsidian mirror from Mesoamerica. (Neg. #312721. Courtesy of Dept. of Library Services, American Museum of Natural History.)

and was widespread in Africa during the past 2,000 years, and in the ancient Americas as well. A famous example is the *kula* ring of Melanesia in the southwestern Pacific. An elaborate network of gift exchanges passes shell necklaces in one direction, arm shells in the other. They are passed as ceremonial gifts from one individual to another, in gift partnerships that endure for decades. These gift exchanges enjoy great prestige, yet serve as a framework for the regular exchange of foodstuffs and other more day-to-day commodities. This sporadic interaction between individuals and communities reduced people's self-sufficiency and eventually made them part of a larger society in which people depended on one another not only for basic commodities but also for social purposes.

Reciprocity, the mutual exchange of goods between two individuals or groups, is at the heart of much gift giving and barter trade. It can happen year after year at the same place, which can be as humble as someone's house. Such "central places" become the focus of gift giving and trade. When a village becomes involved in both the production of trade goods and their exchange with other communities, it probably will become an even more important center, a place to which people will travel to trade.

Redistribution of trade goods from a central place throughout a culture requires some form of organization to ensure that the redistribution is equitable. A redistributive mechanism may be controlled by a chief, a religious leader, or some form of management organization. The chief, whose position is perhaps reinforced by religious power, has a serious responsibility to his community that can extend over several villages. His lines of redistribution stretch out through people of lesser rank to the individual villager. A chief will negotiate exchanges with other chiefs, then redistribute the exotic materials and objects he or she obtains to individual households.

Markets are both places and particular styles of administering and organizing trade that encourage people to set aside one place for trading and relatively stable, almost fixed prices for staple commodities. No literate civilization ever developed without strong central places, where trading activities were regulated and monopolies developed over both sources of materials and trade routes themselves. The Tenochtitlán market, described at the beginning of this chapter, is an example. Successful market trading required predictable supplies of basic commodities and adequate policing of trade routes. It is significant that most early Mesopotamian and Egyptian trade was riverine, where policing was easier. When the great overland caravan routes opened, the political and military issues—tribute, control of trade routes, and tolls—became paramount. The caravan of camels, donkeys, or other beasts, predating the great empires, was a form of organized trading that kept to carefully defined routes set up and maintained by state authorities (see Figure 13.12 on page 276). The travelers moved along these set routes, looking neither left nor right, bent only on delivering and exchanging imports and exports. Markets were also, and still are, places for gathering information from people living at a considerable distance. In West Africa, Fulani cattle herders spend much time hanging around markets, not because they are idling away time, but because they are acquiring valuable information about grazing grass and water supplies.

Studying Ancient Trade: Sourcing

Obtaining evidence of long-distance trade involves far more sophisticated inquiry than merely plotting the distribution of distinctive artifacts hundreds of miles away from their place of manufacture. Research into the sources of raw materials is sometimes called **sourcing** or **characterization** because it involves identifying the characteristic properties of the distinctive raw materials used to fashion, say, stone axes. We should stress the word *distinctive*, for the essence of these methods is that we are able to identify the specific source with great accuracy. For example, obsidian from Lipari Island off Sicily was traded over a wide area of the central Mediterranean. It is an obsidian with highly specific characteristics that show it came from Lipari and nowhere else (see Figure 13.13 on page 277).

Figure 13.12 A camel caravan. The domestication of the camel in southern Arabia in about 1000 B.C. and the development of saddles for both fighting and carrying loads on their backs revolutionized both desert travel and commerce in southwest Asia at about the time of Christ. Those who bred camels and controlled trade routes acquired great political power. The famous city of Petra in present-day Jordan was one major caravan terminus.

Sourcing methods include microscopic examination of thin sections of stone axes or potsherds that use **trace element analysis** and other methods to source raw materials and identify constituents in pottery clays or metal artifacts. Trace element analysis employs a variety of techniques such as neutron activation analysis and x-ray spectrometry. All of them produce tables of individual elements—for example, antimony, lead, tin, and so on. Matching such tables with sources is extremely difficult and requires a careful research strategy, usually involving statistics and several elements.

Some spectacular results have been obtained, especially with obsidian. For instance, we now know that obsidian from the Admiralty Islands in the Bismarck Archipelago in the southwestern Pacific was traded no less than 1,860 miles (2,976 kilometers), as far as Vanuatu in Micronesia, and 2,200 miles (3,520 kilometers) to Borneo in the west. We also know of no fewer than fifty obsidian sources in California alone, their stone exchanged over long distances. The use of source data enables us to conceive of exchange on a regional basis.

Prehistoric quarries, such as those in Greece, Mesoamerica, and Australia, are potentially valuable sources of information on the exchange of exotic materials. Archaeologist Robin Torrence studied the Aegean obsidian trade and found that the exchange was noncommercial and noncompetitive in 5000 B.C.: The prehistoric stoneworkers visited quarries and prepared material for exchange with minimal concern for economical use of the raw material. On the island of Melos, for example, the visitors simply quarried what they wanted and left. There is no evidence of specialized production.

Long-Distance Trade and the Uluburun Ship

Artifact distributions and characterization techniques have helped provide a unique portrait of prehistoric trade from a Bronze Age shipwreck at Uluburun, off southern Turkey. The heavily laden ship was sailing westward from the eastern Mediterranean

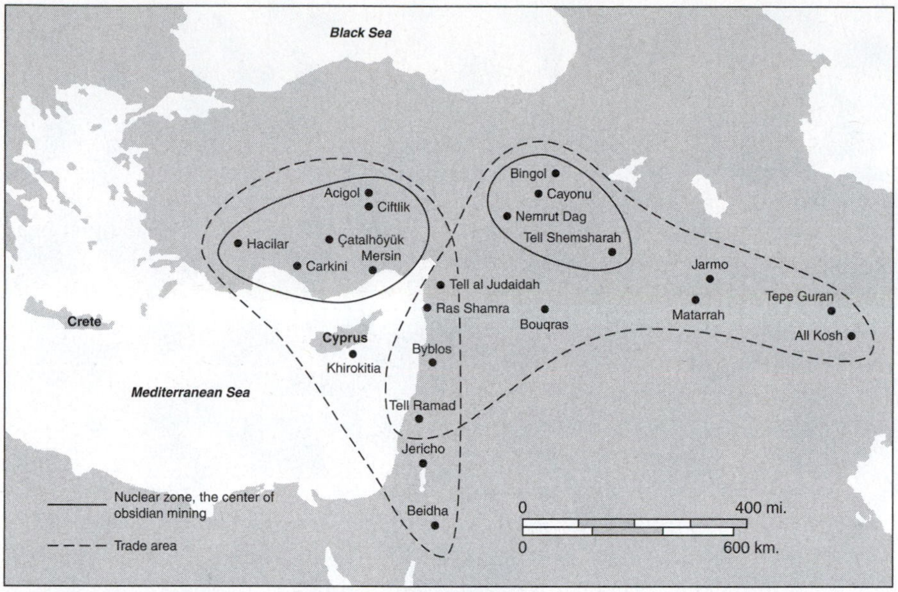

Figure 13.13 Obsidian trade in the eastern Mediterranean region. Sourcing studies reveal that early farming communities in Cyprus, Anatolia, and the Levant obtained their obsidian from two sources in central Anatolia. Meanwhile, villages like Jarmo in the Zagros Mountains and Ali Kosh far to the southeast relied on sources in Armenia. Settlements like Çatalhöyük in Anatolia were so close to obsidian sources that they probably collected their own supplies. More than 80 percent of their stone artifacts are made of the material. Obsidian tools are much rarer down the line, the further one travels from the source. In the 1960s, Colin Renfrew and others used **spectrographic analysis** to identify no fewer than 12 early farming villages that had obtained obsidian from the Ciftlik area of central Turkey. This pioneer study showed that 80 percent of the chipped stone in villages within 186 miles (298 kilometers) of Ciftlik was obsidian. Outside this "supply zone," the percentages of obsidian dropped away sharply with distance, to 5 percent in a Syrian village and 0.1 percent in the Jordan Valley. If these calculations were correct, each village was passing about half of its imported obsidian further down the line.

in 1305 B.C. when it was shattered on the jagged rocks of Uluburun, near Kas. It sank in 151 feet (46 meters) of water. Archaeologists plotted the exact position of every timber, every item of the ship's equipment and cargo, before lifting any artifacts from the seabed. They found that the ship was laden with 6 tons (5,455 kilograms) of copper ingots, probably mined in Cyprus; also with tin ingots and artifacts (see Figure 13.14 on page 278). The tin may have come from southern Turkey. Canaanite jars from Palestine or Syria held olives, glass beads, and resin from the terebinth tree, used in religious rituals. The ship's hold contained Baltic amber that probably reached the Mediterranean overland, ebony-like wood from Africa, elephant and hippopotamus ivory and ostrich eggshells from North Africa or Syria. Egyptian, Levantine, and Mycenaean daggers, swords, spearheads, and woodworking tools lay aboard, as well as sets of weights, some fashioned in animal forms. There were costly glass ingots, Mesopotamian cylinder seals, a Mycenaean seal stone, even a gold cup and parts of a tortoiseshell lute. The ship carried Egyptian scarabs, dozens of fishing weights, fishhooks, and twenty-three stone anchors, vital when anchoring in windy coves. Even the thorny burnet shrub used to pack the cargo was preserved.

Figure 13.14 Excavations on the Uluburun ship, southern Turkey.

By using find distributions from land sites and a variety of sourcing techniques, archaeologists George Bass and Cemal Pulak have reconstructed the anonymous skipper's last journey. He started his voyage on the Levant coast, sailed north up the coast, then crossed to Cyprus and coasted along the southern Turkish shore. The ship called at ports large and small on its way west along a well-traveled route that took advantage of changing seasonal winds, to Crete, some Aegean islands, and perhaps to the Greek mainland. The skipper had traversed this route many times, but on this occasion his luck ran out and he lost his ship, the cargo, and perhaps his life on Uluburun's pitiless rocks. From the archaeologist's perspective, the Uluburun shipwreck is a godsend, for it allows us to fill in many details of an elaborate trade network that linked the eastern Mediterranean with Egypt, the Aegean, and Greece more than 3,300 years ago.

The study of ancient trade is a vital source of information on social organization and the ways in which societies became more complex. Trade itself developed a great complexity, in both goods traded and the interactions of people involved. Colin Renfrew has identified no fewer than ten types of interaction between people that can result from trading, ranging from simple contact between individuals to trading by professional traders, such as the *pochteca* of the Maya and the Aztec, who sometimes acted as spies.

Interactions: Religious Beliefs

Religious beliefs also involve interactions, between people and between the living and supernatural worlds. In Chapter 12, we discussed sacred landscapes, which define the relationships between people and the cosmos, but evidence for religious beliefs goes back at least to the time of the Neanderthals some 70,000 years ago, when the evidence for human burial comes to light. Some of the earliest religious objects in the world are

Figure 13.15 Haunting ancestral figurines from 'Ain Ghazal, Jordan, dating to c. 7500 B.C., some of the earliest religious objects in the world.

the ancestral figurines made at the early farming village of *'Ain Ghazal,* Jordan, before 7500 B.C. (see Figure 13.15).

Belief in an afterlife reflects a view of human existence that connects the world of the living with the supernatural realm in a seamless continuum. For this reason, both burial rites and commemoration of ancestors have played important roles in ancient life. For instance, hundreds of Adena and Hopewell burial mounds dot the landscape of the Midwest, holding the graves of thousands of leaders and lesser personages, each buried with distinctive grave furniture, some with elaborate, highly prestigious artifacts such as mica and copper ornaments. The building of the Hopewell mounds was carried out step by step as the dead were deposited on an earthen platform that was later covered with a large mound. The famed Great Serpent Mound in Ohio is a later ceremonial earthwork whose exact religious significance still escapes us (see Figure 13.16 on page 280).

Most societies' religious beliefs were interpreted and maintained through regular religious rituals conducted at specific times of the year, as at harvests and plantings. These regular ceremonies were vital to the elaborate organization of newly emerging complex societies. The predictable yearly round of religious life gave society an orderly framework for redistributing food, disposing of surplus cattle, accumulating wealth, and other economic functions. The long-term effects of these new, unifying religious beliefs were startling.

Between 1150 and 850 B.C., Mesoamerican society began to undergo rapid transformation. Administrative and religious authority came together in the hands of leaders of a newly ranked society, with specialists and a hierarchy of settlements. This organization contrasted with the dispersed villages of earlier times. More elaborate public buildings appeared as temples and monumental buildings began to reflect individual communities' common involvement in public works (see Figure 13.17 on page 280). In Mesoamerica and elsewhere, the ultimate sacred beliefs and rituals of a society are linked to the processes of social and environmental change that act upon it.

Figure 13.16 The Great Serpent Mound, Hopewell, Adams County, Ohio, built by the Mississippian people as a ceremonial earthwork. (Courtesy of National Museum of the American Indian, Smithsonian Institution [N21598]. Photo by Major Dache M. Reeves.)

Figure 13.17 Four figures grouped deliberately to form a scene, found buried beneath a house of about 1200 B.C. at San José Mogote, Oaxaca, Mexico.

Studying Religion and Ideology

In recent years, many researchers have turned to ethnohistorical and historical records to decipher ancient religious beliefs. Only a few years after the Spanish Conquest of Mexico, missionary Fray Bernardino de Sahagun (c. 1499–1590) laboriously recorded a mass of information about Aztec life and civilization gleaned from Indian survivors of the Conquest. In his great work, *A General History of the Things of New Spain,* he described not only early Aztec history, but minute details of Indian religion, even Aztec philosophy and poetry. Modern scholars are interpreting his writings and discovering that Aztec religious beliefs were at least as sophisticated and complex as the Catholic beliefs that replaced them.

David Lewis-Williams is an expert on the prehistoric rock art of southern Africa, an art tradition painted on the walls of caves and rockshelters for thousands of years until Europeans came in the eighteenth and nineteenth centuries A.D. This art depicts animals, hunters during the chase, and scenes of camp life and religious ceremonies, as well as complex signs and symbols (see Figure 11.7 on page 233). No painters survived into this century, but Lewis-Williams dug into early oral traditions of the paintings collected by nineteenth-century investigators, who also recorded some of the San oral traditions about the paintings. His research has enabled him to evaluate some of the paintings of eland and other animals in their ancient symbolic context. The paintings were integral to the symbolic world of the San, a world intimately tied to the animals they hunted.

David Friedel and Linda Schele's work on Maya cosmology is a fine example of this type of research. They have used changes in Maya images and hieroglyphs to study the meaning of symbols associated with political power. For example, the religious symbolism of Maya society in 100 B.C. was based on the passage of Venus as morning and evening star with the rising and setting of the sun. The people of any Maya community could identify and verify their cosmos simply by observing the sky. As time went on, Maya cosmology was expanded and elaborated. Initially, the names of rulers were not recorded publicly. Perhaps such permanent verification on public monuments was not yet deemed necessary. After A.D. 200, Maya rulers followed a quite different strategy. They legitimized their rule through genealogies, public ceremonies, and monuments—much art was commissioned as part of this process of legitimizing rulers, who claimed identity with gods in the Maya cosmos. Friedel and Schele believe that the metaphor of the twin ancestors—Venus and the sun—provided a potent image for lateral blood ties between lineages, communities, and everyone who believed in the same myths. Because twins are of the same womb and blood, so the Maya are all of common ancestry and blood.

This Maya research shows that we should never think of religion and ritual in isolation but rather as integral to social organization, economic life, and political systems. The ideas and beliefs, the core of all religions, are reflected in many aspects of human life, especially in art and architecture. Every society has its own model of how the world is put together, its own ultimate beliefs. These sacred propositions are interpreted for the faithful through a body of theology and rituals. The rituals are more or less standardized religious acts often repeated at regular times of the year: at harvests, plantings, and other key times. Others are performed when needed: marriages, funerals, and the like. Some societies, such as those of the ancient Egyptians and the Maya, made regular calendars to time religious events and astronomical cycles. These regular ceremonies performed important functions not only in integrating society but also in such activities as redistributing food, controlling population by infanticide, and dispersing surplus male cattle in the form of ritually accumulated wealth.

Religious experiences are predominantly emotional, often supernatural and awe inspiring. A religion operates through sanctified attitudes, values, and messages—an ethic that adds a sacred blessing, derived from the ultimate sacred propositions of the society, to elicit predictable responses from the people. Such predictability, sparked by directives from some central religious authority, ensures the orderly operation of society. In time, as in Mesopotamia, that authority can become secular as well. The institutions and individuals associated with these messages can become sanctified, for they are associated with the sacred propositions that lie at the heart of the society's beliefs. As societies become more complex, so does the need for a stable framework to administer the needs of the many increasingly specialized subgroups that make up the society as a whole. Religious beliefs are intangible and survive only in the form of temples, ritual paraphernalia, and art. Viewed in isolation, the study of ancient religion seems a hopeless task—if archaeological finds are the only source of information available. But if one views religion and ritual as integral to a society and closely tied to all other aspects of its activities, there is some hope that we may be able to look at ritual and religious artifacts in the context of a society as a whole.

One example comes from the Valley of Oaxaca, Mexico. Between 1400 and 1150 B.C., modest temples appear in local villages, built on adobe and earth platforms. Rare conch-shell trumpets and turtle-shell drums traded from the coastal lowlands were apparently used in public ceremonies in such buildings. Clay figurines of dancers wearing costumes and masks that make them look like fantastic creatures and animals, as well as pottery masks, also appear at the same time. So does another religious artifact, the stingray spine imported from the Gulf of Mexico, used in personal self-mutilation rituals of bloodletting. The Spanish described how the Aztec nobles would gash themselves with knives or with fish and stingray spines in religious acts of mutilation that were penances before the gods. Thus, argued archaeologist Kent Flannery, there were three levels of religious ceremony: personal bloodletting; dances run by kin groups, which cut across household lines; and public rituals in ceremonial buildings, involving a region wider than one village.

The most effective way to study such intangibles as social organization or religious beliefs and rituals is to consider them as integral to a society, closely tied to all other aspects of its activities. The rituals that ensured the continuity of religious belief are reflected in architecture and art, and the presence or absence of sacred artifacts in the archaeological record may reveal valuable information on prehistoric religion, provided that research designs are carefully made.

In these and many other ways, archaeologists are trying to unravel the complex and little-understood symbolic world of the ancients. The task will never be an easy one, and it requires large data sets, excellent preservation, and sophisticated theoretical approaches. Australian historian Inga Clendinnen, the author of a superb book on the Aztecs, calls us "Ahabs pursuing our great white whale." She aptly writes the following:

> We will never catch him . . . it is our limitations of thought, of understandings, of imagination we test as we quarter these strange waters. And then we think we see a darkening in the deeper water, a sudden surge, the roll of a fluke—and then the heart stopping glimpse of the great white shape . . . there on the glimmering horizon. (Clendinnen, 1991: 275)

We have described many of the basic principles and methods of archaeology. In Chapter 14, we turn to another aspect of archaeology—the management of the past for future generations.

SUMMARY

1. Humans spend their lives interacting with one another as individuals and as groups. This chapter explains how archaeologists study such interactions, beginning with individuals, then groups.
2. In studying social organization, archaeologists use exotic artifacts and human burials to identify social ranking, by examining the differences in wealth and ornamentation. They use distinctive artifact patterns, historical documents, and symbols of political and religious power to study social ranking and ideologies of domination, as well as resistance to power.
3. Important studies of African-American societies in the southern United States have shown how many such communities maintained their beliefs and culture for many generations.
4. In recent years, some archaeologists have analyzed gender relations in ancient societies, using artifacts, monumental architecture, and the changing status of women as revealed through artifacts and changing food patterns.
5. Archaeologists define several broad levels of sociocultural evolution in prehistory, which provide a general framework for tracing human organization through time. Prestate societies include bands, tribes, and chiefdoms, small-scale societies that vary greatly in their degree of political integration. State-organized societies, the preindustrial civilizations, operate on a large scale, with centralized social and political institutions and social classes.
6. Exchange systems were used by ancient societies to acquire goods and services from outside their own site catchment areas. Much ancient trade depends on reciprocity, the mutual exchange of goods between two individuals, and the redistribution of trade goods from a central place throughout a culture. Such exchange differs from markets, which were places for administering and organizing trade, found in more complex societies.
7. Trade appears in the archaeological record in the form of such exotic objects as seashells far inland or metals far from their original sources.
8. A variety of characterization, or sourcing, techniques allow archaeologists to identify the specific sources of some raw materials like copper and obsidian, thereby allowing them to study ancient trade routes. These methods include spectrographic and neutron activation analysis, as well as artifact distributions.
9. Religious beliefs can sometimes be discerned from traditional histories, and also from art traditions and through the decipherment of early scripts, such as Maya glyphs. Such beliefs were integral to all societies and are best studied with careful research designs.

FOURTEEN

Managing the Past

CRM excavation in the center median of Interstate 10, Tucson, Arizona.

CHAPTER OUTLINE

PREVIEW

Chapter 14 moves away from the basic principles of archaeological research and looks at the management of the archaeological record through Cultural Resource Management. We summarize the key U.S. federal legislation that encompasses the protection of archaeological sites, then describe the three stages of CRM investigation that constitute compliance with federal law. Then we cover issues that confront CRM, issues of research as opposed to management, and the four basic issues surrounding effective management of the past. Native Americans play an important role in CRM, while Public Archaeology is a rapidly expanding part of the discipline, reflected in a new concern for stakeholders in the past, as well as in archaeological tourism.

Make a public example of any one in your company you catch defacing a monument, either by scribbling his name or by taking fragments of it away. Posterity will bless you.

—Canon Hardwicke D. Rawnsley, *Notes for the Nile,* 1892

Archaeology is under siege and has been for generations. The fragile and finite archives of the past have been under accelerating threat ever since the rapid expansion of industrial civilization in Europe and the Americas during the nineteenth century. The problem has assumed epochal proportions since the 1960s. The pace of wholesale destruction has accelerated as urbanization has become universal and global populations have mushroomed. Add a frenzy of road construction to ease traffic congestion, rapid urban expansion, and the intensification of strip mining and industrial-scale deep plowing to the equation and you have a scenario for wholesale destruction. The looting of sites for salable antiquities further threatens the rapidly evaporating record of the past. In many areas, the very future of the past is in question. Less than 5 percent of the pre-1850s archaeological record of Los Angeles County remains undisturbed. At least 25 percent of the sites that existed in Arkansas in 1750 were destroyed by agricultural and other land use, to say nothing of looters, between 1962 and 1972. Despite herculean efforts to stem the tide, the destruction has continued since then.

In many parts of the world, we're now at the point at which the management and **stewardship** of finite archaeological resources is the overwhelming priority. Most archaeologists of the future will spend their careers attempting to save the past for future generations. So far, *Archaeology* has described the basic principles, methods, and techniques of archaeological research. In this chapter we turn our attention to the management of the past and to cultural resource management and public archaeology (see the Discovery box on page 286).

Legislating the Past

Cultural resources are the human-made and natural features associated with human activity. They are the unique and nonrenewable sites, structures, and artifacts that make up the material record of the human past. **Cultural Resource Management (CRM)** is the application of management skills to preserve important parts of our cultural heritage,

Discovery

African-American Burial Ground, New York City, 1991

Cultural Resource Management projects sometimes yield unexpected discoveries. In 1991, the federal government planned to build a thirty-four-story office building in the heart of Lower Manhattan, New York. The responsible agency, the General Services Administration, retained a team of archaeologists to study the cleared site. When they examined eighteenth-century city maps of the area, the researchers found that the proposed construction site was located in an area that surveyors of the day had called the "Negro Burial Ground." They assumed that the basements of nineteenth-century buildings had destroyed most, if not all, the graves in the abandoned cemetery and thus concluded that it was safe to proceed with construction.

Unfortunately, much of the cemetery had been buried beneath thick layers of fill, and many burials remained intact beneath the basements of the nineteenth-century buildings (see Figure 14.1). Just weeks before the contractors were due to start construction, dozens of undisturbed burials were discovered. Four hundred and twenty graves, some stacked one on top of the other, were eventually recovered from one small portion of the cemetery. The discovery provides the largest American skeletal collections and one of the most significant eighteenth-century sites studied by archaeologists. Intense controversy erupted over the discovery, as New York's black community expressed outrage at the way in which the survey, excavations, and human remains had been handled without consultation with African Americans. The site itself became a focus of community protests and cultural inspiration. Eventually, the skeletons were handed over to biological anthropologist Michael Blakey of Howard University for study and eventual reburial.

Figure 14.1 The African-American burial ground in New York City.

Few archaeological discoveries are as controversial as the Negro Burial Ground, where much bitterness and political activity could have been avoided by more thorough field research well ahead of time. Nevertheless, this celebrated find highlights the great complexity of archaeological survey, especially in urban areas, where historical records and sites of all kinds form a tangled archive for the modern scholar. Many of the world's largest cities, among them Amsterdam, London, and San Francisco, have offices specifically concerned with the identification and preservation of archaeological resources.

both historic and prehistoric, for the benefit of the public today and in the future. A considerable body of legislation at the federal and state level protects antiquities on public lands. The United States is one of the few countries that extends virtually no protection to archaeological sites found on privately held or owned land.

Efforts to protect American antiquities go back to as long ago as the Antiquities Act of 1906, which was aimed at controlling a lucrative trade in painted pots from Southwestern pueblos. Since World War II, the accelerating destruction of archaeological sites throughout North America has resulted in a jigsaw pattern of legislation that serves as a framework for cultural resource management. CRM has emerged as a sophisticated phenomenon, its practice surrounded by an elaborate framework of laws, regulations, and statutes, not only at the federal and state levels but also at the county, city, and Native American tribal levels.

CRM archaeology is now an enormous enterprise, ranging in scope from multimillion-dollar projects to small-scale operations involving no more than a small urban plot or a simple survey of a few acres of farmland.

Cultural resource legislation is not the only protective tool. Other laws may be invoked to protect archaeological sites, particularly in cases where the sites are on private lands. In some instances, private groups have also played central roles in the protection of resources. The Archaeological Conservancy is a bright hope, a privately funded membership organization formed in the early 1980s to purchase threatened archaeological sites and manage them as permanent archaeological preserves on hundred-year management plans (see Figure 14.2). The sites this organization has purchased include the Hopewell Mound group in Ohio; Savage Cave in Kentucky, a site with human occupation from Paleo-Indian to Mississippian times; and San Marcos Pueblo in New Mexico, a 200-room pueblo near Santa Fe. (You can join by writing to the Archaeological Conservancy at 5301 Central Ave NE, Suite 902, Albuquerque, NM 87108, or go to www.americanarchaeology.com.)

We don't have the space to describe the mosaic of cultural resource management legislation in any detail, but the Laws box on page 288 lists the major laws.

All this legislation has led to a dramatic explosion in the amount of archaeological effort, much of it contracted by government agencies, as well as by private companies undertaking development work. Whereas fifty years ago museums or universities employed nearly all archaeologists in the United States, most now work in a variety of federal and state departments and private companies concerned with cultural resource management. The money expended on the salvage and mitigation of archaeological sites has resulted in some of the largest excavations in recent history and in some the most innovative approaches to remote sensing and scientific applications.

Figure 14.2 Mound City National Monument, Ohio. Each of these Hopewell mounds covers a charnel house where the cremated dead were deposited.

Laws

Some Cultural-Resource-Management Legislation in the United States, 1960 Onward

This is a summary of some of the key features of federal legislation, which built on the Historic Sites Act of 1935. This baseline act gave the National Park Service a broad mandate to identify, protect, and preserve cultural properties. Numerous state, local, and Native American tribal laws amplify and complicate this already complex legislative picture.

Reservoir Salvage Act of 1960

This act authorized archaeologists to dig and salvage sites that were in danger of destruction as a result of federally owned and funded dam projects.

Historic Preservation Act of 1966 (Amended in 1976 and 1980)

This act was responsible for setting up a national framework for historic preservation, requiring the federal government to establish a nationwide system for identifying, protecting, and rehabilitating what are commonly called "historic places." The act called for the establishment of the National Register of Historic Places. A "historic place" could include prehistoric and historic archaeological sites.

National Environmental Protection Act (NEPA) of 1969

NEPA laid down a comprehensive policy for government land-use planning and resource management. NEPA ordered all federal agencies to take the lead in historic preservation and to locate properties that might qualify for the National Register.

Executive Order 11593 (1972)

Executive Order 11593 and NEPA defined requirements that made it essential for archaeologists to prepare and maintain extremely comprehensive information on archaeological resources on state, federal, and privately owned land. This information would enable them to assess, at short notice, the potential effects of development on these resources.

Archaeological Resources Protection Act (ARPA) of 1979

ARPA gave more stringent protection to archaeological sites over one hundred years old on federal land.

Abandoned Shipwrecks Act of 1988

This act extends protection to shipwrecks and defines ownership of abandoned vessels in state and federal waters.

Native American Grave Protection and Repatriation Act (NAGPRA) of 1990

NAGPRA requires all museums and institutions receiving federal funds to inventory their holdings of Native American human remains, funerary objects, sacred objects, and what are called "objects of cultural patrimony" in the collections with a view to repatriation and reburial. NAGPRA also protects all Native American graves and other cultural objects found within archaeological sites on federal and tribal land. It also requires anyone carrying out archaeological investigation on federal and tribal lands to consult with affiliated or potentially affiliated Native Americans concerning the treatment and disposition of any finds (see Chapter 7).

What Is Protected?

Most Americans likely assume that the nation's historic sites and archaeological resources are well protected and safe for archaeologists to study and future generations to enjoy. However, the actual protection that cultural resources are afforded differs from state to state and from site to site. The legal compliance process on a project is, at best, an attempt to see that cultural resources threatened by the project are properly managed—recorded, evaluated, protected, or, if necessary, salvaged.

Figure 14.3 A Mimbres painted bowl from the Southwest depicting a man spearing a large fish, perhaps a whale. Almost all major Mimbres sites, including those on federal and state land, have been ravaged in recent years, many with backhoes. The pace of damage is accelerating.

In general, archaeological sites on government lands, including national and state parks, forests, reservoirs, and military bases, are well protected. These areas are required by law to have management plans in place, and an active effort is made to document and protect their archaeological resources. Government archaeologists oversee development and contract private archaeologists to conduct work. Some of the nation's best documented and protected archaeological sites, albeit somewhat inaccessible to the public, are located on military reservations. A case in point is the China Lake Naval Air Weapons Station in southern California, site of the Coso Petroglyphs National Historic Site, which includes some of the nation's most spectacular rock art. The sites are open to the public only through special arrangements on a limited basis.

The largest gap in cultural resource protection in the United States is on private lands. In many countries, antiquities are considered the property of the state regardless of where they are found. In contrast, the law in the United States is ambiguous because the Fifth Amendment to the U.S. Constitution forbids the seizure of private property for public use without just compensation. Private property is almost sacrosanct, and over the years, archaeological resources on private land have come to be thought of as part of that land and, therefore, the private property of the owner. Although many owners take the preservation of archaeological resources on their land very seriously, others do not. Unrecorded sites may be unknowingly plowed over, while others are destroyed by landowners who regard sites as sources of income. As legal and official pressures on looters and pothunters increase, prices in the auction room and on the illegal market go up (see Figure 14.3).

It is in the West that the most extensive damage has been done, for the stunning basketry and pottery of Southwest Native Americans have attracted collectors and dealers for more than a century. One Ancestral Pueblo basket alone went for $152,000 in a London auction room some years ago, while a Mississippian stone ax was sold in New Orleans for $150,000. Even relatively prosaic vessels may be worth several hundred dollars, so there is a flourishing commercial, but underground, trade, which is probably a network of well-connected operators. Their work may not lead to fabulous profits, but it does yield enough to keep the enterprise alive. The situation is eerily like that of the drug trade. A crackdown in the field leads to higher prices; in the case of American Indian artifacts, there are plenty of wealthy private collectors at home and overseas who care nothing about ethics. Native Americans have long fought against such activities, which they regard as sacrilege, theft of their native patrimony, and common greed. Today, archaeologists and Native Americans are developing a sometimes uneasy alliance against a common enemy—the looter.

Assessment, Mitigation, and Compliance

The process of identifying, assessing, and managing archaeological resources is often discussed in terms of three phases that reflect increasing levels of archaeological fieldwork and research.

Phase 1: Identification and Preliminary Assessment

Phase 1 provides the preliminary identification and assessment of cultural resources within a project area. An overview of cultural resources within the project area is compiled, ideally including environmental background, the known culture history of the area, a review of previous research, and a description of relevant historical and ethnographic information. The survey area is clearly laid out on maps, and landowners within the study area contacted. Using surface survey and limited subsurface testing, the researchers assess the potential presence of undisturbed archaeological deposits, and make management recommendations. If the assessment indicates that the area has been highly disturbed by previous construction, or if no evidence of cultural materials is found, the Phase 1 report may conclude that no further work be undertaken, and development work begin. Alternatively, the preliminary study may identify significant resources and recommend a Phase 2 investigation.

Phase 2: Assessing Significance

The focus of Phase 2 research is on determining the significance of the archaeological resources present and their potential for listing in the National Register of Historic Places. Fieldwork may include clearly specified surface collection, limited test excavations, deep trenching to identify buried deposits, and the stripping of disturbed surface deposits to reveal buried features. The specific objective is to determine the presence of stratigraphically intact archaeological deposits and to assess the potential significance of the site in terms of its contribution to the understanding of an important person or event, or culture. The completed Phase 2 report discusses the cultural resources identified with regard to relevant CRM legislation and makes recommendations for additional research if necessary to determine their eligibility for the National Register of Historic Places.

Phase 3: Management Plans and Mitigation

This is the final and most intensive stage of cultural resource management work. The proposal for Phase 3 work spells out a management plan for cultural resources eligible for listing in the National Register of Historic Places that will be affected or destroyed by the planned development. It establishes suitable mitigation measures for the protection of the archaeological sites that minimize the impact of development or for excavation to salvage data from sites that will be inevitably destroyed.

Mitigation may include changing the design of a building so that it avoids archaeological resources, or the total excavation of sites, or portions of sites, that cannot be preserved, with the aim of recovering as much information as possible. The final report on Phase 3 work, submitted to the appropriate government agency or contracting firm, describes and synthesizes the data recovered, providing a record of the archaeological resources studies.

The compliance process (often called the **Section 106 process** after the clause of that number in the National Historic Preservation Act of 1966) can be complex, involving the archaeologist in both recommending management strategies and conducting delicate negotiations with several government agencies at once. To be effective, a management plan has to be a constantly evolving document, maintained and changed as archaeologists continue to manage and monitor the area. For example, Phase 3 excavation may reveal the presence of archaeological resources that were not identified in previous work, and consequently a new mitigation plan providing for additional research must be developed.

The same process involves both federal and state agencies in other management duties as well. They have the responsibility for protecting sites against vandalism, a major problem in some areas. The value of each individual resource must also be assessed, either on the basis of its scientific value established within the context of a research design, or because it merits preservation in situ. Agencies must also consider how a site can be utilized for the public good. This responsibility means interpreting it for the public, who may either visit the location, as they do at, say, Chaco Canyon, or learn about it through books, television programs, and popular articles.

Management versus Research

Cultural resource management for the most part involves gathering and assessing archaeological data from very specific areas dictated by development concerns, such as the site of an oil-drilling pad or the locations of pylons along a power line corridor. Often the areas covered may be small and encompass no cultural material or only portions of sites, but larger scale projects can sometimes embrace entire regions or river drainages. The very nature of CRM work means a heavy emphasis on survey and limited excavation, on basically descriptive investigations aimed at satisfying compliance requirements. The identification and preservation of the archaeological record have sometimes been seen as the first and only priority of CRM. This is a relatively theory-free and descriptive approach in which management decisions about land use are based on a catalog of sites within an area.

Many academic archaeologists thought, and some still think, of the descriptive, salvage archaeology that characterizes CRM as entirely inconsistent with the problem-oriented nature of research. As a result, there has been a dangerous and often unthinking tendency to segment archaeology into two broad camps: academic researchers taking on specific problems on one side, and the contract archaeologists involved with salvage, management, and compliance on the other. This insidious distinction is, of course, a gross simplification that fails to recognize the importance of CRM archaeology. CRM archaeology, especially when conducted on a large scale, offers unique opportunities for answering basic questions about the past. The challenge is to grasp these opportunities and to exploit them to the fullest (see Figure 14.4). Any notion that

Figure 14.4 CRM excavation goes on year-round. Excavations at the Howorth-Nelson site in southwestern Pennsylvania were carried on through the cold winter months under a heated inflatable shelter.

academic archaeology is somewhat superior to CRM research at its best is arrogant nonsense. North American archaeology *is* CRM.

Today, there is constant feedback between emerging archaeological theory and methodology and the realities of contract work. Many cultural resource management projects are redefining the way North American archaeologists go about their work, in part because of sound research designs and also because they are often funded at a far higher level than even the most ambitious academic projects—not only for survey and excavation but for analysis and, sometimes, for publication as well. A problem-oriented approach regards CRM as part of contemporary archaeology with all its sophisticated theoretical apparatus for studying and evaluating the past.

Some CRM projects have involved massive archaeological operations and the expenditure of millions of dollars in survey and excavation. The as yet unpublished Ballona Wetlands project in Los Angeles that is still under way, the Lower Verde Valley project in Arizona, and the Black Mesa project in the Southwest have all yielded important methodological contributions and, sometimes, major theoretical perceptions. CRM work on historic period sites has also involved some large-scale meticulous excavations that have greatly enhanced our understanding of the past.

Some of the most successful of these projects have been conducted by large private companies that specialize in environmental impact work or by CRM archaeologists with close ties to academic institutions. For instance, researchers at the Institute of Archaeology and Anthropology at the University of South Carolina have developed a strong partnership with the university that allows them to carry out major CRM projects in an academic setting. With their excellent technical resources and large project budgets, they are able to conduct detailed research and fine-grained field and laboratory investigations that are beyond the budgetary scope of all but a few purely academic research projects.

As a long-term project, some scholars are pulling together enormous quantities of raw settlement data and other culture-historical information into detailed syntheses of the southeastern United States. One such example is a comprehensive study of Paleo-Indian sites in the entire region, an invaluable, if unspectacular, contribution to knowledge. Such efforts maximize the value of local CRM projects and bring the vast amounts of data they accumulate into a meaningful summary of great intellectual value.

CRM archaeology is the only viable way to identify and document rapidly vanishing archaeological resources in North America, the very kinds of data required to fulfill one of archaeology's major objectives—the explanation of culture change over long periods of time. This is not only a matter of economic realities but also one of perceiving the opportunity to make major intellectual advances in archaeology while still meeting the requirements of individual contracts. Some CRM companies are beginning to work with large scale land developers to complete surveys and mitigation recommendations years ahead of actual development of raw land. This strategy has the advantage of allowing plenty of time to complete archaeological work far in advance of construction deadlines.

Strategies of CRM Research

With CRM the dominant force in archaeological fieldwork in North America, the problem of ensuring quality research is of major concern. For all the debate about conflicting approaches, and, to be frank, a good deal of dubious research, CRM has brought extensive methodological benefits to basic research, among them a much greater emphasis on prehistoric settlement patterns, sampling procedures, computer applications, and, above all, remote sensing. The major methodological contributions come in three areas: geomorphology, safety, and technology.

Geomorphology

CRM projects have combined geomorphological expertise with four-dimensional views of landscapes (time being the fourth dimension) to better understand the development of ancient landscapes and for locating and evaluating deeply buried sites. For example, the Upper Mississippi Valley has experienced much sustained CRM work that combines studies of landscape change with paleoecology and buried site archaeology. The result: maps of Late Ice Age and Holocene landforms for a 300-mile (480-km) stretch of the valley. This is a superb basis for accurate assessment of cultural resource potential.

A similar approach has been used by researchers with the Cultural Resource program at Fort Drum, New York. Initially established in 1908, today Fort Drum is home to the Tenth Mountain Division and covers 10,000 acres (4,046 ha), just northeast of Watertown, New York. Military training can have serious impacts on cultural resources, and the base encompasses a diversity of prehistoric and historic archaeological sites. To ensure that cultural resources are not damaged, the Fort Drum Cultural Resources program follows an Integrated Cultural Resources Management Plan, which changes as cultural resources are identified and the base's needs evolve (see Figure 14.5).

The first challenge to effective management is identifying sites before they are impacted. Thus far, six abandoned villages, more than 360 Historic Period farms, and over 200 prehistoric sites have been identified. While some of the historic sites could be located using maps and documentary sources, many had to be identified through archaeological survey, test excavations, and nonintrusive subsurface detection methods, such as ground-penetrating radar, electrical restitivity, and magnetometer surveys. Drawing on geomorphological studies, archaeologists were able to trace the boundaries of Glacial Lake Iroquois, which has receded over the past 10,000 years. By tracing ancient shorelines, they were able to predict areas that were likely locations for early settlements. Special attention is paid to areas that are likely to be impacted by base activities. To mitigate damage to sites, a variety of options are employed. In some cases, areas that contain or potentially contain cultural resources are placed off-limits. In other cases, historic foundations or sites are "hardened": covered with filter fabric and buried with layers of sand and gravel. When this is done, sites are strong enough even to withstand tank traffic. Another protective measure involves the re-vegetation of areas with indigenous plant species to prevent

Figure 14.5 Archaeology at Fort Drum, New York, involved close collaboration with the U.S. Army.

erosion. In these cases, vehicle traffic and digging may be prohibited, but low-impact pedestrian traffic is allowed. In areas of high use, the excavation and salvage of archaeological material may be the only option. For example, barracks construction required the partial excavation of Fort Drum prehistoric site number 1093, a Middle Woodland village.

The work at Fort Drum illustrates the far-ranging concerns and methodologies that must be employed in the management of cultural resources. The researchers are fortunate in that the vast area they are concerned with is under the purview of a single authority and governed by a uniform policy. They also benefit from excellent technical and equipment support. Sadly, many cultural resources do not receive such treatment.

Safety

Whatever their fieldwork, archaeologists face special safety issues. CRM researchers have taken the lead in introducing high safety standards to the field, which has brought archaeology more in line with guidelines in other fields such as construction, engineering, and drilling. Occupational Safety and Health Administration (OSHA) regulations and various local laws may be relevant to archaeological fieldwork. For example, excavation units extending more than 4 to 5 feet (1.2 to 1.5 m) deep must be shored up to ensure the safety of workers. In some instances, archaeologists have to evaluate sites that may be polluted by toxic waste, and fieldworkers have to wear protective clothing.

Technology

CRM archaeologists lead their colleagues in applications of high-technology remote-sensing devices, computer-based data collection, and data management systems. Because of the often-pressing need to quickly identify and excavate sites, CRM projects often employ ground-penetrating radar, magnetometers, and resistivity surveys to locate sites and features without time-consuming excavation. Problems of data storage and the dissemination of information, faced by all archaeologists, are made especially pressing by the volume of CRM work. CRM archaeologists have led the way in the innovative use of computer databases and data management programs to address these concerns. Geographic Information Systems (GIS) have also played a leading role in many CRM projects, as does the technology of site protection.

To these innovations may be added a diversity of other developments that have largely emerged within the context of CRM research. Some truly remarkable investigations combine these and other innovations under often severe all-weather conditions. For example, a CRM project on a Civil War–era foundry in New York State was undertaken under heated domes, with heaters operating twenty-four hours a day. The research combined computerized GIS remote-sensing techniques with computer transit mapping, image analysis, and three-dimensional photogrammetry. The field conservation and curation facility processed as many as five thousand artifacts a week, each being washed, X-rayed, computer inventoried, decontaminated where appropriate, and conserved. All this activity was carried out under OSHA and EPA hazardous materials procedures and precautions, then combined with documentary evidence to provide a story of intelligence operations that were carried out under President Lincoln's direct authority.

Management Challenges

Although CRM has transformed American archaeology—for the most part, for the better—it has also brought its own set of problems. While these difficulties to a large extent are problems faced by all archaeologists, some are particularly challenging because of the scale and volume of CRM work.

Issues of Quality

Some of the most pressing problems concern the quality of the archaeological research. Although federal legislation spells out guidelines, their implementation varies in different states and community settings. State Historic Preservation Offices (SHPOs), the state institutions mandated by the Historic Preservation Act to oversee CRM work, are often understaffed, and many find it difficult to keep up with oversight. The amount of activity is so great that the only long-term solution to the crisis of quality lies in the increasing integration of the goals and research techniques of scientific archaeology, on the one hand, and the realities and demands of cultural management and contract archaeology, on the other.

Attempts have been made at self-regulation. Organizations such as the Register of Professional Archaeologists (www.rpanet.org) and the American Cultural Resources Association (www.acra-crm.org) have stringent guidelines for research, as well as for the archaeologists' responsibilities to the public, clients, and fellow archaeologists. If adhered to, these would ensure uniformly high standards of behavior and research. Unfortunately, the value of the guidelines is only as good as the organizations' memberships, which are entirely voluntary. Rather like the Better Business Bureau, enforcement of ethics is difficult and censure limited.

The Issue of Site Records

The recording of archaeological data is especially important, as the study of community and archaeological site distributions is integral to effective cultural resource management. Only when sites are identified and the information is provided to development planners can sites be protected or salvage work undertaken. The collection and organization of these data can, however, be challenging. Information on archaeological sites within a region is often obtained from a variety of sources that may vary tremendously in terms of detail and quality and be scattered in a diversity of different reports, archives, and publications. For example, information on academic projects and archaeological work by amateurs may not be located in the same repositories as CRM reports.

Fortunately, computerized databases and electronic media such as CD-ROMs and the Web hold great potential for the future. At the national level, there is the National Archaeological Data Base, an online system that contains almost 15,000 records of archaeological reports. Any archaeologist with a telephone line or an electronic mail system can now access the database, which also provides comprehensive site distribution from many states and background environmental information through the Geographic Resources Analysis Support System (GRASS), the GIS system used by the National Park Service. This resource is really a database of databases; it allows managers to acquire information on everything from county-level site data to progress on reburial and repatriation of burials. The National Archaeological Data Base is managed by the Center for Advanced Spatial Technology at the University of Arkansas, Fayetteville. This powerful resource is an invaluable tool for North American archaeologists of all specialties and is mirrored by others being developed in other countries, notably Denmark. There are also state and local data bases of great value.

The Issue of Curation

Curation is the management, storage and conservation of artifacts and other data recovered in the course of archaeological activities. Once artifacts from a site have been excavated and analyzed, what happens to them? Archaeological surface collections and excavations can easily amass hundreds of thousands of artifacts, many of which require conservation if they are to be preserved. While in the past artifacts were sometimes discarded after analysis, keeping the collections for future study or additional analysis is clearly desirable: Material from previous studies may be reexamined as part of new projects, and new methods of analysis may yield information undreamed of by the original excavators.

Many archaeological organizations and institutions have established guidelines for the curation of materials. The National Park Service, for example, has issued regulations for the curation of federal collections, as required under amendments to existing legislation. Unfortunately, curation is expensive, and the costs of providing permanent conservation and storage are prohibitive. Many museums and other designated repositories are grappling with seemingly insurmountable mountains of archaeological finds that pour in from CRM projects. Aside from the space they occupy, the finds must be labeled, cataloged, and placed in plastic bags or boxes that will neither disintegrate nor damage poorly preserved materials. The conservation—cleaning, stabilizing, and preserving—of deteriorating artifacts is a huge problem with some artifacts such as ancient baskets or metal objects that will disintegrate unless properly treated.

Curation is an easily surmountable problem—given time and resources. Archaeologists and museum technicians know what needs to be done, but realization is another issue. Efforts to inventory and curate collections have led to improved guidelines and new facilities. However, there is simply not enough space to house many collections, and there are not enough funds to pay the real costs of curation. Consequently, curation will likely be an issue of continuing concern.

The Issue of Publication and Dissemination

Proliferating contract archaeology and CRM work have caused an explosion not only of raw data but also of publications and reports on completed projects. The essence of publishing archaeological data is, of course, to make them available to as wide an audience of archaeologists as can make use of them. This distribution is achieved through books and national and international journals, and regional periodicals such as the *Plains Anthropologist* or the *New Hampshire Archeologist*. Many of these are widely distributed, peer-reviewed publications, where the submitted contributions are read, evaluated, and edited prior to publication. Ideally, this type of process would be used for all CRM reports and the results of important projects published, but this is clearly impracticable.

Reports on many smaller projects are often purely descriptive and incorporate limited synthesis of data outside of the narrow scope of the project. Although some such reports are potentially useful, many more are sterile, rote descriptions that add little to our understanding of the past and are solely designed to meet CRM legislation. Many of them are literally archaeology by formula, as if the investigators are filling in a form. Even reports on important studies do not receive the degree of external, editorial peer review found in academic journals. This is one reason that archaeologists such as Ian Hodder have insisted on the vital importance of a marriage between theory and excavation that is not merely a sterile recording process.

Another problem lies with the availability of CRM reports. Even many excellent CRM reports are either restricted-circulation documents deeply buried in the files of government agencies or private companies or, at best, photocopied publications that have a severely limited circulation—the so-called "gray literature." One authority estimated that there were about 200,000 gray literature reports in existence in the early 1990s, with an additional 10,000 to 20,000 reports accruing annually. The number has proliferated since then. Sometimes within months they are forgotten, even destroyed, and the vital data in them are as good as lost to science. The problem of failure to publish CRM data in more widely accessible forums is enormous. Ironically, now that awareness about destruction of the archaeological record is greater than ever, the results of much of this anxiety are being buried, almost as effectively as if they had been destroyed, in inaccessible publications. The advent of the World Wide Web has helped ease the situation somewhat, but there are issues of permanence to be considered with

Web sites. The archaeological record is finite, which means that *permanent* records of its excavation must be the exact opposite. The issue of publication and dissemination remains a critical one for the archaeology of the future.

Native Americans and CRM

Most archaeological research in the Americas has involved the excavation of Native American sites, though the majority of the researchers have been of non-Native ancestry. Generations of archaeologists have assumed that the knowledge obtained from their research is of benefit to all, including indigenous peoples. CRM concerns about the protection and management of archaeological sites would also seem to place Native Americans and archaeologists on the same side. Despite these presumed common interests, Native American views about what sites should be preserved, how archaeological research should be conducted, and the ways in which archaeological remains should be treated are often dramatically different from those of archaeologists. NAGPRA, the reburial and repatriation act passed in 1990, still raises occasional violent controversies that often end up in the courts, notably the case of Kennewick Man (see Chapter 7).

Some Native American groups like the Hopi of the Southwest have founded their own cultural preservation offices. The Hopi office preserves "spiritual and cultural essence of the Hopi, encompassing . . . archaeology, ethnology, recovery of stolen sacred artifacts, farming, and the preservation of the Hopi language" (T. J. Ferguson et al., 1995: 13). Intensive consultation with community representatives helps overcome suspicions of archaeologists and their work.

The Hopi definition of a site worth preserving is far more wide-reaching than found in federal and state legislation. In legal terms, they, and other Native American groups, define every ancestral archaeological site as a traditional cultural property to be protected and left alone. The same term, *traditional cultural property*, applies to shrines, sacred sites, springs, quarries, and prehistoric landforms with place names commemorating prehistoric or historic events—some of which bear no visible traces of human activity. Thus, archaeological sites play a central role in the transmission and retention of Hopi culture. Agreement between archaeological and traditional data is often explained in the context of Hopi ritual knowledge. For instance, Hopi prophecies of a time when even the ash left by the ancestors will be used to prove their claims have been connected to the flotation methods used to dissect ancient hearths.

Major controversies surround ritual sites and artifacts, also burials. While we archaeologists see such items as important clues to past religious beliefs, social organization, and health, many Native groups view our excavations as sacrilegious and disrespectful of their cultural heritage. In response, ethics statements by professional organizations now include statements concerning the rights of indigenous peoples and the need to consider Native American concerns in archaeological research.

Public Archaeology

A great deal of the effectiveness in protecting archaeological sites depends on public attitudes toward the past. As archaeology itself has become ever-more specialized, and CRM projects practically universal, so the danger of the study of the past becoming divorced from its public constituency has increased. Both archaeologists and others have asked whether the public is benefiting in practical ways from the enormous sums spent on CRM, when many people perceive of it as a luxury. In response, **public archaeology**, a form of archaeology open and accessible to the public through television, state-sponsored "archaeology weeks," special museum displays and activities, and the Internet, as well as popular publications, has become a growing part of today's archaeology. Public archaeology encompasses a myriad of activities; museum workshops for children run by archaeological societies and museums, the publication of leaflets and Web pages summarizing new work, and many superb public outreach programs run by cities. In areas such as historic Alexandria, Virginia, and Annapolis, Maryland, archaeologists have worked closely with historians and the local communities to provide walking tours, lectures, and other educational programs that share archaeological discoveries and management concerns with visitors.

Archaeological Tourism

Public archaeology brings archaeologists in touch with a wide range of **stakeholders** in the past, from scholars to rangers, curio sellers, science journalists, local farmers, and home owners, this apart from government agencies. These stakeholders have a wide variety of interests in the past—financial, legal, and emotional. A great deal of public archaeology is concerned with the interface between the archaeologist and these diverse stockholders. And much of it revolves around archaeological tourism.

Today, cultural tourism, which includes archaeology, is one of the fastest growing segments of the travel business. Today, thanks to the jumbo jet and the cruise ship, the past is under siege by visitors. Today, more people visit the Pyramids of Giza in a month than visited them in years even a century ago. The scale of visitor counts has exploded. Persepolis in Iran was the seat of the Achaemenid kings, among them Darius I (521–486 B.C.), an architectural masterpiece famous for its columned buildings high on a terrace and a stairway adorned with friezes of subject peoples bringing tribute (see Figure 14.6). In

Figure 14.6 The stairway of the Apadana at Persepolis, Iran, climbed on horseback by Colonel Sykes in 1914.

1914, English Colonel P. M. Sykes scaled the stairway on his sixteen-hand horse and was overwhelmed by the view from the top. He had the place to himself. Today, you arrive in an air-conditioned bus and spend a tightly scheduled two hours in a fenced and controlled archaeological environment. The quality of the experience is completely different.

What was once an adventure enjoyed by a few has become mass-market tourism. Today, even hitherto relatively inaccessible sites like the Khmer palaces and temples at Angkor Thom and Angkor Wat in Cambodia are on the international tourist circuit (see Figure 4.5 on page 77). One forecast projects that 4.3 million tourists will visit Angkor Wat by 2020, a quantum jump over today's figure of some 250,000. The economic impact on the nearby town of Siam Reap has already been significant. Luxury hotels are mushrooming; shanty shacks line the road to the ruins; the infrastructure is under stress. Unfortunately, the huge investment required to make the area a true global tourist destination is beyond Cambodia's ability to afford. But the long-term impact of archaeology here, and at other sites, like, for example, Rapa Nui (Easter Island) in the Pacific with its giant statues, is potentially enormous.

We archaeologists face an appalling dilemma. On the one hand, it's wonderful that millions of people are being exposed to the major sites of antiquity. On the other, the sites themselves are slowly destroyed by visitor traffic, to the point that many of them are becoming less accessible to the public. You can no longer walk among the stones at Stonehenge, except with a special permit. The 15,000 year-old paintings at Lascaux in France are inaccessible. Visitors descend into a superb, accurate replica, which for most people, is as good as the original. As visitor counts increase, so people are being kept at a distance. You can no longer walk among the columns of the Temple of Poseidon at Sounion on Greece, a place famous for its spectacular sunsets when the columns glow with a deep rosy hue from the setting sun. What will the future hold? Will the world's most spectacular archaeological sites be off limits to everyone except professionals? Such a solution is unthinkable, but there seem to be few other affordable options, and visiting a replica of, say, Stonehenge would hardly be a satisfying experience (see Figure 14.7).

Figure 14.7 Today's archaeology is sometimes mechanized. CRM archaeology relies heavily on earthmoving machinery, used carefully and responsibly. Using a backhoe to strip sterile overburden at the Lohmann site, Illinois. The mechanical stripping is followed by manual scraping.

Archaeology has become a major moneymaker on the international tourist scene, but few countries can afford to spend the money to protect major sites from overcrowding. Nor are prospective tourists going to be happy if they are diverted to less well-known, not-so-spectacular locations. So the siege may end in destruction.

If this is allowed to happen, the loss to humanity will be incalculable, both in material and emotional terms. What will be the world be like if our descendants never have the chance to walk through Olympia's temples of Tikal's soaring pyramids? We would lose our past, the collective and magnificent cultural legacy of humankind—and that is unthinkable. Just as important, we would never have the chance to communicate with our forebears in emotional terms, through a timeless sunset at Sounion, or the chorus of a Greek tragedy whispered in the theater at Epidauros. Such moments are rare in our crowded world of package tours, but they can be found. And if we lose these opportunities, we will lose one of the priceless threads that connect us to the past that helped make us what we are. For we are, in the final analysis, all human beings.

SUMMARY

1. Cultural resource management (CRM) involves the development of overall strategies for conservation priorities and management of a finite resource, the archaeological record.
2. Federal legislation, in combination with many state, local, and tribal laws, provides the legal means of protecting the country's archaeological heritage.
3. In the United States, federal legislation, notably the National Historic Preservation Act of 1966, the National Environmental Policy Act of 1969, and the Archaeological Resources Protection Act of 1979, laid down regulations for land use and resource policies and also defined archaeological resources as any artifact more than a century old.
4. Some of the best protected archaeological sites in the United States are on government lands, where management plans require the identification and protection of archaeological resources. The biggest gaps in the protection of archaeological resources in the United States are on private lands.
5. The primary concern of CRM archaeology has been the identification, description, and protection of archaeological resources. Larger-scale projects often provide opportunities for major archaeological excavations and surveys that have important bearing on the development of archaeological method and theory.
6. CRM is having an increasingly important impact on the future direction of American archaeology, on account of both its large budgets and its unique opportunities for large-scale field and laboratory research.
7. The sheer volume of CRM research has led to problems. In some cases inadequate oversight has allowed inadequate archaeological research to be accepted. The recording of sites, the curation and storage of artifacts, and the publication and dissemination of important discoveries are also issues that need to be addressed.
8. Native American groups have demanded that many Indian skeletons in public and private collections be returned to them, a movement that culminated in the passing of the Native American Grave Protection and Repatriation Act of 1990. Archaeologists are now working more closely with Native American communities when excavating sites where burials are likely to be found.
9. One of the most important benefits of CRM has been the increasing input from the public into archaeological research. To inform the public about archaeology, many archaeologists now talk of public archaeology, a form of archaeology open and accessible to the public through television and other means.
10. Archaeological tourism poses serious problems for archaeology, owing to overcrowding and damage done to major sites by visitors.

FIFTEEN

So You Want to Become an Archaeologist?

Edwardian tourists of a century ago pose with their camels and drivers in front of the Pyramids of Giza.

CHAPTER OUTLINE

PREVIEW

So you're thinking about archaeology as a career? Chapter 15 discusses some of the career opportunities, training, and personal qualities needed to become an archaeologist. We also examine some of the ways you can contribute without becoming one and end with a summary of the basic ethics of archaeology for everyone.

> *I fell in love with Ur, with its beauty in the evenings, the ziggurat standing up. . . . I enjoyed the workmen, the foremen, the little basket-boys, the pick-men—the whole technique and life. The lure of the past came up to grab me. To see a dagger slowly appearing, with its gold glint, through the sand was romantic. The carefulness of lifting pots and objects from the soil filled me with a longing to be an archaeologist myself.*
>
> —Agatha Christie, *An Autobiography,* 1977

I became an archaeologist by accident, having entered Cambridge University in England without any idea of potential careers. I was admitted on condition I study anything except Greek and Latin, for which I had no aptitude whatsoever! So I made a list of potential subjects and chose archaeology and anthropology on a whim, with no intention of making it a career. My first lecturer was an archaeologist named Miles Burkitt, a specialist in the Stone Age, who was famous for his classroom stories. He had studied late–Ice Age rock art before 1910 under a legendary French archaeologist named Henri Breuil, the first scholar to copy the art systematically—and had the stories to match the experience. Burkitt's enthusiastic reminiscences triggered my interest in the past. By chance, while still an undergraduate, I met another famous archaeologist, the African prehistorian Desmond Clark, and ended up working in a museum in central Africa after I graduated. I have been an archaeologist ever since, a career choice I have never regretted.

Archaeology as a Profession

I gave up saying I was an archaeologist at cocktail parties after learning the hard way! Say you are an archaeologist and immediately your questioner brightens up. "How exciting! What a fascinating job," your new acquaintance almost invariably says. They think you are some kind of Indiana Jones, perpetually traveling to remote lands in search of some archaeological Holy Grail. When you tell them you study stone tools and recently spent three months searching for fossil rodents (which is usually the truth), their eyes glaze over and they often do not believe you. There's another scenario, too, where the questioner's eyes light up when they learn of your occupation and he or she asks you, confidentially: "Is it true that the Egyptian Sphinx is twelve thousand years old?" Or, "What about the Lost Continent of Atlantis? Isn't it in the Bahamas?" Or, most common of all: "What's the latest on the Dead Sea Scrolls?" I must confess I am a coward and I usually say I am a historian, which, in a sense, I am. My interlocutor soon loses interest.

Archaeology still has an aura of romance and spectacular discovery about it, which probably accounts for why many of you took the course that assigned this book in the first place. You learn pretty fast that modern-day archaeology, while often fascinating and sometimes conducted in remote lands, is a highly technical discipline in which spectacular discoveries are few and far between. An Indiana Jones type of personality is certainly not a qualification for archaeology, indeed it has never been. Today's archaeologist is about as far from Professor Jones as you can get and probably works a long way from the halls of academe.

What, then, are the qualities that make a good archaeologist in these days of highly specialized research and wide diversity of career options? Qualities of character are as important as academic qualifications—which we discuss subsequently—for you will never become rich as an archaeologist. This is a profession that has its own unique rewards. Money is not one of them.

Anyone wanting to become an archaeologist needs far more than academic credentials. Here are some essentials:

- *Enthusiasm,* indeed a passion for archaeology and the past, is the baseline for anyone who enters this field. The best archaeologists are those with the kind of fire in their bellies that enables them to raise money, overcome major practical obstacles, and carry out their work.
- *Infinite patience* to carry out fieldwork and other research that can involve slow-moving, repetitive tasks and dealing with sometimes-difficult people.
- *A mind that thrives on detail,* since a great deal of archaeology is minutiae—small attributes of stone tools and potsherds, analyzing computerized data, studying tiny details of the past for weeks on end.
- *Adaptability,* an ability to put up with long journeys, sometimes uncomfortable fieldwork, and often primitive living conditions. You need to be fit enough to walk long distances and to thrive on improvisation under difficult conditions. Imagine, for example, filing Land Rover wheel bearings out of nails when you are several hundred miles from a service station so you can get home. I know archaeologists who have done that. They had to.
- *Good organizational skills,* since a great deal of archaeology is logistics and organization—of field crews, site archives, even camp kitchens. A good mind for organization is a great asset.
- *Cultural sensitivity and good people skills* are essential. Many of archaeology's most successful practitioners invest enormous amounts of time in cultivating people and communicating with Native Americans and other cultural groups. This is one reason why a background in anthropology is so important to an archaeologist.
- *A commitment to ethical archaeology* is also necessary. Do not become an archaeologist unless you are prepared to adhere to the ethical standards demanded of such professionals, some of which are spelled out in this book.
- *A sense of humor* may seem self-evident, but it is vital, for many archaeologists take themselves far too seriously. Have you ever spent a week writing a paper, then had your computer implode before you have backed up your text? Moments like that beset all field research. That's why archaeologists need a sense of humor, because sometimes everything that can go wrong goes wrong—all at once.

The most important considerations are commitment and enthusiasm, which will carry you through almost anything.

Deciding to Become an Archaeologist

I became an archaeologist almost by chance, for the occasional fieldwork experiences I had as an undergraduate were interesting and left me wanting more. You can ease your way into the field up to the point when you apply to graduate school, and have a great time doing so.

Almost everyone I meet who is contemplating a career in archaeology either encountered the subject in high school or became interested as a result of taking an introductory course at college or university. What, then, should you do next once your appetite for the past is whetted?

First, take more courses in archaeology at the upper-division level from as broad a cross section of instructors as possible. Begin with an advanced method and theory course (if that does not turn you off, then you know you are on to something, for such courses are not remarkable for their excitement). Then take a selection of area courses, so you can find out what general areas of specialty interest you and what do not. Remember, if you apply to graduate school, you will need some specific interest as the potential focus of your degree.

Second, give yourself as thorough and as broad an education in general biological and cultural anthropology as possible, both to focus your interests and to see if living people interest you more than dead ones.

Third, take as many courses as you can in related disciplines, so that you emerge with strongly developed multidisciplinary interests. The most important and fascinating problems in archaeology—for example, the origins of agriculture—can only be approached from a multidisciplinary perspective. Much CRM archaeology is strongly multidisciplinary.

Last, gain significant field and laboratory experience while still an undergraduate. Such experience looks good on graduate applications, especially if it is broadly based. Even more important, it allows you to experience the challenges, discomforts, and realities of field and laboratory work before they become your job (and you should think of graduate school as a job).

If you take the trouble to acquire a broad-based experience of archaeology in your undergraduate years, you will be well equipped for graduate education and its pathways to a professional career. Do not consider applying to a graduate program unless you have well above average grades, a specific interest that coincides with that of the department you are applying to, and people to write letters of recommendation for you who really know you and your archaeological potential well.

Gaining Fieldwork Experience

"How do I go on a dig?" I was asked this question dozens of times a year, especially when I taught the introductory archaeology course. The good news is that there are more opportunities to go in the field as an undergraduate than ever before, provided you are prepared to make the effort to find them. Begin by taking your department's field course, if it offers one; then look further afield, using personal contacts and departmental bulletin boards as a start. The World Wide Web is a useful source of information on such opportunities, as is your department bulletin board, which advertises fieldwork opportunities. You can attend a university field school. The most popular and rigorous field schools are in heavy demand and are filled by competitive application, sometimes by graduate students. General field schools are worthwhile because they combine excavation, laboratory analysis, and academic instruction into one intensive experience. And the camaraderie among participants in such digs can be memorable. Many of my students receive their first fieldwork experience by working as laborers on local CRM projects. Many of them begin as volunteers and are later paid for their work. It is worth checking with any private-sector CRM firms in your area, or consult your instructor, who may have contacts.

Career Opportunities

This is not a good time to become an academic archaeologist, for jobs are rare and the competition intense. But it is certainly an excellent moment to consider a career in government or the private sector, both of which effectively administer or carry out most archaeology in North America.

Academic Archaeology. This field is shrinking. A generation ago, almost all archaeologists were faculty members at academic institutions or worked in museums or research institutions. Purely academic archaeology still dominates both undergraduate and graduate training, and there are many people who enter graduate school with the resolute ambition of becoming a "traditional" research scholar. But growth in academic positions is now very slow. Some programs are even shrinking.

Most archaeology in North America and many parts of Europe is now conducted as CRM projects, much of it mandated by law. This means that most (but certainly not all) academic archaeology in American universities is carried out overseas, most commonly in Europe, Mesoamerica, or the Andes. Over the years, this means that there is intense competition for the rare vacant academic jobs in well-trodden areas such as Mesoamerica, and even more applicants for academic positions in North American archaeology.

A recent study of American archaeologists found that only about 35 percent worked in academia, and the number is diminishing every year. The moral is simple: If you want to become an academic archaeologist, beware of overspecializing or of working in too-crowded fields, and have other qualifications such as CRM or computer skills at your disposal.

Museum jobs are rare, especially those that are purely research positions. A career in museum work is rewarding, but hard to come by and requires specialized training in conservation, exhibits, curation, or some other aspect of collections care in addition to academic training.

Cultural Resource Management and Public Archaeology. These offer almost open-ended opportunities to those who are seeking a career managing and saving the archaeological record. Time was when academic archaeologists looked down on their CRM colleagues and considered them second-rate intellectual citizens. The reverse has been true, too, for I have met CRM archaeologists who consider academics tweed-suited dilettantes! All this is nonsense, of course, for all archaeologists are concerned with careful stewardship of the human past. Some of the greatest opportunities in archaeology during the next century lie in the public archaeology arena and in the private sector, where the challenges are far greater than the traditional academic concerns. Adapting to this reality will lead to many changes in undergraduate and graduate curricula in coming years.

If you are interested in public archaeology or CRM, you have the choice of working either in government or for some form of organization engaged in CRM activity, which can be either a nonprofit group, perhaps attached to a museum, college, or university, or a for-profit company operating entirely in the private sector. The latter come in many forms and sizes, with larger companies offering the best opportunities and career potential, especially for entry-level archaeologists. Most public archaeology activity operates through government, although a few private-sector firms also specialize in this work. If you choose to work in the public sector, you can find opportunities in many federal government agencies, among them the National Park Service and the Bureau of Land Management. Many archaeologists work for state archaeological surveys and other such organizations. Historical societies, such as that in Ohio, often employ archaeologists.

Whichever career track you choose, you will need a sound background in academic archaeology and fieldwork experience, as well as suitable degrees, to follow a career in these areas. Although you may receive some background training in CRM or public archaeology during your undergraduate or graduate career, much of your training will come on the job or through specialized courses taken as part of your work.

Whatever your interests in professional archaeology, I strongly advise you to obtain a background and experience in CRM fieldwork and laboratory work as part of your training.

Academic Qualifications and Graduate School

An undergraduate degree in archaeology qualifies you to work as a gofer on a CRM excavation or an academic dig and little else, except for giving you a better knowledge than most people have of the human past—not something to denigrate as a source of enlightenment and enjoyment in later life. Many people work on CRM projects for a number of years and live in motels—they even have their own informal newsletter!

Any form of permanent position in archaeology requires a minimum of an M.A. (Master of Arts), which will qualify you for many government and private-sector positions. All academic positions at research universities and, increasingly, teaching posts, require a Ph.D.

Typically, an M.A. in archaeology requires two years of course work and some form of field or data-based paper and, at some institutions, an oral examination. The M.A. may have a specialized slant, such as CRM or historic preservation, but most are general degrees, which prepare you to teach at some two- or four-year colleges and universities and open you to many CRM or government opportunities. The advantage of the M.A. degree is that it gives you a broad background in archaeology, which is essential for any professional. It is the qualification of choice for many government and CRM or public archaeology positions.

The Ph.D. is a specialized research degree, which qualifies you as a faculty member to teach at a research university and at many institutions that stress teaching and not research. This is the professional "ticket" for academic archaeologists and is certainly desirable for someone entering government or the private sector, where complex research projects abound and management decisions are often needed. The typical Ph.D. program requires at least two years of seminar, course, and field training, followed by comprehensive examinations (written and often oral), M.A. papers, then a formal research proposal and a period of intensive fieldwork that, in written form, constitutes the Ph.D. dissertation. The average doctoral program takes about seven years to complete and turns you into a highly specialized professional, with some teaching and research experience. After these seven years, you then have to find a job in a highly competitive marketplace. Yes, it is a daunting prospect to face seven years or more of genteel poverty, but the intellectual and personal rewards are considerable for someone with a true passion for archaeology and academic research.

Thoughts on Not Becoming a Professional Archaeologist

Over many years of teaching archaeology, I have introduced thousands of people to the subject. Only a handful became professional archaeologists. Most students who pass through my courses go on to an enormous variety of careers—army rangers, bureaucrats, international businesspeople, lawyers, politicians, real estate tycoons, teachers, and even chefs and pastry cooks. At least two of my former students are in jail! But every one of them is aware of archaeology and its role in the contemporary world and of the remarkable achievements of our ancient forebears. This is by far the most important part of my teaching, of far greater significance than any amount of professional training one may give graduate students.

One's task as a beginning teacher is not to recruit people to the field—to create an "in-group" who know all about radiocarbon dating or the archaeology of the central Ohio valley or eastern Siberia—but to help create what the National Science Foundation calls "an informed citizenry." Some of one's students end up with no interest in archaeology whatsoever; they find it boring and irrelevant to their lives. But you can be sure they have heard of the subject and its remarkable achievements and have decided where it fits in their lives. This is, after all, one of the objectives of an undergraduate education.

Having said this, many people take a single course in archaeology and develop an active interest in the subject that endures through the rest of their lives. If you are one of these individuals, you can stay involved, at least tangentially, with archaeology in many ways.

Archaeology depends on informed amateur archaeologists (often called "avocationals"), who volunteer on excavations, in laboratories, and in museums. Many highly important contributions to archaeology come from amateur archaeologists, often members of local archaeological societies, who participate in digs and keep an eye out for new discoveries in their areas. There is a strong tradition of amateur scholarship in archaeology, especially in Europe, where some avocationals have become world authorities on specialized subjects such as ancient rabbit keeping or specific pottery forms—and they publish regularly in academic journals.

Archaeology could not function without volunteers, whether on Earthwatch-supported excavations or through quiet work behind the scenes cataloging artifacts or running lecture programs. If you have a serious interest in volunteering and pursuing archaeology on a regular basis as an amateur, there are many ways to become involved through local organizations such as colleges, museums, archaeological societies, and chapters of the Archaeological Institute of America. In these days of highly specialized research and professional scholarship, it is easy to say that there is no place for amateurs. This arrogant statement is nonsense and misses the point. Amateurs bring an extraordinary range of skills to archaeology. During my career, I have worked with, among others, an accountant (who straightened out my excavation books), an architect, a professional photographer and artist (who was a godsend in the field), a jeweler (who analyzed gold beads for me), and an expert on slash-and-burn agriculture (who had a passion for environmental history). Your talents are invaluable, and don't take no for an answer! I showed this passage to a colleague, who pointed out that some of his students have gone on to highly successful and lucrative careers in business. Their quiet philanthropy has endowed professorships, paid for excavations, and supported students. Enough said!

Many people develop an interest in the past that comes to the fore when they travel. Their background in archaeology, obtained as undergraduates, enables them to visit famous sites all over the world as informed observers and to enjoy the achievements of ancient peoples to the fullest (see Figure 15.1 on page 308). My files are full of postcards and letters from obscure places and well-known sites, like one mailed from Stonehenge: "Thank you for introducing me to archaeology," it reads. "I enjoyed Stonehenge so much more after taking your course." This postcard made my day, for archaeology cannot survive without the involvement and enthusiasm not just of professionals but of everyone interested in the past. We are all stewards of a priceless and finite resource, which is vanishing before our eyes.

Our Responsibilities to the Past

All of us, whether professional archaeologist, avocational field-worker, casually interested traveler, or basically disinterested citizen, share a common responsibility for the past. It is our collective cultural heritage, whether considering the Parthenon, the pyramids of Giza, *Cahokia,* or the tomb of Chinese emperor Shihuangdi. This past extends back deep into the Ice Age, for more than 2.5 million years, a precious legacy of cultural achievement that is unique to humanity and something that we must cherish and pass on to generations still unborn. The word *steward* is overused, but we are as much

Figure 15.1 Stonehenge, Wiltshire, England. A celebrated Stone Age and Bronze Age shrine that developed over many generations after 3000 B.C. and was used for more than 1,500 years.

stewards of the past as we are of the oceans, forests, and every part of the natural environment. Archaeology is different in one important respect: Once destroyed, its archives can never be reconstructed. They are gone forever. Professional archaeologists subscribe to strict and explicit ethics in their dealings with the past, but, in the final analysis, preserving the past for the future is the responsibility of us all.

As I have emphasized many times in these pages, the world's archaeological sites are under attack from many sources: industrial development, mining, and agriculture, as well as treasure hunters, collectors, and professional tomb robbers (see Figure 15.2 on page 309). The war in Iraq resulted in wholesale looting of archaeological sites and museums. Demand far exceeds the supply, so even modest antiquities fetch high prices in international markets. No government can hope to free the necessary funds to protect its antiquities adequately. And such countries as Egypt, Guatemala, and Mexico, with rich archaeological heritages, have almost overwhelming problems protecting even their well-known sites. As long as there is a demand for antiquities among collectors and we maintain our materialistic values about personal possessions, destruction of archaeological sites will continue unabated. Even the necessary legal controls to prevent destruction of archaeological sites are just barely in force in most parts of the world. Yet there is still hope, which stems from the enormous numbers of informed people who have gained an interest in archaeology from university and college courses or from chance encounters with archaeologists or the past. If sufficient numbers of laypeople can influence public behavior and attitudes toward archaeological sites and the morality of collecting, there is still hope that our descendants will have archaeological sites to study and enjoy.

I am very glad I became an archaeologist and that my passion for the past remains unabated after many years in the field, laboratory, and classroom. I have met many extraordinary people and been challenged by complex research problems that have taken my career in unexpected directions. But the moments I cherish most are those rare occasions when you stand on an archaeological site or among some deserted earthworks or weathered buildings, and the past suddenly comes to life. I am lucky to have experienced this many times: at Mesa Verde's Cliff Palace the day after the first snowstorm of winter, when icicles hung from the trees and I could imagine the smell of ancestral Pueblo wood smoke and the barking of dogs; on cloud-mantled earthworks in Britain where I could almost hear the cries of Roman legionaries advancing into battle; and on a coastal shell midden in southern California where I could imagine planked canoes landing on a fine summer evening. These moments come without warning and are deeply emotional, triggered by evocative sunsets, effects of cloud and light, or even by a chance thought, but they are utterly precious.

Figure 15.2 Two possibilities for the future of the past: *Top*: Archaeologists work on a stone-strewn hillside at the reputed site of Camelot, King Arthur's palace at *Cadbury,* southwestern England. *Bottom*: Pothunters at work do irreparable damage to a site. Compare this scene of devastation with the excavations illustrated in Chapter 7.

The past is personal to us, however dedicated as scientists we are, or however casually we visit a site. If the archaeological record vanishes, with all its great achievements and moments of brilliant success and long-forgotten tragedy, our successors will never be able to learn from the experience of our forebears or to enjoy the powerful and extraordinarily satisfying emotional pull of the past. We owe this legacy to our grandchildren.

A Simple Code of Archaeological Ethics for All

Is there a future for the past? Yes, but only if we all help, not only by influencing other people's attitudes toward archaeology but also by living by this simple code of ethics that applies to all of us, professional archaeologist or not:

- Treat all archaeological sites and artifacts as finite resources.
- Never dig an archaeological site.
- Never collect artifacts for yourself or buy and sell them for personal gain.
- Adhere to all federal, state, local, and tribal laws that affect the archaeological record.
- Report all accidental archaeological discoveries.
- Avoid disturbing any archaeological site, and respect the sanctity of all burial sites.

SUMMARY

1. Chapter 15 summarizes the essential qualities of someone seeking to become an archaeologist and lays out some of the career opportunities.
2. Career opportunities for professional archaeologists can be found in universities, colleges, museums, government service, and private businesses both in the United States and abroad.
3. Most archaeological jobs require at least an M.A. and many require a Ph.D.
4. Do not consider becoming a professional archaeologist unless you have an above-average academic record, some field experience, strong support from your professors, and a moral commitment not to collect artifacts for profit.
5. Even people who don't want to become professional archaeologists can gain digging experience by attending a field school or by digging overseas.
6. Archaeology gives you insight into the past and the potential for involvement as an informed layperson. It also enables you to enjoy the major archaeological sites of the world in a unique way and to aid in archaeologists' attempts to preserve the past.
7. All of us have ethical responsibilities to the past: not to collect artifacts; to report new finds; and to obey federal, state, and tribal laws that protect archaeological sites.
8. Unless we all take our responsibility to the past seriously, the past has no future.

SITES AND CULTURES MENTIONED IN THE TEXT

These brief descriptions give some background on prehistoric sites and cultures mentioned in the text; they are not meant to be precise definitions. Ask your instructor for more information and references if you need them. Some sites mentioned in passing are not included in the list if their significance is self-evident.

Abbeville, France A town in the Somme Valley famous for its nearby gravels containing Stone Age artifacts.

Abri Pataud, France Large rockshelter near the Vezère River in the Dordogne region of southwestern France, occupied by Neanderthal and Cro-Magnon hunter-gatherers between about 50,000 and 19,000 years ago.

Abu Hureyra, Syria One of the earliest farming villages in the world, where archaeologists documented the changeover from hunting and gathering to food production.

Abu Simbel, Egypt Ancient Egyptian temple erected by Ramses II in Nubia, c. 1250 B.C. The site with its seated figures of the pharaoh was moved to higher ground to prevent its flooding by Lake Nasser in 1968 at a cost of $40 million.

Abydos, Egypt Abydos in Upper Egypt was the ancient Egyptian gateway to the underworld and a sacred city. Egypt's earliest pharaohs were buried here before 3000 B.C.

Acheulian Widespread early Stone Age culture named after the town of St. Acheul in northern France. The Acheulian flourished in Africa, western Europe, and southern Asia from before a million years ago until less than 100,000 years before the present. The Acheulians made many types of stone artifacts, including multipurpose butchering hand axes and cleaving tools.

Adena, Ohio Distinctive burial cult and village culture in the Ohio Valley of the U.S. Midwest. It flourished between about 700 B.C. and A.D. 200 and was remarkable for its long-distance trading and distinctive burial cults expressed in large earthworks and mounds.

'Ain Ghazal, Jordan A farming settlement near Amman, dating to c. 7500 B.C., famous for its ancestral figurines.

Ali Kosh, Iran Early farming site on the Deh Luran plain in Iran, where evidence for cereal cultivation was found by flotation techniques. The site dates to as early as 7500 B.C.

Ancestral Pueblo (Anasazi) Pueblo peoples who flourished in the American Southwest in the late first and early second millennium A.D. Builders of large pueblos.

Angkor Wat, Cambodia A Hindu shrine built by the Khmer ruler Suryavarman II in A.D. 1117 as a representation of the Hindu universe.

Ashkelon, Israel An important Bronze Age city and city-state of the Philistines in the eleventh century B.C. Destroyed by the Babylonians in 605 B.C.

Avaris, Egypt Palace and trading site in Lower Egypt celebrated for its Minoan (Cretan) wall paintings—evidence of trade between Egypt and Crete in about 1500 B.C.

Ban Na Di, Thailand Trading settlement and farming village dating from about 1400 to 400 B.C., with a cemetery showing evidence for social ranking.

Benin, Nigeria West African state ruled from the city of Benin from before A.D. 1400 to modern times.

Cadbury, England Reputed site of King Arthur, of Round Table fame.

Cahokia, Illinois A prominent Mississippian ceremonial center that reached its apogee in about A.D. 1250.

Çatalhöyük, Turkey Early farming village in central Turkey, first occupied before 7000 B.C. and famous for its house shrines.

Cerén, El Salvador Maya village buried by an unexpected volcanic eruption in A.D. 684. The ash mantled the village so completely that entire household inventories, even crops, are preserved in the archaeological record.

Chaco Canyon, New Mexico Complex of Ancestral Pueblo structures including both pueblos and kivas dating to the late first millennium A.D.

Chavín, Peru A distinctive art style, and set of religious beliefs, which spread widely over highland and lowland Peru between 900 and 200 B.C.

Chavín de Huantar, Peru An important religious shrine of the first millennium B.C., center of the Chavín religious beliefs and cults.

Chichén Itzá, Mexico A major Maya ceremonial center in the northeastern Yucatán dating to about the ninth century A.D., when it came under Toltec influence from the highlands.

Clovis Paleo-Indian culture that flourished in North America, and perhaps further afield, about 11,000 B.C. and somewhat earlier.

Colonial Williamsburg, Virginia Reconstruction of Virginia's first capital city, carried out partly with the aid of archaeological research.

Copán, Honduras Classic Maya city, A.D. 435 to 900.

Danger Cave, Utah Long-visited desert cave in the western United States, occupied sporadically by Archaic foragers from c. 9000 B.C. to recent times.

Duch, Egypt Egyptian desert village of the first millennium B.C., famous for its cemeteries.

Easton Down, England Long barrow, built as a communal sepulcher by Stone Age farmers, c. 2500 B.C.

Epidauros, Greece Famed Classic Greek amphitheater first built in the fifth century B.C.

Eridu, Iraq Early city in the Mesopotamia delta that boasted of a major temple as early as 4000 B.C. One of the earliest cities in the world.

Flag Fen, England Late Bronze Age field system and ceremonial center in eastern England dating to c. 1100 B.C., famous for its wooden artifacts and timber posts and trackways.

Folsom Paleo-Indian culture that flourished on the North American Plains after 11,000 B.C.

Fort Mose, Florida The first free African-American community in North America, occupied from 1738 to 1763.

Galatea Bay, New Zealand Important shell midden site, about 500 years old, in New Zealand's North Island, famous for exemplary excavation methods and data recovery.

Garnsey, New Mexico Bison kill site dating to A.D. 1550, where hunters selected males for their higher fat content.

Giza, Egypt The pyramids at Giza were built in the desert near Cairo during Egypt's Old Kingdom, around 2550 B.C. The Great Pyramid is 481 feet (146.6 meters) high and covers 13.1 acres (5.3 hectares).

Grasshopper Pueblo, Arizona Important Pueblo site occupied in the fourteenth and fifteenth centuries A.D.

Grotte de Chauvet, France A spectacular painted cave in southeastern France, used between about 31,000 and 24,000 years ago.

Hadar, Ethiopia Region of northeastern Africa where numerous hominin discoveries have been made, including *Ardipithecus ramidus,* dating to about 4.5 million years ago.

Hadrian's Wall, England Frontier fortification wall built by the Emperor Hadrian between A.D. 122 and 130 to keep the Scots out of northern England and the northernmost Roman province.

Halieis, Greece Classical town of the fourth century B.C. famous for its olive oil.

Harappan civilization, Pakistan Urban civilization based in the Indus Valley that flourished from before 2500 to 1500 B.C.

Herculaneum, Italy Roman town destroyed by an eruption of Mount Vesuvius in A.D. 79.

Hissarlik, Turkey Site of Homeric Troy in northwestern Turkey, which was an important Bronze Age city during the second millennium B.C.

Hochdorf, Germany Iron Age burial mound of a chieftain interred in about 550 B.C., remarkable for its rich grave furniture.

Hogup Cave, Utah Dry cave in the Great Basin occupied from c. 9000 B.C. until recent times, famous for its excellent dry preservation of organic artifacts such as fiber sandals.

Hohokam, Arizona Southwestern cultural tradition that originated as early as 300 B.C. and lasted until A.D. 1500. The Hohokam people were farmers who occupied much of what is now Arizona. Their cultural heirs are the O'odham Indians of today.

Hopewell, Ohio Between 200 B.C. and A.D. 600, the "Hopewell Interaction Sphere" flourished in the Midwest. Hopewell religious cults and distinctive burial customs were associated with an art tradition that spread far and wide through long-distance trading connections.

Huaca del Sol, Peru A powerful capital of the Moche state on Peru's north coast, occupied c. A.D. 500 and extensively damaged by El Niños.

Jomon tradition, Japan Japanese cultural tradition dating from before 8000 B.C. until about 300 B.C., remarkable for its early manufacturing of pottery and complex hunter-gatherer culture.

Karnak, Egypt Site of the temple of the ancient Egyptian sun god Amun, which reached the height of its glory in the New Kingdom, c. 1500 B.C.

Kennewick, Washington Location of a Native American burial dated to more than 9,000 years ago, the subject of ongoing controversy.

Khorsabad, Iraq Palace of Assyrian King Sargon, eighth century B.C.

Kish, Iraq A city of the Sumerian civilization in southern Iraq, which was one of the first cities founded, in the fourth millennium B.C.

Klasies River Cave, South Africa Middle Stone Age cave, occupied c. 120,000 to 100,000 years ago, that yielded fossil and cultural evidence for very early modern humans.

Knossos, Crete Palace and shrine complex in northern Crete, which started life as a small village in about 6000 B.C. and became the major center of Minoan civilization, being finally abandoned in the late second millennium B.C.

Koobi Fora, Kenya Location on the eastern shores of Lake Turkana in northern Kenya, where early traces of human culture have been found, dating to more than 2.5 million years ago.

Koster, Illinois From before 7000 B.C. until less than 1,000 years ago, hunter-gatherers and later farmers settled at this location on the Illinois River to exploit the fertile river bottom. The site is unusual for its long stratigraphic sequence of Archaic and Woodland settlements and abundant food remains.

Kourion, Cyprus Small Roman port in southwestern Cyprus in the eastern Mediterranean overwhelmed by a great earthquake early on the morning of July 21, A.D. 365. Excavations at the village have revealed many details of a long-forgotten disaster.

Laetoli, Tanzania This East African site yielded the earliest hominin footprints, potassium-argon dated to more than 3.5 million years ago.

La Madeleine, France Late Ice Age rockshelter containing extensive, stratified Stone Age occupation dating back about 18,000 years. The type site of the Magdalenian culture, famous for its mobile and rock art.

Lascaux Cave, France Painted cave of the Magdalenian culture of southwestern France dating to about 15,000 years ago.

Lovelock Cave, Nevada Desert site in the far western United States, occupied as early as 7000 B.C. Located near a desert marsh, it has yielded minute details of prehistoric desert adaptations over a long period.

Maeshowe, Scotland Stone Age passage grave on the Orkney Islands, c. 3100 to 2900 B.C.

Maiden Castle, England A large Iron Age hill fort attacked and overrun by a Roman legion in A.D. 43. Site of classic excavations before World War II.

Marki, Cyprus A Bronze Age village dating to c. 2200 B.C.

Meer, Belgium A Mesolithic hunter-gatherer camp in a sandy clearing in northern Belgium, dating to c. 7600 B.C.

Mesa Verde, Colorado Deep canyon area famous for its pueblos, notably the Cliff Palace, which reached their heyday in the twelfth century A.D.

Mesoamerica That area of Central America where state-organized societies (civilizations) arose.

Minoan civilization, Crete Bronze Age civilization on Crete, c. 2000 to 1450 B.C., famous for its widespread trading activities.

Moche civilization Coastal state in northern coastal Peru, which reached its height after A.D. 400.

Moundville, Alabama A Mississippian ceremonial center that reached its apogee after A.D. 1100.

Mycenae, Greece Major palace of the Mycenaean civilization, c. 1500 B.C., famous for its royal graves and beehive tombs.

Neanderthal, Germany Cave that yielded the first Neanderthal skull (named after the site) in 1856.

Nelson's Bay, South Africa Late Stone Age coastal cave in southeastern Africa, occupied c. 5000 B.C.

Nimrud, Iraq Assyrian city, the biblical Calah.

Nineveh, Iraq Assyrian capital, famous for the palace of King Assurbanipal in the seventh century B.C.

Nippur, Iraq Sumerian city in southern Iraq, c. 2800 B.C., celebrated in archaeological circles for its clay tablet archives.

Olduvai Gorge, Tanzania Stratified lake beds with associated artifact scatters and kill sites, also early hominins, dating from slightly before 1.75 million years ago up to 100,000 B.P.

Olmec One of the earliest lowland Mexican state-organized societies, Olmec culture flourished from around 1500 B.C. to 500 B.C. Olmec people traded widely, had a distinctive art tradition that depicted human-like jaguars and both natural and supernatural beings, and developed many of the religious traditions that were to sustain the Maya and other Mesoamerican civilizations such as Teotihuacán.

Olsen-Chubbuck, Colorado An 8,000-year-old bison kill site on the North American plains that revealed many details of Paleo-Indian hunting and butchering techniques.

Olympia, Greece Site of the Olympic Games in the northern Peloponnese, c. 400 B.C.

Ozette, Washington Coastal settlement in Washington State occupied for at least 1,000 years by ancestors of the present-day Makah Indians. Ozette suffered disaster two centuries ago when houses were buried by mud slides, which preserved them in perfect condition for archaeologists to investigate in the 1970s.

Palenque, Mexico Classic Maya city and ceremonial center, which reached its height in the mid first millennium A.D.

Paracas, Peru A large cemetery complex on Peru's southern coast, where textiles are exceptionally well preserved in mummified burials dating to between 600 and 150 B.C.

Pecos, New Mexico Ancestral (Anasazi) pueblo in the southwest United States that was occupied for much of the past 2,000 years and provided the first stratigraphic sequence for Southwestern prehistory as a result of A. V. Kidder's excavations.

Petra, Jordan A trading city and camel caravan terminus built by the Nabateans and then controlled by the Romans in the early Christian era.

Pompeii, Italy Italian town destroyed by an eruption of Mt. Vesuvius in A.D. 79.

Pueblo Bonito, New Mexico Ancestral (Anasazi) pueblo first constructed about A.D. 850 and in its heyday in the twelfth century A.D.

Ring of Brodgar, Scotland Stone circle associated with Maeshowe and the Stones of Stenness, c. 2900 B.C.

San José Mogote, Mexico Farming village in the Valley of Oaxaca, which flourished after 1350 B.C. and contained four residential wards and a small shrine.

Schoningen, Germany A northern German hunting site that yielded 400,000-year-old wooden spears.

Shang civilization, China Early Chinese civilization that flourished from as early as 2700 B.C., when the Xia dynasty arose in the north. The Shang dynasty rose to power around 1766 B.C. and ruled until 1122 B.C. Its rulers occupied a series of capitals near the Yellow River, the most famous being Anyang, occupied around 1400 B.C.

Sipán, Peru Site of four spectacularly adorned warrior-priest graves of the Moche civilization, c. A.D. 400.

Skara Brae, Scotland Stone Age farming village on the Orkney Islands, occupied c. 3100 to 2500 B.C.

Snaketown, Arizona Major community of Hohokam people in southern Arizona, famous for its ball court and extensive trade with other regions. In its heyday during the early second millennium B.C.

Sounion, Greece A temple to the Greek sea god Poseidon dating to the fifth century B.C., sited on a headland as a conspicuous landmark for mariners.

Star Carr, England Postglacial hunting site in northeast England dating to about 9200 B.C., remarkable for the bone and wooden artifacts recovered from a small birch-bark platform at the edge of a small lake.

Stonehenge, England Stone circles in southern Britain that formed a sacred precinct as early as 2700 B.C. and remained in use until about 1600 B.C. Some authorities believe Stonehenge was an astronomical observatory, but this viewpoint is controversial.

Stones of Stenness, Scotland Stone circle on the Orkney Islands associated with Maeshowe mound, 3100 to 2900 B.C.

Tehuacán Valley, Mexico Valley in which evidence for a gradual shift from hunting and gathering to deliberate cultivation of squashes and other minor crops, then maize, has been documented. Tehuacán was occupied as early as 10,000 B.C., with maize agriculture appearing before 2700 B.C.

Telloh, Iraq Sumerian city where the civilization of that name was first recognized in the 1870s.

Tenochtitlán, Mexico Spectacular capital of the Aztec civilization in the Valley of Mexico, founded in A.D. 1325 and destroyed by Spanish conquistador Hernán Cortés in 1521.

Teotihuacán, Mexico A vast pre-Columbian city in highland Mexico that flourished from as early as 200 B.C. until it declined in around A.D. 750. Teotihuacán maintained extensive political and trade contacts with the Maya civilization of the Yucatán and is famed for its enormous public buildings and pyramids.

Tepe Yahya, Iran Important trading city on the Iranian Plateau, famous for its steatite markets in the third millennium B.C. Maintained trade connections with Mesopotamia and the Indus Valley.

Tikal, Guatemala Classic Maya city in the Guatemalan lowlands that reached its height in about A.D. 600.

Tiwanaku, Bolivia An important ceremonial center and state that flourished near Lake Titicaca in the Andean highlands in the first millennium A.D.

Tollund, Denmark Site of a bog corpse dating to the Danish Iron Age, c. 2,000 years ago. The man was strangled, apparently a sacrificial victim.

Tsoelike River Rockshelter, Lesotho A rockshelter famous for a painting of a fishing scene of people spearing their catch from boats or canoes. Date unknown, probably the last 1,000 years.

Ubar, Saudi Arabia Desert city of the first millennium A.D. Celebrated for its spice trading.

Uluburun, Turkey Spectacular Bronze Age shipwreck dating to 1305 B.C. with cargo from all over the eastern Mediterranean.

Ur, Iraq Biblical city in southern Iraq that grew from a tiny farming hamlet founded as early as 4700 B.C., known for its Early Dynastic Sumerian burials, where a ruler's entire retinue committed institutionalized suicide.

Uxmal, Mexico Late Classic Maya city and ceremonial center in the northern Yucatán.

Valley of the Kings, Egypt Narrow, dry valley where Egypt's New Kingdom pharaohs, including Tutankhamun, were buried.

Wroxeter, England Roman city in west-central England dating to the first few centuries after Christ.

GLOSSARY OF TECHNICAL TERMS

This glossary gives informal definitions of key words and ideas in the text. It is not a comprehensive dictionary of archaeology. Jargon is kept to a minimum, but a few technical expressions are inevitable. Terms such as *adaptation* and *mutation,* which are common in contexts other than archaeology, are not listed. A good dictionary will clarify these and other such words.

absolute chronology Dating in calendar years before the present.

accelerator mass spectrometry (AMS) Method of radiocarbon dating that counts actual 14C atoms. Requires much smaller samples for precise dates.

activity area Patterning of artifacts in a site indicating that a specific activity, such as stone toolmaking, took place.

agency The assumption that a person or group of people is responsible for cultural change.

analogy Process of reasoning whereby two entities that share some similarities are assumed to share many others.

analysis Stage of archaeological research that involves describing and classifying artifactual and nonartifactual data.

anthropology Study of humanity in the widest possible sense. Anthropology studies humanity from the earliest times up to the present, and it includes cultural and physical anthropology and archaeology.

antiquarian Someone interested in the past who collects and digs up antiquities unscientifically, in contrast to the scientific archaeologist.

archaeobotanist An archaeologist who studies ancient plant remains.

archaeological context See *context.*

archaeological data Material recognized as significant evidence by the archaeologist and collected and recorded as part of the research. The four main classes of archaeological data are artifacts, features, structures, and food remains.

archaeological record Material remains of the past, archaeological sites, artifacts, food remains, and so on, which form the surviving database for the study of the human past.

archaeological survey Systematic attempts to locate, identify, and record the distribution of archaeological sites on the ground and against the natural geographic and environmental background.

archaeological unit Arbitrary unit of classification set up by archaeologists to conveniently separate in time and space one grouping of artifacts from another.

archaeologist Someone who studies the past using scientific methods, with the motive of recording and interpreting ancient cultures rather than collecting artifacts for profit or display.

archaeology Special form of anthropology that uses material remains to study extinct human societies. The objectives of archaeology are to construct culture history, reconstruct past lifeways, and study cultural process.

area excavation Excavation of a large horizontal area, usually used to uncover houses and prehistoric settlement patterns. See *horizontal excavation.*

artifact Any object manufactured or modified by human beings.

assemblage All the artifacts found at a site, including the sum of all subassemblages at the site.

association Relationship between an artifact and other archaeological finds and a site level or other artifact, structure, or feature in the site.

Assyriologists Scholars who study Assyrian civilization.

attribute Well-defined feature of an artifact that cannot be further subdivided. Archaeologists identify types of attributes, including form, style, and technology, in order to classify and interpret artifacts.

attritional age profile Distribution of ages in an animal population that results from selective hunting or predation.

band Simple form of human social organization that flourished for most of prehistory. Bands consist of a family or a series of families, usually ranging from 20 to 50 people.

biblical archaeologist A student of the archaeology of the Bible, specializing in southwestern Asia.

blade In stone technology, a term applied to punch-struck flakes, usually removed from a cylindrical core. Often characteristic of prehistoric societies after 35,000 years ago.

cambium Viscid substance under the bark of trees, in which the annual growth of wood and bark takes place.

catastrophic age profile Distribution of ages in an animal population as a result of death by natural causes.

characterization Methods of identifying the sources of prehistoric artifacts, especially those in clay, metal, and stone.

chiefdom Form of social organization more complex than a tribal society that has evolved some form of leadership structure and some mechanisms for distributing goods and services throughout the society. The chief who heads such a society and the specialists who work for the chief are supported by the voluntary contributions of the people.

chronological types Types defined by form that are time markers.

chronometric chronology Dating in years before the present as statements of statistical probability that yield date ranges. Principal methods are potassium-argon and radiocarbon dating.

civilization See *state-organized society.*

Classical archaeologist A student of the Classical civilizations of Greece and Rome.

classification Ordering of archaeological data into groups and classes, using various ordering systems.

cluster sampling Sampling using clusters of elements.

cognitive archaeology See *cognitive-processual archaeology.*

cognitive-processual archaeology Theoretical approach to archaeology that combines processual approaches with other data to study religious beliefs and other intangibles.

community In archaeology, the tangible remains of the activities of the maximum number of people who together occupy a settlement at any one period.

compliance process In CRM, the process of ensuring that legal requirements surrounding archaeological resources are fulfilled.

component Association of all the artifacts from one occupation level at a site.

conchoidal fracture Type of fracture characteristic of crystalline rocks used for ancient stone tool manufacture.

conservation archaeology See *Cultural Resource Management.*

context Position of an archaeological find in time and space, established by measuring and assessing its associations, matrix, and provenance. The assessment includes study of what has happened to the find since it was buried in the ground.

coprolite Excrement that is preserved by desiccation or fossilization.

core In archaeology, a lump of stone from which human-struck flakes have been removed.

crop mark Differential growth in crops and vegetational cover that reveals from the air the outlines of archaeological sites.

cross-dating Dating of sites by objects of known age, or artifact association of known age.

cultural anthropology Aspect of anthropology focusing on cultural facets of human societies. A term widely used in the United States.

cultural ecology Study of the dynamic interactions between human societies and their environments. Under this approach, culture is the primary adaptive mechanism used by human societies.

cultural process Deductive approach to archaeological research that is designed to study the changes and interactions in cultural systems and the processes by which human cultures change throughout time. Processual archaeologists use both descriptive and explanatory models.

Cultural Resource Management (CRM) Conservation and management of archaeological sites and artifacts as a means of protecting the past.

cultural system Perspective on culture that thinks of culture and its environment as a number of linked systems in which change occurs through a series of minor linked variations in one or more of these systems.

culture Theoretical concept used by archaeologists and anthropologists to describe humankind's external means of adapting to the natural environment. Human culture is a set of designs for living that help mold our responses to different situations. A "culture" in archaeology is an arbitrary unit meaning similar assemblages of artifacts found at several sites, defined in a precise context of time and space.

culture history Approach to archaeology assuming that artifacts can be used to build up a generalized picture of human culture and descriptive models in time and space, and that these can be interpreted.

curation The conservation, management, and storage of archaeological data.

data acquisition The process of acquiring archaeological data from excavation, survey, or laboratory analysis.

dendrochronology Tree-ring chronology.

descriptive types Types based on the physical or external properties of an artifact.

diffusion (diffusionism) Spread of a culture trait from one area to another via contact between people.

direct historical approach Archaeological technique of working backward in time from historic sites of known age into earlier times.

ecofact Object not modified by human manufacture brought into a site (e.g., an unworked pebble brought into an early human occupation site).

ecosystem Environmental system maintained by the regulation of vertical food chains and patterns of energy flow.

Egyptologist An archaeologist specializing in the archaeology of ancient Egypt.

electromagnetic survey Subsurface detection method that measures conductivity of the soil to aid in locating buried features.

electronic spin resonance (ESR) A dating method that measures radiation-induced defects or the density of trapped electrons within bone or shell.

element sampling Sampling that uses an arbitrary grid system.

epiphysis Articular end of a long bone, which fuses at adulthood.

ethnoarchaeology Living archaeology, a form of ethnography that deals mainly with material remains. Archaeologists carry out living archaeology to document the relationships between human behavior and the patterns of artifacts and food remains in the archaeological record.

ethnographer An anthropologist who studies the culture, technology, and economy of human societies.

ethnographic analogy Use of analogies from living societies and cultures to interpret those from the past.

ethnologist An anthropologist who engages in the comparative study of human cultures.

excavation Digging of archaeological sites, removal of the matrix, and observance of the provenance and context of the finds therein, and the recording of them in a three-dimensional way.

exchange system System for exchanging goods and services between individuals and communities.

experimental archaeology Use of carefully controlled modern experiments to provide data to aid in interpretation of the archaeological record.

feature Artifact, such as a house or storage pit, that cannot be removed from a site; normally, it is only recorded.

feces Excrement.

feedback A concept in archaeological applications of systems theory reflecting the continually changing relationship between cultural variables and their environment.

fission track dating Dates minerals containing uranium by measuring the fission tracks in the material, damage caused by particle fragmentation.

flotation In archaeology, recovering plant remains by using water to separate seeds from their surrounding deposit.

functional type Type based on cultural use or function rather than on outward form or chronological position.

general systems theory The notion that any organism or organization can be studied as a system broken down into many interacting subsystems, or parts; sometimes called cybernetics.

geoarchaeology Study of archaeology using the methods and concepts of the earth sciences.

Geographic Information Systems (GIS) Computer-generated mapping systems that allow archaeologists to plot and analyze site distributions against environmental and other background data derived from remote sensing, digitized maps, and other sources.

ground-penetrating radar See *subsurface (ground-penetrating) radar.*

half-life Time required for one half of a radioactive isotope to decay into a stable element. Used as a basis for radiocarbon and other dating methods.

hermeneutics The art of interpretation.

historical archaeology Study of archaeological sites in conjunction with historical records. It is sometimes called historic sites archaeology, or text-aided archaeology.

history Study of the past through written records.

Holocene From the Greek word *holos,* meaning "recent," and covering geological time since the end of the Ice Age 15,000 years ago.

horizon Widely distributed set of culture traits and artifact assemblages whose distribution and chronology allow one to assume that they spread rapidly. Horizons are often formed of artifacts that were associated with widespread, distinctive religious beliefs.

horizontal (area) excavation Archaeological excavation designed to uncover large areas of a site, especially settlement layouts.

household group Arbitrary archaeological unit defining artifact patterns reflecting the activities that take place around a house and assumed to belong to one household.

human culture See *culture.*

industrial archaeologist An archaeologist who studies artifacts, buildings, and technology of the Industrial Revolution.

industry All the particular artifacts made of different materials found at a site that were made at the same time by the same population.

inevitable variation The notion that cultures change and vary with time, cumulatively. The reasons for these changes are little understood.

inorganic materials Material objects that are not part of the animal or vegetable kingdom.

interpretation Stage in research at which the results of archaeological analyses are synthesized and we attempt to explain their meaning.

invention Creation or evolution of a new idea.

landscape A perception of an environment created by humans.

landscape of memory A perception of landscape retained by people during their lifetimes, including memories of earlier perceptions.

LIDAR Light detection and ranging based on laser altimetry, an optical equivalent of radar that measures height with a laser range finder.

linguistic anthropology The study of human languages and culture.

lithic analysis The study of stone technology and artifacts.

magnetometer survey Measures magnetic fields on archaeological sites, producing subsurface contour maps of buried features.

market Place where people congregate to buy, sell, and exchange goods and commodities, usually with relatively stable prices.

Matuyama-Brunhes event Moment 780,000 years ago when the earth's magnetic polarity reversed; named after the two geologists who identified it.

Mayanists Scholars who study ancient Maya civilization.

Mesolithic ("Middle Stone Age") From Greek *mesos,* middle; rather dated term sometimes applied by Old World archaeologists to the period of transition between the Paleolithic and Neolithic eras. No precise economic or technological definition has ever been formulated.

mica Mineral that occurs in a glittering, scaly form; widely prized for ornament.

microlith From Greek: small stone; a distinctive form of small tool, often an arrow barb, used by Mesolithic peoples in the Old World.

midden In archaeology, an accumulation of food remains and other occupation debris. Often used to describe accumulations of shells and mollusks, hence "shell midden."

middle-range theory A way of seeking accurate means for identifying and measuring specified properties of past cultural systems.

migration Movements of entire societies that decide to change their own sphere of influence.

mitigation The process of minimizing damage to cultural resources such as archaeological sites as part of the management of the archaeological record.

multilinear cultural evolution Theory of cultural evolution that sees each human culture evolving in its own way by adaptation to diverse environments. Sometimes divided into four broad evolutionary stages of social organization (band, tribe, chiefdom, and state-organized society).

natural type Archaeological type coinciding with an actual category recognized by the original toolmaker.

neutron activation analysis The study of trace element clusters in clay vessels by activating neutrons.

noncultural processes Events and processes of the natural environment that impact on the archaeological record.

normative view View of human culture arguing that one can identify the abstract rules regulating a particular culture; a commonly used basis for studying archaeological cultures throughout time.

obsidian Volcanic glass.

obsidian hydration A dating method that measures the build-up of hydration layers on obsidian fragments.

Oldowan tradition The earliest stoneworking tradition, dating from about 2.6 million to 2 million years ago. Named after Olduvai Gorge.

optical stimulated luminescence (OSL) A form of thermoluminesence dating that uses laser technology to date the emissions from quartz and feldspar grains in archaeological sites.

oral tradition Knowledge, in the form of histories, practical knowledge, and traditions and values, passed orally from one person to another.

organic materials Materials such as bone, wood, horn, or hide that were once living organisms.

paleoanthropology The multidisciplinary study of archaic humans and their behavior.

paleobotanist One who studies prehistoric botany.

palynology (pollen analysis) The study of ancient vegetation using minute pollen spores.

paste In ceramic studies, the type of clay used to fabricate a vessel.

patterns of discard Remains left for investigation after natural destructive forces have affected artifacts and food remains abandoned by their original users.

permafrost Permanently frozen subsoil.

petrological analysis Sourcing of toolmaking stone using trace elements and other characteristics of the rock. Widely used to trace the extent of ax trade in Stone Age Europe.

phase Archaeological unit defined by characteristic groupings of culture traits that can be identified precisely in time and space. It lasts for a relatively short time and is found at one or more sites in a locality or region. Its culture traits are clear enough to distinguish it from other phases.

physical anthropology Basically, biological anthropology, which includes the study of fossil human beings, genetics, primates, and blood groups.

Pleistocene The last major geological epoch, extending from about 2.5 million years ago until about 13,000 B.C. It is sometimes called the Quaternary, or the Great Ice Age.

postprocessual archaeology Theoretical approaches to archaeology that are critical of processual archaeology and emphasize social factors in human societies.

potassium-argon dating Absolute dating technique based on the decay rate of potassium 40K, which becomes 40Ar.

potsherd A fragment of a clay vessel.

prehistoric archaeologists (prehistorians) Archaeologists who study the prehistory of humankind.

prehistory Millennia of human history preceding written records. Prehistorians study prehistoric archaeology.

prestate society Small-scale society based on the community, band, or village.

primary context An undisturbed association, matrix, and provenience.

probabilistic sampling Means of relating small data samples in mathematical ways to much larger populations.

process See *cultural process.*

processual archaeology An approach to archaeology that uses deductive research methodology—research design, and the scientific method to analyze conditions of cultural change.

public archaeology Archaeological education to inform the general public about archaeology and the past.

Quaternary See *Pleistocene.*

radiocarbon dating Absolute dating method based on measuring the decay rate of the carbon isotope carbon 14 to stable nitrogen. The resulting dates are calibrated with tree-ring chronologies, from radiocarbon ages into dates in calendar years.

random sampling Sampling method using random choice of samples to obtain unbiased samples.

reciprocity In archaeology, the exchange of goods between two parties, implying obligation to give a gift in exchange.

redistribution Dispersal of trade goods from a central place throughout a society, a complex process that was a critical part of the evolution of civilization.

reductive technology Technology in which an artisan acquires material, then shapes it by removing flakes or other fragments until it is shaped to the finished product. Normally applied to stone technology.

refitting (retrofitting) Reassembling of flaked stone waste fragments and cores to reconstruct ancient lithic technologies.

relative chronology Time scale developed by the law of superposition or artifact ordering.

remote sensing Reconnaissance and site survey methods using such devices as aerial photography to detect subsurface features and sites.

research design Carefully formulated and systematic plan for executing archaeological research.

resistivity survey Measurement of differences in electrical conductivity in soils, used to detect buried features such as walls and ditches.

sampling Science of assessing the reliability of data through the use of probability theory.

satellite sensor imagery Method of recording sites from the air using infrared radiation that is beyond the practical spectral response of photographic film. Useful for tracing prehistoric agricultural systems that have disturbed the topsoil over wide areas.

secondary context A context of an archaeological find that has been disturbed by subsequent human activity or natural phenomena.

Section 106 process See *compliance process.*

seriation techniques Methods used to place artifacts in chronological order; artifacts closely similar in form or style are placed close to one another.

settlement archaeology Study of ancient settlements and settlement distributions in the context of their landscape.

settlement pattern Distribution of human settlement on the landscape and within archaeological communities.

shovel pits Test pits, typically laid out in lines, excavated with a few shovel strokes. Used to define the limits of shallow sites.

site Any place where objects, features, or ecofacts manufactured or modified by human beings are found. A site can range from a living site to a quarry site, and it can be defined in functional and other ways.

site catchment analysis Inventorying natural resources within a given distance of a site.

site-formation processes The processes, natural and humanly caused, that modify the material remains of the past in the ground after their abandonment.

social anthropologist Anthropologists who study social organization.

sourcing See *characterization.*

spatial analysis Analysis of spatial relationships in the archaeological record.

spectrographic analysis Chemical analysis that involves passing the light from a number of trace elements through a prism or diffraction grating that spreads out the wavelengths in a spectrum. This enables researchers to separate the emissions and identify different trace elements. A useful approach for studying metal objects and obsidian artifacts.

stakeholder An individual or group with a vested interest in an archaeological site or finds.

state-organized society Preindustrial civilization marked by cities, centralized government, and social stratification and large-scale social complexity. Often called a *civilization.*

stewardship The process of managing the archaeological record for future generations, in perpetuity.

stratified sampling Probabilistic sampling technique used to cluster and isolate sample units when regular spacing is inappropriate for cultural reasons.

stratigraphy Observation of the superimposed layers in an archaeological site.

stratum Single-deposited or cultural level.

stylistic type Type based on stylistic distinctions.

subassemblage Association of artifacts denoting a particular form of prehistoric activity practiced by a group of people.

subsistence How people acquire food and make their living.

subsurface (ground-penetrating) radar Radar sets used to detect subsurface features on archaeological sites without excavation.

subtractive technology See *reductive technology.*

superposition The principle, borrowed from geology, that states that a stratigraphic layer overlying another is younger than the one below it.

surface collection Collection of archaeological finds from sites, with the objective of gathering representative samples of artifacts from the surface. Surface survey also establishes the types of activity on the site, locates major structures, and gathers information on the most densely occupied areas of the site that could be most productive for total or sample excavation.

taphonomy Study of the processes by which animal bones and other fossil remains are transformed after deposition.

taxonomy Ordered set of operations that results in the subdividing of objects into ordered classifications.

tell Arabic word for an occupation mound; a term referring to archaeological sites of this type in the Near East.

temper In ceramic studies, the fine, coarse elements such as sand or ground-up shell, added to clay to help it bind during firing.

test pit Excavation unit used to sample or probe a site before large-scale excavation or to check surface surveys.

theory In archaeology, a body of theoretical concepts that provides both a framework and a means for archaeologists to look beyond the facts and the material objects for explanations of events that took place in prehistory.

thermoluminescence (TL) Chronometric dating method that measures the amount of light energy released by a baked clay object when heated rapidly. Gives an indication of the time elapsed since the object was last heated.

Three-Age System Technological subdivision of the prehistoric past developed for Old World prehistory in 1816.

total data station An electronic surveying device used for surveying sites and excavations.

trace element analysis Means of identifying the sources of artifacts and raw materials using x-ray spectrometry and other techniques that identify distinctive trace elements in stones and minerals. Trace element analysis is used to study the sources of obsidian and other materials traded over long distances.

tradition Persistent technological or cultural patterns identified by characteristic artifact forms. These persistent forms outlast a single phase and can occur over a wide area.

transect In archaeology, a corridor of statistically selected landscape intensively examined during field survey.

tribe A larger group of bands unified by kinship and governed by a council of representatives from the bands or kin groups within it.

type In archaeology, a grouping of artifacts created for comparison with other groups. This grouping may or may not coincide with the actual tool types designed by the original manufacturers.

typology Classification of types.

underwater archaeology Study of archaeological sites and shipwrecks beneath the surface of the water.

uniformitarianism Doctrine that states the earth was formed by the same natural geological processes operating today.

unilinear cultural evolution Late-nineteenth-century evolutionary theory envisaging all human societies as evolving along one track of cultural evolution, from simple hunting and gathering to literate civilization.

uranium series dating A dating method that measures the steady decay of uranium into other elements in formations made up of calcium carbonates, such as limestone.

vertical excavation Excavation undertaken to establish a chronological sequence, normally covering a limited area.

zooarchaeology Study of animal remains in archaeology.

GUIDE TO FURTHER READING

The technical literature of archaeology is immense and proliferating daily, to the point that no one, least of all this author, can possibly keep up with it all. Here, I can guide you to no more than a few key references on each of the major topics covered in this book. For more detailed information, consult one of the major summaries listed here or ask your instructor.

General Summaries

Several major college texts provide a comprehensive background on the method and theory of prehistoric archaeology. This text is a much shortened version of Brian Fagan, *In the Beginning,* 12th ed. (Upper Saddle River, NJ: Prentice Hall, 2009) and the first half of *Ancient Lives,* 3rd ed. (Upper Saddle River, NJ: Prentice Hall, 2007). The most comprehensive survey of archaeological methods available is Colin Renfrew and Paul Bahn, *Archaeology: Theories, Methods, and Practice,* 4th ed. (New York: Thames and Hudson, 2004). The major developments of world prehistory are described in my *People of the Earth,* 12th ed. (Upper Saddle River, NJ: Prentice Hall, 2007), and in my *World Prehistory: A Brief Introduction,* 7th ed. (Upper Saddle River, NJ: Prentice Hall, 2007). Another excellent account is Douglas Price and Gary Feinman, *Images of the Past* (New York: McGraw Hill, 2006).

Special Fields of Archaeology

For historical archaeology, James Deetz, *In Small Things Forgotten,* 2nd ed. (New York: Natural History Press, 1996), is a minor classic. Charles Orser, *Historical Archaeology* (Upper Saddle River, NJ: Prentice Hall, 2004), and Barbara Little, *Historical Archaeology* (Walnut Creek, CA: Left Coast Press, 2006) are basic texts. Classical archaeology is summarized in Simon Hornblower and Anthony Spawforth, eds., *The Oxford Classical Dictionary,* 3rd ed. (New York: Oxford University Press, 1996). For biblical archaeology, see T. E. Levy, ed., *The Archaeology of Society in the Holy Land* (New York: Facts on File, 1995). Underwater archaeology is covered by George Bass, *Archaeology Underwater* (New York: Praeger, 1966), and by the same author's magnificent *A History of Seafaring Based on Underwater Archaeology* (London: Thames and Hudson, 1972) and *Ships and Shipwrecks of the Americas* (London: Thames and Hudson, 1988). For Cultural Resource Management, see Thomas W. Newmann and Robert M. Sanford, *Cultural Resources Archaeology* (Walnut Creek, CA: AltaMira Press, 2001). A wide-ranging series of essays on archaeological method and theory appear in Herbert D. G. Maschner and Christopher Chippindale, eds. *Handbook of Archaeological Methods.* 2 vols. (Lanham, MD: AltaMira Press, 2005).

Atlases and Encyclopedias

A flood of reference books on archaeology has appeared in recent years, few of them comprehensive, and most of them far from authoritative. The best atlas for the general reader is still Chris Scarre, ed., *Past Worlds: The Times Atlas of Archaeology* (London: Times Books, 1988). *The Oxford Companion to Archaeology* (New York: Oxford University Press, 1996) is a comprehensive guide to the field on a global scale and tells you all you want to know about archaeology, and perhaps some things you don't.

Major Archaeological Journals

There are dozens of international, national, and local archaeological journals. Among those carrying occasional popular articles on archaeology are *Discover, National Geographic, Natural History, Smithsonian,* and *Scientific American. Archaeology* is a well-illustrated magazine for enthusiasts. *Current World Archaeology* is a British magazine that is rapidly acquiring an international readership. *Antiquity, the Journal of World Prehistory* and *World Archaeology* carry articles of wide interest to serious archaeologists. American archaeologists rely heavily on *American Antiquity* and *Latin American Antiquity,* the journals of the Society for American Archaeology. *American Anthropologist* and *Current Anthropology* sometimes carry archaeological pieces, and Old World archaeologists publish in *Nature* and the *Proceedings of the Prehistoric Society.* More specialized archaeological journals abound, among them the *Journal of Anthropological Archaeology* and the *Journal of Archaeological Science and Geoarchaeology. The Journal of Field Archaeology* is of high technical value and carries regular articles on looting issues.

Web Sites

The World Wide Web is becoming a preferred medium of communication for archaeologists, as for everyone else. This is a confusing universe for those unfamiliar with the Internet, especially because so much is changing all the time. However, the major Web sites are here to stay and offer links to other important locations. Please realize that Web pages and addresses change frequently, so this information may already be out of date. Many departments of anthropology and archaeology have Web sites, which you can access through ArchNet. Everything operates on Uniform Resource Locators (URLs), some of which we list here. A good search engine like Google.com is excellent for finding sites, new discoveries, and departments.The Virtual Library for archaeology worldwide is ArchNet: http://archnet.asu.edu. This is both geographically and subject-matter based, covering everything from the archaeology of

Australia to method and theory and site tours. There are also listings of academic departments, museums, and other archaeological organizations, even of journals. ArchNet is an extraordinary resource, which does not claim to be comprehensive but covers a huge range of topics. ArchNet and ARGE (Archaeological Resource Guide for Europe) have links to virtually any kind of archaeology you are looking for. For more information, please consult this book's Web site. And you can contact the author at brian@brianfagan.com if you have a question.

Chapter 1: Fossils, Cities, and Civilizations

Beyond the general summaries mentioned, the history of archaeology is easily accessible. Paul Bahn, ed., The *Cambridge Illustrated History of Archaeology* (Cambridge, England: Cambridge University Press, 1997), is a lavishly illustrated global summary of the subject. Brian Fagan, *A Brief History of Archaeology* (Upper Saddle River, NJ: Prentice Hall, 2005), is just that, for beginning students. Gordon Willey and Jeremy Sabloff, *A History of American Archaeology,* 2nd ed. (New York: W. H. Freeman, 1990), is widely quoted. Bruce Trigger's *A History of Archaeological Thought*, 2nd ed. (Cambridge, England: Cambridge University Press, 2006) is the definitive work on the subject. For firsthand accounts of major discoveries, see Brian Fagan, ed., *Eyewitness to Discovery* (New York: Oxford University Press, 1996). Marilyn Zeder, *The American Archaeologist: A Profile* (Walnut Creek, CA: Altamira Press, 1998) offers an authoritative portrait of an academic and professional community. Alternative archaeologies are discussed in Joe Watkins, *Indigenous Archaeology: American Indian Values and Scientific Practice* (Walnut Creek: AltaMira Press, 2001) and Roger C. Echo-Hawk, "Ancient History in the New World: Integrating Oral Traditions and the Archaeological Record," *American Antiquity* 65 (2) (2000): 267–290.

Chapter 2: Introducing Archaeology and Prehistory

James Deetz, *Invitation to Archaeology* (Garden City, NY: Natural History Press, 1967), is a gem of an essay on archaeology and covers many of the points in this chapter. So does Grahame Clark, *Archaeology and Society* (New York: Barnes and Noble, 1965)—an old account dealing with the political uses of archaeology that has never been bettered. Gordon Willey and Philip Phillips, *Method and Theory in American Archaeology* (Chicago: University of Chicago Press, 1958), is a standard work. Kenneth L. Feder, *Frauds, Myths, and Mysteries,* 5th ed. (Mountain View, CA: Mayfield, 2005), is a survey of pseudoarchaeology. Rose Macaulay, *The Pleasure of Ruins* (London: Thames and Hudson, 1959), is a delight for tourists. Massimo Pallotino, *The Meaning of Archaeology* (New York: Abrams, 1968), is a thoughtful account of the issues raised in this chapter. Karl Meyer, *The Plundered Past,* 2nd ed. (New York: Athenaeum, 1993), is a popular account of the international antiquities trade that makes for sobering reading. Things are even worse today. Regrettably, there is little modern writing on the role of archaeology in today's world. We have become too specialized. On world prehistory, see previously recommended books.

Chapter 3: Culture and Context

Few archaeologists have dared to write a summary of the controversial issues covered in this chapter. Gordon Willey and Philip Phillips, *Method and Theory in American Archaeology* (Chicago: University of Chicago Press, 1958), is fundamental. So is V. Gordon Childe's insightful *Piecing Together the Past* (London: Routledge and Kegan Paul, 1956), an old book, but right on the money in many respects. R. L. Lyman and R. C. Dunnell, *The Rise and Fall of Culture History* (New York: Plenum, 1997), is a recent assessment of the history of this approach. See also Bruce D. Trigger, *A History of Archaeological Thought,* 2nd ed. (Cambridge, England: Cambridge University Press, 2006).

Chapter 4: Explaining the Past

The literature is enormous and sometimes acrimonious. Two good starting points are Bruce D. Trigger, *A History of Archaeological Thought*, 2nd ed. (Cambridge, England: Cambridge University Press, 2006), and Lewis Binford's *In Pursuit of the Past,* rev. ed. (Berkeley: University of California Press, 2002). Also, P. J. Watson, Steven A. LeBlanc, and C. L. Redman, *Archaeological Explanation* (New York: Columbia University Press, 1984). Postprocessual archaeology has generated a profuse literature, critiqued and surveyed by Matthew Johnson, *Archaeological Theory: An Introduction* (Oxford: Blackwell, 1999). A series of essays on cognitive-processual archaeology appears in Colin Renfrew and others, "What Is Cognitive Archaeology?" *Cambridge Archaeological Journal* 3 (2) (1993): 247–270. A useful introduction to general anthropological theory is Robert Layton, *An Introduction to Theory in Anthropology* (Cambridge, England: Cambridge University Press, 1997). For a contemporary view, see Ian Hodder, *The Archaeological Process: An Introduction* (Oxford: Blackwell, 1999). An excellent anthology of writings about archaeological theory over the past 20 years is Robert Preucel and Ian Hodder, eds., *Contemporary Archaeology in Theory: A Reader* (Oxford, England: Blackwell, 1996). For a dispassionate analysis of current theoretical approaches, see Michele Hegmon, "Setting Theoretical Egos Aside: Issues and

Theory in North American Archaeology," *American Antiquity* 68 (2) (2003): 213–243. Also Bruce Trigger, "Archaeological Theory: The Big Picture," Grace Shallit Memorial Lecture (Provo, UT: Brigham Young University, 2003).

Chapter 5: Space and Time

Thomas Hester, Harry J. Shafer, and Kenneth L. Feder, *Field Methods in Archaeology,* 7th ed. (Mountain View, CA: Mayfield, 1997), contains invaluable essays on stratigraphy and dating. No one has yet rivaled Sir Mortimer Wheeler's classic description of stratigraphy in his *Archaeology from the Earth* (Oxford: Clarendon Press, 1954). E. C. Harris and M. R. Brown III, *Principles of Archaeological Stratigraphy,* 2nd ed. (New York: Academic Press, 1989), offer a more technical analysis. Dating techniques are mainly described in journal articles, but M. J. Aitken, *Science-Based Dating in Archaeology* (New York: Longman, 1990), is informative. R. E. Taylor, *Radiocarbon Dating: An Archaeological Perspective* (Orlando, FL: Academic Press, 1987), is an excellent account. A. G. Wintle's paper "Archaeologically Relevant Dating Techniques for the Next Century," *Journal of Archaeological Science* 23 (1996): 123–138, is up-to-date, technical, and invaluable. On the topic of space, once again, V. Gordon Childe, *Piecing Together the Past* (London: Routledge and Kegan Paul, 1956), is one of the few general accounts. Kent V. Flannery, ed., *The Early Mesoamerican Village* (New York: Academic Press, 1976), covers some key concepts, but is better read in the context of Chapter 12. For the law of association, read John Rowe's classic paper, "Worsaae's Law and the Use of Grave Lots for Archaeological Dating," *American Antiquity* 28 (2) (1962): 129–137. Much of the literature for this chapter is scattered in periodicals: Consult an expert.

Chapter 6: They Sought It Here, They Sought It There

Here we introduce a wonderful set of small paperbacks that summarize the process of archaeological research. Larry J. Zimmerman and William Green, *Archaeologist's Toolkit* (Walnut Creek, CA: AltaMira Press, 2003), is a set of seven short volumes that cover the essentials of doing archaeology in the field and laboratory. The volumes in the series are written by real dirt archaeologists of considerable experience. Each volume has a strong ethics orientation and is concerned as much with CRM archaeology as it is with academic research. Any serious student should buy the whole series. Stephen L. Black and Kevin Jolly, *Archaeology by Design,* the first volume in the series, offers a wonderful summary of the basics of research design. The second volume, James M. Collins and Brian Leigh Molyneaux, *Archaeological Survey,* does the same for survey, with a strong emphasis on nonintrusive methods.

Thomas Hester, Harry J. Shafer, and Kenneth L. Feder, *Field Methods in Archaeology,* 7th ed. (New York: McGraw Hill, 1997), contains invaluable essays on aspects of survey and excavation, including stratigraphy and dating. Any serious student will likely encounter this book at some stage in his or her career. More specialized works include E. B. Banning, *Archaeological Survey* (Norwell, MA: Kluwer, 2002), and Irwin Scollar and others, *Archaeological Prospecting and Remote Sensing* (Cambridge, England: Cambridge University Press, 1990). For sampling, see Clive Orton, *Sampling in Archaeology* (Cambridge, England: Cambridge University Press, 2000). H. D. G. Maschner, ed., *New Methods, Old Problems: Geographic Information Systems in Modern Archaeological Research* (Carbondale: Southern Illinois University Press, 1996), is a very useful volume on GIS. See also A. Clark, *Seeing Below the Soil* (London: Batsford, 1996), and the more technical Lawrence B. Conyers and Dean Goodman, *Ground Penetrating Radar: An Introduction for Archaeologists* (Walnut Creek, CA: AltaMira Press, 1997).

Chapter 7: Excavation

Again, a volume in the *Archaeologist's Toolkit* is an admirable starting point: David L. Carmichael, Robert H. Lafferty III, and Brian Leigh Molyneaux, *Excavation,* is volume 4 in this important series, with a strong conservation ethic and CRM orientation (Walnut Creek, CA: AltaMira Press, 2003). Thomas Hester, Harry J. Shafer, and Kenneth L. Feder, *Field Methods in Archaeology,* 7th ed. (New York: Mayfield, 1997), contains invaluable essays on excavation and is a standard work for American archaeologists. H. S. Dancey, *Archaeological Field Methods: An Introduction* (Minneapolis: Burgess, 1981), is also valuable. Mortimer Wheeler, *Archaeology from the Earth* (Oxford: Clarendon Press, 1954), is a timeless account of basic principles, based on larger sites. Quite apart from its other merits, it is readable! Phillip Barker, *Understanding Archaeological Excavation* (London: Batsford, 1986), has a strong European orientation, but is very perceptive. The same author's *The Techniques of Archaeological Excavation,* 2nd ed. (London: Batsford, 1995), and Martha Joukowsky, *A Complete Manual of Field Archaeology* (Englewood Cliffs, NJ: Prentice Hall, 1981), are basic sources for the serious student. For sampling, see John A. Mueller, ed., *Sampling in Archaeology* (Tucson: University of Arizona Press, 1974). Two exemplary case studies of archaeological excavation in historical settings are Ivor Noel Hume, *Martin's Hundred* (New York: Alfred Knopf, 1983), and Kathleen Deagan, *Spanish St. Augustine: The Archaeology of a Colonial Creole Community* (New York: Academic Press, 1983).

Chapter 8: Archaeological Classification and Technology

A general account of artifact analysis for beginners can be found in Charles R. Ewen, *Artifacts* (Walnut Creek, CA: AltaMira Press, 2003), the fourth volume in the *Archaeologist's Toolkit* series. This should be read in conjunction with Lynne P. Sullivan and S. Terry Childs, *Curating Archaeological Collections* (Walnut Creek, CA: AltaMira Press, 2003), the sixth volume in the same series. V. Gordon Childe, *Piecing Together the Past* (London: Routledge and Kegan Paul, 1956), is still one of the best accounts of the problems of ordering. So is Gordon Willey and Philip Phillips, *Method and Theory in American Archaeology* (Chicago: University of Chicago Press, 1958), which describes some of the archaeological units used in the New World. Robert Whallon and James A. Brown, eds., *Essays on Archaeological Typology* (Kampsville, IL: Center for American Archaeology, 1982), updates the earlier literature and is a fundamental source. The latest major treatment is W. Y. Adams and Ernest W. Adams, *Archaeological Typology and Practical Reality* (Cambridge, England: Cambridge University Press, 1991). For quantitative methods in archaeology, try Stephen Shennan, *Quantifying Archaeology,* 2nd ed. (Orlando, FL: Academic Press, 1996), which is intelligible to a beginner, as is Robert Drennan, *Statistics for Archaeologists: A Commonsense Approach* (New York: Plenum, 1996). For lithics, see William Andrefsky, Jr., *Lithics: Macroscopic Approaches to Analysis* (Cambridge, England: Cambridge University Press, 1998). For ceramics, see Prudence Rice, *Pottery Analysis: A Sourcebook* (Chicago: University of Chicago Press, 1987). James Muhly and Theodore Wertime, eds., *The Coming of the Age of Iron* (New Haven, CT: Yale University Press, 1980), is somewhat dated but a good starting point on early metallurgy. For textiles, see Penelope E. Dooker and Leanne D. Webster, eds., *Beyond Cloth and Cordage* (Salt Lake City: University of Utah Press, 2000).

Chapter 9: The Present and the Past

The study of site-formation processes is fundamental to this chapter. Michael Schiffer, *Site Formation Processes of the Archaeological Record* (New York: Academic Press, 1987), is a good starting point. For preservation, Nicholas Reeves, *The Complete Tutankhamun* (London: Thames and Hudson, 1990), tells you all you want to know about the boy pharaoh and more. Walter Alva and Christopher Donnan, *The Royal Tombs of Sipán* (Los Angeles: Fowler Museum of Cultural History, 1992), is a comprehensive account of one of the most spectacular archaeological discoveries of the twentieth century. P. V. Glob, *The Bog People* (London: Faber and Faber, 1969), describes a number of well-preserved prehistoric corpses from waterlogged Danish bogs; even the skin and intestines survive. The remarkable Ozette site is described by Ruth Kirk, with Richard Daugherty, in *Hunters of the Whale* (New York: Morrow, 1975). Payson D. Sheets, *The Cerén Site* (New York: Harcourt, Brace, Jovanovich, 1992), offers a clear and well-written account of this remarkable site. Middle-range theory is best summarized by Lewis Binford, *In Pursuit of the Past*, rev. ed. (Berkeley: University of California Press, 2002). His *Nunamiut Eskimo Ethnoarchaeology* (New York: Academic Press, 1977), is a detailed account of his own attempts to grapple with issues of middle-range theory and ethnoarchaeology. For living archaeology, see Nicholas David and Carol Kramer, eds., *Ethnoarchaeology in Action* (Cambridge, England: Cambridge University Press, 2001). For the !Kung San, see Richard B. Lee, *The !Kung San* (Cambridge, England: Cambridge University Press, 1979). John Yellen, *Archaeological Approaches to the Present* (Orlando, FL: Academic Press, 1977), covers ethnoarchaeological work in the Kalahari. This book provides background on all aspects of !Kung San lifeways referred to in these pages. John Coles, *Archaeology by Experiment* (London: Hutchinson University Press, 1973), is the best summary of this subject. For a project combining both approaches, see Brian Hayden, ed., *Lithic Studies among the Contemporary Highland Maya* (Tucson: University of Arizona Press, 1987).

Chapter 10: Ancient Climate and Environment

Karl Butzer, *Archaeology as Human Ecology* (Cambridge, England: Cambridge University Press, 1982), is fundamental; so is his *Environment and Archaeology,* 2nd ed. (Chicago: Aldine, 1971). Jared Diamond's *Guns, Germs, and Steel* (New York: W. W. Norton, 1997), argues for the importance of environment and climate change in the past in a stimulating essay for the general reader. A growing literature deals with shorter-term climatic change, best summarized for the general reader in two books: William Ryan and Walter Pitman, *Noah's Flood: The New Scientific Discoveries about the Event That Changed History* (New York: Simon & Schuster, 1998), describes the extraordinary detective work that went into the reconstruction of the Black Sea catastrophe of 5500 B.C. This book describes cutting-edge paleoclimatic research little known outside specialist circles. My own *The Long Summer* (New York: Basic Books, 2004) analyzes the impacts of long-term and short-term climatic change on human societies since 18,000 years ago. For the Moche, read Walter Alva and Christopher Donnan, *The Royal Tombs of Sipán* (Los Angeles: UCLA Fowler Museum of Cultural History, 1983). Andean ice core research is described by L. Thompson and others, "El Niño—Southern Oscillation and Events Recorded in the Stratigraphy of the Tropical Quelccaya Ice Cap," *Science* 225: 50–53, and in "A 1500-Year Tropical Ice Core Record of Climate: Potential Relations to Man in the Andes," *Science* 234 (1986): 361–364. Tree-ring research is well described by Jeffrey

Dean, "Demography, Environment, and Subsistence Stress," in Joseph A. Tainter and Bonnie Bagley Tainter, eds., *Evolving Complexity and Environmental Risk in the Prehistoric Southwest* (Reading, MA: Addison-Wesley, 1996), pp. 25–56. Also see his "A Model of Anasazi Behavioral Adaptation," in George Gumerman, ed., *The Anasazi in a Changing Environment* (Cambridge, England: Cambridge University Press, 1988), pp. 25–44.

Chapter 11: Come Tell Me How You Lived

For an introduction to the topics covered in this chapter, see Kristin D. Sobolik, *Archaeobiology* (Walnut Creek, CA: AltaMira Press, 2003), the fifth volume in the *Archaeologist's Toolkit* series. Zooarchaeology is well served by S. J. M. Davis, *The Archaeology of Animals* (London: Batsford, 1987). See also Elizabeth J. Reitz and Elizabeth Wing, *Zooarchaeology* (Cambridge, England: Cambridge University Press, 1999). Richard Klein and Kathryn Cruz-Uribe, *The Analysis of Animal Bones from Archaeological Sites* (Chicago: University of Chicago Press, 1984), and Donald Grayson, *Quantitative Zooarchaeology* (New York: Academic Press, 1984), are more advanced essays. Lewis Binford's widely read and controversial *Bones* (New York: Academic Press, 1981) is an essay about the basic problems of animal bones in archaeological sites. For plants, Deborah Pearsall, *Paleoethnobotany: A Handbook of Procedures,* 2nd ed. (San Diego: Academic Press, 2000), is an excellent starting point. For the origins of agriculture, see Bruce Smith, *The Emergence of Agriculture* (New York: Scientific American Library, 1994). David Hams and Gordon Hillman, eds., *Foraging and Farming* (London: Unwin Hayman, 1989), is a fundamental source on plant remains of all kinds. Andrew Moore, Gordon Hillman, and Anthony Legge, *Village on the Euphrates* (New York: Oxford University Press, 2001), is not only a monograph on this important site, but a seminal foray into early farming. For shell middens, see Julie Stein, ed., *Deciphering a Shell Midden* (Orlando, FL: Academic Press, 1992).

Chapter 12: Settlement and Landscape

K. C. Chang, ed., *Settlement Archaeology* (Palo Alto: National Press, 1968), is a basic, if outdated, source, and Kent V. Flannery, ed., *The Early Mesoamerican Village* (New York: Academic Press, 1976), is essential reading for everyone interested in this subject, if only for the fascinating and hypothetical dialogues that communicate different viewpoints about the archaeology of the day. For households, Penelope M. Allison, ed., *The Archaeology of Household Activities* (London: Routledge, 1999) gives some useful examples. For Teotihuacán, see René Millon and others, *Urbanization at Teotihuacán,* Mexico, vol. 1 (Austin: University of Texas Press, 1973). A superb monograph on settlement archaeology is W. T. Sanders, Jeffrey R. Parsons, and Robert S. Santley, *The Basin of Mexico: Ecological Processes in the Evolution of a Civilization* (New York: Academic Press, 1979). More recent survey projects are usually summarized in periodical literature. Ask your instructor for details. Jefferson Reid and Stephanie Whittlesey, *Grasshopper Pueblo* (Tucson: University of Arizona Press, 1999), is an excellent popular account of pueblo settlement archaeology. For ancient landscapes, Christopher Y. Tilley, *The Phenomenology of Landscape* (Oxford, England: Berg, 1994), is informative, but not for the weak.

Chapter 13: The Archaeology of People

The Ice Man is well described by Konrad Spindler, *The Man in the Ice* (London: Weidenfeld and Nicholson, 1994), although new and obscurely published articles are updating the portrait in Spindler's summary. Simon Mays, *The Archaeology of Human Bones* (New York: Routledge, 1998), is an invaluable manual on this complex subject. Clark Spencer Larsen, *Skeletons in Our Closet* (Princeton: Princeton University Press, 2000), is a lively introduction. For a text, see Jane Buikstra and Lane Beck, *Bioarchaeology: The Contextual Analysis of Human Remains* (San Diego: Academic Press, 2006). The literature on social evolution and complexity is enormous and very confusing. Elman Service, *Primitive Social Organization* (New York: Random House, 1973), is a (now outdated) classic that discusses socioeconomic classification of human societies. Social ranking is well covered by Robert Chapman et al., eds., *The Archaeology of Death* (Cambridge, England: Cambridge University Press, 1981). See also Sarah Tarlow, *Bereavement and Commemoration: An Archaeology of Mortality* (Malden, MA: Blackwell Publishers, 1999). Ethnic diversity is a relatively new concern in archaeology. There are some excellent essays in Randall McGuire and Robert Paynter, eds., *The Archaeology of Inequality* (Oxford: Blackwell, 1991), pp. 64–78. These include articles on the examples cited here. Leland Ferguson, *Uncommon Ground* (Washington, D.C.: Smithsonian Institution Press, 1991), is a fascinating essay on African-American archaeology that reveals some of the potential of this approach to historical archaeology. See also Sian Jones, *The Archaeology of Ethnicity: Constructing Identities in the Past and Present* (London: Routledge, 1997). Also: Teresa Singleton, ed. *I, Too, Am American* (Charlottesville, VA: University Press of Virginia, 1999), for essays on African-American archaeology.

The literature on the archaeology of gender is proliferating rapidly. Joan Gero and Margaret Conkey, eds., *Engendering Archaeology* (Oxford: Blackwell, 1991), is still a definitive starting point. Sarah Nelson, *Gender in Archaeology* (Walnut Creek, CA: AltaMira Press, 1997), is a critique of gender in archaeology with a comprehensive bibliography. Another useful book is Marie Louise Stig Sørensen, *Gender Archaeology* (Oxford: Blackwell, 2000). See also Sue Hamilton et al., eds, *Archaeology and Women*

(Left Coast Press, 2007). Jeremy A. Sabloff and Karl Lamberg Karlovsky, eds., *Ancient Civilizations and Trade* (Albuquerque: University of New Mexico Press, 1975), and E. Brumfiel and T. K. Earle, eds., *Specialization, Exchange, and Complex Societies* (Cambridge, England: Cambridge University Press, 1987), discuss long-distance exchange; Robin Torrence, *Production and Exchange of Stone Tools* (Cambridge, England: Cambridge University Press, 1986), is an admirable study of the obsidian trade of the Aegean Sea. On prehistoric religion, I have attempted a summary in my *From Black Land to Fifth Sun* (Reading, MA: Perseus, 1998). Two of the best studies come from Maya civilization: Linda Schele and Mary Miller, *The Blood of Kings* (New York: Thames and Hudson, 1992), is based on art and hieroglyphs and is excellent on attitudes and beliefs of the Maya. Linda Schele and David Friedel, *A Forest of Kings* (New York: William Morrow, 1991), is a popular if sometimes controversial account of Maya civilization that is a mine of information on religion, iconography, and social ranking. The same authors' *Maya Cosmos* (New York: William Morrow, 1993), is an informative sequel. The best set of essays on the whole area of the intangible appears under the title "What Is Cognitive Archaeology?" in the *Cambridge Archaeological Journal* 3 (2) (1993): 247–270.

Chapter 14: Managing the Past

Cultural Resource Management is a complex subject, which draws on many disciplines and is remarkable for the complexity of its jargon. A widely used basic textbook is Thomas W. Neumann and Robert M. Sanford, *Cultural Resource Archaeology* (Walnut Creek, CA: AltaMira Press, 2001). Thomas F. King, *Doing Archaeology: A Cultural Resource Management Perspective* (Walnut Creek, C: Left Coast Press, 2005) is a very good basic manual. Stephanie M. Whittlesey and others, eds., *Vanishing River: Landscapes and Lives of the Lower Verde Valley* (Tucson: SRI Press, 1998) is an exemplary synthesis based on large-scale CRM research. See also Thomas F. King, *Cultural Resource Laws and Practice: An Introductory Guide* (Walnut Creek, CA: AltaMira Press, 1998) and the same author's *Places That Count: Traditional Cultural Properties in Cultural Resource Management* (Walnut Creek, CA: AltaMira Press, 2000). King's *Federal Palling and Historic Places: The Section 106 Process, 2001 Updated Printing* (Walnut Creek, CA: Left Coast Press, 2001) is widely consulted. These are essential guides to current legislation and practice that should be on every CRM archaeologist's bookshelf. I strongly advise you to consult a CRM archaeologist before going further into the technical literature. Technical discussions of public archaeology exist largely in edited volumes, most of which are case studies, and., again, a specialist guide is advisable. Cornelius Holtorf's *Archaeology Is a Brand* (Walnut Creek, CA: Left Coast Press, 2007) is a provocative take on the subject that everyone should read and digest.

Chapter 15: So You Want to Become an Archaeologist?

There is surprisingly little literature on career prospects in the field. Marilyn Zeitlin's *The American Archaeologist: A Profile* (Walnut Creek, CA: AltaMira Press, 1997) is essential reading for any aspiring professional. The literature on ethics and archaeology in the modern world is also sparse. More's the pity, for it is a major issue in contemporary archaeological scholarship. Karl Meyer, *The Plundered Past*, 2nd ed. (New York: Athenaeum Press, 1993), is required reading for everyone. Charles McGimsey, *Public Archaeology* (New York: Seminar Press, 1972), highlighted the crisis in North American archaeology a generation ago and is still relevant. Colin Renfrew, *Loot, Legitimacy, and Ownership* (London: Duckworth, 2001), looks at the problem of international trade in antiquities. Archaeological ethics in general are explored by Mark J. Lynott and Alison Wylie, eds., *Ethics in American Archaeology: Challenges for the 1990s* (Washington, D.C.: Society for American Archaeology, 1995), and in Lynott's admirable "Ethical Principles and Archaeological Practice," *American Antiquity* 61 (1997): 589–599. Karen Vitelli, ed., *Archaeological Ethics* (Walnut Creek, CA: AltaMira Press, 1997), is a useful anthology of writings on the subject.

REFERENCES

Belzoni, Giovanni Battista. 1820. *Narrative of the Operations and Recent Discoveries in Egypt and Nubia.* London: John Murray.

Binford, Lewis R. 1983. *Working at Archaeology.* Orlando, FL: Academic Press.

Bintcliff, John. 1991. "Post-Modernism, Rhetoric, and Scholasticism at TAG: The Current State of British Archaeological Theory." *Antiquity* 65 (247): 274–278.

Black, Stephen L., and Kevin Jolly. 2003. *Archaeology by Design.* Walnut Creek, CA: AltaMira Press.

Chauvet, Jean-Marie, Eliette Deschamps, and Christian Hillaire. 1996. *Dawn of Art: The Chauvet Cave.* New York: Abrams.

Chippindale, Christopher. 1994. *Stonehenge Complete.* 2nd ed. London: Thames and Hudson.

Christie, Agatha. 1977. *An Autobiography.* London: Collins, 1977.

Clendinnen, Inga. 1991. *The Aztecs.* Cambridge, England: Cambridge University Press.

Deetz, James. 1967. *Invitation to Archaeology.* Garden City, NY: Natural History Press.

Ewen, Charles R. 2003. *Artifacts.* Walnut Creek, CA: AltaMira Press.

Ferguson, T. J., et al. 1995. "WorkingTogether: Hopi Oral History and Archaeology." *SAA Bulletin* 13 (2): 12–15.

Flannery, Kent, ed. 1976. *The Early Mesoamerican Village.* Orlando, FL: Academic Press.

———, and Joyce Marcus. 1993. "Cognitive Archaeology." *Cambridge Archaeological Journal* 3 (2): 260–267.

Hegmon, Michele. 2003. "Setting Theoretical Egos Aside: Issues and Theory in North American Archaeology." *American Antiquity* 68 (2): 213–243.

Higham, Charles. 1994. *Khok Phanom Di: Prehistoric Adaptation to the World's Richest Habitat.* New York: Harcourt.

Layard, Austen Henry. 1849. *Nineveh and Its Remains.* London: John Murray.

Mouhot, Henri. 1872. *Travels in the Central Parts of Siam, Cambodia, and Laos, 1858–1861.* Paris: Hachette.

McPherson, R. S. 1992. *Sacred Land, Sacred View: Navajo Perceptions of the Four Quarters Region.* Provo, UT: Brigham Young University.

Schiffer, Michael. 1987. *Site Formation Processes of the Archaeological Record.* Albuquerque: University of New Mexico Press.

Specter, Janet. 1983. *What This Awl Means.* St. Paul: Minnesota History Society.

Stephens, John L. 1841. *Incidents of Travel in Chiapas and Yucatan.* New York: Harper's.

Tedlock, Dennis. 1996. *Popol Vuh.* New York: Simon and Schuster.

Trigger, Bruce. 1991. "Distinguished Lecture in Archaeology: Constraint and Freedom." *American Anthropologist* 93 (3): 551–569.

Tylor, Sir Edward. 1871. *Anthropology.* London: Longman.

Wheeler, Mortimer. 1943. *Maiden Castle.* London: Society of Antiquaries.

Woolley, Sir Leonard. 1982. *Excavations at Ur.* New York: Barnes and Noble.

PHOTO CREDITS

Frontmatter Page xix: Lesley Newhart.

Chapter 1 Page 1: © Bettmann/Corbis, All Rights Reserved; page 3: © The Trustees of the British Museum; page 5: Photography by Egyptian Expedition, The Metropolitan Museum of Art; page 6: Courtesy of the Library of Congress; page 8: Corbis/Bettmann; page 11: © Gianni Dagli Orti/Corbis, All Rights Reserved; page 12: Corbis/Bettmann; page 14: Courtesy of the Library of Congress; page 15: Buddy Mays/Corbis/Bettmann; page 18: Courtesy of Salisbury & South Wiltshire Museum, © Anthony Pitt-Rivers.

Chapter 2 Page 22: C. Bowman/Robert Harding World Imagery; page 24: © The Trustees of the British Museum; page 25: English Heritage National Monuments Records; page 26: Robert Frerck/Odyssey Productions, Inc.; page 30: Peter Buckley/Pearson Education/PH College; page 34: George Holton/Photo Researchers, Inc.; page 35: Photo by Susan Einstein, Courtesy of UCLA Fowler Museum of Cultural History; page 36: The Ancient Art & Architecture Collection Ltd.; page 40: Courtesy of Clark Erikson; page 41: Ruggero Vanni/Corbis/Bettmann; page 44: Neg./Transparency no. 4936(7), Photo by D. Finnin/C. Chesek, Courtesy of the Dept. of Library Services, American Museum of Natural History.

Chapter 3 Page 47: Fanny Broadcast/ZUMA Press–Gamma; page 49: Yutaka Yoshii/Izumi Shimada; page 52: © The Field Museum, Neg. #A90925, Chicago; page 55: Painting by Percy Fiestas, Courtesy of Bruning Archaeological Museum, Lambayeque; page 62: Hillel Burger/Peabody Museum, Harvard University; page 63: Dr. Steven A. LeBlanc.

Chapter 4 Page 65: Bas-relief of the Goddess Maat, painted stone relief, Egypt, nineteenth dynasty, Museo Archeologico, Florence, Italy, Copyright Scala/Art Resource, NY; page 68: Photograph by the Egyptian Expedition, The Metropolitan Museum of Art; page 69: Franklin Graham; page 70: Chuck Carter/NGS Image Collection; page 77: Tim Hall/Getty Images, Inc.–Photodisc; page 79: Courtesy of the Qatna Project of the Altorientalisches Seminar of Tubingen University; page 82: Courtesy of the UCLA Fowler Museum of Cultural History.

Chapter 5 Page 85: R. Sheridan/The Ancient Art & Architecture Collection Ltd; page 90: © Society of Antiquaries of London; page 100: Richard A. Cooke/Corbis/Bettmann; page 107: © Gail Mooney/Corbis, All Rights Reserved.

Chapter 6 Page 109: Buddy Mays/Corbis/Bettmann; page 111: Used with permission of Merle Greene Robertson, copyright 1973; page 116: Arizona State Museum; page 117: Neg./Transparency no. 326597, Courtesy of the Dept. of Library Services, American Museum of Natural History; page 118: © British Museum/Art Resource; page 120: © Stephanie Maze/Corbis, All Rights Reserved; page 122: © Crown copyright NMR; page 124: Satellite Image Courtesy of GeoEye, © 2008, All rights reserved; page 129: Dr. Vincent Gaffney, University of Birmingham, England; page 130, top: Professor Payson Sheets, Department of Anthropology, University of Colorado, Boulder.

Chapter 7 Page 131: Crown copyright Historic Royal Palaces, Reproduced by permission of Historic Royal Palaces under license from the Controller of Her Majesty's Stationery Office; page 133: Charles Higham; page 137: Penn Museum image #07458; page 138: © The Society of Antiquaries of London; page 139, top: The Danebury Trust; page 139, bottom: James A. Tuck; page 140: Photo by A. Chopping/Museum of London Archaeology Service; page 144: David Brill/Brill Atlanta; page 145: Hilary John Deacon; page 146: Courtesy of Ashkelon Excavations, The Leon Levy Expedition; page 147: Yann Arthus-Bertrand/Corbis/Bettmann; page 148: Mr. Francis Wilfred Shawcross; page 149: Peter Arnold, Inc.

Chapter 8 Page 153: Feline effigy, Moche site of Huaca de la Luna (c.a. 500 A.D.), excavated by Santiago Uceda, photograph by Steve Bourget; page 156: David L. Brill/Brill Atlanta; page 160, top: Courtesy of the Phoebe Hearst Museum of Anthropology and the Regents of the University of California; page 162: Courtesy of the Library of Congress; page 165: Bodleian Library, University of Oxford (MS. Arch. Selden. A.1, fol. 67r); page 172: Corbis/Bettmann; page 174: © The Trustees of the British Museum; page 175: Courtesy of the Dept. of Library Services, American Museum of Natural History; page 176: Dumbarton Oaks, Pre-Columbian Collection, Washington, D.C.

Chapter 9 Page 178: Courtesy of the Library of Congress; page 180: Moodboard/Corbis–Moodboard; page 181: Ashmolean Museum, Oxford, England, U.K.; page 187: Perfectly preserved moccasins, the larger moccasin from Hogup Cave, Utah (42B036) with catalog number FS47.7, a Fremont-style moccasin ca. 500 A.D., the smaller moccasin from Promontory Cave, Utah (42B01) with catalog number 9764, a Puckered Toe child's moccasin ca. 1260 A.D., Courtesy of the Utah Museum of Natural History; page 188: © Silkeborg Museum, Denmark; page 189, top: Professor John Coles; page 189, bottom: Copyright Werner Forman/Art Resource, NY; page 191: National Archives and Records Administration; page 193: Professor F. L. Van Noten, Belgium; page 194: Brian Hayden, Department of Archaeology, Simon Fraser University.

Chapter 10 Page 198: Thomas Nash; page 201: Steve Bourget, Department of Anthropology, University of Texas, Austin; page 212: Dumbarton Oaks, Pre-Columbian Collection, Washington, D.C.

Chapter 11 Page 217: Charles & Josette Lenars/Corbis/Bettmann; page 219: Adam Woolfitt/Corbis/Bettmann; page 221, left: © Courtesy of Dr. Klaus Schmidt, DAI; page 221, right: © DAI, Irvingard Wagner; page 229, top: Cambridge Museum of Archaeology and Ethnography, Cambridge University.

Chapter 12 Page 234: © Adam Woolfitt/Robert Harding World Imagery/Corbis, All Rights Reserved; page 236: © Dept. of Environment, Heritage and Local Government, Ireland; page 243: Courtesy of David Frankel and Jennifer Webb; page 244, bottom: Caroll Boltin; page 251: Kevin Fleming/Corbis/Bettmann; page 252: Courtesy of James M. Harmon, National Park Service, Mark P. Leone, University of Maryland, Stephen D. Prince, University of Maryland, and Marcia Snyder, University of Maryland; page 254, top: © Adam Woolfitt/Corbis, All Rights Reserved; page 254, bottom: © Kevin Schafer/Corbis, All Rights Reserved; page 255: © Adam Woolfitt/Corbis, All Rights Reserved.

Chapter 13 Page 257: Courtesy of Jane Brayne and Wessex Archaeology; page 259: Copyright Atlantic Productions Ltd.; page 261: The Biological Anthropology Research Centre, Archaeological Sciences, University of Bradford; page 263: Wieslav Smetek/Stern/Black Star; page 264: O. Louis Mazzatenta/NGS Image Collection; page 265: Roger Wood/Corbis/Bettmann; page 266: © Angelo Hornak/Corbis, All Rights Reserved; page 267: Bronze cline from the Celtic grave at Eberdingen-Hochdorf (Germany), 2.75 m length, second half of sixth century B.C., photo by Keltenmuseum Hochdorf; page 269: South Carolina Institute of Archaeology and Anthropology, University of South Carolina, Columbia; page 274: Neg. #312721, Obsidian mirror, Courtesy of the Dept. of Library Services, American Museum of Natural History; page 276: Holton Collection/SuperStock, Inc.; page 278: Institute of Nautical Archaeology/D. Frey; page 279: Photograph from The Arthur Sackler Gallery, Washington, D.C., reproduced with the permission of the Jordan Department of Antiquities; page 280, top: The Great Serpent Mound, Hopewell, Adams County, Ohio, Courtesy of the National Museum of the American Indian, Smithsonian Institution (N21598), photo by Major Dache M. Reeves; page 280, bottom: Kent Flannery.

Chapter 14 Page 284: © Copyright, All rights reserved, Adriel Heisey Photography; page 286: AP Wide World Photos; page 287: Van Bucher/Photo Researchers, Inc.; page 289: Neg./Transparency no. 29.1/288 1919–31, Courtesy of the Dept. of Library Services, American Museum of Natural History; page 291: Dr. J. M. Adovasio/Mercyhurst Archaeological Institute; page 293: Dr. Laurie Rush/Fort Drum Archaeology, Courtesy of the U.S. Army; page 298: © Gianni Dagli Orti/Corbis, All Rights Reserved; page 299: Courtesy of the Illinois Transportation Archaeological Research Program (ITARP), University of Illinois.

Chapter 15 Page 301: © Chris Hellier/Corbis, All Rights Reserved; page 308: Fritz Henle/Photo Researchers, Inc.; page 309, top: Hester A. Davis, "Is There a Future for the Past?" *Archaeology* 24: 4, Copyright © 1971 Archaeological Institute of America; page 309, bottom: British Tourist Authority.

INDEX

Page numbers followed by *f* indicate figures. Page numbers in bold type indicate glossary entries.

D

E

F

T